An Introduction to Child Theology

An Introduction to Child Theology

EDITED BY
James M. Houston

CASCADE *Books* • Eugene, Oregon

AN INTRODUCTION TO CHILD THEOLOGY

Copyright © 2022 Wipf and Stock. All rights reserved. Except for brief quotations in critical publications or reviews, no part of this book may be reproduced in any manner without prior written permission from the publisher. Write: Permissions, Wipf and Stock Publishers, 199 W. 8th Ave., Suite 3, Eugene, OR 97401.

Cascade Books
An Imprint of Wipf and Stock Publishers
199 W. 8th Ave., Suite 3
Eugene, OR 97401

www.wipfandstock.com

PAPERBACK ISBN: 978-1-7252-8562-0
HARDCOVER ISBN: 978-1-7252-8561-3
EBOOK ISBN: 978-1-7252-8563-7

Cataloguing-in-Publication data:

Names: Houston, James M., editor.

Title: An introduction to child theology / James M. Houston, editor.

Description: Eugene, OR: Cascade Books, 2022 | Includes bibliographical references.

Identifiers: ISBN 978-1-7252-8562-0 (paperback) | ISBN 978-1-7252-8561-3 (hardcover) | ISBN 978-1-7252-8563-7 (ebook)

Subjects: LCSH: Children (Christian theology).

Classification: BT705 .I50 2022 (print) | BT705 (ebook)

In memory of Katie Hughes (1928–2013), whose childhood was victimized by the Holocaust

Katie Hughes had a horrendous childhood and a hard life. From a wealthy, happy family in Berlin, she and her younger brother were put on a Red Cross train to London, a day before the outbreak of war. Upon their arrival in London, separate couples volunteered to "adopt" the children. But immediately Katie began to be sexually abused by the husband. Desperately, she learned English as quickly as she could, to facilitate escape, which within six weeks she managed, to join the kind Christian family who had adopted her brother. Meanwhile, her parents escaped into Switzerland, and from there hired, with a large number of wealthy refugees, a boat to take them to safety. But country after country refused them asylum, until the established Jewish community bribed the government of Chile to accept them. For years, her physician father could only medically treat the diseases of prostitutes. In despair, after his death Katie's mother committed suicide. Meanwhile, Katie had married and emigrated with her husband to Vancouver. But after the death of her husband, their eldest son disowned his mother, wanting to avoid being recognized as a "Jew." Katie died of a broken heart.

Table of Contents

Preface—James M. Houston ix

List of Contributors xi

Introduction: "But I Am Only a Child!":
Christian Formation Transforms Childhood—James M. Houston 1

Chapter 1: The Childhood of Humanity in the Biblical Narrative
—Jonathan Lipps 7

Chapter 2: Isaac the Son and the Shadow of Ishmael
—Andrew Zack Lewis 19

Chapter 3: Fear and Love in the Book of Ruth—Kelly Lamb 36

Chapter 4: Wise Child-Rearing According to Proverbs—Bruce Waltke 41

Chapter 5: "*Only* a Boy"?: Jeremiah's Protest from the Perspective of Child Theology—Jonathan D. Bentall 61

Chapter 6: While Knit in My Mother's Womb:
The Theology of Infancy in Psalm 139—Keith Bodner 76

Chapter 7: The Genius of the Greek Mind:
Education of Greek and Roman Children—Shirley Sullivan 87

Chapter 8: Scripture on the Birth and Infancy of Jesus
—Markus Bockmuehl and Evangeline Kozitza 104

Table of Contents

Chapter 9: Childhood in Islam and the Heritage of Shame
—Mark Robert Anderson 122

Chapter 10: Memory and Character Formation:
The Ark in Hugh of Saint Victor—Hans Boersma 139

Chapter 11: The Child in the Early Middle Ages—James M. Houston 165

Chapter 12: "Let the Little Children Come to Me":
Evangelicalism as a Young People's Movement—Bruce Hindmarsh 177

Chapter 13: John MacMurray's Vision of the Personal Based on Child Development—Marty Folsom 186

Chapter 14: Child Resilience Despite Extreme Trauma/Deprivation
—Robert and Suzanne Taylor 204

Chapter 15: My Childhood Theology: For the God of My Life
—Leighton Ford 212

Chapter 16: And That is What We Are: Embracing the Child
—Mike Mason 220

Chapter 17: To Be a Christian Was to Be a Child to God:
Kierkegaard's View—Tetsuya Shimada 230

Chapter 18: "A Childhood into Which We Have to Grow":
George MacDonald and Childlikeness
—Sharon Jebb Smith and Kirstin Jeffrey Johnson 245

Chapter 19: To the Time before Time Began:
The Spiritual Vocation of Childhood—Patrick Calvo 264

Chapter 20: The Child in the Midst—Preston Manning 279

Bibliography 293

Preface

WHY "CHILD THEOLOGY"? ONE of my students at Oxford was John White, whose family for over a century had created a family community in a suburb of London. Together, we discussed "child theology," and he subsequently wrote much about its advocacy. For the community was a haven for battered mothers, abused and adopted children, and penniless families.

This book is further born out of much human suffering. I was flying across the Pacific from Vancouver, Canada to Singapore, having prepared for a Business Leaders Forum, but my sermon was not finished. So I arrived with no sleep. But I had the Advent symphony music ringing in my ears: "For unto us a Child is born, unto us a Son is given, and the government shall be upon His shoulders". So I stood up to preach the next morning, making the pastors immediately nervous about my theology. For I started by saying I had introduced "spiritual theology" into the teaching of Regent College, in lieu of systematic theology, and now I was replacing that with "child theology."

Immediately after the service, three business ladies approached me. Two of them were devout members of the Methodist cathedral where I had preached. The other was a cynical secular Buddhist who had "no place for religion." Many times her friends had urged her to come to church, but the day before this occasion, she suddenly asked to be taken to church. Why? She explained that she had been awakened on the previous night and the child Jesus was placed in her bosom. Now she wanted to come, not knowing the topic of the sermon. The coincidence was too remarkable for her not to believe. God was arresting her attention.

Shirley Sullivan, emeritus professor of classical studies, was lying dangerously ill of pneumonia in hospital; the doctors did not think she would live long. But lying in bed she had the faith that God would heal her, and that she would be able to write her essay.

Preface

Marty Folsom had just lost his teenaged daughter to suicide when he wrote his contribution.

The teenaged daughter of Keith Bodner was killed just before he was invited to write on the child in the Psalms.

Leighton Ford, the brother-in-law of Billy Graham, has movingly described his zig-zag adoptions from the breakup of his parents' marriages, in his memoirs *A Life of Listening*. Then he and his wife suffered the grief of losing their son Sandy in a failed heart operation. He summarizes his sufferings in his essay.

Tetsuya Shimada has had to face his troubled childhood by identifying with the deeply depressed childhood of Søren Kierkegaard, on whom he is writing his doctoral thesis. Tetsuya is finding the essay of Kirstin Jeffrey Johnson, whose parents divorced as a child, therapeutic for his own needs.

My wife and I had the grief in 1967 of learning our fifth child, Jonathan, was born with Down's syndrome, and then losing him under surgery for a blocked stomach a week later. The loss of Jonathan has made a big impact on our family ever since.

Indeed, we hope this book of testimonies of suffering will become a therapeutic community for our readers, with each essayist and reader helping "the other."

I am indebted to Wipf and Stock Publishers and to Kelly Lamb, Shirley Sullivan, Steven Gomez, and Tetsuya Shimada for their help with the manuscript.

James M. Houston

List of Contributors

Mark Anderson (MA Theology, Westminster Theological Seminary, and MA Islamic Studies, McGill University) was with the Sudan Inland Mission in Cairo for many years.

Jonathan D. Bentall (PhD, Durham) is instructor of University Foundations, Seattle Pacific University, and adjunct professor at Northwest University.

Markus Bockmuehl (PhD, Cambridge) is the Dean Ireland Professor of the Exegesis of Holy Scripture at the University of Oxford, and a fellow of Keble College.

Keith Bodner (PhD, Aberdeen and Manchester) is professor of religious studies and Stuart E. Murray Chair of Christian Studies at Crandall University, New Brunswick.

Hans Boersma (ThD, Utrecht) is the Saint Benedict Servants of Christ Professor of Ascetical Theology at Nashotah House Theological Seminary.

Patrick Calvo (ThM, Regent College, Vancouver) is a pastor and currently a psychotherapy intern.

Marty Folsom (PhD, Otago) teaches as an adjunct at Seattle Pacific University, Northwest University, Trinity Lutheran College, and other schools.

Bruce Hindmarsh (DPhil, Oxford) is the James M. Houston Chair of Spiritual Theology at Regent College, Vancouver.

List of Contributors

Leighton Ford, evangelist, was an associate of Billy Graham and is the founder of Leighton Ford Ministries.

James M. Houston (DPhil, Oxford) was founding principal of Regent College, Vancouver, and is an emeritus professor of spiritual theology there.

Kirstin Jeffrey Johnson (PhD, St. Andrews) is the director of Linlathen, a conference and lecture series, and a George MacDonald scholar.

Evangeline Kozitza (DPhil, Oxford) is stipendiary lecturer in theology at St. John's College, Oxford.

Andrew Zack Lewis (PhD, Cambridge) is sessional lecturer in biblical languages and Old Testament at Regent College, Vancouver.

Kelly Lamb (MA, King's College London; MA, Fuller Theological Seminary) has built companies, traveled the world, and pastored.

Jonathan Lipps (MPhil, Oxford; MA, Stanford) is engineering director at HeadSpin, Inc., and a ThM student at Regent College, Vancouver.

Mike Mason is a professional writer and graduate of Regent College, Vancouver.

Preston Manning was leader of the Reform Party of Canada and Leader of the Opposition in the Canadian federal parliament.

Tetsuya Shimada (ThM, Regent College, Vancouver) is lecturer at Jesus to Japan Missionary Seminary and a vision coordinator at Murasaki Sports Co.

Sharon Jebb Smith (PhD, St. Andrews) is a freelance lecturer and speaker on literature, theology, and Christian spirituality.

Shirley Sullivan (PhD, Toronto) is emeritus professor of classics, University of British Columbia.

LIST OF CONTRIBUTORS

Robert Taylor (MD) is emeritus professor of surgery, the University of British Columbia.

Suzanne Taylor is former adjunct professor of nursing, University of British Columbia.

Bruce Waltke (PhD, Harvard) is emeritus professor of Old Testament Regent College, Vancouver.

INTRODUCTION

"But I Am Only A Child!"
Christian Formation Transforms Childhood

THE PURPOSE OF THIS collection is to draw the skilled resources of many scholars from diverse disciplines to expose child abuse as systemic to the human condition, yet to reveal the creative resources of childhood, to overcome evil by good. Our writers are all Christian scholars, and their work here is born on the premise that God became a child, which we celebrate every Advent season.

We may well wonder when the final "exposé" of child abuse will finally have been accomplished, in the cellars not only of the Vatican, but of global societies. Bleakly, they may never end, for all human emotions are determined by fear, and fear is an addictive emotion. "The child" is the scapegoat of fear, as the first fratricide began with Cain and Abel, Joseph and his brothers, and has been never-ending since! But God's devices are contrastive with human will, as we shall explore in this book.

Just as a mighty oak begins with an acorn, so does our life and Christian witness begin with a child's faith. In the book of Jeremiah, the word of the Lord comes to the prophet, words that echo Psalm 139, "Before I formed you in the womb I knew you, and before you were born I consecrated you; I appointed you a prophet for the nations." The prophet's response was like that of Moses at the burning bush—that he was helpless to think he could ever take up the call of the Lord.

"Ah, Lord God! Truly I do not know how to speak, for I am only a boy." But the Lord said to me, "Do not say, 'I am only a boy,' for you shall go to all to whom I send you, and you shall speak whatever I command you. Do not be afraid of them, for I am with you to deliver you, says the Lord." Then the Lord touched my mouth; and the Lord said to me, "Now, I have put my words into your mouth. See, today I appoint you over nations and kingdoms, to pluck up and pull down, to destroy and to overthrow, to build and to plant." (Jer 1:4–10)

I was privileged to meet in Brasilia, Maria da Silva, who was then leading an opposition party for a previous presidential election in Brazil. An Amazonian Indian by birth, illiterate until she was sixteen years old, with her frail diminutive body wracked by seven malarial attacks, and later escaping four serious assassination attacks, she was given strength to be an inconceivable agent of God to clean up the systemic corruption of Brazilian culture. We never know when God will take up a child to be his redemptive servant, as the following essays illustrate so well.

So how did I ever get involved in "child theology"? It happened one Advent season on a transpacific flight from Vancouver to Singapore. I prayed, "Lord, what can I say in the Sunday morning services of the Methodist Cathedral in Singapore, when I am arriving at midnight, weary and empty?" As I tried to sleep, the words of Bach's *Messiah* kept ringing through my heart, *"For unto us a child is born, unto us a son is given."* It seemed a fitting text to preach. I confessed that I had long debated about the legitimacy of "systematic theology" and had introduced a more comprehensive use of "spiritual theology," but now I was scrapping both to introduce "child theology."

After the service, I was told that a secular Buddhist was converted by the address. I met her the next evening and asked, "What has happened?" Her friends answered, "We have begged her for years to come to church, but she always scornfully refused. But on the Saturday before the sermon, she phoned us to request, 'Please take me to church tomorrow.'" Then the Buddhist explained: "On the Friday night, I was awakened to find the baby Jesus placed in my bosom, and then on Sunday morning you explained it all! What else can I do but accept Christ in my life?"

In turn, that has made me think, what else can I now do, but teach and preach and write on "child theology"!

INTRODUCTION

WHAT ARE THE NORMS OF CHILD SPIRITUALITY?

Since the concept of "spirituality" became popular, it felt it was like an air balloon: it needed to be anchored. As Rabbi Hugo Gryn wisely observed, "'Spirituality' is like a bird; if you hold it too tightly, it chokes; if you hold it too loosely, it flies away. Fundamental to spirituality is the absence of force." Spirituality cannot be confined by words, for it is literally "inspiring," and yet it can so easily sweep writers into apostasy. The former Archbishop of Canterbury, Rowan Williams, puts it soundly in saying, "each believer making his or her own engagement with the questioning of the heart of faith . . . must constantly be allowed to challenge the fixed assumptions of religiosity."[1]

For this study, the first norm must be biblical. It is what the Holy Scriptures say about childhood.

What then is children's spirituality? Rebecca Nye puts it beautifully: "It is God's ways of being with children and children's ways of being with God." It all starts with God, as the birth of a child all starts with the parents. It is all about being like a child, as Jesus exhorts us: "Truly I tell you, unless you change and become like children, you will never enter the kingdom of heaven" (Matt 18:3). Mark's Gospel puts it just a little differently: "Amen I say to you. Whoever does not receive the Kingdom of God like a child will not enter into it" (Mark 10:15).

Yet Nicodemus is amazed one should require so paradigmatic a shift of life as to be "born again" (John 3:10). So Jesus challenges us all to take a *metanoia*, that is a paradigm shift, beyond our conversion, to see our Christian life in a radical new way.

As the twelfth-century Cistercian monk, Guerric of Igny, a disciple of Bernard of Clairvaux, says in a Christmas sermon, "God did not humble himself to become a man, but God came as a child," wrapped in swaddling clothes, a newborn baby. God knew how deeply dangerous such an act would be, as Herod tried to exterminate all small children in Palestine, just as Pharaoh had done with the incipient people of Israel in Egypt. It became a scandal to the Jews, that the whole corpus of the Law of the Covenant should now be placed by God in the heart and mind of a small child. Yet God placed his own Holy Spirit into the spirit of the child Jesus.

We can devote the rest of our lives to pondering these things, perhaps with the meditations of Hans Urs von Balthasar, one of the great

---

1. Williams, *The Wound of Knowledge*, 11.

theologians of the twentieth century, in his small book *Unless You Become Like This Child*.

What then are some of the marks of a child's spirituality?

- Children have a more holistic way of seeing things; they don't think and analyze as much as adults, so their perception is more mystical.
- Thus children are more open and curious, not critical, but living in wonder.
- Their emotional life is as strong as their intellectual life, so they cannot hide their feelings, and they are aware of transcendent forces they cannot control.
- So much is unknown, so mystery is everywhere, and so much more needs to be trusted.
- They know words are not adequate to describe everything, so they are comfortable with the power of the ineffable.

Through children's literature, adults today are beginning to see new dimensions of reality that are only available through the eyes and spirit of a child. A Finnish researcher, Kalevi Tamminen, has found that 60 percent of eleven-year-olds and 80 percent of seven-year-olds speak of being aware of God's presence. By comparison only 30 percent of adults are aware of similar experiences. Again, in contrast, the everyday consciousness of a child is more unitive, whereas the adult world is much more fragmented. The rule of life for a child is simple: it is just being a child. Whereas for an adult, most have no idea what is their rule of life! Yet for the Christian, the everydayness of life should wholly be "in Christ," as the apostle exhorts 166 times. The child has just one identity, "a child," whereas adults wear multiple personae.

The Gospels do not treat the childhood of Jesus the ways our curiosity tends to do. They are totally silent about Jesus' childhood. Rather the sayings and actions of Jesus with children fit into a theological frame centered around the theme of the coming of the kingdom of God. This "kingdom" was not a territory but the sphere of the activity of God acting as the King of Kings. It is what many of the Psalms anticipated. That activity was already present, but it would finally be disclosed by God in apocalyptic terms as described in the book of Revelation. Many of Jesus' parables anticipate this future. And the children were the models of true discipleship in preparation for the fulfilment of the kingdom of heaven.

INTRODUCTION

To enter into the kingdom, in Mark 10:13–16, Jesus took children as his model. For entry into the kingdom is not by way of privilege, status, or merit, but in the helplessness of a child. So Jesus "puts his arms around them, laying his hands upon them and blessing them." (See also Matthew 19:1–15; 18:3; and Luke 18:15–17.) The child, instead of the adult, is a total reversal of human attitudes. Again, as the incident of Mark 8:27–10:45 reveals, children are given as much access to Jesus as adults, which we still do not practice publicly! Like the disciples, we want to place children where "they will be seen, but not heard."

Was Jesus idealizing children, or was he expressing deeper truths, when he declared: "the kingdom of heaven belongs to such as these"? Clearly, it is the latter. The poet Wordsworth seemed to hint at this in his poem, *Ode on Intimations of Immortality from Recollections of Early Childhood*:

> Not in entire forgetfulness,
> And not in utter nakedness,
> But trailing clouds of glory do we come
> From God who is our home:
> Heaven lies about us in our infancy.

Matthew 11:25 and 18:10 both suggest Jesus regarded children as more open to revelation of the truth than adults might be. Jesus was speaking specifically about how a person enters the kingdom of God. Looking at children, it was not their subjective characteristics but their objective position in society that made them models for discipleship. Socially, children occupy a small and humble role in society, dependent upon others. Likewise, Christ's disciples are to be content with being at others' beck and call, often a hidden role, expressive of humility. Actually, both in Aramaic and Greek, the language of the Gospels, the word *child* and the word *servant* are the same.

Radically, Jesus is saying God uses disciples who are like himself, humble in heart and lowly in spirit. So Jesus adds, "Whoever does not accept the kingdom of God as they would accept a child, will never enter it." This indicates the kingdom of God has to be received in a childlike way. Elsewhere Jesus had condemned double-mindedness, and again the child is the opposite of this, in the single-minded pursuit of "one thing," without holding back. In contrast, this is immediately followed by the story of the rich young ruler, who could not follow Jesus for he had too much to lose (Matt 19:16–30; Mark 10:17–31; Luke 18:18–30).

But this raises one of the most acute problems of the child theology of the Gospels. Is Jesus literally speaking of the child, or is he using the imagery of the child to instruct adults? Clearly, he is using both, in teaching adult disciples basic lessons on the nature of his ministry and kingdom. This seems the correct exegesis of Matthew 11:25 and Luke 10:21, where new translations interpret "little ones" as *nepioi* or "simple ones," for many times Jesus is speaking to both children and adults.

For Jesus is creating a new community, radically expressed in Matthew 12:46–50, Mark 3:31–5, and Luke 8:19–21. "Who are my mother and brothers?" he is asking, and replies himself: "Whoever does the will of God is my brother and sister and mother." Children will be part of the new community, but as Jesus commits the care of his mother to John as he was dying on the cross, so a whole new understanding of the Christian community was being created.

In the late second century, the brilliant biblical scholar Origen pursued this element of spiritual growth that 1 John had first developed, in his distinction of children, youth, and fathers (1 John 2:12–14), while at the same time using it in Christ's connotations for all believers: "And now little children, abide in him" (1 John 2:28). John then explores what the Father's love has revealed to the believers, that they should become "the children of God" (1 John 3:1).

Origen then picked up the theme of growth in his exegetical studies of Paul's epistles. The young Paul, as a missionary to the young church of Corinth, wrote exhortations to his quarrelling children in Corinthians, with moral exhortations appropriate to the young in faith. Then he wrote more maturely to the house churches at Rome that had become more mature in handling diverse ethnicity in their communities. Finally, he composed his letter to the Colossians as a model of Christian maturity. Possibly, a late writer, modeling on the Colossian letter, then composed Ephesians, to a church that had matured through much suffering.

This then, is the purpose of this book, to give a fresh and realistic way of interpreting the Christian life, through the eyes and the wounds of the child. This is what the contributors of this book are demonstrating, for in the context of Henri Nouwen and the L'Arche movement of crippled children: we are all wounded readers, yet we can become "wounded healers." This gives depth to the good news of the gospel, that we do not hear frequently enough in our churches.

Chapter One

The Childhood of Humanity in the Biblical Narrative

Jonathan Lipps

It is a truism that we can only understand ourselves with reference to some larger narrative within which our lives are placed. For many Christians, the cosmic narrative of which we are a part goes something like this: an eternal God created a perfect world. On this world he placed two fully mature and perfect human beings. He then prohibited one specific action within the world—eating the fruit of a certain tree. The humans were, unfortunately, persuaded by an evil being to disobey God and eat this fruit. As a result, the humans were punished by God. We live in the echo of that punishment today, both within ourselves (in the form of "original sin") and globally (through conflict with other people and nature, and the inevitability of death).

Finally, after a long story having to do with the ancient Israelites, God decided to intervene in the mess we'd made of things, becoming a human himself in the form of Jesus. Jesus ultimately died by state execution, but this was actually a blessing for us. Since Jesus *was* God, his death counted as payment for every sin every human had committed or was yet to commit. His death "soaked up" God's anger towards our evil actions, from the fruit-eating onward. All we have to do to live in this state of forgiveness is to agree that Jesus did in fact do the things just mentioned. This of course is eminently desirable, because unless our wrongs are forgotten by God, we will be punished eternally after we die.

Narratively, this story has the shape of a large capital letter "U," with Eden at the top left, heaven at the top right, and most of human history sunk somewhere in the trough between. It is not, as we shall see, the best way of understanding the narrative of the cosmos as expressed in the Bible. Instead, the best way of understanding the arc of the human race in the biblical cosmos is arguably an analogy with the arc of a single human life, from birth to childhood to maturity. Rather than reading the Genesis account as describing a fall from mature perfection, we should read it as an exceedingly tragic, but only eventually catastrophic, tale of childhood innocence lost in the attempt to grow up too soon. The rest of the history of God's relationship with humanity revolves around God's attempts to restore humanity's childlike trust (if not their innocence), and to heal them of the consequences of their premature adulthood, so that the original purposes of creation might once more come into view. We must therefore begin by understanding the story of creation.

Creation

From a literary perspective, the creation narrative may be regarded as a polemic for the Yahwist conception of God, since it borrows freely from preexisting ancient Near Eastern mythological resources but then makes radically different points with them.[1] What emerges clearly and distinctively through this lens is a depiction of a God who creates *ex nihilo*, and who acts as a continuous, sustaining ground for the existence of the whole cosmos. As Walter Brueggemann puts it, "Israel's testimony to Yahweh as creator concerns Yahweh's ultimate power to work an utter novum, one that on any other terms is impossible."[2]

This "utter novum" is described by its Creator as "good." In fact, it is described as "good" at many points along the process of creation, not only at the end. The distinction between land and sea is "good." The growth of seed-bearing plants is "good." And so on. Finally, before God rests from the creation, the result of all his work is described as "very good." What we can learn from this observation is that we should not equate "good" with the conceptual intersection of "final," "finished," and "perfect."

Theologians like Colin Gunton and biblical scholars like John H. Walton agree with early Christian thinkers (Irenaeus of Lyons, for one) that

1. See Provan, *Seriously Dangerous Religion*.
2. Brueggemann, *Theology of the Old Testament*, 146.

creation's goodness lies not in its perfection but in its appropriateness for its current stage, relative to the order that God has set up.³ Gunton urges us to "recover the notion of creation as project. That is to say, we need to understand it as something God creates not as a timelessly perfect whole, but as an order of things that is planned to go somewhere; to be completed or perfected, and so *projected* into time."⁴

In the second century CE, Irenaeus made more or less the same point, arguing that Adam and Eve were to be regarded not as paragons of maturity, but rather as children, even infants. As infants, they were "unaccustomed to, and unexercised in, perfect discipline."⁵ This perspective paints a very different picture of Eden from that of static perfection. The first humans are placed in a world that is a *project*, and they are invited to join in the project by adding their own brushstrokes to the canvas that God has not yet completed. God constantly calls human beings to work with him towards his purposes, which, as Irenaeus insightfully observes, appear to center on the fashioning of humans themselves!⁶ This is a radical inversion of the neighboring philosophies of the ancient Near East. The place of humans in these other mythologies is that of fulfilling the needs of the gods, as slaves or as food.⁷ Yahweh, by contrast, has no need of human work for his continued existence. Rather, his orientation is one of self-giving, creative, sustaining love. In line with this kind of love, humans were created immature, with a path to maturity laid out before them.⁸

This brief sketch is an outline of how we should conceive of the basic facts of creation according to the biblical narrative: the world was created as an "utter novum" by a good and loving God. It was created "good," in line with its early stage in the unfolding drama. Humans were also created good, as children, and invited to work with God as participants in the story as cultivators of the garden. This invitation was, according to the story, given to humans uniquely among all the creatures of the world, and helps to define human nature itself.

---

3. Walton, *The Lost World of Adam and Eve*, 55.

4. Gunton, *The Promise of Trinitarian Theology*, 181.

5. Irenaeus, *Against Heresies*, 4.38.1. Of course Irenaeus agrees that it was *possible* for God to have made humanity perfect from the start, but he did not.

6. Irenaeus, *Against Heresies*, 5.15.2.

7. Provan, *Seriously Dangerous Religion*, 78.

8. Irenaeus, *Against Heresies*, 4.38.3.

An Introduction to Child Theology

Imago Dei

What does it mean to be human? On the story offered in the introduction as a foil to our argument, what is important about humanity is that we have an immortal soul, and this is what the *imago dei* (the "image of God") means. It matters greatly, then, what ultimately happens to this soul, and the choice between eternal punishment or eternal bliss is the most important choice a human can make. As was argued in the previous section, we should be suspicious of any such reading of creation (and any associated anthropology) that depends on the static perfection model of creation. What shall we put in its place? Following the insights of trinitarian theologians like Colin Gunton or John Zizioulas, the *imago dei* is best understood as participation in the relational personhood of God. While the biblical narrative does not discount the human faculty of reason that is so often touted as the distinguishing feature of humanity, and therefore often identified with the *imago dei*, reason is not that which is most constitutive of God, and so we should not think that to be "like" God is to be rational.

Instead, we should take advantage of the theological work done from the time of the church fathers, who needed a category to describe the reality of God's trinitarian existence, and so co-opted the dramatic term of art *persona*.[9] What God granted human beings in the *imago dei* was first of all personhood, defined as an existence that consists of relationality prior to any other mode. In essence, God invites humanity into something of the trinitarian relationship, which grounds our beings as "persons," outside of any particular set of features we might use to describe ourselves.

This relationship between God and humanity has a definite character. Part and parcel of personhood is *vocation*, which we have already mentioned in the concept of participating in the great project of God. Humans are called uniquely to steward the earth and care for the other creatures, in other words to do the kinds of things that God is already doing! God cares for and sustains his creatures. He loves them and cultivates them in the direction of flourishing. So humankind's God-given responsibility is not somehow unrelated to the character of God; humans are called precisely to adopt the loving character of God to the rest of God's creation.

We thus "image" God in two ways: first, via our essence (as persons), and second, via our actions (as stewards, vice-regents of God meant to care for the world in line with his character). The best analogy for understanding

---

9. Balthasar, "On the Concept of Person," 20.

this "likeness" is that of the similarity between parents and children. When our children are born, they in some way receive our essence—they are of the same "kind" as us (biologically as well as theologically). As they grow, we ask them and teach them to also be of the same "kind" as us when it comes to our typical (and ideally typically *good*) modes of acting in the world.

Of course, we are not biologically related to God. The biblical story is clear that there is a wide gulf of being between God and creation. Humans are not divine. We are merely part of creation, along with all other creatures. God is the totally other, which is why he cannot be depicted in any form within the world, even the form of humankind.[10] And yet God has bridged that gulf in the gift of the *imago dei*, which is not itself the divine substance but rather personhood, God's own relationality.

From the focus on growth in the story of creation, we can infer that our nascent personhood and vocation were *also* meant to grow into something greater. Children are not meant to stay children, but to become more and more like their parents in their maturity, freedom, and autonomy. Contrary to the common assumption that humans innately possess an eternal soul (which derives ultimately from Platonism), there is no indication in the biblical story that Adam and Eve were immortal. The tree of life was present in the garden, but we are never told that its fruit has been eaten. Irenaeus agrees that we are not naturally immortal, arguing that we should never suppose "that the incorruptibility which belongs to [us] is [our] own ..., as if [we] were naturally like to God."[11] It is in fact the supposition that we *could* compare ourselves with God in this way that led to the fall, which we will discuss in detail shortly.

The trajectory of the *imago dei*, then, is that God intended for us to grow more and more into his likeness through the work of stewarding creation. This work necessarily involves learning what it is to care for other creatures and to love them in a self-giving fashion, which is precisely what typifies Yahweh. "Growing up," in other words, is growing more like God. Following church fathers like Athanasius, we will refer to this eventual, mature "greater communion" as *theosis*. We must be careful here, as there is obviously a danger of conceiving *theosis* Platonically, as if some preexisting divine spark in each of us will one day fly back to union with God. We must not be so careful, however, as to miss the observations of orthodox

10. Brunner, *Christianity and Civilisation*, 78.
11. Irenaeus, *Against Heresies*, 3.20.1.

theologians across the ages, especially when they make sense of the biblical story. These theologians are themselves usually careful enough. John Zizioulas, for example, asserts that *theosis* is *not* a deification of human nature, but unity in personhood with God.[12] St. John of the Cross agrees that while the human being is transformed in *theosis*, it is still "as distinct from the Being of God as it was before."[13]

Irenaeus is clear that *theosis* was in view from the beginning, otherwise we would not "cast blame upon [God], because we have not been made gods from the beginning, but at first merely men, then at length gods."[14] Athanasius upholds the same perspective in his famous formula, this time centered around the redeeming actions of Christ: "He was incarnate that we might be made god."[15] So, to the story of biblical creation we have been developing, we can add the concept of *theosis*, which amounts to the mature state of grown-up humankind as it emerges from childhood. However, for good or (as most Christians through the ages have had it) for ill, this straightforward narrative arc of gradual growth and eventual *theosis* was rudely interrupted.

The Fall

The fall is often made to bear prime explanatory weight for many streams of religious anthropology. We should make sure, then, to understand it well. Iain Provan reads this story as one not of instant catastrophe but rather of gradual alienation, consisting of other milestones of human choice just as significant as the fall. Even *after* the fall, human freedom matters: "Cain himself is clearly presented with a *choice* in Genesis 4:7. He might well submit to sin, which is pictured as a wild animal crouching at his door, *or* perhaps he will 'master' it. There is nothing inevitable about his submission."[16] Even *after* the fall, humans have a kind of immediate relationship with God we have apparently lost at some point since then: "The expulsion of human beings from the garden does not mean, in Genesis, that they cannot 'walk with God.'"[17]

12. Zizioulas, *Communion and Otherness*, 243.
13. John of the Cross, *The Ascent of Mount Carmel*, book 2, chapter 5, section 7.
14. Irenaeus, *Against Heresies*, 4.38.4.
15. Athanasius, *On the Incarnation*, 93.
16. Provan, *Seriously Dangerous Religion*, 136.
17. Provan, *Seriously Dangerous Religion*, 136.

The Childhood of Humanity in the Biblical Narrative

So, what *is* the fall? In the story, it occurs after the humans eat the fruit of the tree of knowledge of good and evil. This was the fruit that had been forbidden to them, but was held up by Satan as a vehicle for making the humans "like God."[18] It is offered as a strategy for the adoption of certain divine attributes (in this case, knowing what is truly good and evil).[19] In this sense it is precisely a shortcut, a way around the God-ordained path to *theosis*. It is tiresome to perform the slow work of stewarding creation, learning only over eons of human history what it is to truly love as God loves. Rowan Williams makes the same sad observation: we want "ways of knowing, ways of mastery, which didn't depend on the contingency of taking time."[20] Thus the crux of the matter was the decision to forcibly take some aspect of divinity outside the established path of the maturation of the *imago dei*. If we conceive (along with Irenaeus) of Adam and Eve as children, then their taking the fruit was a bid for adulthood: an adulthood not attained naturally by growing more deeply into the image of their divine Father, but as an instantaneous jump.

It is therefore a mistake to see the tree of knowledge of good and evil as some kind of necessary negative space for free will. The better analysis sees the sin in the motive and means of disobedience: to become like God on our own, out of a distrust in God's good processes. We can only speculate as to God's purpose for placing the tree in the garden, as his reasoning does not figure into the narrative. The interpretation offered here is one that sees God's prohibition as probably temporary, and not arbitrary, but for the humans' own good. In other words, the fruit of that tree was not yet ripe for Adam and Eve, or put perhaps more accurately, *they* were not ripe for *it*.

With our own human children we frequently prohibit the consumption or use of this or that thing, even knowing the thing to be good at some time and in some way. Electricity is a useful and powerful source of energy, and yet we routinely cover up the electrical outlets in our homes when we have babies crawling around. There are inappropriate times at which, and motives for which, to engage with many good things. God's warning that the humans will surely die when they eat of the tree can thus be seen as a *helpful* warning describing the *reality* of the tree and its power, not a description of

---

18. Gen 3:5.

19. As Dietrich Bonhoeffer points out, the desire to know what is truly good and evil is a desire for self-justification, which is inimical to trust in God. See Clark J. Elliston, *Dietrich Bonhoeffer and the Ethical Self*, 60.

20. Williams, *Being Human*, 64.

God's willingness to inflict capital punishment on those who transgress this boundary. But humans ignored God's warning, choosing self-dependence over God-dependence. The crucial point is that humans have *grasped after*, have *taken* their *theosis* rather than accepting it in childlike dependence from the hand of their creator. The quite natural result is a loss of relationality not only with God (expressed in their act of hiding), but with each other (expressed in their act of blaming), and eventually the world.

Despite this admittedly momentous shift in orientation for humankind, God did not respond (as many people assume) with swift vengeance. He first sought out the humans and asked them questions.[21] He then pronounced a series of curses, though it is only the serpent who is cursed directly (the only party to whom it is said, "cursed are *you* . . .").[22] The human beings themselves are not cursed, but rather it is peripheral aspects of their life in the world that receive the brunt. Even after the cursing, Adam and Eve still inhabit a good world, and God's providence will still sustain them, but because of their premature adulthood, they will not experience an easier and more gradual introduction to the art of cultivation.[23]

The ultimate problem of the fall is that sin (defined at root as the choice of a delusional self-dependence rather than God-dependence), hardened itself at the core of human existence. This is a process that happened over time, continuing from Adam and Eve through Cain, Lamech, and their antediluvian offspring. Continued sin was not initially viewed as inevitable, though it is now difficult to argue against its practically determining force in our lives. It results ultimately from our woeful habit of constantly setting our sights too low, on the kinds of gods we imagine we can become through our own efforts. As C. S. Lewis famously said, "We are half-hearted creatures, fooling about with [sin] when infinite joy is offered us, like an

---

21. Gen 3:8–13.

22. Gen 3:14.

23. Gen 3:16–19. The human pair's expulsion from paradise is likewise not described as punitive in the text, where God says, "The man has now become like one of us, knowing good and evil. He must not be allowed to reach out his hand and take also from the tree of life and eat, and live forever" (Gen 3:22). This locking up of the tree of life is viewed instead as a mercy, as Irenaeus points out: "Wherefore also He drove him out of Paradise, and removed him far from the tree of life, not because He envied him the tree of life, as some venture to assert, but because He pitied him, [and did not desire] that he should continue a sinner for ever, nor that the sin which surrounded him should be immortal, and evil interminable and irremediable" (Irenaeus, *Against Heresies*, 3.23.6). In other words, it would not be good for *us* to add immortality to a human character that was vulnerable to evil!

ignorant child who wants to go on making mud pies in a slum because he cannot imagine what is meant by the offer of a holiday at the sea. We are far too easily pleased."[24]

The sad fact is that we, being these "ignorant children," have grown up! We have become adults, but the wrong kind of adults, and far too soon on top of that. We did not grow into the image of our heavenly Father, but worshiped everything else in the world that we thought might make us wiser or more powerful. Dietrich Bonhoeffer made a similar point when he described us as living in a "world come of age," where we now have to reckon with the consequences of our adult freedom, without the benefit of having developed adult character along the way.[25] The fall, then, threw a twist into the simple narrative of creation leading towards *theosis*. After the fall, humans were on a different trajectory, attempting self-made divinity. The original story did not need to be thrown away entirely as a result of this fork in the narrative, but clearly God's project of "fashioning the human being" had become more complicated, now that sin constantly cropped up as a barrier to the childlike trust in God that is prerequisite for true human maturity. What could God do to help get us back on the original path?

Redemption

Thankfully, the biblical story did not end with a fatalistic acceptance of humankind's choice, though God's optimism could be described as foolhardy, when recalling the almost comical parade of human failure and forgetfulness throughout the duration of his efforts to work with humans beginning with Abraham. We must regrettably leave out a detailed exploration of God's work with Israel. Suffice it to say that the entire narrative is one attempt after another at redeeming the inner character of humanity as the first step in redeeming the world. Ultimately, the story culminates in the incarnation of Christ, where God himself becomes a human being in the form of Jesus of Nazareth.

If the incarnation is in some way a solution to the problem of human sin, it must ultimately provide humans a path to the original process of maturation that leads to godlikeness and therefore God's gift of *theosis*. It must fix the problem of human *character*. And so the incarnation should be primarily understood as God's making visible the kind of childlike life

---

24. Lewis, *The Weight of Glory and Other Addresses*, 26.
25. Bonhoeffer, *Letters and Papers from Prison*, 324–29.

of faith that we were always supposed to live. In Philippians 2, Jesus is explicitly described as passing the test that Adam and Eve failed: "Being in very nature God, [he] did not consider equality with God something to be used to his own advantage; rather, he made himself nothing by taking the very nature of a servant, being made in human likeness. And being found in appearance as a man, he humbled himself by becoming obedient to death—even death on a cross!"[26]

Jesus perfectly embodied the posture of a child, not seeking premature adulthood in the way that Adam and Eve did. As Hans Urs von Balthasar has observed, Jesus is the model of the child who matures *without* discarding basic trust, even in the face of apparent abandonment.[27] When faced with death and the silence of God, Jesus accepts suffering, even though he had the power within himself to avoid it. Jesus accepted God's judgment of death on a cross in the way that a trusting child does not care whether her actions were right or wrong, but looks simply to the loving gaze of her parent.[28]

In the crucifixion, then, God reconciled the world to himself not primarily by paying for the cosmic debt of human sin. Jesus, as the second Adam, remained a faithful child of God to the point of death, thus reopening the path of *theosis* that necessarily begins with such faith. After the crucifixion, a door was opened to a *new* path, a path of faithfulness through death. This faithfulness, as St. Paul puts it, stole away death's "sting."[29] Traversing the door of death does of course involve dying, but dying is now only an intermediate point, thanks to God's vindication of Jesus in the resurrection.

On its own, the crucifixion can only bear so much weight. A faithfully crucified Christ is an inspiration, but not a solution to the problem of sin. Wonderfully, death could not hold Jesus; after a short time God granted him new life, and indeed a new *kind* of life, one totally different from what we currently experience. As the model of the child who had grown into a mature adult following the path of trust in God, Jesus was given the fruit of the tree of life—an immortal and incorruptible body. This astonishing and unexpected outcome makes visible, for the first time in the history of creation, what the human being was ultimately intended to become! Faithful obedience to God in the way of Christ is therefore a path that starts with

---

26. Phil 2:6–8.
27. Balthasar, *Unless You Become Like This Child*, 31.
28. Bonhoeffer, *Ethics*, 38.
29. 1 Cor 15:55.

birth, passes through childhood, leads to maturity, and ultimately traverses death. Church fathers like Irenaeus and Athanasius would have felt very much at home in this understanding, and it unifies all aspects of the biblical narrative, making sense of creation, fall, incarnation, crucifixion, and resurrection. These are not just arbitrarily conjoined doctrines, but rather the unfolding of the loving intention of the God who created and sustains the cosmos.

If we balk with Nicodemus about the language of becoming a child again, we should remind ourselves that being dependent children of God is not in any way like placing ourselves under the absolutism of another human being. Depending on God, says Rowan Williams, is not like losing autonomy to other human beings, because God is not a greedy, controlling ego.[30] Indeed, Balthasar has noted that the world of the Father's pleasure is not narrow (as the serpent would have us believe) but exceedingly wide, "so that the Son always does what pleases the Father and 'exactly fulfills his command' (Jn 14:31)."[31] It is possible, as Jesus proved, to retain the trust and dependence of a child while growing beyond ignorance and incapacity into mature adulthood. Our *trying* to be adults, on the other hand, is ultimately much more dangerous, because it amounts to Gnosticism, the anti-child religion.

Redemption, of course, is not eschatology. Jesus may have shown us a path of childlike trust leading eventually to *theosis*, but the journey is not the destination. We still have to walk the path, to get on with the work of stewarding creation, and to grow into mature, godlike adults. We still have to choose faithfulness at the price of death in this broken world, at least for now.

Conclusion

We began this essay with the point that being able to articulate an overarching biblical narrative is essential, for otherwise we end up simply laundering our cultural anthropology through Scripture. God's creation is not best understood as an act that led to a statically perfect Eden, which was subsequently shattered by human disobedience in the face of an arbitrary prohibition, and which metaphysically poisoned our immortal souls. The

---

30. Williams, *Being Human*, 83.
31. Balthasar, *Unless You Become Like This Child*, 35–36.

point of human life is not for these souls to become purified and allowed to join God in heaven.

The story we find ourselves in is rather the story of a loving Father and his beloved children. Our Father desperately wants us to remember that we are children, to forget our obsession with self-dependence, and to allow a true maturity to blossom that remains rooted in childlike trust. Our Father wants us to learn how to become more and more like him, by doing the kinds of things he does in the playground of this world. And ultimately, our Father wants to give us even more of his life than he did at the beginning.

When a relatively inexperienced King Solomon admitted to God that he was only a little child in need of wisdom, God blessed him with wisdom and all manner of other gifts. Later in his life, when he found his confidence and sustenance in his wisdom and in his gifts, having "grown out" of his childlike faith, he thereby sowed the seeds of Israel's eventual downfall. Jesus, by contrast, cried "Abba, Father!" even until the point of death. To him, God granted not only wisdom but an entirely new kind of life, as the model of what he has in mind for all of us. Therefore let us too cry "Abba, Father!" along with Jesus, trusting that *theosis* as the gift of God, and given in his time, is far better than any bid for independence and divinity we might contemplate on our own.

Chapter Two

Isaac the Son and the Shadow of Ishmael

Andrew Zack Lewis

The haunting effect of the opening lines of Genesis 22 hinges largely on the triple accusative attached to the imperative "take." Abraham is to take "your son," "your only one, whom you love," "Isaac." Each of these phrases is delineated in the Hebrew by the untranslatable definite direct object marker "*eṯ*."[1] The difficulty of the act proposed by God grows with each accusative phrase. The delay in naming Isaac creates a sense of possibility that Isaac may not be the object of the taking. The sparseness of the grammar—the single verb, ellipsed for the second and third direct objects—increases the weight of what is being asked of Abraham. As Claus Westermann explains it, "[To] the first command, 'Take your son, Isaac,' is added, 'your only son, whom you love' so as to underscore the difficulty and harshness."[2]

Westermann's assessment, as insightful as it seems, relegates the power assigned to the passage only to the immediate context. That is, by reading the second accusative as "your only son, whom you love" as merely modifying "your son, Isaac," Westermann ignores an important factor in the narrative as a whole, namely, that Isaac is not Abraham's only son. In the previous chapter the reader is brought into the destiny of Abraham's other son, his firstborn, Ishmael. Ishmael continues to live and, even though he is sent away with his mother Hagar to another place, Ishmael does not cease to be Abraham's son in the narrative of Genesis or the Bible as a whole. In

1. "*eṯ-binəḵā ʾeṯ-yəḥîḏəḵā ʾăšer-ʾāhaḇtā ʾeṯ-yiṣḥāq*"
2. Claus Westermann, *Genesis 12–36*, 357.

fact, in Genesis 25, in the context of Abraham's death and burial by both Isaac and Ishmael, the narrator twice calls Ishmael Abraham's son.[3]

The rabbis did not fail to note the problems with the command laid down on Abraham in Genesis 22:2. In as early as the fourth century CE *Bereshit Rabba* 55:7 explores the triple accusative with the following midrash:

> Said God to him: "Take, I beg you . . . Your son." "Which son? I have two sons" he said. "Your only son," replied He. "This one is the only one of his mother, and this one is the only one of his mother." "The one you love"—"Is there a limit to the affections?" "Itzchak" said He. And why did God not reveal it to him without delay? In order to make him even more beloved in his eyes and reward him for each and every word spoken.[4]

The story of the binding of Isaac reveals its power in the history of interpretation. As in Westermann's commentary, the most well-known of these interpretations—from the author of Hebrews to Maimonides to Kierkegaard—treat the story isolated from the larger context in the book of Genesis. There is great value in focusing on the story under a microscope, as it were. Such great value, as it happens, that I am not convinced I could contribute much more to the philosophical depth generated by the story than, say, Maimonides, Kierkegaard, or the interpreters of Maimonides and Kierkegaard. Rather, I am struck by the line describing Isaac before the call to sacrifice him has even been fully announced. While many have rightly wondered about the lasting psychological effect on young Isaac of being a few inches from death at the hand of his father, the larger context of the biblical story should also direct one to wonder about the effects of being the beneficiary of a type of sacrifice in the previous chapter. While Isaac is moments away from being sacrificed on an altar, he had already witnessed his brother treated like a proto-scapegoat, sent into the wilderness to help fulfill his own promise.[5]

We know, however, that Ishmael returns. He joins Isaac to bury Abraham. The text remains silent as to how Ishmael learns of his father's death. Abraham has six other sons besides Isaac and Ishmael (Gen 25:2). As with Ishmael, Abraham sends these sons away "from his son Isaac" to another land so that Isaac can receive Abraham's full inheritance (Gen 25:5–6). But

---

3. Gen 25:9, 12. Cf. 1 Chr 1:28.
4. Bereshit Rabbah 55:2. Cf. Rashi, who quotes the above midrash in his commentary.
5. Lev 16:10.

when Abraham dies, Ishmael returns to bury him. There is no mention of the other sons in the text. Ishmael is again called Abraham's son and he and Isaac are seen as brothers. Perhaps Isaac stays in touch with Ishmael throughout his adulthood. There is no way to know. That Isaac bears a knowledge of his older brother must be considered, though, for Ishmael lurks in the shadows of Isaac's life in striking ways, including in his relationship to his own children.

As many students of the Pentateuch will note, the stories of Abraham, Ishmael, and Isaac that make up the middle parts of Genesis seem to have come from different traditions. Most commonly understood as written by either the so-called Yahwist on one hand and the priestly writer on the other, Genesis and Exodus, in particular, are made difficult to interpret in light of the development of the final product. Whatever the developmental history of the text of Genesis, I am interpreting the book through a narrative-critical lens. That is, I am choosing to read the Abram/Abraham of the Yahwist as the same Abram/Abraham of the priestly writer. Source criticism, while not a perfect science, can perhaps help explain some puzzling aspects of a wide-scoped story like Isaac and Ishmael's. For instance, perhaps the story of Abraham's sons from his concubines in 25:2 are from the pen of a different author than the story of Ishmael's return for Abraham's burial.[6] These explanations are largely unsatisfactory for a whole army of reasons that have been hashed and rehashed the last several decades. Narrative criticism has been a necessary corrective for those of us who view the redacted text itself as authoritative. A narrative critical reading not only invites readers to explore the text as it has been read for millennia, but the characters that emerge from said text bear a complexity that proves to be more real psychologically than the simplistic folktales source criticism intends to unearth. The humanity of Isaac as Abraham's son, Ishmael's brother, and Jacob and Esau's father need not be unearthed, for humanity is earthy.[7]

Ishmael as son

In order to understand the earthy Isaac, we must begin years before his birth, when his parents still believe the existence of Isaac to be an impossibility. In Genesis 16, Sarai and Abram become frustrated enough with their inability to conceive that Sarai gives Abram her slave girl Hagar as a

6. Von Rad, *Genesis*, 260–63.
7. See Gen 2:7.

surrogate for his child. When Hagar finally conceives, Sarai turns jealous to the point that Hagar runs away. For reasons unclear, the angel of the Lord appears to Hagar to tell her to return and submit to Sarai. Along with that command the angel of the Lord gives Hagar a promise strikingly familiar to readers of Genesis: "I will so greatly multiply your offspring that they cannot be counted for multitude" (Gen 16:10). The careful reader cannot help but hark back to Genesis 13:16, when the Lord promises Abram: "I will make your offspring like the dust of the earth; so that if one can count the dust of the earth, your offspring also can be counted." Two chapters later in 15:5, just before Hagar's exile and what may have spurred Hagar into Abram's harem, the Lord brings Abram outside under the night sky and says, "Look toward heaven and count the stars, if you are able to count them. . . So shall your descendants be." Hagar, induced to return to her mistress, gives birth and names her son Ishmael, meaning "God hears," because "the LORD has given heed to [*lit.* heard] [her] affliction."

In chapter 17, God reiterates his promise to Abraham, telling him, "And I will make my covenant between me and you, and will make you exceedingly numerous" (Gen 17:2). Along with this covenant, God declares that the sign of the covenant will be the circumcision of all the males in Abraham's household. Though the reader learns of the eventual birth of Isaac in this chapter, Abraham circumcises Ishmael after his dialogue with God. Even though Abraham learns that the covenant will be established with Isaac, he brings Ishmael into the covenant family through the sign of the covenant. In this story, God blesses Ishmael in order to "make him fruitful and exceedingly numerous; he shall be the father of twelve princes, and [God] will make him a great nation" (Gen 17:20). Though Abraham's circumcision of Ishmael is not described as a direct response to the blessing God promises Ishmael, the two events—the blessing of Ishmael and the circumcision of Ishmael—appear to the reader as related. God blesses Ishmael with a blessing similar to the covenant with Abraham and then Abraham gives Ishmael the sign of the covenant. Notably, Abraham, perhaps concerned by Sarah's barrenness, asks for Ishmael to receive the covenant, which God denies him. Ishmael's blessing then seems to act as a concessionary prize for Abraham.

At the end of Genesis 17, the narrator describes the circumcision of Ishmael three times in consecutive verses:

> [23]Then Abraham took his son Ishmael and all the slaves born in his house or bought with his money, every male among the men of

Isaac the Son and the Shadow of Ishmael

Abraham's house, and he circumcised the flesh of their foreskins that very day, as God had said to him. ²⁴Abraham was ninety-nine years old when he was circumcised in the flesh of his foreskin. ²⁵And his son Ishmael was thirteen years old when he was circumcised in the flesh of his foreskin. ²⁶That very day Abraham and his son Ishmael were circumcised. (Gen 17:23–26, NRSV)

Note also that the narrator calls Ishmael Abraham's son three times in the above four verses. All of which is to say, that despite Ishmael not receiving the covenant promised to Abraham's line, he bears the *sign* of the covenant *and* receives a promise strikingly similar to Abraham's covenant *because* he is Abraham's son. This is made explicit later in the larger narrative of Abraham, in Genesis 21:13, when God tells Abraham directly regarding Ishmael, "I will make a nation of him also, because he is your offspring." It must be said that Ishmael is still clearly to be considered secondary to the progeny of Abraham and Sarah. Ishmael is Abraham's son. He receives a blessing due to his status as the son of Abraham. However, the covenant of Abraham is reserved for the son of Sarah.[8]

Sarah does give birth to a son a few chapters later in the narrative. This is, of course, Isaac. Isaac is a miracle, a fact reflected in his name—"He laughs." Both Abraham and Sarah laugh at the ridiculous thought of having a child so late in life (Gen 17:17; 18:12), but one gets the sense that they laugh with relief when the son is finally born. The relief that Sarah feels, though, soon shades to paranoia. In order to guarantee Isaac's inheritance, Sarah forces Ishmael to leave Abraham's household with his mother Hagar. On this occasion, as in chapter 16, Sarah instigates Hagar's departure to the wilderness. As in chapter 16, God appears to Hagar near a spring of water.[9] In contrast to the earlier experience with the divine, God does not beckon Hagar to return to the household of Abraham. Rather, God stays with Ishmael in the wilderness where Ishmael becomes an expert with the bow and marries an Egyptian woman.

While Ishmael's departure from the household of Abraham after the birth of Isaac ends the latent suspense that Ishmael could receive the covenant of Abraham along with his inheritance, his stamp does remain on the rest of the story.

---

8. Leon Kass writes, "To overstate the point, Abraham is here with Ishmael undergoing basic training, as it were, just practicing to become the father of Isaac" ("Educating Father Abraham," 35).

9. In chapter 16, "the Angel of YHWH" finds Hagar by a spring in the wilderness; in chapter 21, "*ĕlōhîm*"—translated "God" in English Bibles—hears the boy's voice.

Consider the beginning of the story of Isaac. While Isaac is still a toddler, the only thing we readers know about him is his name. Isaac receives his name (*yiṣəḥāq*) when his father laughs at the prospect that he and his wife could conceive at such an advanced age (17:17-19; cf. 18:12ff.). After the weaning of Isaac, Sarah witnesses Ishmael jesting (*məṣaḥēq*).[10] The letter *mem* at the front of the root, accompanied by a particular vocalization in the Masoretic Text, indicates the *piel* stem of the verb. The name Isaac is vocalized as a *qal* stem, so it appears that Ishmael is not laughing, but, perhaps more making something worthy of laughing at.[11] The same verb in the same *piel* stem had been used in Genesis 19:14, when Lot's sons-in-law believed Lot to be joking about the coming destruction of Sodom. The suggestion with Ishmael could be that he is making fun of Isaac, but since Isaac is not present in the verse the Masoretic Text must be arguing something else. The LXX adds that Ishmael was playing with Isaac (παίζοντα μετὰ Ισαακ), but the MT lacks any object of Ishmael's play.[12] Rather, it lets the participle describing Ishmael's actions do the work. It is clearly a pun on Isaac's name, seemingly used to provoke Sarah into jealousy. Perhaps Sarah witnesses Ishmael's joy and is reminded that, as the firstborn son of Abraham, Ishmael is set to inherit more of his father's inheritance than her son Isaac.[13] But as the firstborn son in the larger narrative of Genesis, Ishmael finds himself as an object of narrative patterning.

---

10. See Joshua Schwartz, "Ishmael at Play," for a survey of how this event has been interpreted in the history of Judaism.

11. The effect of the stem system in Semitic languages generally affects the agency of the action. The qal stem is the simplest and tends to indicate an active verb. The piel stem is, unfortunately, the most complicated of the main seven stems in biblical Hebrew. One of the more common effects it has on a qal verb is to put something else in the state of the verbal root. So, qal "laugh" presumably means "to make something laughable" in the piel. See Waltke and O'Connor, *An Introduction*, 203-21.

12. It is unusual for verbs in the piel stem to act as intransitive verbs, but not in the case of *ṣḥq* apparently, for in two other places in the Pentateuch (Gen 19:14 and Exod 32:6) is its use similar to that in Genesis 21:9. When it does take an object, the verb in the piel means "to fondle." It means "to make fun of" with an object preceded by a preposition.

13. See Deuteronomy 21:15-17, whose principle may have influenced Sarah's fear that Ishmael would receive a "double portion" of all Abraham has: "If a man has two wives, one of them loved and the other disliked, and if both the loved and the disliked have borne him sons, the firstborn being the son of the one who is disliked, then on the day when he wills his possessions to his sons, he is not permitted to treat the son of the loved as the firstborn in preference to the son of the disliked, who is the firstborn. He must acknowledge as firstborn the son of the one who is disliked, giving him a double

Exile and the Older Son

The story about tension between two brothers leading to the exile of one has both an archetype in Cain and Abel and antitype in Jacob and Esau and Joseph and his brothers.[14] In the story of Cain and Abel, both brothers present offerings to the Lord, but only Abel's is accepted. In his jealousy, it seems that Cain tricks his brother to go into the field under false pretenses, where he kills Abel.[15] Cain then goes into exile to the land of Nod, where he becomes a builder of cities. Cain's mother, Eve, laments the loss of her son Abel through the naming of her son Seth (*šēṯ*), because God has provided (*šāṯ*) another seed. Though Cain's sin is egregious to the Lord, he receives a mark of some sort which grants him protection on his journey. However, the line that leads to Noah and the covenants that follow comes from Seth. Cain is protected as long as he lives, but his lineage is forgotten in Genesis beyond his great-great-great grandson Lamech.

Similar but distinct patterns occur in the stories of Ishmael and Isaac, Jacob and Esau, and Joseph and his brothers. Jacob, whose name ostensibly reflects his grabbing Esau's heel during birth, comes to reflect his trickery in betraying his brother out of his blessing. Joseph's brothers trick their father Jacob into believing Joseph has been torn to pieces by a wild animal. Ishmael's trickery is much less clear. As noted above, though the action Sarah witnesses Ishmael doing has its root in the verb "to laugh," in the *piel* stem—thus, perhaps to put something in a state of laughter, or ridicule— the lack of an object of his ridicule makes the offense ambiguous. Other uses of the word in the Bible evoke possibilities of Ishmael's actions that have been explored in rabbinic texts. *Bereshit Rabbah* posits a host of suggestions, ranging from Ishmael practicing sexual immorality (cf. the use of the same word in Genesis 39:17 where Potiphar's wife accuses Joseph) to practicing idolatry (cf. the use of the same word in the golden calf episode in Exodus 32:6 where the Israelites participate in revelry). Rabbi Azariah, along with rabbis in several other Midrashim, connects Ishmael's facility

---

portion of all that he has; since he is the first issue of his virility, the right of the firstborn is his."

14. A detailed examination of this pattern can be found in Jon Levenson's *The Death and Resurrection of the Beloved Son*, 55–60.

15. The MT introduces speech by Cain but lacks the speech itself. A literal translation reads, "And Cain said to Abel his brother. And it happened, when they were in the field . . ." The LXX and Samaritan Pentateuch both include a brief quote by Cain: "Let us go to the field," suggesting a corrupted MT.

with the bow to this scene, proposing that Ishmael pretends to shoot his younger brother with an arrow, thus threatening his life.[16] Such an interpretation cannot be entirely justified by the language of the text in the verse alone, but it does connect the dots with respect to the other examples of fraternal tension in the book of Genesis, for not only does Cain murder Abel, but Esau threatens to kill Jacob, instigating Jacob's exile. Similarly, Jacob's own sons pretend to kill Joseph, Jacob's beloved son, out of jealousy and then send him off to an exile of sorts. Incidentally, Joseph is sold to descendants of his great uncle Ishmael.

We will return to the story of Jacob and Esau in more detail below with the above narrative patterning in mind. Before we do that, it is important to consider here more differences between Ishmael and Isaac and the other sibling rivalries. In each of these stories, one brother is favored over the other in some way. The Lord accepts Abel's offering over Cain's (Gen 4:4–5). Isaac loves Esau while Rachel loves Jacob (Gen 25:28). Jacob loves Joseph more than his brothers (Gen 37:3). The contrast between Abraham's love for Isaac over Ishmael, however, is not made explicit by the narrator. I look closer at Abraham's love for Isaac below.

Though all four examples describe one brother going into exile, the brother who goes into exile is not necessarily related to his favorability. For instance, while the older brother leaves the home of the father in the case of Cain and Ishmael, the younger brothers, Jacob and Joseph, are the exilic parties in the later stories.

Another disparity is found in the role of the covenant. Abel, while favored over Cain (and favored in the eyes of the Lord, at that) dies before he has children, so Seth's line adopts the role as covenant partner with the Lord. Joseph's older brothers are definitively a part of the covenant family and it is the line of Judah, one of the older brothers, which bears the line that will give the Israelites King David. Thus, Isaac and Jacob are the only younger sons who bear the covenant line at the exclusion of their older brothers.

Thirdly, the threats of death that lead to exile are distinct in each episode. Cain follows through with his murderous desires and must go into exile because the ground is too cursed for him to work it. While Esau, like

---

16. Note also Galatians 4:29. Though Paul is allegorizing the story of Hagar/Ishmael and Sarah/Isaac, he writes that "the one born according to the flesh was persecuting the one born of the spirit." Paul does not specify how he believes Ishmael was persecuting Isaac, but it would be reasonable to assume he is familiar with the traditions that give birth to the medieval rabbinic texts.

Cain, conspires to kill his younger brother, it is Jacob who flees into exile in order to escape Esau. Likewise, Joseph, the younger brother, is forced into exile by his murderous kin, though the circumstances are obviously distinct from his father's. Ishmael, while an older brother like Cain, and while sent into exile like Cain, not only does not kill his brother; as noted above, it is unclear what he does. Also, while Cain must leave the land because he is more cursed than the cursed ground, Ishmael is sent into exile by his father's jealous or fearful wife. Like Cain, who receives a mark of protection from God, Ishmael is saved from death by God and receives a promise of a great nation from his own loins.

While the pattern—which includes one son favored over another, trickery, exile, and threat of murder—weaves through four generations,[17] none of the stories repeats any previous one with obvious consistency. Rather, each successive story surprises the reader, subverting expectations established by the previous similar story.

Excursus: "your only son whom you love"

In the introduction to this essay, I note the potentially confusing command by God to Abraham instigating the *aqedah*. Beyond the challenging command to sacrifice his son, God calls Isaac Abraham's "only son." I want to revisit the phrase in the midst of the command—"your only son, whom you love"—to determine the meaning of the phrase as finely as possible in the context of the narrative as given in Genesis. The author of *Bereshit Rabba* sees the second accusative, "your only son," as limiting the meaning of "your son," the relative clause "whom you love" as limiting the meaning of "your only son," and "Isaac" as limiting the meaning of all the previous phrases. Such an interpretation works best, however, in the context of a midrash, where the interpreter is encouraged to fill in the gaps. The discourse *Bereshit Rabba* recounts is not found in the text itself. The rabbis perceive a problem and contend with the problem without solving the problem. Not that the problem is possible to solve, but other witnesses from antiquity deal with the problem in other ways.

The Hebrew word translated as "only son" in most familiar English Bibles—*yāḥîḏ*—occurs in nine passages in the Hebrew Bible outside of Genesis 22. Most of these examples are in poetic passages. Examples from

---

17. A shade of this pattern exists in the Noah story (9:21–27) but it is incomplete.

the Psalms describe the suppliant's life, so should be understood as "only."[18] The prophets use the word to describe a son that a parent is mourning,[19] perhaps alluding to the *aqedah*, but not necessarily meaning "only son" based on the context. In the case of Judges 11:34, however, the context certainly indicates that Jephthah's daughter is his only child.

The Septuagint deals with the problem of "your only son" by translating the Hebrew word rendered as such in English as τον αγαπητον, namely, "beloved." Such a translation is awkward, considering that the relative clause following "beloved" is translated as ον ηγαπησας, or, "whom you love." The Hebrew words the translator of the Septuagint is presumably reading are not related (*yāḥîḏ* for "only son" and *'hḇ* for the verb "love") and so the Greek reads like a strained way of avoiding the awkwardness of calling Isaac Abraham's only son by calling him loved twice. Ishmael is not forgotten, just unloved.

The authors of the Septuagint were not limited to such a translation of the Hebrew word. While several other passages render *yāḥîḏ* as "beloved" (αγαπητος),[20] the Septuagint translator(s) of the Psalter regularly interpret *yāḥîḏ* as μονογενης,[21] which is often translated as "only begotten."[22] This translation of the Hebrew is how Josephus seems to understand God's command to Abraham. In *Antiquities*, book I, chapter 13, Josephus calls Isaac his father's "only begotten son." This language is picked up by the author of Hebrews, a contemporary of Josephus, in 11:17. The author of Hebrews likely did not know Hebrew, but rather is making a theological point regarding the patriarchs.[23]

Regarding these Greek renderings, we see there is no real consensus on how to understand Abraham's relationship to Isaac in Genesis 22:2. The narrative of Genesis does not lend itself to the idea that beloved, only begotten, and firstborn can be equated at all. Abraham loves Isaac, his second-born son. Jacob loves Joseph, the son of his old age. Rachel loves Jacob, her second born. The only beloved firstborn son in Genesis is Esau by Isaac.

---

18. Pss 22:21; 25:16; 35:17; and 68:7.

19. Jer 6:26; Amos 8:10; and Zech 12:10.

20. Prov 4:3, Jer 6:26, Amos 8:10, and Zech 12:10. Note especially the Zechariah passage where αγαπητος is parallel with the Greek word πρωτοτοκος, that is, "first born."

21. Psalms 21:21/22:20 Heb; 24:16/25:16 Heb; and 34:17/35:17 Heb.

22. See John 3:16.

23. Such a move is typical in Hebrews (Guthrie, "Hebrews," 922-23).

Based on the above data and the narrative context where one son is generally favored over the others, whether they be Abel, Esau, or Joseph, and given that Isaac is the second-born son, whose brother still lives, it seems appropriate to understand *yāḥîd* as meaning "favored" or something similar and not "only son" despite its understanding in other texts as such.[24] The Septuagint attempts a similar, if inelegant reading, repeating the root for "love" in successive words. Though one might argue that Isaac acts effectively as Abraham's only son once Ishmael is forced to leave Abraham's household, it holds that Ishmael remains Abraham's son, returning to bury Abraham with Isaac after Abraham's death.

One must also consider the spare, poetic nature of the phrasing:

> Take your son
> Your favored one, whom you love
> Isaac...

Each successive line limits the meaning of the previous, but it also bears a parallelism familiar in the Hebrew Bible, especially in quoted speech. In the command we read a brief poem organized in a chiasm where "your son" is parallel with "Isaac." The middle phrase, while still describing the same son, has a relative clause parallel with but not identical to the main clause. Your favored one is another way of saying "whom you love."

Keep in mind that the word in question, which we are rendering "your favored," is repeated two more times in the narrative, in 22:12 and 22:16. The repetition of the phrase "your son, your favored one" maintains the memory of Ishmael throughout the episode. Ishmael, therefore, is not forgotten. Nor can Ishmael be forgotten to the attentive reader, for throughout the episode of the binding of Isaac are allusions to the scapegoating of Ishmael.

The Binding of Ishmael

Though Isaac and Abraham were not present for most of the episode recounting Ishmael's ostensible near-death experience in the wilderness of Beersheba, the parallels between the episode and the *aqedah* force the reader

---

24. Note, however, Levenson, who writes that "when Hagar finds Ishmael an Egyptian wife (Gen 21:21), the boy's severance from the chosen lineage is complete... Only after the elimination of Ishmael can Isaac be called Abraham's 'favored' son" (Levenson, *Death and Resurrection*, 109).

An Introduction to Child Theology

to consider the continued connections between the two brothers. In both stories, Abraham "rises early in the morning" in order to send his son on an uncertain journey (21:14; 22:3). Levenson posits that Abraham's placing (*śām*) bread and water on the shoulder of Hagar foreshadows him placing (*wayyāśem*) "the wood for the burnt offering" on Isaac (21:14; 22:6).[25] Once on the journey the parallels become more striking. In both cases, the narrator points to the perspective of the parent and not the child despite the fact that the child's life is the one in peril. At the time when all hope seems lost, the angel of God/YHWH calls "from heaven" (21:17; 22:11) to save the boy from death at the last moment possible.[26] Once initiating the conversation from heaven, God makes the saving implement known to the parent. God opens the eyes of Hagar, who then sees a well where she can provide water for Ishmael (21:19). No less miraculous is the event where Abraham looks up to see a ram caught by its horns in a thicket (22:13).[27] The purpose of the salvation event by God and his angel in both cases is a promise of a great nation (21:18; 22:16–18).

These parallels, both linguistic and thematic, are in stories situated a mere twelve verses from each other. The similarities are striking, both perhaps detailing an initiation rite of sorts[28] and further reinforcing the idea that Ishmael's shadow looms larger in the life of Isaac than often understood. One of these parallels, however, bears an equally striking difference, accentuated by the aforementioned similarities. When the angel of God saves Ishmael from his near-death event, the angel says that God will make Ishmael into a great nation. Note, however, the differences in the great nation promised by the angel of the Lord in 22:16–18. In chapter 22 the promise is directed at Abraham. Though the line will certainly go through Isaac, the descendents belong to Abraham. "I will certainly bless *you* [Abraham]," the angel of the Lord says, "and I will surely make your seed great like the stars of the sky and the sand which is on the shore of the sea. Your seed will possess the gate of your enemies.[29] And all the nations

---

25. Levenson, *Death and Resurrection*, 104.

26. Pardes, "Modern Literature," 192.

27. There may also be some connection between Ishmael saved from a bush and Isaac saved by a thicket, but the linguistic relationship is tenuous.

28. Hugh C. White, "The Initiation Legend of Isaac," quoted in Levenson, *Death and Resurrection*, 110.

29. The verb for "possess," *yrš*, echoes in the mind of the reader from Sarah's command to Abraham to drive out "this slave woman and her son, for this slave woman's son will not possess (*yrš*) with my son Isaac." Perhaps there is another allusion when

of the earth will be blessed by your seed, because you have listened to my voice." Isaac is merely an instrument in this promise to Abraham. Ishmael is the recipient of his own promise.

As if empowered by his promise and the presence of God in his life (21:20), Ishmael becomes a skilled archer while living in the desert. One must wonder if his destiny—a great nation from his loins—has spurred him to greatness in his own right.[30] The promise to Abraham, for not withholding his son from death, mentions Isaac only collectively with the rest of Abraham's seed. Though one cannot draw too much from the contrast in these different promises, it remains tempting to consider Isaac's story subsequent to the promise also in contrast to his brother's. As we read on, we find that many years pass between the *aqedah* and Isaac's finally taking Rebekah as his wife. In Genesis 25:20 we learn that Isaac is forty years old when he marries Rebekah, though there are very few stories regarding his life before marriage. While Isaac's age is not conspicuously advanced to take a wife for the first time,[31] his life otherwise is uneventful compared to his father's. The passivity he displays at the conclusion of the *aqedah*, whether it is his fault or not, bears a resemblance to the next several decades of his life, and even beyond the eventual birth of his children.

One event that is recorded is the aforementioned burial of Abraham in 25:9.[32] Isaac is reunited with his brother, certainly learning about Ishmael, though the narrator offers no record of the reunion besides the burial itself. One can surmise, however, that while his interactions with his brother have been limited to the opening of chapter 21, they have remained consequential in some respects. As described above, Ishmael's shadow looms over Isaac's near-sacrifice in the language of the narrator. Furthermore, Ishmael, the scapegoat whose own sacrifice actuates the favored status of the son

---

Abraham is told his seed will possess the gates of his enemies. Ishmael is excluded from possessing the gates of Abraham's enemies.

30. "His bow also serves as a mark of divine protection—an endowment of power, indicating that although God has assigned Isaac the privileged position of the chosen son of Abraham, Ishmael too is destined to become a great resilient nation" (Pardes, "Modern Literature," 188).

31. Esau, in fact, is said to be forty as well at the time of his marriage in 26:34.

32. See Wenham, *Genesis 16–50*, 151–52, who discusses the somewhat confusing chronology of events between Abraham's enlisting his servant to find a wife for Isaac in 24:3 and his subsequent marriage in 25:20. Abraham seems to have died while the servant was in Nahor.

whom Abraham loves, somehow influences Isaac's relationship with his own children.

Isaac Loved Esau but Rebekah Loved Jacob

Before Isaac and Rebekah's children are born, Rebekah learns from the Lord that "two nations are in [her] womb" (Gen 25:23). In successive lines of poetic prophecy Rebekah learns that the twins she will bear will be in conflict. The language used, however, suggests that each of the boys will issue nations in their own right. "Nations" (*gōyîm*) in the first line becomes a poetic word for "peoples" (*lə'ummîm*) in the second. The word for peoples is used almost exclusively in poetry and almost always parallel with plural or collective singular nouns for people groups or nations.[33] One of these people groups she will bear "will be stronger than the other and the older will serve the younger." The pattern of the favored younger son, established with the very first brothers in Genesis and reestablished with Isaac himself, is destined to continue with Isaac's children.

The language in the prophecy also points back to the promise to Abraham in 12:2 to make a great nation (*gōy*) from him. The promise is repeated several times, the most recent to Rebekah's prophecy being in 22:16–18 in response to the *aqedah*. We recall the parallels between Isaac's near-sacrifice and Ishmael's exile, both climaxing in a promise of great nations. The pattern reasserts itself here, in the lives of Jacob and Esau. Thus, the reader is invited to find parallels between the two sets of brothers in conflict.

Many of the parallels have been noted already: the younger son is the favored one; one son will go into exile after a some sort of trickery. However, the parallels between these two generations stand out over the larger pattern. Note that younger son is particularly favored by the matriarch. The circumstances differ, of course. Sarah is jealous of another woman's son and acts as the agent of her son's destiny, while Rebekah's favoring follows the prophecy to which she, and not Isaac, is privy. However, the pattern holds. Esau, therefore, resembles Ishmael while Jacob bears a similarity to his father Isaac. For instance, Esau is hairy. While the narrator never describes the appearance of Ishmael, we do learn one thing from the angel of the Lord's description of Ishmael in 16:12. The angel says that Ishmael will be a "wild donkey of a man."[34] Esau's hairiness, in fact, makes his skin feel like

---

33. E.g., Ps 2:1; Jer 51:58; Isa 60:2, etc.
34. The term "wild donkey" is a single Hebrew word.

a wild animal. We know this because Jacob fools Isaac into believing Jacob is Esau by fitting the skins of a goat onto his hands. Once the boys grow up we learn that Esau becomes a hunter, literally, "a man knowing game, a man of the field" (Gen 25:27). In a later chapter we learn that Esau uses a bow to hunt for his game (27:3), thus making his resemblance to Ishmael, a great bowman, more striking.

Jacob, on the other hand, is described in 25:27 as "a civilized man, dwelling in tents."[35] The description of Jacob and Esau in these verses is meant to show the contrast between the two brothers—Esau in the field and Jacob in the house. That Jacob is further described as "civilized," "mild" (TNK), "quiet" (NRSV), "plain" (KJV), or "simple" (LXX), suggests that Esau was wild, a description recalling the prophecy to Hagar regarding Ishmael. In Genesis 16:12, the angel of the Lord tells Hagar that Ishmael, the "wild donkey of a man," will live a life of conflict and, in a particularly ambiguous phrase, "he will dwell against the face of all his brothers." This last phrase can be interpreted as "live among all his brothers" (KJV) or, recognizing the previous phrase as parallel, "live in hostility toward all his brothers" (NIV).[36] The latter interpretation seems the most likely given the poetic context of the prophecy. Note that such an interpretation also resembles the one given to Rebekah, wherein she will give birth to sons in conflict with each other.

That Jacob is described as "living in tents," in contrast to Esau's hunting in fields, brings up the possibility of Jacob being purposefully compared to Isaac. There is no obviously direct correlation between the two, but it is possible that Isaac's uneventful life between his near-sacrifice on Mount Moriah and the birth of his sons suggests that he, like Jacob, favors a quiet life. In the long narrative of chapter 24, Isaac is absent almost entirely from the action as his father's servant finds him a wife in Nahor. When the servant brings Rebekah back Isaac is in the field, like Esau will be, but what he is doing there is ambiguous. In fact most early interpretations render

---

35. This translation, "civilized," of the adjective *tām* is unique in the Hebrew Bible. In normal parlance, *tām* means perfect or blameless (Job 1:8). However, its usage in Genesis 25:27 is determined by its contrast with the description of Esau. See the entry in Koehler, Baumgartner, et al., *The Hebrew and Aramaic Lexicon of the Old Testament*. See also Von Rad, *Genesis*, who explains, "The adjective means actually belonging to the solidarity that the hunter does not know because he is much more dependent on himself" (266). Therefore, Jacob is civilized in contrast.

36. It is also possible to interpret the phrase as "live to the east of all his brothers," which is intriguing, given that Esau's descendents are the Edomites, who live in the east.

his action as meditating—hardly the activity of a wild man. At most he is walking around, perhaps aimlessly.[37]

These parallels between Esau and Ishmael and between Jacob and Isaac lead the reader to recognize a great irony in the story.[38] One would think that, given the similarities Isaac shares with Jacob that he would favor Jacob. The pattern established by Abraham in 22:2 and continued by Jacob, whom we are told loved Joseph more than his brothers because Joseph was "the son of his old age" (Gen 37:3), skips a generation, for Isaac loves Esau. It is Rebekah who loves Jacob. The reason for Isaac's love of Esau is that he likes the food Esau brings him. In particular, Isaac loves the food Esau acquires through hunting. While Esau's hairiness and status as hunter will play into the narrative, Esau's appearance and vocation are no mere plot devices but point to character. However, while they may tell us about Esau, they tell us just as much about Isaac.

Isaac's love for Esau over Jacob, which we learn of a mere chapter after he and Ishmael bury Abraham, shows us how large a shadow Ishmael casts over the life of Isaac. Note Isaac's love of game, the purported reason for his love of Esau. It strikes one as a superficial basis for love. Interestingly it also does not hold as the story unfolds. Rebekah is able to fool Isaac into believing he is eating game when she has merely prepared goats from the family's own herd (Gen 27:9). How great is Isaac's love of game that he cannot recognize domesticated meat? Though it is not made explicit, Isaac loves Esau not for the game, but because he reminds him of Ishmael. Esau recognizes Isaac's admiration for Ishmael, too, for in 28:8–9, Esau takes "Mahalath, the daughter of Ishmael, Abraham's son" as a wife in order to please his father, Isaac. Isaac does not recognize Ishmael as a rival the way Sarah presumably did when they were still children.

Isaac has his blessing from the Lord. He secures his blessing because Sarah witnesses Ishmael playing and perceives it as a threat to her son. There is a connection from the beginning. Isaac means "he laughs," but Ishmael is the subject of the verb *maṣaḥēq*. Ishmael is putting something or someone in the state of laughter. Sarah may believe she witnesses a threat,

---

37. The verb in question, *śûaḥ*, is a hapax legomena, but Koehler, Baumgartner et al., *The Hebrew and Aramaic Lexicon of the Old Testament*, note that in verse 65, Rebekah asks who the man is "who is walking in the field to meet" her and the servant. The narrative, however, suggests that he was in the field doing something when he sees them in the distance. Whatever he is doing he stops it when he sees Rebekah and his father's servant.

38. One other parallel between Jacob and Isaac are that their names can both work as puns on tricking, but it is Ishmael who tricks with Isaac's name.

but the threat is not on Isaac's life. Rather, she admits that it is a threat on his status in the family. But Isaac never expresses any pleasure over his status. His status leads him to a near-death experience at the hand of his father. The promise, the covenant, with world historical ramifications, he receives only vicariously until he is much older. When the time comes to bless the next generation with the covenant transmitted through his line, he believes he is blessing Esau (27:29), the firstborn, the bowman, the wild animal, so much like Ishmael that one wonders if he feels the blessing should have been Ishmael's from the beginning.

One tends to read the Bible for the theology it espouses. In the case of Isaac, while the individual stories matter, the broader picture remains the important one. Isaac receives the covenant of Abraham. He receives a blessing from the Lord. He blesses Jacob, who reestablishes the covenant with God while on the run from his brother. The covenant is what is important to the reader of Genesis. We read for the covenant, afraid to miss the forest for the trees. But God makes the covenant with people, whose experiences speak to the reader, too. Jacob receives the blessing and the birthright in place of the firstborn, Esau, father of the Edomites (Gen 36:43). Jacob/Israel is favored over Esau/Edom—an etiology for the Israelites' relationship with the Edomites throughout the two people groups' histories[39] and another parallel with Isaac, father of Israel, and his brother Ishmael, father of the Ishmaelites. But Jacob/Israel eventually returns to his brother. They reconcile their relationship, Jacob bowing to the ground seven times while Esau embraces him (Gen 33:3, 4). They both weep, setting aside any resentment, because they are brothers. One is intrigued by the reunion of Isaac and Ishmael at their father's death. Do they embrace? Do they weep?

---

39. Von Rad, *Genesis*, 265.

Chapter Three

Fear and Love in the Book of Ruth

Kelly Lamb

FEAR IS OUR BASIC human emotion. Even when we are dogmatic about how we should read and teach the Bible, this too reveals concealed fear. That is why the book of Ruth is so human, so realistic of family life, in its disarming simplicity, to remove fear and to substitute love.

The book is playing out the high drama of the Old Testament covenant God had made with his people Israel, in the role of the kinsman redeemer. But it is all featured in one extended family, where the central role is being played out by three women, the widow Naomi and her two daughters-in-law, Ruth and Orpah.

In a profound sense we can only read the Bible stories metaphorically, because the language about God can only be expressed in metaphor, since the depth of biblical revelation is so profound. God is like a Father, we are like his children. Likewise, Psalm 1 defines "the Way of the Righteous" as simply being "right-related," as being in love with God.

Ruth, is then, a lovely love story about God's love to three women, two who responded with and in his love, and the other concerned only with her self-love. This is all so universally human that we are all drawn into the story.

There are ten movements of the soul being portrayed.

1. **Loss in bereavement**, as no doubt many of you remember the loss of family members.

2. This brings **change**, so that our life becomes a mosaic whose original design is altered. The widow Moab faces changes that she has to share with her two daughters-in-law. We experience the same. We believe in God, but we don't expect him to change our lives, when he is himself the unchanging One; yet we do find him turning us upside down. If change was progressive, that would be bearable, but often it seems painfully regressive!

3. A **transformed life** blessedly comes when we change to our circumstances, by humility and trust. Then it is like a reformation or a revolution of the soul. Ruth had done all the right things for all the right people, but she had not been true to herself. Her life had been defined by duty, not by God; by her culture, not by her trust in God. She had been a dutiful wife, a faithful daughter-in-law, a devout Moabite. But the old comes crashing down in rebirth, renewal, metanoia, or a paradigm shift in her new awareness of who she really was before God.

4. **Aging** comes to us all. Our children grow up and leave the house. Our faces now show wrinkles in the mirror, our bones ache. We begin to face the fact that it's no fun growing old! We become more extravagant with face balm, and begin to take our diet and our exercise more seriously. Yet age is a mirror also before God, to take our devotions more seriously, to cultivate the sense of the presence of God, which we never did before; now he is always with us! Older, wiser, closer to God, Naomi has become.

5. **Independence** truly comes when we no longer trust ourselves, but God alone. Then the narcissistic self that Orpah, her sister-in-law became, is contrastive with Ruth. Independence demands so much, yet gives so little. Yes, we can sustain ourselves but then it isolates us from others. So it is so easy to fall into depression.

6. **Respect** then follows, as Boaz, catching sight of the strange woman in his field, Ruth, asks: "To whom does she belong?" She is her own, a unique human being, whom he then respects, and later the elders at the gate, also begin to "respect her." It is what is being seen today with ethnic minority women in our society. Their attitude is gratitude, no different from the basic gratitude that we should all have, that God has called us into being.

7. **Recognition** then follows. In Ruth 2:10–17, Ruth prostrates herself on the ground, saying to Boaz: "Why have I found favor in your sight,

that you should take notice of me, when I am a foreigner?" Boaz answers her: "All that you have done for your mother-in-law since the death of your husband has been fully told me, and how you left your father and mother and your native land and came to a people that you did not know before.

"May the Lord reward you for your deeds and may you have a full reward from the Lord, the God of Israel, under whose wings you have come for refuge!" Then she says, "May I continue to find favor in your sight, my lord, for you have comforted me, and spoken kindly to your servant, even though I am not one of your servants." Then at mealtime, Boaz says to her, "Come here, and eat some of the bread, and dip your morsel in sour wine." So Ruth sits down, eats until she is satisfied, and has some left over.

The truth is that recognition is the source of our identity, so that to be recognized by Christ is truly to have a Christian identity. Every child in a family struggles to be recognized. Children love to play hide and seek, not just to hide—that is no fun—but to be found, to be recognized.

So Boaz assured Ruth, "Because I recognize the good you do." It is the basis of creation, "when God saw that it was good."

To withhold recognition, as we daily do with people we sense are hostile to us, is to express fear, fear of their hostility. Sadly, it is a deep sign of personal insecurity.

8. Next comes **insight**. Too readily we diminish people, either by praising them for accomplishments we envy, or by criticizing them in prejudice when we scarcely know them. Naomi, in her wizened length of life, teaches Ruth to be a real woman, meeting in Boaz a true man. For he makes the world safe for everyone around him.

The book of Ruth teaches, then, that the spiritual life is to fullfil the purpose of creation to be fruitful in all our relationships, with a life grounded on the will of God for creation. We must all learn that to be a man or woman of God is more than being sexual; it is to do the will of God in and through our relationships with others.

9. What follows is **empowerment**. Naomi continues to teach Ruth, saying: "My daughter, I need to seek some security for you, so that it will be well with you. Now here is our kinsman Boaz, with whose young

women you have been working. See, he is winnowing barley tonight at the threshing floor."

Now wash and anoint yourself, and put on your best clothes and go down to the threshing floor; but do not make yourself known unto the man until he has finished eating and drinking. When he lies down, observe the place where he lies; then go, and uncover his feet and lie down; and he will tell you what to do. [Ruth] said to [Naomi]: 'All that you tell me, I will do'" (Ruth 3:4–5).

Empowerment is reciprocal. Naomi needed Ruth as much as Ruth needed Naomi. Both need and value empowerment. The daughter who is not a daughter is needed by the mother who is not her mother. Naomi, whose name for God is Shaddai, i.e. "the God with breast," the nurturing God, is nurturing Ruth.

10. Also arriving is **self-definition**. Reading Ruth 3:6–14, we follow Ruth onto the threshing floor, to lie down with Boaz. Awakened and startled, he asks, "Who are you?" She answers him: "I am Ruth, your servant; spread your cloak over your servant, for you are next of kin". He responds: "May you be blessed of the Lord, my daughter; this last instance of loyalty is better than the first; you have not gone after young men, whether rich or poor. And now, my daughter, be not afraid, I will do all that you ask, for all the assembly of my people know you are a worthy woman."

As with the winnowing of the barley, Ruth and Naomi are like the husks left over following tragedy after tragedy, being marginalized women, women without a life ahead. But Boaz is not sure if he is next of kin. This has to be found out. There is one closer kinsman but he has limited resources; he cannot act as "a kinsman redeemer." So often people cry out for help, but we cannot help, for we are not like God with unlimited resources, "above all that we can ask or think"! But we have to do our part; we need to strategize how we can help.

11. So a next step involves **invisibility**. We have to get out of sight to allow the kinsman redeemer to fulfill his obligation. Boaz honors Ruth's rights, far more than subsequent history has honored the rights of women. They needed the suffragette movement in Europe. They are still not honored in Islam. They are still not fully granted equality in the business world around us. Ruth is still suffering badly at our own city gates.

12. But lastly comes **fulfillment**. "So Boaz took Ruth and she became his wife. When they came together, the Lord made her conceive, and she bore a son" (Ruth 4:13–17). Then Ruth did an incredible thing, by giving her little son to be nurtured by her mother-in-law. We all know the jokes about mothers-in-law! Ruth was wholly countercultural, as she trusted God not the culture that had been so cruel to her. The book of Ruth is turning our world upside down, as the Apostle Paul was accused of doing with his preaching. In all ages, the gospel unmasks the pretenses, exposes the hypocrisy, that claim to be the will of God, as Muslims do in reciting "as Allah wills it!"

Think then of this simple story as the prelude for the incarnation. For through Ruth, the genealogy of Jesus Christ is traceable, and Ruth foreshadows the Virgin Mary in her barrenness, that God used for the birth of his Son.

Chapter Four

Wise Child-Rearing According to Proverbs

Bruce Waltke

THIS ESSAY AIMS TO set forth a theory of wise child-rearing according to "The Proverbs of Solomon son of David, king of Israel"[1] (hereafter Proverbs). The essay is developed firstly by defining wise child-rearing; secondly, Proverbs is established as the authority by reflecting on epistemology; thirdly, the book's fundamental concepts of child-rearing are analyzed; and finally, a theory of wise child-rearing is given. The essay is drawn to a conclusion with a final encouragement for flawed parents.

The Goal of Parenting

A website on parenting defines child-rearing as "the process of promoting and supporting the physical, emotional, social, and intellectual development of a child from infancy to adulthood."[2] That definition, however, is woefully deficient because it fails to state the shape and goal for the child's development. Proverbs rectifies this lack. It aims to develop the child in the way of wisdom and righteousness,[3] and its goal is *shalom* ("peace and prosperity") and *ḥayyîm* ("life"):

1. The NIV is the basis of the translation of Proverbs in this essay, and citations of chapter and verse are from Proverbs, unless otherwise indicated.

2. Globalshopcliq.

3. Wisdom and righteousness are correlative terms—that is to say, they are inseparably to the same referent, albeit belonging to the different semantic domains, namely

> My son, do not forget my teaching, but keep my commands in your heart,
> For they will prolong your life many years and bring you peace and prosperity.
> (3:1–2)

Of personified wisdom, a figure of the book's teachings, it claims:

> Long life is in her right hand; in her left hand are riches and honor. (3:16)

By "life" is meant more than clinical life. For the righteous, clinical death is nothing more than being hit by the shadow of a truck:

> When calamity comes, the wicked are brought down, but even in death the righteous seek refuge in God. (14:32)

Shalom and *ḥayyîm* are achieved through righteousness (i.e., serving the best interest of others as defined by the LORD in Proverbs):

> In the way of righteousness there is life; along that path is immortality. (12:28)

Since being wise and righteous is the book's desired shape of a child's development and abundant life is the goal, we should assume that these inform the shape and goal of wise child-rearing. That way, however, may not safeguard the wise child against suffering:

> Do not lurk like a thief near the house of the righteous, do not plunder their dwelling place;
> for though the righteous fall seven times, they rise again, but the wicked stumble when calamity strikes. (24:15–16)

"Seven times" signifies that the righteous are out, flat on the mat, for the count of ten.

In the New Testament, Christ is the Way, the wisdom and righteousness of God, and the goal is clearly revealed as eternal life. Moreover, the New Testament clarifies that the Holy Spirit develops the child of God into the image of Christ. In Proverbs wisdom is personified as Woman Wisdom (e.g. chapter 8); in the New Testament wisdom and righteousness become incarnate in the Lord Jesus Christ.[4] This canonical context should

---

wisdom and ethics. If a person is righteousness, they are wise, even as the vice president of the United States is inseparably the head of the senate.

4. Waltke, *Proverbs 1–15*, 834–85.

be assumed in the rest of this essay, albeit the essay will use the language of Proverbs.

The Epistemological Basis for a Theory of Wise Child-Rearing

Paul D. Wenger notes that child-rearing is a hotbed of contending notions.[5] A fundamental divide in these notions is accepting the authority of human reason or of Proverbs, which claims its teachings are revealed by God through the words of inspired sages:

> For the LORD gives wisdom; from his mouth come knowledge and understanding. (2:6)

The sage Agur, who claims divine inspiration (30:1–2), argues cogently that true wisdom cannot be gotten apart from the revelation of Scripture:

> Surely I am only a brute, not a man; I do not have human understanding.
> I have not learned wisdom, nor have I attained to the knowledge of the Holy One.
> Who has gone up to heaven and come down? Whose hands have gathered up the wind? Who has wrapped up the waters in a cloak? Who has established all the ends of the earth? What is his name, and what is the name of his son? Surely you know!
> "Every word of God is flawless; he is a shield to those who take refuge in him."
> Do not add to his words, or he will rebuke you and prove you a liar. (30:1–5)[6]

Neither Agur nor any other biblical sage attempts to validate by reason their authority. If such an attempt were made, it would make finite, fallible reason the final arbiter of truth, turning the argument back on itself and of necessity ending in skepticism. Without comprehensive knowledge the finite mind can neither derive nor certify absolute truth. Moreover, the sage's words are certified as true by the discerning, which presumes their divine illumination as the first cause. Woman Wisdom claims:

> My mouth speaks what is true, for my lips detest wickedness.

---

5. Wenger, "Discipline in the Book of Proverbs," esp. 415.
6. For an exposition of this text see Waltke, *Proverbs 15–31*, 466–72.

> All the words of my mouth are just; none of them is crooked or perverse.
> To the discerning all of them are right; they are upright to those who have found knowledge. (8:7–8)

From revelation to reception, wisdom is a gift of God.

Many stumble over Proverbs' credibility on account of Solomon, the book's primary sage. He died a fool (1 Kgs 11:4). "How could he be so wise and die such a fool?" they ask. His own proverb provides the answer:

> Stop listening to instruction, my son, and you will stray from the words of knowledge. (19:27)

Being wise today is no guarantee of being wise tomorrow; becoming wise is a constant process:

> Let the wise listen and add to their learning, and let the discerning get guidance. (1:5)

Fundamental Truths for a Theory of Wise Parenting

Having laid our epistemological foundation for a theory of wise child-rearing, we now build upon it fundamental truths of the theory. Wise parents recognize that "the fear of the LORD" is foundational to the child's development; that the generations are mutually dependent; that the child is born an ignoramus; and that their training is effective.

"The fear of the LORD"

"The fear of the LORD" is the quintessential expression of the spiritual grammar for learning wisdom:

> The fear of the LORD is the beginning of knowledge, but fools despise wisdom and instruction. (1:7)
> The fear of the LORD is the beginning of wisdom, and knowledge of the Holy One is understanding. (9:10)

Briefly stated, the collocation "the fear of the LORD" signifies a spiritual attitude of submission to the LORD's teachings in the Holy Bible out of recognition that its Author has the keys of life and death.[7] What the alphabet

---
7. Waltke, "The Fear of the Lord."

is to reading, notes to music, and numerals to mathematics, the fear of *I AM* is to gaining the book's wisdom and instruction. In his second lecture to the son (2:1–22), the father states the mental and spiritual rudiments of gaining the fear of the Lord:

> My son, if you accept my words and store up my commands within you, turning your ear to wisdom and applying your heart to understanding—indeed, if you call out for insight and cry aloud for understanding, and if you look for it as for silver and search for it as for hidden treasure, then you will understand the fear of the Lord and find the knowledge of God. For the Lord gives wisdom; from his mouth come knowledge and understanding. (2:1–6)

In other words, effective learning of wisdom takes place within the religious context of faith. This context reinforces youth's intuitive grasp of right and wrong. Elsewhere we wrote: "Tragically, . . . secular educators and politicians unrelentingly seek to silence this religious instruction in the public square. The consequences have been grim: unprecedented school shootings, the alarming rise of birthing children without a nurturing home, teenage suicides, and drug addiction."[8]

Generations are Mutually Dependent on One another

The Creator made human beings social creatures and ordained a hierarchical order in their best interest. Some are employers, others workers; some are governors, others subjects. These social relationships entail mutual dependence and a hierarchy of authority and submission. Proverbs addresses these relationships and pounds home the truth that to function properly hierarchical relationships must be informed by righteousness, to wit, disadvantaging self to serve others. If they are informed by wickedness—disadvantaging others to serve self—they produce strife that destroys community.

This notion of mutual dependence also pertains to parenting:

> The glory of young men is their strength, gray hair the splendor of the old. (20:29)

"Gray hair" is a symbol of wisdom and righteous living;

---

8. Waltke and de Silva, *Proverbs: A Shorter Commentary*.

> Gray hair is a crown of splendor; it is attained in the way of righteousness. (16:31)

So the Creator has adorned the generations, the aged and youth, each with unique splendors: the wisdom of the older generation and the strength of the younger. These adornments inferentially signify their mutual dependence. Without strength the wisdom of the aged cannot effect good, and without wisdom the strength of youth can effect evil. Though physically weak, the aged lay down the tracks along which the engine of youth arrives at the station of *shalom* and *ḥayyîm* (cf. 2 Cor 4:16–18).

Children Are Born Morally Corrupt

Wise parenting is essential because children are born depraved; by nature a child serves self, not God or others, albeit they know better. David, Solomon's father, confessed:

> Surely I was sinful at birth, sinful from the time my mother conceived me.
> Yet you desired faithfulness even in the womb; you taught me wisdom in that secret place. (Ps 51:5–6)

Solomon agrees implicitly and explicitly:

> Where there is no revelation, people cast off restraint; but blessed is the one who heeds wisdom's instruction. (29:18)
> Folly is bound up in the heart of a child. (22:15)

There are degrees of evil among people, but all do evil, except the Lord Jesus Christ:

> Who can say, "I have kept my heart pure; I am clean and without sin"? (20:9)

This doctrine of human depravity is validated empirically. The Minnesota Crime Commission wrote, albeit with some immoderate humor:

> Every baby starts life as a little savage. He is completely selfish and self-centered. He wants what he wants when he wants it: his bottle, his mother's attention, his playmate's toys, his uncle's watch, or whatever. Deny him these and he seethes with rage and aggressiveness which would be murderous were he not so helpless. He's dirty, he has no morals, no knowledge, no developed skills. This means that all children, not just certain children but all children,

Wise Child-Rearing According to Proverbs

are born delinquent. If permitted to continue in their self-centered world of infancy, given free rein to their impulsive actions to satisfy each want, every child would grow up a criminal, a thief, a killer, a rapist.[9]

Similarly, the Houston Texas Police Department published a leaflet that gives twelve surefire principles of parenting guaranteed to produce delinquent children:

1. Begin with infancy to give the child everything he wants. In this way he will grow to believe the world owes him a living.
2. When he picks up bad words, laugh at him. This will make him think he's cute. It will also encourage him to pick up "cuter" phrases that will blow off the top of your head later.
3. Never give him any spiritual training. Wait until he is twenty-one and then let him "decide for himself."
4. Avoid use of the word "wrong." It may develop a guilt complex. This will condition him to believe later, when he is arrested for stealing a car, that society is against him and he is being persecuted.
5. Pick up everything he leaves lying around—books, shoes, and clothes. Do everything for him so that he will be expecting it.
6. Let him read any printed matter he can get his hands on. Be careful that the silverware and drinking glasses are sterilized, but let his mind feast on garbage.
7. Quarrel frequently in the presence of your children. In this way they will not be too shocked when the home is broken up later.
8. Give a child all the spending money he wants. Never let him earn his own. Why should he have things as tough as you had them?
9. Satisfy his every craving for food, drink, and comfort. See that every sensual desire is gratified. Denial may lead to harmful frustration.
10. Take his part against neighbors, teachers, and policemen. They are all prejudiced against your child.
11. When he gets into real trouble, apologize for yourself by saying, "I never could do anything with him."

---

9. Harmless Online.

12. Prepare for a life of grief. You will be likely to have it.[10]

Training Is Effective

Proverbs assumes that its teachings reorient children from their innate way of selfishness to the way of trusting God and serving others. According to its preamble, this is the aim of the book:

> For giving prudence to those who are simple, knowledge and discretion to the young. (1:4)

"Prudence" signifies "shrewdness"—that is to say, to have a goal and a plan to attain it. The "simple" are those who have neither decisively oriented their lives to the way of wisdom nor committed themselves to the teachings of Proverbs. The book's knowledge is as essential to wisdom as knowing the laws of aerodynamics are to building an airplane.

"The young" (Heb. *na'ar*) refers to the inexperienced; it can refer to baby Moses (Exod 2:6; 1 Sam 1:22, 24; 4:21), a seventeen-year-old Joseph (Gen 37:2; cf. 1 Sam 30:17), and young adults: Zadok, the priest (1 Chr 12:28); Absalom (2 Sam 18:5) and Solomon (1 Kgs 3:7), sons of David. Men were registered in the military and held accountable at twenty years of age (Num 1:3; 14:29) and the son addressed in the prologue has likely reached puberty.

The sages assume their teaching reorients the depraved child toward wisdom and parents should assume the same. Indeed Proverbs teaches that parental instruction or discipline is necessary:

> Discipline your children, for in that there is hope; do not be a willing party to their death. (19:17)

It also teaches that child-rearing is effective:

> Start children off on the way they should go, and even when they are old they will not turn from it. (22:6)[11]

This proverb admonishes the wise pedagogue to heal the child from humankind's endemic folly by dedicating them to the fear of the LORD; the effects will last a lifetime. "Even" signifies that even after attaining old age

---

10. Catholic Education.

11. For a rebuttal of the interpretation that the child's way here refers to the child's nature, see Waltke, *Proverb 15–31*, 205.

the youth will not cease to be fashioned by the instruction. The proverb is famous, however, for its teaching seems out of touch with reality. Children raised by the same parents and in the same way differ morally: some are wise and others foolish. This skepticism, however, mistakenly infers from the proverb that parents have the sole responsibility for the child's moral choices. If that were the case, Proverbs would be addressed to parents, but the book's preamble (1:1–7) states it is written for youth (1:4). In the book's prologue the father lectures the son; the sage does not lecture the parent. Moreover, the book recognizes the freedom of a child to choose sin and apostatize by joining with villains (1:11–15) and whores (5:11–14). Also, a proverb by its epigrammatic form expresses a truth but cannot nuance it. All the book's proverbs and sayings must be heard together to hear these nuances:

> Pay attention and turn your ear to the sayings of the wise; apply your heart to what I teach,
> for it is pleasing when you keep them in your heart and have all of them ready on your lips. (22:17–18)

So Proverbs 22:6 must be heard in tension with the profligate's confession at the end of his life, when his flesh and body are spent:

> How I hated discipline! How my heart spurned correction!
> I would not obey my teachers or turn my ear to my instructors.
> (5:12, 13)

In sum, Proverbs 22:6 teaches that parental training has its effect, but that is not the only factor in the child's development. Christians are not produced by the will of parents, but by the will of God (cf. John 1:12–13).

A Theory of Effective Child-Rearing

Proverbs presumes that moral education takes place in the home for it constantly identifies the pedagogues as the parents and children as their students. To be sure, Woman Wisdom in her two sermons addresses the masses in the public square (1:2–27; 8:1–31), but her fictional sermons are given for the benefit of the son: implicitly in 1:28–33; explicitly in 8:32–36. Those who propose a school setting—a place outside the home and staffed by professional sages—argue on the basis of Egyptian analogies. But there is no unambiguous evidence of a school setting in ancient Israel before the time of Ben Sirach's "house of instruction" in the early second century BC (Sir 51:23).[12]

Trust the LORD

Another famous proverb is:

> Trust in the LORD with all your heart and lean not on your own understanding; in all your ways submit to him, and he will make your paths straight. Do not be wise in your own eyes; fear the LORD and shun evil. (3:5–7)

"Trust in the LORD" signifies relying on him out of a sense of security, often in the presence of danger or difficulty. The command is a platitude, however, without defining who the LORD is. In this context he is defined by his revelation of the way in which a person should walk. Proverbs is a collection of the teachings of his inspired sages to mark out that way. In short, trusting the LORD is inseparable from trusting his inspired proverbs and sayings. Correlatively, Proverbs is good only to the extent that the LORD backs it up; so the parent's trust is ultimately in God, not in Proverbs per se. In fact, Proverbs is written to teach a life of faith in Israel's covenant-keeping God:

> So that your trust may be in the LORD, I teach you today, even you. (22:19)

Wise parents trust the Lord to uphold the moral order taught in Proverbs sovereignly (i.e., in his own time and way) and contingently (i.e., in response to human actions). This is so despite appearances to the contrary, such as the wicked prospering and the godly suffering. "With all your heart" refers to all your being and actions, for all actions flow from it (see 4:23). Entire commitment entails exclusive commitment. "In all your ways" adds to them exhaustive commitment.

This teaching heads our theory of wise child-rearing according to Proverbs because it entails a wholehearted commitment to all that Proverbs teaches about the goal of parenting, its divine authority, and its spiritual foundation.

---

12. Lucas, *Exploring the Old Testament*, 82. Similarly, see M. V. Fox, "The Social Location of the Book of Proverbs." Fox states (231): "Apart from the supposed Egyptian analogy, there is nothing in Proverbs to point to a school origin."

Prayer

Proverbs is not usually connected with prayer, but prayer is a corollary of faith. Here are three proverbs to sustain the notion that wise parenting involves prayer:

> The LORD detests the sacrifice of the wicked, but the prayer of the upright pleases him. (15:8)
> The LORD is far from the wicked, but he hears the prayer of the righteous. (15:29)
> Commit to the LORD whatever you do, and he will establish your plans. (16:3)

Teach with Conviction

Moses famously taught parents how to teach the Book of the Law:

> These commandments that I give you today are to be on your hearts.
> Impress them on your children. Talk about them when you sit at home and when you walk along the road, when you lie down and when you get up.
> Tie them as symbols on your hands and bind them on your foreheads.
> Write them on the doorframes of your houses and on your gates. (Deut 6:6–9)

"Impress"(*shānan*) is related to the Hebrew term *shēn*. If you will allow a bit of midrash, we could render it "teach with a bite." In Proverbs, the father's fictional lectures model teaching with a bite. Each lecture begins with a stern command to listen:

> My son, pay attention to my wisdom, turn your ear to my words of insight. (5:1)

Its prologue (1:8–9:18) also contains two sermons by personified wisdom. These too model teaching with stern exhortation. Personified wisdom cries out with a loud voice and full lungs:

> Out in the open wisdom calls aloud, she raises her voice in the public square;
> on top of the wall she cries out, at the city gate she makes her speech. (1:20–21)

"Lady Wisdom," says Aitken, "is no gentle persuader. She shouts, pleads, scolds, reasons, threatens, warns, and even laughs . . . Pulpit bashing and hell-fire preaching if ever there were! All quite unladylike; and nowadays also quite unfashionable, even frowned upon."[13]

Parents teach with urgency because obedience to their teaching is a matter of life and death.

> Thus you will walk in the ways of the good and keep to the paths of the righteous.
> For the upright will live in the land, and the blameless will remain in it;
> but the wicked will be cut off from the land, and the unfaithful will be torn from it. (2:20–22)

Both Parents Involved

The first lecture to the son (1:8–19) mentions the mother as a teacher alongside of the father:

> Listen, my son, to your father's instruction and do not forsake your mother's teaching. (1:8)

And the first proverb of the first collections of proverbs (10:1–22:16) also involves both father and mother:

> The proverbs of Solomon:
>
> A wise son brings joy to his father, but a foolish son brings grief to his mother. (10:1)

Plausibly, considering the epigrammatic nature of Proverbs, the mention of the mother at the seams of the first two collections of Proverb allows us to infer that the remaining lectures and proverbs that mention only the father include the mother. Moreover, the book's final poem is an encomium to a real wife and mother. One of her glories is she teaches her children wisdom:

> She speaks with wisdom, and faithful instruction is on her tongue.
> She watches over the affairs of her household and does not eat the bread of idleness. (31:26–27)

---

13. Aitken, *Proverbs*, 22.

Proverbs assumes that to teach wisdom one must first be taught its knowledge. Inferentially, if the mother is a teacher, she was taught as a daughter along with the son.

Loving and Exemplary

To teach with tender affections for the child and to teach by example are two distinct notions in developing a theory of wise child-rearing. They are combined here because they are combined in the fifth lecture of the father (4:1–9), which gives us a beautiful peek into a pious Israelite home:

> Listen, my sons, to a father's instruction; pay attention and gain understanding.
> I give you sound learning, so do not forsake my teaching.
> For I too was a son to my father, still tender, and cherished by my mother.
> Then he taught me, and he said to me, "Take hold of my words with all your heart; keep my commands, and you will live." (4:1–4)

The plural "sons" addresses the entire lineage of sons, not just siblings, suiting well a lecture about the generational transfer of wisdom. The father's comment, "I too was a son to my father," seems on the surface tautological, but it connotes the parent-child spiritual—not just biological—relationship. J. E. Barrett states, "In Hebrew thought sonship was understood not as a matter of biology but as a matter of obedience."[14] Teaching began soon after the child was weaned.[15] So the father presents himself as a model son who was dedicated to his parents' wisdom from his earliest years. He further exemplifies a wise son by his relationship to his mother as "tender" (i.e., pliable). To be effective a parent must model the teaching. If parents teach their children not to smoke tobacco, and yet themselves smoke, the child will likely smoke.

The father's rearing also demonstrates that wisdom is learned in a context of a loving home. "Cherished" highlights the child's incomparable and beloved status.

---

14. Barrett, "Can Scholars Take the Virgin Birth Seriously?," 15. The LXX paraphrases 4:3 as "obedient son."

15. Weaning probably occurred at the age of three years. The Egyptian *Instruction of Any* (7:19), speaks of "the mother's breast in your mouth for three years."

Levels of discipline

The sage says that out of their delight in their children and their love for them both the Lord and parents discipline their children:

> The Lord disciplines those he loves, as a father the son he delights in. (3:12)

As analysis of the book's teachings, however, reveals there are levels or degrees in the severity of discipline. The Hebrew term for "instruction" (*mûsār*) signifies both verbal admonitions to prevent acts of folly and corporal discipline to prevent their repetition. Note these two poles in these proverbs:

> A wise son heeds his father's instruction (*mûsār*), but a mocker does not respond to rebukes [*gĭ'ārāh*, "a morally indignant protest against wrong"]. (13:1)
> Whoever spares the rod hates their children, but the one who loves their children is careful to discipline (*mûsār*) them. (13:24)

Indebted somewhat to Wenger's analysis of seven levels of discipline in Proverbs, this essay finds five levels of severity in instructing children: four pertain to verbal discipline and one to corporal punishment.

Level 1. Encourage proper behavior by noting the benefits of wisdom

Wenger comments on this level: "A wise parent encourages a child to see the benefits of proper behavior. When a child actually sees the benefits of proper behavior, it is logical that he or she would choose this behavior." In the prologue of Proverbs (1:8–9:18), the father's first seven lectures (1:8–19; 2:1–22; 3:1–13, 14–35; 4:1–9, 10–19, 20–27) motivate the son to heed his instruction by promising the benefit of heeding it:

> Listen, my son, to your father's instruction and do not forsake your mother's teaching.
> They are a garland to grace your head and a chain to adorn your neck. (1:8, 9)

In her second sermon (8:1–36) Woman Wisdom, a personification of Proverbs, claims:

> I have riches and honor, as well as enduring wealth and justice.

My gifts are better than gold, even the purest gold, my wages better than sterling silver! (8:18–19)

*Level 2. Encourage proper behavior
by noting the negative consequences of folly*

Following Wenger we have distinguished motivating children to do right by promises from motivating them not to do wrong by threats. In fact the two motivations are often juxtaposed in antithetical parallels:

> If you ignore criticism [*qālōn*], you will end in poverty and disgrace; if you accept correction [*tōkaḥat*], you will be honored. (13:18)
> Only a fool despises a parent's discipline [*mûsar*]; whoever learns from correction [*tōkaḥat*] is wise. (15:5)

As the father's first seven lectures promised benefits for obedience, his last three lectures threaten dire consequences for doing evil (5:1–23; 6:20–33; 7:1–27):

> For your ways are in full view of the LORD, and he examines all your paths.
> The evil deeds of the wicked ensnare them; the cords of their sins hold them fast.
> For lack of discipline they will die, led astray by their own great folly. (5:21–23)

In a supplement to his proverbs, Solomon adds a striking allegory on the woes of laziness:

> I went past the field of a sluggard, past the vineyard of someone who has no sense;
> thorns had come up everywhere, the ground was covered with weeds, and the stone wall was in ruins.
> I applied my heart to what I observed and learned a lesson from what I saw:
> A little sleep, a little slumber, a little folding of the hands to rest—
> and poverty will come on you like a thief and scarcity like an armed man. (24:30–34)

Even more striking is the poem he adds on the danger of lingering over wine (23:29–36).

An Introduction to Child Theology

Level 3: Be proactive: motivate against follies before encountering them

Far from advocating being "helicopter parents"—that is to say, overly safeguarding the child from real world evil—the father takes the risk and allows the son to feel the tempting power of seducers by recreating the words of wicked men and of the unfaithful wife, while simultaneously building repulsion to them. These scenarios reinforce motivating proper behavior by noting the wages of sin is death. In his first lecture the father takes his son into the conspiring of thieves and warns the son against accepting their invitation to join them:

> My son, if sinful men entice you, do not give in to them.
> If they say, "Come along with us; let's lie in wait for innocent blood,
> let's ambush some harmless soul;
> let's swallow them alive, like the grave, and whole, like those who go down to the pit;
> we will get all sorts of valuable things and fill our houses with plunder;
> cast lots with us; we will all share the loot"—
> my son, do not go along with them, do not set foot on their paths.
> . . .
> These men lie in wait for their own blood; they ambush only themselves!
> Such are the paths of all who go after ill-gotten gain; it takes away the life of those who get it. (1:10–19)

In the father's last lecture he shares with his son his observation of the tactics of an adulteress to warn his son that going to bed with her will ruin him:

> "My son, keep my words and store up my commands within you.
> . . .
> They will keep you from the adulterous woman, from the wayward woman with her seductive words. . . .
> At the window of my house I looked down through the lattice.
> I saw among the simple, I noticed among the young men, a youth who had no sense.
> He was going down the street near her corner, walking along in the direction of her house
> at twilight, as the day was fading, as the dark of night set in.
> Then out came a woman to meet him, dressed like a prostitute and with crafty intent. . . .
> Now in the street, now in the squares, at every corner she lurks.

> She took hold of him and kissed him and with a brazen face she said:
> "Today I fulfilled my vows, and I have food from my fellowship offering at home.
> So I came out to meet you; I looked for you and have found you!
> I have covered my bed with colored linens from Egypt.
> I have perfumed my bed with myrrh, aloes and cinnamon.
> Come, let's drink deeply of love till morning . . .
> Come, let's drink deeply of love till morning; let's enjoy ourselves with love! . . ."
> With persuasive words she led him astray; she seduced him with her smooth talk.
> All at once he followed her like an ox going to the slaughter, like a deer stepping into a noose
> till an arrow pierces his liver, like a bird darting into a snare, little knowing it will cost him his life." (7:1–21)

Level 4: Correct folly

The Hebrew root *ykḥ* (verb *yākaḥ*, noun *tōkaḥat*) means "to correct," "correction," which expresses disapproval and aims to right a wrong and reorient a child to wisdom. The root's connoted severity ranges from "correction," meaning "disapproval and corrective criticism," to "rebuke," meaning "disapproval and harsh criticism." It clearly means "rebuke" in the Woman Wisdom sermon against unrepentant youth who love being open to everything and committed to nothing:

> How long will you who are simple love your simple ways? How long will mockers delight in mockery and fools hate knowledge? Repent at my rebuke [*tōkaḥat*]! Then I will pour out my thoughts to you, I will make known to you my teachings.
> But since you refuse to listen when I call and no one pays attention when I stretch out my hand,
> since you disregard all my advice and do not accept my rebuke [*tōkaḥat*],
> I in turn will laugh when disaster strikes you; I will mock when calamity overtakes you—
> when calamity overtakes you like a storm, when disaster sweeps over you like a whirlwind, when distress and trouble overwhelm you. (1:22–27)

Agur warns his son, Ithiel, about God's rebuke of those who compose pseudepigrapha:

> Do not add to his [God's] words, or he will rebuke [*yākaḥ*] you and prove you a liar." (30:6)

In some contexts with regard to child-rearing, English versions use "rebuke," but that translation is questionable. The NIV (1983) used "rebuke" for elegant variant with "correction" in 15:31–32:

> Whoever heeds life-giving rebuke [*tōkaḥat*] will be at home among the wise.
> Those who disregard discipline despise themselves, but the one who heeds correction [*tōkaḥat*] gains understanding." (15:31–32)

But the NIV (2011) changed "rebuke" in v. 31 to "correction." No text clearly teaches parents to be harsh with their children and the tenor of the book censors that translation. Rather, correction is given with love and respect for the child, as taught in the conclusion of the father's third lecture (3:1–12):

> "For whom the LORD loveth he correcteth [*yākaḥ*]; even as a father the son *in whom* he delighteth." (KJV)

In this case, the LORD's correction may involve inflicting pain (cf. Heb. 12:3–11); that entailment is less certain in the father's correction.

Finally with regard to correction in child-rearing, it is folly to correct mockers. They are so full of themselves and contemptuous of others that they are unable to humble themselves.[16] Since the effort to correct will be futile, it is foolish even to try.

> Whoever disciplines [*yāsar*] a mocker invites insults; whoever corrects [*yākaḥ*] the wicked incurs abuse.
>
> Do not correct [*yākaḥ*] mockers or they will hate you; correct [*yākaḥ*] the wise and they will love you. (9:7, 8, my translation).

The wise aim to reorient a person to the path of life and thereby form a spiritual relationship with them (cf. Amos 3:2). If correcting a person defeats this aim, then better not to correct that person (cf. 17:14).

---

16. See Waltke, *Proverbs 1–15*, 114.

Wise Child-Rearing According to Proverbs

Level 5. Use corporal punishment when verbal correction is inadequate

Finally, when verbal motivation fails, corporal punishment is necessary. Elsewhere we wrote:

> The time-tested English proverb, "Spare the rod and spoil the child," is biblical. The New Testament does not abrogate it and the church should not abandon it (cf. Eph. 6:4; Heb. 12:5–11). "A hard way to wisdom is better than a soft way to death."[17] The apostate West's failure to discipline its children has left it in moral chaos with the result that in the end the parent "will hate his son, for he will see him ... going forth to evil deeds."[18]

Several proverbs clearly teach that corporal punishment, the most severe level of instruction, may be necessary and so appropriate to restore a child to proper conduct. The symbol of this instruction is the rod, not the hand.

> Whoever spares the rod hates their children, but the one who loves their children is careful to discipline them. (12:24)

Importantly, the rod is used out of love. An ancient Egyptian wisdom text, Papyrus Insinger, teaches: "No instruction can succeed if there is dislike" (8:24).[19] Flogging out of love for and with respect for the child (see 4:3) is not cruel; withholding it is. But parents who brutalize their children cannot hide behind the "rod" doctrine of Proverbs.

Parents instruct their children to be themselves disciplinarians:

> Do not withhold discipline from a child; if you punish them with the rod, they will not die.
> Punish them with the rod and save them from death. (23:13–14)

Spanking the child out of love and with respect for him or her morally cleanses them (20:30), prevents repeated folly (19:25), and saves them from

---

17. Kidner, *Proverbs*, 51.

18. Rashi, *Proverbs*, 76. Recently, Jordan B. Peterson, a clinical psychologist, has addressed this problem in his popular book *12 Rules for Life*, under the provocatively titled chapter, "Do Not Let Your Children Do Anything That Makes You Dislike Them." His argument is that if parents, who love their children, allow them to do things that make the parents dislike them, how much more will strangers dislike them. "Those other people will punish them, severely, by omission or commission. Don't allow that to happen. Better to let your little monster know what is desirable and what is not, so they become sophisticated denizens of the world outside the family" (144).

19. Lichtheim, *Ancient Egyptian Literature*: "Dislike" means "resentment, blame" (214n28).

death. Bridges asks, "Is it not better that the flesh should smart, than that *the soul should die?*"[20]

Conclusion

No parent is either all-knowing or without sin in child-rearing. Invariably, in spite of their best intentions, they discipline in anger; frustrate their children; or fail to discipline out of apathy. But let every Christian parent recall that they are the beloved children of a merciful God. So let them heed the proverbs:

> Whoever conceals their sins does not prosper, but the one who confesses and renounces them finds mercy.
> Blessed is the one who always trembles before God, but whoever hardens their heart falls into trouble. (28:13–14)

And let them remember, as my mother often reminded me: "prayer changes things."

---

20. Bridges, *Proverbs*, 429.

Chapter Five

"Only a Boy"?
Jeremiah's Protest from the Perspective of Child Theology

JONATHAN D. BENTALL

Introduction

THE ACCOUNT OF JEREMIAH's call and commission to prophetic ministry in Jeremiah 1:4–10 has been, and will no doubt continue to be, a source of valuable insight into the interpretation of the book of Jeremiah as a whole.[1] Many interpreters have noticed the significant ways in which this opening narrative sets the stage for various themes that are central to the message of the entire book, from the prophet's dual role with regard to the destruction and restoration of nations and kingdoms (vv. 4, 10), to his conflicted relationships with both this prophetic vocation and the God who has assigned it to him (vv. 6–8).[2] Especially owing to the influence of historical-critical

---

1. For the most part, I will follow convention and refer to Jeremiah 1:4–10 as the prophet's call narrative; however, it is worth noting at the outset that there is some debate over whether or not this is the best description of the form of the passage. For a useful discussion, see Carroll, *From Chaos to Covenant*, 31–58. In a subsequent section of this essay I explore the argument for understanding this text to be of a "mixed genre" in Strawn, "Jeremiah's In/Effective Plea."

2. Worth noting in these verses is the blend of architectural, agricultural, and political images that indicate the prophet's role in God's action to bring about both destruction

paradigms and concerns arising within the modern period, a distinct focus has often been what light this text (along with the preceding superscription, Jer 1:1–3) might shed upon the situation of the historical prophet, such as the date of Jeremiah's call, his age at the time of his call and early ministry, and his possible role within the context of Josiah's reform movement.[3] Unsurprisingly, somewhat different concerns and emphases were the focus of interpretations of this prophetic book prior to the modern era, and numerous recent interpretations have either resisted the so-called "biographical approach," or else simply been content to pursue other concerns.[4] In contemporary popular Christian practice, specifically within Western evangelical culture, it is not uncommon to hear the call of Jeremiah referred to in sermons and conversations regarding Christian calling and vocation, as well as theological debates about topics such as predestination and ethical discourse concerning abortion.

The focus in this essay will be directed toward the theme of Jeremiah's youth, a feature of the text that is central both to Jeremiah's protest against his call and to YHWH's subsequent response. As I will suggest below, the syntax of both speeches signals the importance of this theme and its relationship to what is arguably *the* central element of the prophetic vocation throughout the Old Testament, namely, speech on behalf of God. However, my focus upon Jeremiah's youth will not primarily be for the purpose of coming to conclusions about the age of the prophet during this episode, or the date that should be ascribed to his call. Instead, I will explore the way in which the call of Jeremiah—in particular, his self-designation as a *naʿar* ("a youth" or "boy")—serves to highlight the prophet's limitations and vulnerability at the outset of the book concerning his prophetic ministry, so as to emphasize his dependence upon YHWH as a key aspect of what it means to be a genuine prophet.

---

and restoration of nations and kingdoms, a theme that recurs throughout the book. Another motif that is signaled here initially (vv. 6-8) and becomes pervasive—not least throughout the so-called 'confessions' (roughly, Jer. 11–20)—involves the interrelationship between the prophet's conflicted relationship with YHWH and his experience of conflict and persecution in relation to his contemporaries, both of which are integrally related to the difficulty of his prophetic vocation.

3. Many of the standard commentaries published in recent decades continue to reflect such concerns. For a representative example, see the discussion in both the introductory remarks and exegetical analysis of Thompson, *The Book of Jeremiah*, 50–56 and 143–47, respectively.

4. For the former, see Carroll, *Jeremiah*, 94–101. A good example of the latter is Moberly, *Prophecy and Discernment*, 43–47.

"Only a Boy"?
A Reading of Jeremiah 1:4–10

At the outset of the book bearing his name, Jeremiah is portrayed as both an insider and an outsider. The superscription (vv. 1–3) situates him firmly within the national story of Judah, as a member of a prominent priestly household, initially active during the critical era of King Josiah's efforts at reform (cf. 2 Kgs 22–23; 2 Chr 34–35), with a prophetic ministry that spans the reigns of numerous descendants of Josiah, until the Babylonian exile. There is a somewhat surprising contrast from the superscription's presentation of this apparently key player in the nation's history to the call narrative's portrayal of a prophet who is set apart (*qdš*) from among his own people and appointed (*ntn*) "to the nations," whose divinely given words will somehow accomplish what he has been appointed (*pqd*) to do concerning "nations and kingdoms" (v. 10; cf. Jer 18:5–11) outside of the realm of Judah itself.[5] Thus, the initial portrait of Jeremiah anticipates an element of tension that will pervade his prophetic ministry as a whole, namely his complex relationship with his own people vis-à-vis the tumultuous international political context within which they find themselves.[6]

Within this initial narrative of Jeremiah's encounter with God, and the first of many dialogues between them, it becomes clear that Jeremiah was *known* by and *formed* by YHWH "in the womb," as well as *set apart* and *given over* to his prophetic vocation prior to his birth. It is worth noting that these four verbs are set in the temporal context of Jeremiah's residence in the womb, whereas the action that takes place within what we might call the narrative present (i.e., "Today," v. 10), includes YHWH speaking to him ("The word of YHWH came to me" v. 4), touching his mouth and putting words in it (v. 9), and then reiterating the purpose of his prophetic vocation (v. 10). Initially, Jeremiah is a passive agent in the text, the object of the four divine actions that have preceded this dialogue; in verse 6, however,

---

5. While it is common for English translations to use the term "appoint" for YHWH's description of Jeremiah's vocation concerning the nations in both vv. 5 and 10 (see, e.g., NRSV, ESV, NAS, NIV), it is worth noting that two different verbs are used here. Both the KJV and the CEB helpfully distinguish between the nuance of God's making/setting up (נתן) Jeremiah as a prophet to the nations (v. 5; notably, this is the same root used to describe YHWH setting/putting his words in the prophet's mouth in v. 9b), and the subsequent idea of God's appointing, or setting (פקד) him over nations and kingdoms (v. 10).

6. Some Greek manuscripts seem to have intended to resolve this tension by rendering the Hebrew plural *goyim* with the singular *ethnos*, so that Jeremiah is understood as a "prophet to the nation," i.e. Judah.

the prophet speaks up in response, expressing a kind of exclamatory distress ("Ah, Lord YHWH") followed by a more reasoned dispute concerning where the dialogue seems to be going ("Look here . . ." [*hinneh*]). The substance and the syntax of Jeremiah's protest highlight both his youth and his perceived incapacity to speak:

> "Ah, Lord YHWH!
> Look, I do not know [how] to speak, for (*kî*) I am [only] a boy (*naʿar*)" (v. 6).[7]

While the voice of the narrator describes him as a son within a prominent priestly family, and YHWH describes him as a prophet to the nations, Jeremiah refers to himself as (merely) a *naʿar*, a youth, or more specifically, a young boy.[8] The Hebrew term has a wide enough semantic range to suggest a degree of ambiguity with regard to the age and social status of the prophet.[9] Despite the common practice among English translations of rendering the thrust of Jeremiah's protest (as well as YHWH's negation of it in v. 7) along the lines of "I am *only* a boy" (NRSV) or "I am *only* a youth" (ESV), the Hebrew text simply states the fact of his youth, without adjectival qualification.[10] In other words, whereas many English translations supply a term that has decisive implications for reading Jeremiah's protest as implying something negative, or at least limiting, about being *merely* a child/youth, the logic of the Hebrew text itself must be determined by close attention to the syntax of the verse and the relationship between the clauses.

The immediate rationale for Jeremiah's protest, indicated by the semantic construction of v. 6, is his inability to speak, which is linked causatively to his self-designation as a *naʿar*. The phrase "Behold, I do not know (*lōʾ-yādaʿtî*) how to speak" should probably not be understood simplistically as a blanket statement regarding a complete lack of verbal ability or linguistic competence, given that the boy is indeed portrayed here as speaking to YHWH; rather, the claim is best understood as signaling a perceived

---

7. Translations are my own unless otherwise indicated.

8. The corresponding feminine term, *naʿarah*, is frequently used in the Hebrew Bible to describe a young girl, suggesting that these terms are less generic designations of youth or childhood, but more specific in relation to gender.

9. See Brown, Driver, and Briggs, *The Brown, Driver, Briggs Hebrew and English Lexicon*, 654–55.

10. KJV and NASB are examples of English versions that do not supply the additional terminology; see also the distinctive rendering of the NIV: "I am *too young*," which is somewhat further down the line of dynamic equivalence than is commonplace.

inability to speak adequately, or appropriately, in relation to the role that has been assigned to him in v. 5.[11] In the subordinate clause, which introduces the explicit relation of causation (*kî*) to the main clause, the young Jeremiah cites his age—or perhaps his status in relation to his age—as the reason for his inability to speak adequately.

This brief exploration of the syntax and rhetorical implications of Jeremiah's objection suggests that the tendency among translators to supplement the Hebrew text along the lines of adjectival qualification ("I am *only* a boy," or "I am *merely* a youth") is not necessarily unwarranted. Careful attention to the logic of the prophet's objection reveals that the self-designation of Jeremiah as a *na'ar* has the potential to be understood as an inherently limiting feature of his identity, which might disqualify (or indeed excuse) him from fulfilling the role to which he has been assigned. Moreover, YHWH's response does not necessarily deny the logic of Jeremiah's objection (i.e., that being a *na'ar*, with insufficient oral abilities, might legitimately stand in the way of serving as a prophet to the nations), but rather *overrules* it by emphasizing that the sending, the speaking, and even the very words that must be spoken will be dependent not upon Jeremiah's own abilities but upon YHWH's sovereign initiative (vv. 7, 9). Moreover, it is promised that this divine initiative of sending and equipping his prophet will be accompanied by divine presence and protection (v. 8; cf. vv. 18–19).

Just as Jeremiah's objection signaled a causative relationship between his not being qualified for his calling and his being a child or a young man, YHWH's response makes a causal link (*kî*) between his negation of Jeremiah's rationale (that he is [merely] a boy) and his assurance that he will direct and ensure the success of the prophetic vocation he is assigning:

> And YHWH said to me: "Do not say 'I am [only] a boy'; for (*kî*) to everyone to whom I send (*šlḥ*) you, you will go, and all that I command (*ṣwh*) you, you will speak. Do not be afraid of them, for (*kî*) I am with you to deliver you"—says YHWH. (vv. 7b–8)

It is noteworthy that YHWH's response to Jeremiah's objection involves not only a negation of the prophet's protest ("*Do not say*, 'I am only a boy'"), and an assurance of sending, equipping, and protecting, but also a kind of

---

11. Note Ellen Davis's admittedly somewhat "free" translation "I am not expert at speaking" (in Davis, *Biblical Prophecy*, 143). A brief reference to Jeremiah 1:6 features within Davis's discussion of Jeremiah as a prophet like Moses, and her translation certainly serves to enhance the connection, given the nature of Moses' own protest in Exodus 4:10.

"doubling down" on precisely what Jeremiah seems to have been afraid of in the first place! The fairly general—perhaps even ambiguous—notion of being set apart and given as a "prophet to the nations" in v. 5 is extended and intensified in v. 10 with the tripartite set of paired infinitives ("to pluck up and pull down; to destroy and overthrow; to build and to plant"), which introduce thematic elements that will recur throughout the book (cf. Jer 12:14–17; 18:5–10; 24:6; 31:28; 42:10; 45:4). That is, YHWH's assurance by no means softens the implications of what Jeremiah initially objected to, but rather gives greater specificity to his vocation in a way that would presumably make the role of "prophet to the nations" that much more daunting and disagreeable. Interestingly, the account does not narrate Jeremiah's agreement or acquiescence, but simply gives YHWH the last word before transitioning into the book's second account of YHWH's word coming to the prophet (1:11–19). The fact that this second account involves Jeremiah acting as a prophet—receiving words, visions, and interpretations of those visions from the Lord, with clear implications for the message he will ultimately take to his own people—leads the reader to presume that YHWH has won the prophet over through the dialogue in vv. 4–10, if not in the sense of actually convincing him, then in the sense of overruling or overpowering his objections.[12]

Jeremiah's Call in Context: Form and Intertextuality

It is highly likely that the account of Jeremiah's protest and YHWH's response is intended to call to mind the similar, if more extensive, debate between Moses and YHWH in Exodus 3:10–4:17. In that account, YHWH expresses his intention to send (*šlḥ*) Moses to the ruler of a foreign nation in order to accomplish what must have seemed like an impossible task—the deliverance of the Israelite people from Egyptian slavery. In response, Moses calls into question his own suitability for this task (Exod 3:11), expresses reservations concerning what he will tell his people regarding the One who has sent him (3:13), worries about whether the Israelites will trust or listen to him (4:1) and, finally, protests by citing his lack of eloquence (4:10). YHWH's counterargument to each of these points takes the form of a promise of divine presence and assurance of having been sent by YHWH

---

12. Further weight is added to this suggestion by language used by the prophet later in the book, describing YHWH as akin to a "deceitful brook" (Jer 15:18) and an overpowering presence (20:7–9). Cf. Crenshaw, *A Whirlpool of Torment*, 38–50.

himself (3:12), a revelation of the divine name in continuity with God's previous revelation to the patriarchs of Israel (3:14–16), instructions regarding a series of miraculous signs that may be used to authenticate his divinely initiated prophetic commissioning (4:2–9), and an assurance that not only is all human speech made possible by God himself, but more specifically that YHWH will be "with" Moses' mouth and that he will teach him what to speak (4:11–12).

It might be suggested that what we find in Jeremiah 1:4–10 is a condensed form of the dialogue between Moses and YHWH from the Exodus narrative. In the story of Jeremiah's call, we have analogues for both the initial and the final elements of Moses' call—i.e., Jeremiah is sent by YHWH with a seemingly impossible prophetic task concerning powerful foreign nations, and his protest involves an emphasis on his inability to speak in a way that will be fitting for this task. YHWH's response to Jeremiah consists of both an assurance that God himself will be the source of the needed words as well as an assurance of God's protective presence in the midst of what will surely be a difficult assignment. Although the middle components of the longer Exodus account are not present, it is reasonable to conclude that the account of Jeremiah's call has been composed with the intention of calling to mind the commissioning of Israel's paradigmatic prophetic figure, Moses.

Moreover, the final stage of the latter episode provides a striking linguistic correspondence between the two texts. Moses' final protest lacks the imaginative character of his previous arguments as he simply blurts out "Oh my Lord, please send someone else!" (4:13). YHWH's response to Moses' final plea is initially described as angry, and yet it quickly takes the form of a kind of compromise, in which the deity proposes that Moses' brother, Aaron, will serve as a kind of prophet on behalf of Moses.[13] YHWH explains that Moses will speak to Aaron and thereby will "put/set (*śym*) the words in his mouth" that are to be spoken. While there may not be precise linguistic correspondence between the two texts (note the use of different verbs), this is precisely the image and phraseology with which YHWH assures Jeremiah, explaining, "Behold, I have put (*ntn*) my words in your mouth" (Jer 1:9b).

Alongside these particular intertextual resonances, it is frequently observed more broadly that Jeremiah 1:4–10 contains common features

---

13. On the theme of Aaron as Moses' "prophet," see Moberly, *Prophecy and Discernment*, 3–4.

of the call narrative form, including the prophet's *objection* or resistance to YHWH's call, and the deity's response of *assurance*, in which he both counters the objection and provides rationale for acceptance of the call.¹⁴ However, Brent A. Strawn offers a compelling argument for regarding this text as being of "mixed genre," incorporating elements of both the call narrative form and also aspects of the generic category of prayers of lament and distress.¹⁵

Strawn resists the interpretive tendency to focus upon what this text might reveal about the chronological and historical details behind the text, seeking to identify the precise age of the prophet at the time of his call, and instead argues that the term *naʿar* is best understood as a rhetorical device intended to highlight the "weak or insignificant status" of a supplicant making an appeal to God, thereby seeking to invoke divine compassion or prompt divine action.¹⁶ Drawing upon the work of Patrick D. Miller concerning prayer in the Hebrew Bible, Strawn claims that Jeremiah not only protests his call but in fact *laments* it, incorporating formal and rhetorical indications of a prayer of distress; extending this line of interpretation, Strawn resists the idea that YHWH's words to Jeremiah should be understood as any kind of refutation or rebuke, instead claiming that God's response here constitutes "nothing short of an oracle of salvation."¹⁷ Thus, according to Strawn, the term *naʿar* is best understood as a "formal or conventional element" that signals a mixed genre; it is a "rhetorical move involving the appeal to נער-status," intended to emphasize not the precise age of the prophet so much as his weakness and insignificance before God.¹⁸

Taking Strawn's argument as my cue, and in the light of the parallels between the commissioning accounts of Jeremiah and Moses, I suggest that Jeremiah's self-designation as a young boy should be understood as a central

---

14. Alongside Exodus 3:10–4:17, note the calls of Gideon (Judg 6:11–18) and perhaps also Isaiah (Isa 6:1–13).

15. Strawn, "Jeremiah's In/Effective Plea," 373–77.

16. Strawn, "Jeremiah's In/Effective Plea," 369. Strawn counters what he regards as problematic attempts to use the term *naʿar* as an indication of the prophet's age, maintaining that the word is "horribly imprecise" (368). Citing a number of examples (Gen 32:11; Num 11:14; Amos 7:2, 5; 1 Kgs 3:7), many of which use a form of the term קטן (small, insignificant), Strawn suggests that comparison with these—esp. 1 Kgs. 3:7—"indicates that Jeremiah's statement that he is a נער may have little to do with his chronological age, or, at the very least, if it has to do with his chronological age, it is not only that" (370).

17. Strawn, "Jeremiah's In/Effective Plea," 372. Cf. Miller, *They Cried to the Lord*, 398.

18. Strawn, "Jeremiah's In/Effective Plea," 373–74.

feature not only of his call narrative, but also of his portrayal as a prophet as a whole. In other words, Jeremiah's *na'ar* status may be understood not so much as an aspect of his humble origins that the prophet "grows out of," as it were, but rather as yet another feature of the call narrative that, alongside other key motifs introduced in Jeremiah 1:4–10, sets the stage for the remainder of the book. Of course, it is undeniable that the book portrays the prophet as a fully matured adult subsequent to the first chapter; thus, my claim is not that the prophet should be understood as literally remaining a child throughout the book.[19] Rather, I wish to explore the potential theological implications of Strawn's insight that the prophet's *na'ar*-status goes beyond biographical information and physiological implications.

Whereas the value of historical, philological, and contextual insights into the nature of childhood, the semantic range of the Hebrew term *na'ar*, and the possible significance of Jeremiah's self-designation as such within the context of ancient Judah are undeniable, perhaps there is a relatively unexplored angle on Jeremiah's call narrative that might further illuminate the text. Thus, I now turn to the horizon of contemporary theological reflection upon the nature and meaning of childhood that might enrich our understanding of this biblical text and its role of introducing the prophet and the book of Jeremiah.

Reading Jeremiah Against the Backdrop of Child Theology

Among the more prominent themes associated with children and childhood in contemporary theological discourse are those of dependence and vulnerability. For example, in *Let the Children Come*, Bonnie J. Miller-McLemore seeks to reclaim the idea of "children as gift," which she claims has a strong basis in Scripture despite the apparent ambivalence or ambiguity surrounding this subject in much of the biblical narrative.[20] Focusing on the Markan accounts of Jesus' interaction with children and claims

---

19. Already in the superscription (Jer 1:1–3) we are told that his ministry spans the reigns of three separate kings. Presumably, readers should regard Jeremiah as having 'grown up' to some extent either between the episodes of 1:4–10 and 11–19 or at least by the time of his encounters with YHWH in 2:1ff., 3:6ff., and/or 7:1ff.

20. Similarly, Berryman, *Children and the Theologians*, discusses what he regards as a high view of children within the Gospel accounts, without denying that this is intermingled with elements of a low view and even indifference. He also takes up the narrative in which the young child is set in the midst of a theological debate, noticing many of the key differences between the three Gospel accounts.

regarding their relation to the kingdom (Mark 9:33–37 and 10:13–16), Miller-McLemore stresses the importance of placing these episodes firmly within their sociohistorical context such that "the imperative to receive the kingdom 'like a child' must be read in light of the imperative to receive children in themselves, in their inferior and vulnerable social status in the first-century world."[21] While it is not at all uncommon for interpreters to notice the motif of *humility* being prominent in these texts, in contrast to the disciples bickering over status and recognition, Miller-McLemore insists that the terminology and conceptualities surrounding humility in this context must not be reduced to romanticized perceptions of sentimentality, but instead must be heard in all of their concrete political and social contextual significance, as indications of insignificance, powerlessness, and vulnerability.

Further insight into the theological significance of humility and vulnerability may be drawn from the rich study of Kristine A. Culp, entitled *Vulnerability and Glory: A Theological Account*.[22] Here, Culp offers a compelling account of the positive capacity of vulnerability as basic to human existence in the presence of God, capable both of tragic devastation and of bearing the glory of God through transformation. Central to Culp's argument is the concept that vulnerability is an "enduring feature of creaturely existence" as opposed to a "temporary condition that can or ought to be overcome."[23] In a number of places throughout her book, she reiterates and expands upon this observation, explaining that "[v]ulnerability is a basic aspect of creaturely existence and a situation wherein the grace and glory of God may be known . . . not a condition to be overcome,"[24] and claiming: "to receive and bear the glory of God cannot mean somehow to deny vulnerability or to escape ambiguity."[25]

Such themes also play central role in Hans Urs von Balthasar's beautiful little study, *Unless You Become Like This Child*, in which he explains, "Childhood is fully vulnerable because the child is powerless."[26] In a way that finds resonance with Culp's discussion, Balthasar suggests that this vulnerable condition of the human child—the "fragility of this originally

---

21. Miller-McLemore, *Let the Children Come*, 96.
22. Culp, *Vulnerability and Glory*.
23. Culp, *Vulnerability and Glory*, 3.
24. Culp, *Vulnerability and Glory*, 94.
25. Culp, *Vulnerability and Glory*, 103.
26. Balthasar, *Unless You Become Like This Child*, 12–13.

"Only a Boy"?

inviolable dimension"—is not so much a state that is entirely transcended or overcome with growth in maturity or the onset of adulthood, but rather "an experience . . . to which we must somehow return."[27] Reflecting upon the dialogue between Jesus and Nicodemus in John 3, Balthasar suggests that participation in the kingdom of God is dependent upon one's ability to enter into this "profound mystery, rooted in the very being of Christ, whose identity is inseparable from his being a child in the bosom of the Father."[28] Thus, the notion of being or becoming a child of God is a matter of participating in the relationship that is established by the incarnation.

The preceding insights offer support for the line of interpretation I have been developing regarding Jeremiah's call narrative, viewing the *naʿar* motif not merely as a feature of Jeremiah's initial call and biographical existence, not as something that he eventually "grows out of," but rather as an element of the prophet's portrayal that, along with other motifs in 1:4–10, sets the stage for the rest of the book. Of course, presumably the prophet does grow up and is no longer a child or a youth as the book progresses; however, what it means for him to be a *naʿar*, and how this functions rhetorically and theologically at the outset of the book, does not cease to shape the portrayal of the prophet and his vocation. In other words, what it means for Jeremiah to be a *naʿar* in relation to God, in relation to his people, and in relation to his vocation remains central to the persona of the prophet throughout the book. Whereas Jeremiah initially regards the vulnerability and dependence associated with his self-designation as a *naʿar* to be a clear-cut indication of his disqualification for the role of "prophet to the nations" (Jer 1:6), YHWH's response may be understood as confirmation that this is precisely the posture with which a genuine prophet undertakes the task of being sent by YHWH to speak his words, on his behalf (Jer 1:7–10; cf. 23:18–22).[29]

---

27. Balthasar, *Unless You Become Like This Child*, 11–12. According to Balthasar, "What is called for is not at all a form of infantilism, but a repetition of the eternal Son's readiness to obey the 'command' (*mandatum*) of the Father . . ." (40).

28. Balthasar, *Unless You Become Like This Child*, 10–11; cf. 43–55. As he puts it, "We never quite outgrow our condition of children, nor do we therefore ever outgrow the obligation to give thanks or to continue to ask for our being" (49).

29. For more on the link between prophetic authority and being genuinely sent by YHWH, see the illuminating study of Moberly, *Prophecy and Discernment*, 41–99.

An Introduction to Child Theology

Reading Jeremiah with Medieval Interpreters

A final avenue to explore is the way in which the insights that I have drawn upon within contemporary forms of theological discourse also find resonances with premodern intuitions and emphases concerning the theological interpretation of Scripture. Joy A. Schroeder's contribution to the series *The Bible in Medieval Tradition* compiles and translates numerous interpretations of the book of Jeremiah from the medieval period.[30] In this volume, selections from Rupert of Deutz (1075–1129) and Albert the Great (ca. 1206–1280) are illustrative of premodern interpretive traditions that, unsurprisingly, reveal a very different set of concerns from those of many modern biblical scholars. Rupert finds it unproblematic, for example, to claim a typological link between God's knowing and foreordaining of Jeremiah prior to his birth (Jer 1:5) and the prologue of John's Gospel, which envisions a preexistent Christ intimately know by God prior to his incarnation (John 1:1).[31]

Albert the Great pursues a similar line of interpretation, yet with a more expansive selection of canonical texts shaping his construal of the divine foreknowledge and predestination that he takes to be on display in Jeremiah 1:5.[32] He also makes much of what he calls the "impediment" to Jeremiah's acceptance of his call in 1:6. First, Albert distances Jeremiah's objection to God's call from those articulated by Moses (Exod 4:10) and Isaiah (Isa 6:5), interpreting these latter examples as based upon a literal speech impediment and a sense of unworthiness, respectively. Albert interprets Jeremiah's words through the lens of Pseudo-Dionysius and his work *The Divine Names*, highlighting the incapacity and irrationality of human language in the presence of God.[33]

Second, Albert addresses the age of Jeremiah as a feature of the impediment. Drawing upon numerous biblical texts as well as the Greek philosophical tradition, Albert stresses that youthfulness and wisdom need not be understood as mutually exclusive. Following Jerome's reasoning that

---

30. Schroeder, ed., *The Bible in Medieval Tradition*.

31. Rupert of Deutz, "On the Holy Trinity and Its Works: On Jeremiah," in Schroeder, ed., *The Bible in Medieval Tradition*, 55, 57. It is worth noting that Rupert's interpretations of the book also involve distressing instances of supersessionism and anti-Semitism.

32. Albert the Great, "Postill on Jeremiah," in Schroeder, ed., *The Bible in Medieval Tradition*, 62–64.

33. Albert the Great, "Postill on Jeremiah," in Schroeder, ed., *The Bible in Medieval Tradition*, 68.

Jeremiah has been "granted the grace of childhood," he suggests that the frailty and modesty that accompanied the prophet's young age by no means precluded him from being "gray-haired" in his understanding or from receiving wisdom and understanding from the hand of God. He offers the following take on YHWH's "removal of the impediment" in v. 7: "It is as if God were saying: Even though you are a child in age, when you obey my spirit you are not a child. For God poured into him the wisdom of venerable aged people."[34]

Albert's approach contributes further to the central insight developed in this essay, namely that Jeremiah's status as a *na'ar* may be understood as much more than a minor hindrance to be dismissed initially by YHWH, and then ultimately left behind as the prophet presumably ages and matures; instead, the typological link between Jeremiah and Jesus reinforces the notion that the limitations, vulnerability, and dependence associated with the prophet's *na'ar*-status participate in a reality that is central to the Christian story itself, involving God's embrace of the humility and limitations of humanity that is on display most strikingly and powerfully in the incarnation.

Conclusion

According to the reading presented here, the introduction of Jeremiah as a child, or perhaps a youth, is not a feature of his identity that is meaningful only within the context of the call narrative but then left behind as the remainder of the book portrays a matured, adult prophetic figure operative within Judahite society; nor is it merely a feature of the prophet's biological childhood or adolescence, primarily of interest for what it reveals about the age of the historical individual at the time of his call. Instead, the humility and vulnerability associated with Jeremiah as a *na'ar* contribute to the role of this programmatic text in constructing a hermeneutical framework through which one is prepared to encounter the book of Jeremiah as a whole. What the prophet sees as a clear indication of his disqualification becomes, from God's perspective, the marker of his preparedness to be used by God and to speak genuinely on his behalf.

---

34. Albert the Great, "Postill on Jeremiah," in Schroeder, ed., *The Bible in Medieval Tradition*, 69.

An Introduction to Child Theology

Jeremiah's dialogue with YHWH in Jeremiah 1:4–10 therefore raises questions such as: What does it mean to be a child?[35] And what might this have to do with not being able to speak? While there is much to be said in favor of interpreting Jeremiah's protest to his calling in connection with that of Moses, such that the primary concern has to do with the subject's lack of skill as an orator and his perceived inadequacy in relation to a divinely ordained task, in this essay I have pursued a slightly different line of reasoning, suggesting that the status of Jeremiah as a *na'ar* may be connected to his inability to speak in a sense that we might express using a figure of speech: the idea of not having a voice.

This approach need not be conceived as a distinct alternative to a reading that sees Jeremiah as concerned with his own inabilities, but it adds an important dynamic that arguably finds resonance in the experience of children in innumerable times and places—i.e., the experience of not being taken seriously, and this precisely because of one's age and consequent status. According to this reading, behind Jeremiah's protest lies not only a self-conscious concern over his own knowledge, skill, or sufficient preparation as a public orator in the mode of a prophet of Judah, but also an uneasy awareness of the way in which his words, his voice, his speech, might be (or, more precisely, might *not* be) received. We might imagine that even as his words focus upon his own self ("I don't know how to speak") the subtext of his concern includes the apprehensive question: "Who would listen?"

In many cultures throughout human history there has been an understandable association of wisdom with age, experience, and maturity. Moreover, it would be an uncontroversial assumption within most cultures that performing a role such as that envisaged by a prophet or spokesperson would seem to require a fair amount of such maturity, wisdom, and discernment. Yet, there is also an important sense in which the profound simplicity of a child's perspective can offer a kind of directness, an unadulterated focus on the core of an issue in a way that has not been clouded by the complexities of supposedly more mature and experienced perspectives. More importantly, with the economy of God's action, often in and through

---

35. For a historical and contextual orientation to the role and status of children in an ancient context, see Garroway, *Children in the Ancient Near Eastern Household*; and Garroway, *Growing up in Ancient Israel*. For useful discussions of the role and portrayal of children and childhood within biblical literature, see the essays in Bunge, Fretheim, and Gaventa, eds., *The Child in the Bible*. An illuminating discussion of the topic that touches on both the story of Scripture and its ancient context, focusing especially on the context of the early church, is Horn and Martens, *"Let the Little Children Come to Me."*

chosen human agents, being or becoming "like a child" may have less to do with a developmental stage that one inevitably leaves behind and more to do with a fundamental posture of humility before God. This position of vulnerability and dependence is not denied, overcome, or abandoned within the context of witnessing and facilitating God's presence in and for the world, but rather may be understood as a prerequisite and a necessary, continuing posture. Not only does the kingdom of heaven belong to children (Matt 9:14), but those who imagine themselves to have surpassed this stage of life and transcended its corresponding status must become like children in order to enter it (Matt 18:1–5).

Chapter Six

While Knit In My Mother's Womb

The Theology of Infancy in Psalm 139

Keith Bodner

Among the various poetic reflections on the experience of childhood in the book of Psalms, the famous words of Psalm 139—"I am fearfully and wonderfully made"—surely hold a certain pride of place. But what are the best options for interpreting these words, how do they work in the context of the psalm, and where are they found with the larger Psalter? In this short essay I will explore the theology of infancy in Psalm 139 by discussing three interrelated elements. First, I discuss recent views of the Psalter that suggest the book is a five-act drama that traces the rise and fall of the Israelite monarchy, and incrementally moves from a preponderance of lament to a symphony of praise over the course of its 150 compositions. Second, I undertake a more detailed readings of the third stanza (vv. 13–18) and the vision of infancy that is presented within the context of Book Five. Third, I conclude by raising several implications for the theology of infancy in light of a wider biblical theology and the pressing concerns of our contemporary age, suggesting that Psalm 139 makes a significant contribution to the story of the Psalter and carries an abiding relevance in the worship tradition of God's people.

While Knit In My Mother's Womb
The Psalter as a Five-Act Drama

In days past the book of Psalms was most often read as an illuminating anthology of Israel's prayers over the centuries. While the array of poetic voices and rich tapestry of theological thought brought comfort and instruction to believers from a host of traditions and an ostensible window on the spiritual and ritual worlds of the ancient Levant for scholars, in terms of organization the collection was not interpreted through the lens of an overarching structure or with much sense of a broader plot movement from start to finish. On the one hand, the inner drama of the Psalter has long been appreciated, with a great cloud of witnesses testifying to divine efficacy in the midst of trials, external attacks, doubts, frustrations, fears, and triumphs. On the other hand, in more recent decades there has been an increased effort to study the Psalter as a book with a plot: rather than a random collage, the book of Psalms is finally designed with a five-book structure that incrementally moves from *petition* to *praise* over the course of the 150 compositions. So, in what follows I will briefly outline the Psalter as a drama in five acts that traces the rise and fall of the Israelite monarchy, and ultimately instructs the community to focus on the kingship of God rather than any earthly alternative.[1]

The opening two psalms can be interpreted as a prologue to the forthcoming drama of the Psalter. At the gateway, Psalm 1 sets the stage by setting before the community two pathways: the way of the Torah that leads to a firmly rooted life, contrasted with the frenetic instability of the wicked path that ultimately vanishes.[2] Akin to Deuteronomy, the opening psalm operates as an encouragement and warning for the entire community (including kings and leaders) to walk under the aegis of divine beneficence and resist the allure of darker pathways. Psalm 2 begins with an image of the raging nations and the inception of Davidic kingship, in a poetic vision of God's promise of an enduring house in 2 Samuel 7; indeed, though the monarchy may fail, the divine assurance will prevail. Psalm 1 begins with the term 'asherê ("Blessed is the one who walks . . ."), and Psalm 2 ends with the same term ("Blessed are all who take refuge in him"), and together these compositions form an overture to the fivefold drama of the Psalter.

---

1. See Wilson, "The Structure of the Psalter"; deClaissé-Walford, "The Meta-Narrative of the Psalter"; and Waltke and Houston, *The Psalms as Christian Worship*, 89–92.

2. As an example of such an approach, see Cole, "An Integrated Reading of Psalms 1 and 2."

Book One unfolds a series of poetic snapshots that variously reflect the vicissitudes of Israel's early experiences with monarchy, and it is bracketed by a pair of programmatic compositions. The superscription of Psalm 3 plunges the reader immediately into the catastrophe of Absalom's rebellion, and strongly indicates from the outset that even a person under great divine promise is not excepted from suffering and strife. Various genres such as *creation* and *thanksgiving* psalms are found scattered throughout Book One, but the percentage of *lament* psalms is disproportionately high, suggesting that Israel's royal experiment was fraught with challenge and crisis from the outset. Psalm 41 can be viewed as a fitting conclusion to Book One especially in comparison with the theology of Psalm 1. In that first psalm, the person who eschews the counsel of the wicked and delights in the *tôrāh* is likened to a transplanted tree, firmly rooted to withstand the storms of life. Similarly, the severe trials of Psalm 41 emphasize the need to trust in the character of God rather than succumb to the schemes of adversaries, and so encourage future leaders among God's people to do likewise (and perhaps even warn about disregarding the poor). A concluding doxology in 41:13 ("Amen and amen") marks the conclusion of Book One, much like the endings of the other books of the Psalter.

Book Two (42–72) begins with the more somber Psalm 42, as the poet is evidently displaced from the promised land and longs for the divine presence, yet the image of a wounded deer (cf. Lam 1:6) escaping a predator casts a faintly ominous mood over this book, and may foreshadow future displacements. Again, there is continuity in Book Two as the highs and lows of the monarchy are poetically intoned with a higher frequency of lament psalms, and overall the spatial setting leans toward Jerusalem. The placement of Psalm 72 at the end of Book Two has a startling effect: it is a prayer that Solomon and other Davidic successors will walk in the Torah and have social justice as a central priority, but given the dismal failure of Israel's forty-two kings, such a prayer has an ironic ring at the end of Book Two. The closing doxology is augmented with a note of finality—"The prayers of David, the son of Jesse, are ended"—and marks the end of Israel's tenure in the land, the destruction of the temple, and a transition to exile.

Book Three has a tenor of comparative bleakness, and reflects the period of exile in the aftermath of the Babylonian invasion. Psalm 73 recounts a story of a poet who nearly experienced a fatal slip due to covetousness, and one wonders if the poet is speaking as the representative of a nation that envied the foreign nations and their kings, and fatally lost their focus.

Hope is possible, exhales the poet, when people return to the *holy places of God* (73:16, *miqdeshê-ʾēl*).[3] The exilic atmosphere of Book Three is palpable in the opening lines of Psalm 74, "O God, why do you cast us off forever? Why does your anger smoke against the sheep of your pasture?" For this poet, however, even the exile is firmly under the aegis of God's sovereignty, and hence the conclusion of the psalm is a call for God to act on the basis of a prior commitment: "Consider the covenant, for the dark places of the land are full of the habitations of violence" (74:20). Psalms 88 and 89 together are a formidable conclusion to Book Three: the final line in 88:18 ("my only companions: darkness") is then extended with a searing assertion in 89:39 ("You have renounced the covenant with your servant; you have defiled his crown in the dust"). With the institutional monarchy in ruins, has the Davidic promise been eschewed?

Book Four (90–106) represents a definitive turning point in the story of the Psalter, and encourages the community to reframe its focus and begin rebuilding their broken world. It is surely no accident that Psalm 90 glances back to a time prior to kings or temple, when the nation had an eminently reliable guide: "Before the wilderness of Babylonian Exile, there had been another wilderness through which Israel had been guided without king by pillars of fire, clouds, and the Ark to reunite with an earlier promise made to Abraham. Before kings and temples there was YHWH, and in staccato fashion Book Four reminds a new wilderness generation: the Lord reigns (Pss 93, 95–99). The answer to the dismal ending of Book Three is the affirmation of YHWH's reign that will call for, in Book Five (Pss 107–150), trust in YHWH."[4] Altogether, Book Four moves to a conclusion with a sequence of creation and historical hymns, recounting various contours of divine sovereignty and beneficence toward a wayward people who will be granted a second chance to return from exile and reoccupy the land of promise.

Book Five commences with a sweeping poetic vision of regathering, as those scattered—whether from desert wastelands, darkness of prisons, deprivations of harsh labor, or even tossed about in tempestuous waters—have not been abandoned in Psalm 107, but rather are the objects of God's steadfast commitment. As one scans Book Five there is much less

3. Note Brueggemann and Miller, "Psalm 73 as a Canonical Marker."

4. Parrish, *A Story of the Psalms*, 5. Cf. Waltke and Houston, *The Psalms as Christian Worship*, 92: "He has been Israel's refuge in the past, long before monarchy existed; he will continue to be Israel's refuge now that monarchy is gone; and blessed are they that trust in him."

reorientation toward any hopes of a restored Davidic monarchy and much more emphasis on trust and worship, as evidenced in Passover *Hallel* collection (113–18), the vast tapestry of *Torah* celebration in Psalm 119 or the rebooted *Songs of Ascents* (120–34). Moving toward the climax of the Psalter in the final sequence leading to Psalm 150, there is a diminution of evil and a communal chorus of orchestral praise: "Psalm 150 is remarkable because it contains no reason or motivations at all. It is the only Psalm which completely lacks motivation. It is the most extreme and unqualified statement of unfettered praise in the Old Testament. Psalm 150 is situated literally at the end of the process of praise; it is also located theologically at the end of the process of praise and obedience, after all of Israel's motivations have been expressed and no more reasons need to be given."[5] Even though this has been just a short sketch of the plot of the book of Psalms, one can discern a movement from *petition* to *praise*, and quite plausibly this is the reason why the book is finally titled *Praises* (*Tehillim*) in Hebrew tradition. The journey of the Psalter leads the people of God away from misplaced confidence in human machinery and toward the throne of God, in anticipation that the promise to David about an eternal king will indeed be fulfilled.[6]

Psalm 139:13–18

Located near the heart of Book Five, Psalm 139 is often classified as an *individual hymn of thanksgiving and petition* in four stanzas. Alternatively, Richard Clifford reports an older theory that has a judicial view of the psalm as "the prayer of an accused person facing an ordeal such as that described in Num 5:11–31," while Erhard Gerstenberger refers to it as a meditation or "a musing, self-centered, theologically reflected prayer."[7] Far more contentious among scholars is the debate about the structure of Psalm 139: the first three stanzas narrate a passionate story about inner creation

---

5. Brueggemann, "Bounded by Obedience and Praise," 67.

6. Cf. Wilson, "The Shape of the Book of Psalms," 136: "The intention of the last two books of the Psalter—to point postexilic Israel away from reliance on human kings toward trust in Yahweh, who alone rules eternally—is already discernible in book three."

7. Clifford, *Psalms 73–150*, 279; and Gerstenberger, *Psalms, Part 2, and Lamentations*, 401. The sufferings of Job might also be compared, for even though "defamed by his friends-turned-enemies, Job held fast to his righteousness against all odds, calling upon God to vindicate his integrity in the presence of his detractors (cf. Job 27:5–12; 31:6 with Ps. 139:23–24)." (Brown, "Psalm 139.")

and soaring divine knowledge, but the violent language and desires for the bloodthirsty to be terminated in the fourth stanza strikes many as out of order. Such apparent disharmony has led to proposals that the psalm has been patched together from two discrete units of material.[8] Similarities can be observed, however, with the neighboring Psalm 137, a composition that likewise begins with famous and meditative lyrics that are followed by abrupt and crushing imprecations, and in both cases it falls on the interpreter to make sense of the whole rather than the parts. While my central interest here is the third stanza of Psalm 139, a few remarks are in order about the first two in order to frame the discussion.

Considering the larger picture, I would suggest that Psalm 139 is an expression of confidence and a prayer for help in the midst of calculated wickedness: the poet variously recounts aspects of the divine character, and on the basis of such realities (i.e., God's incomparable knowledge coupled with spatial and temporal sovereignty) calls on God to eradicate evil that threatens from without and test the veracity of the poet's commitment within. The first stanza (vv. 1–6) unfold a series of parallelisms that underscore the multidimensional contours of divine knowledge; even if such sweeping divine knowledge of every facet of life may seem daunting, for the poet it is something to be celebrated and a source of trust. Not only can God discern the poet's very motives from afar, but words are known even prior to their utterance. Of course, such intimate acquaintance may, for some, be suffocating or unwelcome, just as the image of *besieging* in v. 5 might seem to carry negative connotations.[9] Yet in the light of the next line, as the poet deploys a metaphor whereby God's knowledge is a citadel whose walls cannot be breached in v. 6, he implies that what would be hostile from any other agency is actually a source of confidence when it comes to God. Given the circumstances of violence and distress that surround the poet as adumbrated later in the psalm, the first stanza's stress on divine awareness can be here construed as an antidote to the chaos of the world.

---

8. E.g., the secondary sources cited by Goulder, *The Psalms of the Return*, 238.

9. Cf. the discussion of Zenger and Hossfeld, *Psalms 3*, 540. Perhaps also compare at this point the thoughts of Soelle, "The Onward Journey Concerning the Problem of Identity," 22: "God knows me better than I know myself, he knows me differently from the way my environment knows me, knows me longer and more deeply than anyone who knows something of me. That means that my identity is more and can be more than that which I already know. 'That which we shall be has not yet appeared' (1 John 3:2). It means that every human being is a mystery which is not dissolved within the social identity."

If the first stanza of Psalm 139 focuses on divine knowledge, then the second stanza (vv. 7–12) takes a spatial turn and reflects on the impossibility of any escape from God. One might note some conceptual parallels here to the adventure of Jonah, whose attempt to flee to Tarshish was thwarted by a tempest just as his attempt to descend into the depths is thwarted by the great fish. Whether a horizontal or a vertical axis, this second stanza declares that God is everywhere and spans every compass point: the heights of the heavens, the chaotic expanse of the sea, surprisingly even depths of Sheol, or penetrating the thickest darkness.[10] Nonetheless, some scholars have raised a question about why the poet is considering such matters: there is no escaping from God, but does the poet want to? It seems to me that this stanza is a hypothetical reflection that builds on the previous verses, and since flight from the God who intimately knows the poet is impossible, there is a reassurance that one can never be far from God's presence. Emerging from exile, where the people were again bombarded with competing ideologies about the realm of the gods, the manifold spatial presence of God is striking, and echoes of Genesis 1 abound in Psalm 139. Furthermore, as is evident in the third stanza, God's intimate knowledge of the poet stems from a unique creative activity:

> 13 For You created my innermost parts,
>   wove me in my mother's womb.
> 14 I acclaim You, for awesomely I am set apart,
>   wondrous are Your acts,
>   and my being deeply knows it.
> 15 My frame was not hidden from You,
>   when I was made in a secret place,
>   knitted in the utmost depths.
> 16 My unformed shape Your eyes did see,
>   and in Your book all was written down.
> The days were fashioned,
>   not one of them did lack.
> 17 As for me, how weighty are Your thoughts, O God,
>   how numerous their sum.
> 18 Should I count them, they would be more than the sand.
>   I awake, and am still with You.[11]

---

10. On the sea in particular, see Waltke and Houston, *The Psalms as Christian Worship*, 427: "In Israel's cosmography the land was surrounded by the primeval abyss that existed before the creation of land. Although it can be spoken of neutrally as a part of the cosmos (Gen. 1:2), normally *sea* represents chaotic power hostile to God and the world (Job 26:12f.; 38:8–10; Pss. 46:2f. ;104:6)."

11. This translation is by Alter, *The Book of Psalms*.

In several respects the third stanza of Psalm 139 arguably unfolds a theology of infancy that can be interpreted as a poetic complement to the *imago dei* that is presented in the early chapters of Genesis. Recalling Genesis 2:7, for instance, God *forms* (*yāṣar*) the human being from the dust of the earth, with the verb *form* often used for a potter fashioning a vessel from clay. The same verb is deployed in Psalm 139:16, as not only did God see the poet's unformed substance in the darkness of the womb, but also all the poet's days were *formed* (*yāṣar*) in the divine book long before any of them came to pass. This divine book is variously interpreted, but one option is akin to Revelation 5:1 and the scroll of destiny (cf. other uses of *book* in Pss 56:9 and 69:28).[12] Mention of the *book* is most significant, for even as God is shaping the infant in the womb, so God is endowing a larger purpose for that same human being, much like a potter would plan how the finished vessel is to be effectively put to use. The infant in the womb has already been set apart for divine use in a meaningful life.

A trace of Genesis 3:21 might also be discerned here in the third stanza of Psalm 139, a verse rendered by the NRSV as follows: "And the LORD God made (*'āśah*) garments of skins for the man and for his wife, and clothed them." In Psalm 139:15 the poet's frame is not hidden when being made (*'āśah*) by God in secret and intricately stitched together in the depths of the earth, with the imagery of a divine weaver who thoughtfully embroiders the human person. If there is not a conscious allusion at work here, then certainly we can at least suggest an extension of the theological vision, for just as God makes (*'āśah*) the infant in the womb so God makes (*'āśah*) provisions after the catastrophic choices in the garden. Most standard English translations of Genesis 3:21 opt for the rather generic term *garments*, but the Hebrew term *ketōnet* is more specialized and often used elsewhere for priestly or royal outfits. For example, a *ketōnet* is an inner tunic that is part of the priestly attire in Exodus 39:27 and Leviticus 8:13, compared to 2 Samuel 15:32 and Isaiah 22:21 where a *ketōnet* is worn by high-ranking courtiers. Therefore, when God makes (*'āśah*) royal and priestly garments to clothe humanity, it implies that God does not withdraw the royal or priestly mandates of humanity despite their flawed choices. By extension, the infant in the womb who is formed with a destiny and handcrafted by God is imprinted with a certain royal dignity and priestly vocation when these two texts are read in partnership.

As mentioned in the introductory paragraph at the outset of this essay, among the more famous lines in the Psalter is Psalm 139:14, the poet's

---

12. Waltke and Houston, *The Psalms as Christian Worship*, 431.

declaration of being fearfully (*nôrā' ôt*) or awesomely woven together. Elsewhere in the Psalter, the same participle *awesome* (*nôrā' ôt*) is used to describe major events with redemptive significance. In this regard, one might fruitfully consider passages such as Psalms 65:5 ("By awesome deeds [*nôrā' ôt*] you answer us with righteousness, O God of our salvation, the hope of all the ends of the earth and of the farthest seas) or 106:21-22 (They rejected the God who delivered them, the one who performed great deeds in Egypt, wondrous works in the land of Ham, and awesome deeds [*nôrā' ôt*] by the Red Sea), inviting Richard Clifford to conclude that "God's creation of the psalmist is as wondrous in its own way as other great deeds of God."[13] Weaving together an infant in the womb is audaciously framed within the magnificent events of the redemptive narrative, resulting in the theological conclusion that every child is graced with design and destiny.

If Psalm 139 ended on this note, few readers would complain. But as it stands, such thoughts are a transition to the closing complaint and petition. The fourth stanza (vv. 19-24) presents a twofold petition: the poet desires that God slay the wicked (further defined as those who speak with malicious intent and use the divine name gratuitously), and, ensuring that one's own motives are not deceitful, the poet expresses a further desire to be searched by God and guided in the everlasting and eminently reliable ancient way. To reiterate, some scholars have demurred, and asserted that two disparate compositions have been merged here, but there are good reasons for reading the psalm as a unity. While it may seem abrupt to move from the sublime to the imprecatory, on the contrary it can be maintained that evil is a palpable threat to the fragile lives described in Psalm 139. But are the *wicked* external foes such as Babylonian officers or Persian power brokers or, more disturbingly, are the enemies of God in Psalm 139 those who actually reside within the covenant community? Given the disingenuous use of the divine name (cf. Exod 20:7; Deut 5:11), the latter option is eminently possible. Within the community, then, are those who would deny the very kinds of divine sovereignty and human worth—from infancy onward—that is so passionately expressed, and thus pose a threat to those

---

13. Clifford, *Psalms 73-150*, 282. Cf. Goldingay, *Psalms*, 427: "The terms 'create,' 'set apart,' 'awesome,' 'acts,' and 'extraordinary' are all more familiar in connection with the great deeds whereby Yhwh brought Israel to birth; they are here applied to the birth of an ordinary human being. The obverse of that point is also instructive. Most Israelites did not experience the exodus or the deliverance at the Red Sea, but they did experience the wonder of human birth, and maybe this can help them appreciate the wonder of Yhwh's bringing Israel into being."

who believe that God crafts the human person in the womb and has destined them for a priestly vocation in the world. Verbal links between the various stanzas of the psalm imply that it is to be studied with a unified message. The poet of Psalm 139 is self-aware and realizes that such a temptation is an easy path to follow, then thus prays with the deceitfulness of the heart in mind, and asks for God's guidance in the days ahead.

Book Five and the Child of Psalm 139

There are many questions about this psalm that could be raised. For example, is the poet of Psalm 139 speaking as an individual, or (like many compositions in the Psalter), speaking collectively as a representative of the nation? Is the birth of every human person solely in view, or is the miraculous birth of Israel also touched upon (a community that is as much threatened by evil within as much as enemies without)?[14] Why is there no mention of *Zion* in this psalm?[15] Does the Davidic superscription imply a certain reading strategy? Since the term *king* in Book Five does not refer to an Israelite monarch, is a messianic hope in view, or does Psalm 139 teach that every believer under the aegis of the Davidic promise has a responsibility to ensure the sacredness of human life?[16] But for the purposes of this essay, two particular issues will be raised by way of conclusion about the images of infancy in Psalm 139 within the context of Book Five of the Psalter.

First, if we read Book Five as a reflection of Israel's postexilic world after the traumas of displacement and return, then Psalm 139 provides a fresh inspiration about the breadth and intimacy of divine involvement in

---

14. For Rodd ("Psalms," 402) vv. 13–16 refer "either to divine foreknowledge of the psalmist, even before he was born, or draws on mythological ideas about the creation of the first man from the womb of the earth." Cf. Waltke and Houston, *The Psalms as Christian Worship*, 433.

15. See W. Dennis Tucker Jr., *Constructing and Deconstructing Power in Psalms 107–150*, 146: "Similar to the heavenly construct in the preceding psalm (138:6) that portrays Yahweh as lofty (רָם), the psalmist in Ps 139 repositions Yahweh beyond the domain of Zion. In both constructs, the 'heavenly' and the 'cosmos-theistic' conceptions, the psalmists connect this confession of Yahweh with a desire for deliverance from the 'enemies' (138:7) and the 'men of blood' (139:19). Despite the differing spatial images employed in these constructs, the underlying assumption remains the same. Yahweh's location beyond Zion reinforces the belief that Yahweh remains readily available to deliver his people regardless of location or circumstance (cf. 138:7; 139:19–22)."

16. On the king of Israel in Book Five, see Wilson, "The Structure of the Psalter," 236.

the human life. As God's people rebuild their shattered world and negotiate their status as a minor province under the shadow of the Persian empire (not to mention the challenge of Hellenism to emerging Judaism), this psalm provides an imaginative resource for believing in the comprehensiveness of divine care. The awesome deeds of Israel's past, such as silencing the roaring waves of the chaotic sea in Psalm 56 or the signs and wonders of liberation from Egypt in Psalm 106, are now augmented with the awesome deed elucidated in the third stanza of Psalm 139: human beings are fearfully made and imprinted with a royal dignity and priestly vocation, part of the great redemptive narrative of the Hebrew Bible that is continued in the New Testament.

Second, to further a point made above, those who are heirs of the Davidic promise have an obligation to confer a degree of respect to all human beings, each of whom has been handcrafted in the womb and endowed with regal dignity. Moreover, as the final stanza of Psalm 139 makes clear, there are real and present threats to well-being, as William Brown remarks: "Both Job and Jonah are narrative demonstrations that this psalm is the impassioned cry of praise from an individual whose worth as a child of God is wondrously affirmed as well as vehemently attacked. Indeed, our world, conflicted as it is, hardly permits the former without the latter. Psalm 139 serves as an eloquent cry of praise and pain, the vulnerable voice of holy dignity that must be heard anew whenever the inviolable worth of any human being is called into question."[17] Not only does the theology of infancy have a prominent place in Book Five of the Psalter, but it also carries ethical implications for the contemporary believer in the present day.

17. Brown, "Psalm 139," 281.

Chapter Seven

The Genius of the Greek Mind
Education of Greek and Roman Children

Shirley Sullivan

IN THIS ESSAY I will treat the content of the education for Greek and Roman male children.[1] We are speaking only of the children of the aristocratic class who would be able to provide education by tutors or slaves. Our evidence for the education of Greek children is slim, but we can perhaps reconstruct it from what we know of the education of Roman children. We know that wealthy Romans used educated Greek slaves and freedmen as tutors from Greece to teach their children. Thus, children were taught Greek at an early age and were introduced to the great thinkers among the Greeks. The Roman poet, Horace (65–68 BC), vividly describes the Roman response to Greek literature:[2]

---

1. On the subject of childhood and education in Classical Greece and Rome, see: Beaumont, *Childhood in Classical Athens*; Bonner, *Education in Ancient Rome*; Cartledge, *The Cambridge Illustrated History of Ancient Greece*; Garland, *The Greek Way of Life*; Golden, *Children and Childhood in Classical Athens*; Grubbs and Parkin, *The Oxford Handbook of Childhood and Education in the Classical World*; Joyal, McDougall, and Yardley, *Greek and Roman Education*; Marrou, *A History of Education in Antiquity*; Robb, *Literacy and Paideia in Ancient Greece*; Shelton, *As the Romans Did*; Walker, *Rhetoric and Poetics in Antiquity*; Waterfield, *Creators, Conquerors, and Citizens*; and Wilson, *Encyclopedia of Ancient Greece*.

2. Horace, *Epistles*, 2.1.156.

Graecia capta ferum victorem cepit
Greece captured took captive its fierce victor.

Romans had the humility and wisdom to recognize the genius of the Greek mind.

Paul of Tarsus

We can perhaps discern what young people in Greece were taught from the example of Paul, a Jew living in the Diaspora and clearly given an excellent education. In his speech in Athens (Acts 17:28) he quotes, "For in him we live and move and have our being, as some of your own poets have put it,[3] for we too are his offspring." Although we cannot be sure of the author of the first quotation, the second appears to be from *Phaenomena* 5 of the third-century Stoic poet, Aratus.[4] What is important for us to note is that Paul quotes from a rather obscure poet, not from Homer, Hesiod, the dramatists, Plato, or Aristotle. If Paul had received a traditional Greek education, it was clearly one that covered a wide range of authors.

Early Education

First, let us look at the education of young people. My pattern will be the education of Jerome (347–420 AD).[5] As the child of wealthy parents, Jerome received the education that would have been customary for Roman aristocratic children. His elementary education in his hometown of Stridon, perhaps in a small school or by a tutor, would have included reading and writing in Latin. He would also have learned Greek and memorized quotations from Greek literature.[6]

Grammatica

When he was about twelve, Jerome was sent to Rome for the next three stages of his education: grammar, rhetoric, and philosophy. His first study

---

3. This is a formulaic introduction and could refer to a single author but here we appear to have two quotations.
4. Fitzmyer, *The Acts of the Apostle*, 610; Keener, *Acts*, 2653.
5. Graves, *Jerome*, xxxvi–xl.
6. See the excellent discussion of early education in Keener, *Acts*, 2653–57.

was *ars grammatica*, "the art of grammar," which focused on literary studies. It was much broader in content than its name implies. Its four elements, defined by the Latin scholar Varro (116–27 BC), were *lectio* (reading aloud), *ennaratio* (explanation), *emendation* (textual criticism), and *iudicium* (literary criticism).[7] Students would read a whole range of literature, especially Greek poets, dramatists, and philosophers (who wrote both in poetry and prose). In the case of the Stoics, we have evidence that collections were made of their sayings, and there may have been other anthologies that students were given to read.[8] *Lectio* taught students to read texts out loud correctly. *Ennaratio* involved discussion of the narrative and mythological background of a text (*historia*), linguistic analysis, and explanation of the meaning of a text. Students would be encouraged to explain obscure words by *glossemata*, "glosses." They would also learn to explain features of grammar and syntax. They would be taught to recognize similes, metaphors, and hyperbole. *Emendatio* focused on understanding the text and possible alternate readings. *Iudicium* taught assessment of the stylistic features of a text and comparison with the texts of other authors.

Rhetorica

In the late teens, a student would begin the second stage of study, *rhetorica*. Aristotle says: "Rhetoric then may be defined as the faculty of discovering the possible means of persuasion in reference to any subject whatever."[9] Students learned how to speak and write effectively and how to critically analyze discourse. Attention may also have been paid to the subjects mentioned in Plato's *Republic*: arithmetic, geometry, music, and astronomy.[10] "Music" (*mousike*) had a much wider meaning than our "music" and included all the arts inspired by the muses. Thus, it included all literature.

Philosophia

The final stage of education was *philosophia*, the study of philosophy, and here the students truly encountered the brilliance of the Greek mind. Such

---

7. Graves, *Jerome*, xxxvii, and Graves, *Jerome's Hebrew Philology*, 17–20.
8. Keener, *Acts*, vol. 3, 2659.
9. Aristotle, *Art of Rhetoric* Book 1, 1355 b 2.
10. *Republic*, VII, 525 d–531 d.

philosophical giants—Presocratics, Plato, Aristotle, Stoics, and Epicureans! In this essay, we will now consider in detail some of the different Greek authors whom children would study. We will observe that the Greeks introduced many literary forms: narrative epic, didactic epic, lyric and elegiac poetry, philosophy (in poetry, prose, dialogue, and exposition), history, tragedy, comedy, and oratory. It was to this wealth of literature that Greek and Roman children were introduced.

An important feature of Greek culture was their conviction that all poetry is inspired. Thus, whatever a poet sang was a gift of a divine source, however that was conceived to be. Poetry contained "wisdom" (*sophia*), something that could never obtained by the process of learning. For the first time, in the seventh century, individuals appeared to whom the name "philosopher" ("lover of wisdom") was given. These philosophers especially attempted to explain where the universe came from and why it continues to exist.

Certain features of Greek society help to explain why philosophy developed in Greece.[11] First, Greek society lacked any priest class which, for example, in Babylon and Egypt, formulated and determined what people were to believe. When it came to the subject of the gods, Greeks would probably give a shrug and say: "We do not know." In their literature we find "gods" and "god" used interchangeably to indicate the Divine. Until the end of the fifth century, no one doubted that there was a Divine Power of some sort that was the source of the universe, but Greeks remained open to suggestions of what that Divine Power might be like. As the centuries went by, few accepted the traditional, mythical stories of the gods found in Homer and were fascinated to hear new proposals about divinity. But there was never any dogmatism about divinity and new ideas were always welcomed.

Second, Greece had a long history of oral, formulaic poetry, beginning perhaps around 1500 BC. The form of this poetry was narrative epic. Bards were able to sing very long poems centered around different mythical stories and various heroic figures. "Heroes" were those who had one divine parent from the family of gods, led by Zeus, who lived on Mt. Olympus. Poetry was considered a divine gift, inspired by the Muses who lived on Mt. Helicon. For centuries different tales were sung, but two, it seems, were the favorites: the *Iliad* and the *Odyssey*. Around 750 BC these poems were written down by a poet of Chios called Homer, perhaps as guides for competitions of bardic recitation.

---

11. My discussion is indebted to two timeless classics: Jaeger, *Paideia*, and Fränkel, *Early Greek Poetry and Philosophy*.

The Genius of the Greek Mind

Homer

Homer was to become the chief poet among the Greeks, quoted endlessly by later authors and considered the standard of literary excellence.[12] Already in Homer the question that was to be asked again and again by Greeks is treated: "What makes a person excellent?"[13] The word for excellence is *arete*. Greek observed that one could speak of the *arete* of objects or animals. Their attention then turned to the question: What is the excellence of human beings?

In the *Iliad* heroes are called on "always to be best and to be preeminent over all" (6:208, 11.784). In their youth, they received training so that, like Achilles, they could be a "speaker of words and doer of deeds" (9:443). They fight in single combat in order that they might win glory (12:325) and a bard might sing of them. Only in this way can they find immortality (22:304–5). Human beings are fragile, like "the generation of the leaves" (6:146). At the time of death, their souls (*psychai*), being merely breath, fly to the underworld and float about, uttering unintelligible sounds (1:3). Thus, Achilles says (*Il.* 23:103–7):

> Even in the house of Hades there is something—soul and form—though there is no mind at all; for the whole night long has the soul of unfortunate
> Patroclus stood over me, weeping and grieving, and he gave me instructions
> about each thing and was wondrously like himself.

The amazing thing is: Greeks always believed that some part of a person, namely the soul (*psyche*), would exist forever.

In the *Odyssey*, Odysseus acts like such heroes. He shows himself ever a man of courage, dauntless in facing dangers and challenges. He also shows great versatility in different situations, earning the epithet of "man of many devices" (*polutropon*: 1:1). In the *Odyssey*, therefore, we see courage and versatility as keys to a hero's excellence.

In the *Odyssey*, we also encounter an example of female excellence. Penelope has been a faithful wife to Odysseus for twenty years. She is called "wise" and "prudent" (1:329, 17:36). In order to delay the suitors who have come to woo her, she devises the trick of weaving and unweaving a web (2.93–110). She shows good sense, manages her household well, and cares

---

12. Keener, *Acts*, vol. 3, 2653–54.
13. See especially the discussion in Jaeger, *Paideia*.

for Telemachus, her son (1:356–58). Her excellence lies in her competent management of her household and especially in her fidelity to her husband.

In the chief character of the *Iliad*, we find a different answer to what makes a hero excellent. Achilles is the greatest of all the heroes who have come to Troy. In his case, courage is a given. Many, many times he has fought in single combat and won, stripping off the armor of his opponent. Unlike other heroes, Achilles knows that he will die young at Troy (9:411–13). Like other heroes, he behaves courageously in order to win fame. But at the very beginning of the *Iliad*, Agamemnon arbitrarily deprives him of a rightly won prize. In great anger, Achilles refuses to risk his life in single combat any longer. For seventeen of the twenty-four books of the *Iliad*, he sits on the seashore, playing his lyre. When he does return to battle in Book 18, it is for the wrong motive: he goes to revenge the death of his friend Patroclus, killed by Hector. In Book 22, he slays Hector and drags his body around the walls of Troy. Even the gods are horrified by such barbaric treatment (24:40–45). In Book 24 we find a new form of courage: the aged Priam, father of Hector, although terrified of Achilles, bravely goes to his tent and asks for the body of his son (24:253–85). Achilles is astonished at the courage and love for his son that Priam shows in coming to his tent (24:468–84). He recalls that another father, namely his own, will grieve over the death of his young son (24:522–51). He compassionately agrees to return the body of Hector. In the response of Achilles, we find a new definition of what makes a hero excellent: showing compassion.

Students were taught to read Homer from their earliest years of training. From the *Odyssey*, they would learn about the heroic courage of Odysseus and about the abiding fidelity of Penelope. From the *Iliad*, they would learn that heroic excellence also included pity and compassion for shared suffering. Moral behavior was to be a constant theme in Greek literature. It is profoundly present in its first poems, the *Iliad* and *Odyssey*.

Hesiod, Lyric, and Elegiac Poets, Pindar and Bacchylides

Let us now consider other authors whom students would have studied. I will consider authors from Hesiod (c. 700 BC) until the Stoics (third century). Students would read these authors and often have to memorize portions of them. In this literature we will see that four questions are prominent:[14]

---

14. For the early period, see my book *Psychological and Ethical Ideas*.

- What makes a person excellent?
- What is the divine source of the universe?
- Why does it continue to exist?
- What is the nature of the human personality?

After Homer, students would read a different form of epic: the didactic epics of Hesiod. In his *Theogony*, Hesiod explains the universe in terms of births of gods with a focus on their transformation in morality. The first two gods are "Sky" (*Ouranos*) and Earth (*Gaia*). "Sky" is so unjust that he does not allow his children to be born. "Time" (*Cronos*), who replaces him, is also unjust, swallowing his children down at the moment of their birth. Cronos has a son, "Life" (Zeus[15]), whom his mother saves from being consumed by his father. "Life" proves to be just. He overpowers his father and confines him to the underworld. "Time" continues to exist but now he can swallow human beings down only after they have had a period of life. "Life" himself becomes just by marrying "Themis," the goddess of justice. Zeus's rule is threatened by the Titans, but he proves triumphant, showing that "Life" will continue to rule in the universe. In the *Theogony*, therefore, students would see that Hesiod explained where the universe came from and why it continues in being. In his second work, *The Works and Days*, Hesiod teaches his brother Perses about admirable and just human behavior. What makes a person excellent lies in the justice shown to others.

From an early age, students would also read lyric and elegiac poetry, often called on to memorize these texts.[16] In this poetry, once again, we find authors treating the question: What makes someone excellent? They would be startled to hear Archilochus (c. 650 BC) say that his life was more precious than courage (5) and that people rarely remember the brave (133). In contrast, Callinus (c. 650 BC) and Tyrtaeus (c. 650 BC) encourage a new manifestation of courage: fighting as an army instead of in single combat. No longer were there situations calling for single combat. From the seventh century onward, the place for someone to achieve individual excellence would be in different athletic competitions at the Olympian, Pythian, Nemean, and Isthmian games.

Regarding excellence, Xenophanes (c. 570–470 BC) would suggest something quite new: wisdom (*sophia*) as its highest form. He suggests

---

15. "Zeus" comes from the Greek verb, ζάω, "to live."

16. Concerning the numbering of the lyric and elegiac poets, see West, ed., *Iambi et Elegi Graeci*.

that the wisdom he offers in his poems is much more valuable than any excellence shown in competitive games (B 2 DK). He also introduces a new criterion of excellence: It should be useful for others. Xenophanes foreshadows the suggestion of Socrates during his trial: He says that he has practiced wisdom in Athens and therefore deserves to be treated like a much-honored athlete (*Apology* 37D-E). Like Xenophanes, Socrates claims that he has served Athens better with his wisdom than athletes with their prowess.

When students read the poetry of Theognis (late sixth century), they would see that he, like Hesiod, thought justice the highest form of excellence. In Homer it was assumed that heroes were well-born, handsome, and possessed of wealth. Theognis, an impoverished aristocrat, suggests that only the person born with a noble inner nature can achieve excellence. Its presence was not to be judged by externals but was to be summed up in the just acts a person did (145–148). Another poet, Solon of Athens (fl. 594 BC), also lays great emphasis on justice. For human society to flourish, its members must be just (13). Simonides (c. 556–468 BC) speaks of excellence as something impossible for human beings to achieve or maintain. He sets a new standard: the "sound" or "healthy" (*hugies*) man who "does nothing wrong willingly" (542:21–30).

In contrast, Pindar (c. 522–443 BC) and Bacchylides (c. 518–452 BC) believe that human beings can achieve excellence with divine help. They write victory odes, celebrating the excellence shown by athletes in competitive games. Pindar is convinced that such excellence can be achieved only by those with a capacity inherited at birth (*Olympians* 2:11). Nor is birth enough: athletes must train vigorously (*Olympians* 10:22). If a person show excellence, it is always a divine gift (*Olympians* 9:100–104). Victors must always remember that their achievement was a gift and never boast as if it were their own achievement. Only with this remembrance will they be able to sustain excellence (*Olympians* 1:109). Pindar tells us that human nature is utterly fragile but made glorious when God sends his light upon it (*Pythians* 8:95–97):

> Creatures of a day! What are we? What are we not?
> A shadow of a dream is the human being.
> But when the brightness comes and God sends it,
> A shining light is upon human beings and life is sweet.

The Genius of the Greek Mind

Presocratic Philosophers

In their second stage of study, students would be introduced to philosophy.[17] First, they would encounter several philosophers who lived in the sixth and fifth centuries, whom modern critics have called "Presocratics." These thinkers can be grouped together because they all sought to explain the source and continued existence of the universe in terms of their perceptions. They did not refer to the gods of myth as a source of explanation. In their approach to the universe, they believed that there was only one "truth" (*aletheia*) and, if one found the truth, one would understand reality. They interpreted the word for truth, *aletheia*, as *a-letheia*, an "unveiling" of reality. They showed a passionate curiosity for discovering this "truth."

What is most amazing about the Presocratics is that, by asking questions, finding proposed answers inadequate, and asking new questions, they had, by the end of the fifth century, discovered the truth about the universe that is still taught by modern science. They had done so strictly by the acuity of their thinking, not by any experimentation. The Atomists, the last of the Presocratics, say that the universe is made up of smallest, "uncuttable" particles, which they called "atoms." Scientists incorrectly termed "atom" something that could be split but now call the smallest particles "quarks." The Atomists explained that the particles they called "atoms" could not be split because they had no space within them. "Space" was the second discovery of the Atomists. Up until the Atomists, Greeks imagined that the universe was a single sphere of solid material. Around this sphere was the Divine, which acted as the source for the universe. The idea of space was so alien to the Greeks that Plato, Aristotle, and the Stoics rejected it. The Epicureans, however, accepted the view of the universe given by the Atomists.

An assumption that the Presocratics make will help us to understand their ideas: everything is infused with life. Not until Aristotle would the notion of inert matter appear. When they speak of the Divine Power as Air or Fire, those substances were thought to be alive. We can speak of two groups of Presocratics, one in the sixth century and one in the fifth. In the sixth century, Thales suggests that the Divine Principle is Water and that all things are essentially made of water. Anaximander proposes a Divine Principle called the "Infinite," that surrounds the universe and acts as a source of the opposites that compose it. He also speaks of Justice keeping

---

17. Concerning numbering for the Presocratics, see Diels, *Die Fragmente der Vorsokratiker*.

the opposites in balance. Anaximenes says that the Divine Principle is "Infinite Air" and that all things are made of air.

Xenophanes, whom we mentioned above, lived in both the sixth and fifth centuries. In some of his writings that have been called "philosophical," students would encounter amazing ideas. We heard above that he suggested that wisdom was the highest form of excellence. When he speaks of the universe, he, first among the Greeks, suggests that Divinity is "One, unlike mortals in form and thought" (B 23 DK). This one God governs the universe by the "thought of his mind" (B 25 DK).

Pythagoras (late sixth century) appears to have introduced new ideas about the soul (*psyche*).[18] As mentioned above, people generally thought that the soul, being simply breath, fled at death to the underworld to a very unenviable existence. The Pythagoreans, in contrast, suggest that the soul is the most important part of the living person and that it is on a journey to perfection. They introduce the idea of transmigration of souls: people have several lives during which the soul can become better. The final destiny of the soul appears to be some form of union with the Divine.

The Presocratics of the fifth century approached the question of the Divine Principle in a new way. They assumed that human beings were set off from other creatures because they shared somehow in the Divine Nature. In what did that share consist? By discovering that share, one would also discover that nature of the Divine. Heraclitus (c. 540–480 BC) suggests that the ability of humans to think and to speak puts them on a continuum with the Divine. In Greek, *logos* means "speech reflecting thought." It never refers to a single word; it is always a collection of words, an utterance, or expression. Heraclitus suggests that a Divine *Logos* thinks and speaks the universe, organizing it into opposites in perfect balance (B 1 DK). Human beings with their *logos* organize the opposites that the Divine *Logos* has spoken. We see a refinement on anthropomorphism. Homeric gods were simply human beings writ large. Now Heraclitus focuses on a capacity that humans have, that of *logos*, and writes it large as the Divine Principle. When we have the picture correctly, the Divine *Logos* came first. The fact that human beings have *logos* allows them to understand the universe. Heraclitus also describes this *Logos* as fire. We can see evidence of this Divine Fire at sunrise and sunset.

---

18. Our information on Pythagoras himself is very sparse. His followers, the Pythagoreans, were a secret society and information about their doctrines only became known in the late fifth century. Whatever they taught was always ascribed to Pythagoras himself.

Parmenides (early fifth century) was perhaps the most brilliant Presocratic. He does not speak of a Divine Principle but focuses entirely on the nature of the universe. He was the first to propose what Being must be like: one, unchanging, imperishable, timeless (B 6, B 7). Later, when the Atomists come to speak of atoms, each has Being such as Parmenides describes.

Empedocles (c. 492–432 BC) suggests that there are two Divine Principles, Love and Strife (B 17). The universe is made up of earth, air, fire, and water (B 6). It undergoes cycles of change depending on which Divine Principle is ascendant. Empedocles chooses two human capacities—loving and hating—and projects them large as Divine Principles. Anaxagoras (c. 500–428 BC) teaches that the Divine Principle is the Mind (*Nous*: B 14). It organizes the universe that is made up of very small seeds (B 4). Anaxagoras chooses the human faculty of mind and assumes that it is akin to the Divine Principle. This human *nous* is "mind" in a very special sense. It is the human ability of inner vision and what it perceives is always true.[19] Pindar also suggests that we are akin to the immortals in having *nous* (*Nemeans* 6:1–7).

As mentioned above, the last of the Presocratics, the Atomists, Democritus and Leucippus (late fifth century), introduced the notions of atoms and space as the components of the universe. They do not mention a Divine Principle, but it is clear that the atoms are infused with life.

How the ideas of all the Presocratics must have enlarged and challenged the minds of students! They would see traditional points of view challenged. They would learn new ideas. They would be introduced to critical thinking. They would hear amazing explanations of the truth (*aletheia*), seeing the universe "unveiled" in different ways.

Greek Dramatists

In fifth century Athens a new type of literature appeared: tragedy.[20] The main tragedians were Aeschylus (c. 523–c. 456 BC), Sophocles (c. 497–c. 406 BC), and Euripides (c. 484–406 BC). Aeschylus presented profound themes in his plays. His *Oresteia*, the only example of a surviving trilogy, explores the nature of justice and suggests why human beings are able to

---

19. See my *Psychological and Ethical Ideas*, 18–35.

20. On the dramatists, see my books: *Aeschylus' Use of Psychological Terminology*; *Sophocles' Use of Psychological Terminology*; and *Euripides' Use of Psychological Terminology*.

make judicial decisions. In the *Persians*, he amazed his audience by presenting the Persian point of view, as he explained why little Greece was able to conquer the giant Persia. In the *Seven Against Thebes*, he explores the fate of the sons of Oedipus, each to die at the other's hand.

Sophocles's chief interest is to explore the nature of human greatness. In the *Ajax* and the *Antigone*, he portrays characters endowed with astounding nobility and yet driven by their convictions to end their lives. In the *Oedipus the King*, he describes a man desperately seeking to avoid his horrible destiny and, by the very steps he takes, bringing about that destiny. In the *Philoctetes*, Sophocles affirms his conviction that a good person, even though misled for a time, will still act nobly. In this play he also explores the theme of trust: once broken, never restored.

Euripides again and again challenges traditional ideas in his plays. In the *Medea*, he shocks his audience by having Medea say that she knows that killing her children is evil but is determined to do so. In the *Hippolytus*, Euripides examines the question of fanaticism. In the *Alcestis*, he makes fun of the heroic ideal in having a woman be much braver than her husband. In the *Helen*, he paints Helen as completely self-absorbed and worried only about her reputation, not giving a thought for all the Greeks who died because of her. In the *Trojan Women*, Euripides shows that in war no one is a victor since victory corrupts those who win.

Students reading and memorizing portions from Greek drama would learn the profound thoughts and challenges that different plays presented. They would encounter a whole new way of looking at life.

Sophists

In the middle of the fifth century, a new group of teachers appeared in Greece, who claimed to "practice wisdom" (*sophistes*).[21] Instead of the speculation characteristic of the Presocratic philosophers, these people offered a practical wisdom, based on clever argumentation. They challenged traditional ideas and the morality associated with them. They focused on the effective use of speech as a tool for persuasion. Truth (*aletheia*) interested them little. The only reality that they accepted was appearance. What they claimed to teach people was how to be successful, how to get rich, and how to be powerful. Their aim was to please people and they charged huge sums for their instruction.

---

21. On the Sophists see Jarratt, *Rereading the Sophists*, and Poulakos, *Sophistical Rhetoric in Classical Greece*.

The Genius of the Greek Mind

Plato

In 436 BC a strange man appeared on the Athenian streets, dressed in an old sheet and going barefoot, constantly talking with the people he met. Socrates (c. 470–399 BC) had appeared. Called by the Delphic oracle the "wisest man in Greece," Socrates knew that there must be a hidden meaning in this pronouncement, and he found it. As he explains in his defense during the lawsuit that would condemn him to death, he learned that he was the wisest man in Greece because he knew when he did not know. He took the Delphic oracle as a call for him to teach Athenians to think more clearly and not to claim to know what they did not know. A young man, Plato (428–347), was most impressed with Socrates, so much so that, when he came to write his twenty-one philosophical dialogues, Socrates was the chief character in each. Plato was to establish his school of philosophy, the Academy, in 387 BC, at which Aristotle was to be a student from 367–347 BC.[22]

We do not know the dates of Plato's dialogues and the distribution of his dialogues has been much disputed. Traditionally they have been arranged according to the picture that Plato paints of Socrates: early, middle, and late. In the early dialogues, Socrates is true to his claim of being wise because he does not know. In the middle dialogues, we begin to hear the voice of Plato in that of Socrates as he comes to frame his own philosophical opinions. In the late dialogues, Plato is much less confident of his views and questions them in depth.

What ideas would students encounter in Plato's dialogues? First, Plato teaches that the candidates for excellence found already in earlier Greek literature, such as courage, justice, as well as holiness and moderation, cannot be considered apart from one another but are all inseparable parts of the "Good" (*Euthyphro, Laches, Republic, Cratylus*). This "Good" he identifies as the Divine Principle. Second, the "Good" is also Beauty and Truth (*Timaeus*). The "Good" is the highest of the Forms or Ideas after which all existing things are patterned.

In Plato's dialogues, something remarkable has happened to the notion of "soul" (*psyche*). Like the Pythagoreans, he identifies the soul not merely as the part of a human being that survives death but as having a vital role in the living person. Soul has become the seat of all intellectual, emotional, and volitional activities. It is the personality of a person. People

---

22. On Plato, see Lodge, *The Philosophy of Plato*, and Ritter and Alles, *The Essence of Plato's Philosophy*.

who still held the Homeric view of the soul were perplexed at the new picture that Plato was giving. He also suggests that the soul alone is capable of perceiving the Good, the True, and the Beautiful. It is a person's most valuable possession and should be the constant object of attention (*Apology, Phaedo*). After death, this soul may enjoy the highest destiny of being joined to the Good, the True, and the Beautiful (*Phaedo, Timaeus*).

The soul is made up of three parts (*Republic, Phaedrus*). *Logistikon*, the "rational" portion, is found in the head and is the seat of all our thinking. *Thumoeides*, meaning "form of *thumos*," is found in the upper chest region and is the center of all positive emotions. *Epithumetikon*, related to the verb *epithumeo*, "to desire," is the seat of the lower appetites and is found in the lower chest region. Plato says that the *logistikon* should govern the other two parts of the soul. Its highest activity is to love, that is, to create the beautiful (*Symposium*). The soul undergoes transmigration, increasing in purity in different lives (*Republic*).

In the *Republic*, Plato shared his conviction that a well-ordered state was essential for the development of the rational human being. The constitution of the state must parallel the moral nature of the individual and politics must necessarily be connected with ethics. Only those who have come to the state of knowledge of the Good should be in the position of rulers. He introduces the idea of the "philosopher king," worthy to rule because he is totally free of self-interest.

Thus, in Plato, students would encounter amazing new ideas of the Divine, the soul, and the state. They would also hear of a wealth of other ideas that appear often in different dialogues: the ways in which humans come to move beyond opinion and come truly to know, the origin of the universe, and the nature of ethics. Plato has been called the greatest genius among the Greeks. His philosophical ideas show why this description is apt.

Aristotle

Plato's most famous pupil was Aristotle (384–322 BC).[23] He studied for twenty years at the Academy but, on the death of Plato, left Athens and in 342 BC became the tutor of Alexander the Great in his native city of Stageira in Macedonia. In 335 BC Aristotle returned to Athens and founded his own school. It was called the "Lyceum" or "Peripatetic School," since

---

23. On Aristotle, see Höffe, *Aristotle*; Shields, *Aristotle*; and Wians and Polansky, *Reading Aristotle*.

Aristotle delivered his lectures while walking up and down (*peripateo*). For the next thirteen years until his death Aristotle's school thrived, attracting many students. During this time, he wrote his many philosophical treatises.

What would students encounter in the writings of Aristotle? The whole range of subjects included under the broad scope of "philosophy": aesthetics, astronomy, biology, economics, ethics, linguistics, logic, mathematics, metaphysics, music, physics, poetry, politics, psychology, rhetoric, theater, and zoology. Raphael's masterpiece, "The School of Athens," clarifies well the difference between Plato and Aristotle. Plato's chief interest was the nature of the soul and its destiny: he points to heaven. Aristotle wanted to explain the universe in which he lived: he points downward. Like earlier Greeks, Aristotle wished to understand truth (*aletheia*), that is, to unveil the real nature of the universe. Fascinated by the intrinsic composition of each separate thing within the universe, he sought to show its origin and development. He was also interested in explaining the whole range of human culture, especially the phenomenon of language. He is the first to speak of logic, the operations of abstract reason.

In studying Aristotle, students would also learn his picture of the universe. Like early Greeks, he thought that there was one universe only, composed of fifty-seven concentric spheres, surrounded by a Divine Principle. This Divine Principle was "Mind" (*Nous*), the Unmoved Mover, which imparted motion into the universe.[24] We see that Aristotle has adopted the idea of Anaxagoras, who also called the Divine Principle, "Mind" (*Nous*).

In ethics Aristotle suggested a new answer for the question: what is the nature of excellence (*arete*)? He suggests that happiness (*eudaimonia*) is the highest good that people seek. It "is the active exercise of his soul's faculties in conformity with excellence or virtue, or, if there be several human excellences or virtues, in conformity with the best and most perfect among them."[25] Thus, Aristotle assumes that there can be many "excellences," whose presence are necessary for the achievement of "happiness."

Epicureans

Epicurus (340–270 BC) founded a school of philosophy in Athens in 307 or 305 BC.[26] Since he met with his students in a garden, his school was

---

24. Aristotle, *Metaphysics*, 1072a18–1074a32.

25. Aristotle, *Nicomachean Ethics*, 1094a7.

26. On the Epicureans, see Fish and Sanders, *Epicurus and the Epicurean Tradition*;

known as the "School of the Garden." Aristotle had introduced "happiness" as the goal people seek. Epicurus suggested that this "happiness" consisted in the "absence of pain" (*ataraxia*). The Greek word signifies the absence of both physical pain and emotional distress. What Epicureans were to seek was "pleasure" (*hedone*), which required them to use their minds always to seek that which was free from pain. Their way of life was quite austere and modest, requiring the limitation of desires since these could lead to pain. People, however, could easily misunderstand this pursuit of "pleasure" and fail to see its rigorous demands. Such a misunderstanding might happen especially in Roman society where, in the first century BC, the Epicurean Lucretius (95–55 BC) wrote his didactic epic, "On the Nature of the Universe" (*De Rerum Natura*) and translated *hedone* as *voluptas*. The Latin word has a similar meaning to the English!

In order to remove fear from people's lives, Epicurus adopted the ideas of the fifth century Atomists. This universe, which may be one of many universes, is made up of atoms and space. There are gods but they live in the spaces between universes and show no interest in human beings. They are perfect models for human beings, who should strive ever to be carefree. In order to remove all fear of the afterlife, Epicurus denied that there was one. Human beings are simply atoms and space and dissolve into these at death. The only reason that they may choose to be virtuous is that the opposite behavior causes distress.

The way of life enjoined upon the Epicurean was one of withdrawal from public life. They were to live in such a way that no one would know that they were alive (*lathe biosas*). One is astonished, therefore, to learn that Julius Caesar claimed to be an Epicurean![27] We may wonder what Greek and Roman students thought of the Epicureans, so different from other authors.

Stoics

In the third century, another school appeared in Athens, founded by Zeno of Citium (c. 334–c. 262).[28] Zeno and his students walked in a portico and they were called the "School of the Porch." Above, we heard that Heraclitus

---

Lillegard, *On Epicurus*; and O'Keefe, *Epicurus*.

27. Sallust, *War with Catiline*, 51.

28. On the Stoics, see Brennan, *The Stoic Life*; Farnsworth, *The Practicing Stoic*; and Reydams-Schils, *The Roman Stoics*.

described the Divine Principle as *Logos*, "speech reflecting thought." The Stoics also suggest that the Divine Principle is *Logos*, but they focus on the "thought" element and call *Logos* "Reason." Just as in Heraclitus, *Logos* forms the universe by thinking and speaking it. This *Logos*, composed of fire, surrounds the universe. Human beings all have a portion of the Divine *Logos* and this *logos* puts them on a continuum with the Divine. It allows them to grasp what the Divine Principle is.

The highest goal for Stoics was to live in accord with the Divine *Logos*. They were called to see everything that happens as an expression of *Logos* and to learn to express only a rational response. They were, therefore, to control their emotions, especially their desires and fears. To be Stoic meant that reason ruled supreme in the person.

Stoics also assumed that *Logos* and Nature were one. Excellence was "living in accord with Nature." This behavior constituted "happiness." Living in accord with *Logos*, Stoics would manifest wisdom, courage, justice, and moderation, all the excellences that earlier Greeks had named.

Stoicism proved to be a very popular philosophy, and many called themselves Stoics. The identification of the Divine Principle as *Logos* became a pervasive philosophical idea until the end of the third century AD, with its most prominent adherent being the Emperor Marcus Aurelius (161–180 AD).

Conclusion

In this essay we first discussed the nature of classical education and then focused on the authors students would read. No civilization has influenced the Western world as much as the Greek, with Rome as its first conquest. Until 1945, the study of classics occupied first place for those studying the humanities. Why, we may ask? The Greeks not only introduced all literary forms, but they also composed masterpieces in all of them. Their works speak timelessly to different ages in history because they understood human nature so profoundly. They presented a lofty view of humanity and were convinced of the ability of human beings to become truly noble.

How privileged were Greek and Roman students to encounter the genius of the Greek mind! Perhaps they joyfully memorized the final words of Socrates at his trial: "Keep in mind this one thing that is true: nothing can harm the good person, either alive or dead, nor does God ignore that person's affairs" (*Apology* 41D).

Chapter Eight

Scripture on the Birth and Infancy of Jesus

MARKUS BOCKMUEHL AND EVANGELINE KOZITZA

The Problem with Baby Jesus

TO MANY CONTEMPORARIES, THE birth of Jesus remains today associated with the sorts of infatuation that characterize our inheritance of Victorian Christmas kitsch—complete with "baby Jesus no crying he makes" and "Christian children all must be / mild, obedient, good as he." One suspects such saccharine emetics may have raised some eyebrows even in the nineteenth century; they certainly do so today.[1]

That said, those same misguided seasonal sentiments do in fact grasp one important twin insight about the nature of the incarnation. First, that baby savior's striking vulnerability appears to resonate with universal human experience more easily and analogously than do many other aspects of his subsequent biography—including, perhaps for all but martyrs, his redemptive death on the cross. For all its unquestionable uniqueness, that infancy of the incarnate Word is embedded in familiar but strikingly unprivileged circumstances: multiply challenging pregnancy and birth, poverty, political repression, forced migration, and formative years spent in culturally unpromising provincial obscurity. Second, therefore, there is

---

1. This chapter incorporates material revised from Bockmuehl and Kozitza, "The New Testament." Used by permission of Oxford University Press.

Scripture on the Birth and Infancy of Jesus

clearly a sense in which the aspects of sheer ordinariness palpable in "his wondrous childhood" (as C. F. Alexander's Victorian doggerel had it) at once powerfully sanctify the "inestimable blessing and bother" (Mark Twain) that characterize human pregnancy, birth, infancy, and childhood.

Christian traditions and practices have reflected this point in multiple interesting ways over the centuries. Jesus' experience of human birth, childhood, youth, adulthood, and death encouraged several second-century writers to affirm that he encounters and embraces all believers at the age appropriate to them. For example:

> He sanctified every age by a likeness to himself ... infants, children, youth, young adults, elderly.... Becoming an infant among infants, he sanctified infants; becoming a child among children, he sanctified those having this age and at the same time became for them an example of piety and righteousness and obedience; becoming a young adult among young adults, he was an example for young adults and sanctified them to the Lord. In the same way, he became also an elderly person among the elderly, so that he might be a mature teacher for all, not merely by explaining the truth but also by his age, that is, by at the same time sanctifying the elderly and being an example for them. Lastly, he came even to death so that he might be the "Firstborn from the dead, himself holding the primacy in all things" [Col 1:18], the "Author of life" [cf. Acts 3:15], prior to all and going before all. (Irenaeus of Lyons, *Against Heresies* 2.22.4; cf. e.g. *Acts of John* 89, 91; *Acts of Peter* 20–21; *Acts of Andrew* 18)

"The Lord of glory conformed himself to the infancy of mortals," said Leo the Great in a series of Christmas sermons two and one-half centuries later: the magi came to worship a child who was "small when it came to size, dependent on others for help, unable to speak, and in no way different from the general condition of human infancy." Through his birth and infancy, "the Word of God the Father clearly expressed that human substance belonged to himself both in the power of the divinity and in the weakness of humanity" (Sermons 31.3 [AD 441]; 34.3 [AD 444]; 96.2 [AD 457]). In the nineteenth century, Rome's newly founded children's hospital (to this day a leading pediatric research hospital) was named the "Bambino Gesù" (baby Jesus)—a designation preceded by a fifteenth-century olive wood image of the sacred child (Santo Bambino) that would proceed from its home at the church of Santa Maria in Aracoeli to comfort the sick around the city.

Compared with these affirmations of the baby savior, the New Testament remains at first sight remarkably taciturn about the child Jesus. Most of its writings foreground his death and resurrection, while the four Gospels also report prominently on his ministry of teaching and healing.

Matthew and Luke are the only two writers whose narrative includes any account of the birth of Jesus. Yet even the circumstances they describe strike many readers to stand in considerable tension. The newborn child is introduced as from the family of David, but through different sons of David; only Luke also affirms a connection with the priestly family of John the Baptist. Between Matthew and Luke, readers come away wondering whether Bethlehem or Nazareth is the original home of Mary and Joseph, whether both Mary or Joseph are instructed by angels, whether shepherds from the fields or astrologers from the East first visit the infant; whether the family returns directly to Galilee from Bethlehem or moves to Egypt before eventually setting up home in Nazareth. With one exception in Luke (2:41–52) we hear very little more about the child Jesus, and these opening narratives remain strikingly detached from the following accounts of his baptism and public ministry: none of the persons and events of his birth and childhood are heard from again.

Should we therefore conclude that the birth and infancy of Jesus are of no consequence to the New Testament? In this essay we hope to show that the scant narratives of Matthew and Luke in fact make up just a small part of the New Testament's reflection on the human birth, infancy, and childhood that by which God became man and "Jesus became Jesus."

Here we begin our tour of the New Testament with a brief look at the Gospel of Mark, which New Testament scholars of virtually all stripes agree was the first Gospel to be written. We will then turn to the familiar infancy stories of Matthew and Luke before going on to look at John and then, more briefly, the New Testament's nonnarrative ways of referencing the birth and infancy of Jesus. Our concluding observations will also raise the question of how these New Testament accounts were understood by the earliest Christians who heard and received them.

The Silence of Mark

The New Testament's earliest Gospel begins its story of Jesus without any information about his origin, infancy, or family background. He is immediately identified as "*Christos*" (Messiah) but without any Davidic or other

Scripture on the Birth and Infancy of Jesus

family tree. He emerges suddenly onto the stage as one who responds to John the Baptist's ministry "in the wilderness," reflecting the scriptural prophets (1:1–4, quoting Mal 3:1 and Isa 40:3) and calling the nation to immersion as a mark of repentance (1:1, 9). Mark gives no information about the place of Jesus' birth, although some have considered Nazareth strongly implicit (1:9, 24; 6:1–4; 10:47). There is no family background or line of descent for either parent, no virginal conception or nativity, no childhood or youth.

While Mark never references Bethlehem, the residents of Nazareth express an attitude of open skepticism about a Jesus they have known all his life: he is just "the builder" (or carpenter), with four equally ordinary and well-known brothers and several sisters all still living in the same place but evidently not prominent in speaking up for him (6:3). The words on his Nazareth neighbors' lips are clearly intended to slight and to patronize, but Mark's "disciples'-eye view" narrative never questions their factual accuracy.

That said, one surprising feature of this dispiriting Nazareth encounter is worth a moment's further reflection. Jesus is identified as "Mary's son," not the son of Joseph as we might expect. He does have a *brother* called Joseph (lit. *Joses*, Heb. *Yose*) in this Gospel (6:3), and having a father of the same name would be unsurprising in first-century Jewish settings (as Luke also knows: 1:59–61). Strangely, though, no father ever features in Mark—perhaps because the man who raised him was known not to be his father, or perhaps because he was an older man who had long since passed away, a suggestion first made in the second-century *Protevangelium of James*, where Joseph is a widower with children from a previous marriage. (There is nothing here to suggest specifically the claim of illegitimate birth sometimes suspected in John 8:41 and asserted by later critics like the second-century philosopher Celsus and his Jewish source: cf. Origen, *Against Celsus* 1.32, 69.) Mary, too, has no prominent or continuing role in this Gospel: she is earlier mentioned in passing along with his siblings (3:31–34), but probably nowhere else[2].

This mysterious absence of Jesus' human father is echoed by his equally early and complete disappearance from the other New Testament Gospels. More importantly, Mark's Jesus is nowhere the son of Joseph or any other man; even his Davidic descent is mentioned but seemingly downplayed (12:35–37; cf. 2:25; 10:47–48; 11:10).

2. So, rightly, Marcus, *Mark*, 1060.

Rather than a defensive attempt to conceal illegitimacy, this strange phenomenon must be read in contrast to the sonship that Mark emphatically does affirm for Jesus: he is above all Son of God (1:1 *v.l.*, 11; 3:11; 5:7; 9:7; 12:6–8; 13:32; 14:61–62; 15:39) as well as the Son of Man who will be seated at the right hand of God (13:26; 14:62). Commentators sometimes also compare the ancient literary custom of highlighting the great Homer's obscure background as a way of emphasizing his origins as the son of a god.[3]

Be that as it may, Jesus comes onto Mark's narrative stage from an obscure background, seemingly out of nowhere (1:14, 38; 2:17; 10:45). And this dramatization allows the evangelist to foreground the divine origin and theophany of the Christ and Son of God, who goes on to forgive sin, to preach and enact the kingdom of God, to command and dispel storms and demons, to heal and raise the dead (2:1–12, 18–22; 4:41; 14:61–62).[4]

The Infant Who Is "God With Us" in Matthew

For Matthew, who redeploys and expands Mark's material, the story of Jesus must necessarily be both his "book of origin" (1:1) and also of his continued post-Easter presence to his disciples and their mission (28:8–20). Whether as newborn infant or as empowered Risen One, Jesus is "God with us" (1:23).

Matthew's story of the birth and infancy of Jesus is cast far more explicitly against the backdrop of Israel's history of election, fulfilling scriptural prophecy and bringing to completion the long line of promise from Abraham via David and the exile to the Messiah. It involves the mundane as well as the miraculous, from a catalogue of ancestors to murderous threats against his family, from angels and dreams to the star auguring his birth to pagan astrologers.

With his explicit designation of the Gospel as the "book of origin" of Jesus as Messiah, son of David and son of Abraham (1:1), Matthew alludes to the only two other occurrences of that phrase in Scripture, at Genesis 2:4 (a narrative of creation) and Genesis 5:1 (an account of humanity descended from Adam). Just as those texts addressed a cosmic canvas, so Matthew sets out the origins of Jesus as an equally global reference. He thereby also

---

3. Cf. Collins, *Mark*, 291.
4. See further Bauckham, "Markan Christology"; Frey, "How Could Mark and John"; and Geddert, "The implied YHWH."

Scripture on the Birth and Infancy of Jesus

locates Jesus explicitly as "son of David," key to establishing his messianic identity; and even more basically, as "son of Abraham," an ancestry of covenant and faith that embodies and belongs to the people of Israel. Jesus' human line of descent from these figures (1:2-17) is carefully designed and telescoped to reflect Matthew's priorities, including the 3 x 14 generations pivoting around David and symbolically highlighting the numerical value of fourteen constituted by the three Hebrew letters of the name David (D-V-D). This dramatic portrayal of the line of promise culminates in "Joseph, the husband of Mary, by whom was begotten Jesus, who was called Christ."

But why would Matthew go to all this trouble to craft a genealogy through Joseph, a man who matters little for most of the subsequent narrative, especially when Matthew himself goes on to insist repeatedly that Mary's pregnancy is "from the Holy Spirit" rather than from Joseph (1:16, 18, 20, 25)? Joseph evidently functions in the birth narrative as the key recipient of divine revelation concerning the child's identity, and as the one who enacts divine instructions to protect both Mary and the child (1:20-25; 2:13-14, 19-23). His role is vital if ancillary, both in the narrative and in the Davidic descent he represents. (For Luke and the consistent tradition of the church fathers, by contrast, Joseph is the Son of David but Jesus is biologically Davidic through Mary.)[5]

Matthew punctuates his account of Jesus' birth with the angel's revelation to Joseph about Jesus being conceived through the Holy Spirit (1:18-25), the adoration of the magi (2:1-12) and Herod's persecution of the child, the Holy Family's flight to Egypt, and finally their settlement in Nazareth (2:13-23). These steps in turn are highlighted by means of five so-called "fulfilment quotations" referencing Old Testament prophecy in sometimes unexpected ways. While these prophetic "anchors" are distinctive of Matthew's Gospel as a whole, they are particularly concentrated in his infancy narrative.[6] Matthew makes sense of specific features or events of the life of the infant Jesus by drawing on prophetic texts from Israel's Scriptures. Famously the angel who appears to Joseph in a dream cites Isaiah 7:14 to bolster Mary's virginal conception and to link the child's name, Jesus ("for he will save his people from their sins"), to the name Emmanuel ("God with us"). In similar fashion, when magi call on Herod in search of the "king of the Jews," Micah 5:1 and 2 Samuel 5:2 are invoked to prophesy the

---

5. Cf. Bockmuehl, "The Son of David and His Mother."
6. See further Soares Prabhu, *The formula quotations*.

Messiah's birth in Bethlehem. Hosea 11:1 finds "fulfillment" in the infant Jesus's flight to Egypt until the time of Herod's death; Rachel's weeping for her children in Jeremiah 31:15 anticipates the massacre of the innocents; and an unidentified quotation from "the prophets" serves Matthew to show why the Holy Family settle in Nazareth as the infancy narrative concludes.

Aside from these overt appeals to Jewish Scripture to elucidate specific scenes, Matthew also and more subtly develops parallels between the experiences of the infant Jesus and the infant Moses, Israel's great leader and lawgiver, as these appear both in the Hebrew Bible and in later midrashic traditions. Both children, for example, are saved from a cruel and powerful king.[7] Even beyond the parallels with Moses, Matthew interprets the infant Jesus' flight to Egypt and return as typologically embodying the people of Israel's experience—especially in the rereading of Hosea 11:1, which in its original context unambiguously designates Israel as God's son. From the start, the life of Matthew's Jesus is intimately bound up with that of his people.

But it is also clear from this Gospel's first chapter to the last that the impact of this infant reaches well beyond Israel's borders. The mysterious "magi from the east" have captivated readers since antiquity; indeed, the magi and the star that guides them are among the first motifs to surface in early Christian art.[8] The text intriguingly offers no assistance to readers keen to discover the geographic origin of the magi (whether Arabia, Babylon, Persia, or elsewhere); nor does Matthew lend support to the long-standing tradition that they were three in number. His concern instead focuses on the nature of their pilgrimage to the newborn "king." That story of the magi involves both vision ("we have seen his star at its rising") and devotion ("we have come to worship him"), along with King Herod's inability to find the child and disinterest in paying him homage. The irony of this contrast has not been lost on interpreters: the child's royal importance keenly concerns these foreign astrologers, whereas that insight notably eludes Herod and others among Jesus' own people.

All in all, Matthew's remains a limited, yet significant, picture of the birth and childhood of Jesus. He is the only New Testament writer to detail Joseph's experiences of that birth, and the only one to narrate the story of the star, the magi, and the events surrounding the Holy Family's flight to Egypt. Theologically, Matthew articulates Scripture's first attestation of

---

7. See further examples in Davies and Allison, *Matthew*, 192–93.
8. See Jensen, "Witnessing the Divine."

the foundational Christian belief in the virginal conception of Jesus by the Holy Spirit. He also singles out and interprets the two names, Jesus and Emmanuel, for this messianic child's mission and identity. Emmanuel—"God with us"—encompasses the theological heart of Matthew's infancy narrative, and through it sets the tone for the entirety of the Gospel (cf. 18:20; 28:20). From the start of Jesus' life, therefore, Matthew draws the reader into the mystery of God entering the drama of human history at his birth, combining Jesus' Abrahamic and Davidic family tree with the revelation of his divine conception. By juxtaposing these nativity scenes against a brilliant opening panorama of scriptural citation and allusion, Matthew shows the infant Jesus in close solidarity with his people. At the same time, his accounts of the enigmatic magi from the East and the flight to Egypt already anticipate the extent to which this child's significance as "God with us" would reach out to all Israel and far beyond.

The Child Savior "For All People" in Luke

Luke the evangelist extensively supplements the New Testament account of the infant Jesus with such familiar motifs as the swaddled baby in a manger, hymnic worship including the "Gloria" sung by angels, and shepherds called to his cradle from looking after their flocks by night. Luke's is an artistic composition of profound literary and theological achievement. At the same time, unlike in Matthew, it is more difficult to identify a single line or motif that encompasses the whole. Perhaps the words of the angel to the shepherds on that holy night provide a fitting point of entry: "Do not be afraid. I bring you good news that will cause great joy for all the people. Today in the town of David a Savior has been born to you; he is the Messiah, the Lord. This will be a sign to you: You will find a baby wrapped in cloths and lying in a manger" (2:10–12 NIV). One might say that rather like this angel's message, Luke's infancy narrative has spoken in a particularly compelling and intimate way to readers throughout history, inviting them into its evocative scenes to encounter the mystery of a child who is both Lord and lowly.

Luke accomplishes this in an account that in literary terms is remarkably different from Matthew's. He offers the perspective of Mary rather than Joseph; he introduces numerous characters who do not appear in Matthew (the angel Gabriel, John the Baptist and his parents Zechariah and Elizabeth, shepherds, Simeon and Anna); and does not mention others

An Introduction to Child Theology

whom Matthew does feature (the magi, King Herod). Theologically, however, Luke provides resonance with Matthew's account in several important ways. He affirms the virginal conception of Jesus through the Holy Spirit, and illustrates the child's inextricable connection to his native Judaism while simultaneously asserting his significance for "all people."

Luke begins his Gospel not with Jesus' genealogy (which he provides later, in 3:23–38), but with a short preface (1:1–4). Here he references previously written accounts of Jesus' life, and emphasizes the orderly and reliable nature of his own account, based on eyewitness testimony. Interpreters often wonder how far this claim extends to the infancy narrative: Did Luke have access to any eyewitness sources for the birth and childhood scenes that he relates? One older, yet nonetheless intriguing, suggestion is that Mary herself was a key source; this is based on Luke's ambiguous references to Mary "storing up" and "pondering" events surrounding her son's nativity (2:19, 51), as well as his featuring of her personal experience. More recently, many have doubted Luke's access to any such source; others have raised the possibility of Lukan contact with someone from Jesus' family, even if not Mary herself.[9] However we may construe the redaction history of the infancy narrative, on the purely literary level, at least, Luke's preface sets a tone for its reception as biographically trustworthy.

Following the preface, Luke begins to intertwine the story of Jesus' birth with that of his relative, John the Baptist. The respective annunciations and births of the Messiah's forerunner, and the Messiah himself, are recounted in parallel. Thus the angel Gabriel announces John's birth to Zechariah (1:5–25) before announcing Jesus' birth to Mary (1:26–38); there is a joining of the two families as Mary visits Elizabeth (1:39–56); and Luke completes the parallel in the corresponding nativity of John (1:57–80) and nativity of Jesus (2:1–7). Following the birth of Jesus in Bethlehem, several more scenes are narrated from his infancy and youth: the proclamation of angels and visit of shepherds (2:8–20); the circumcision and presentation of Jesus in the Jerusalem temple, with Simeon and Anna as witnesses (2:21–40); and the finding of the twelve-year-old Jesus in the temple (2:41–52).

Luke's account of Jesus' origins connects the child deeply and intimately with his native Judaism. In agreement with Matthew, Luke repeatedly affirms that Jesus is of Davidic lineage; furthermore, according to ancient interpretations of Luke 1:27, Jesus' connection to the "house of

---

9. For these views, see, respectively, Brown, *Birth of the Messiah*, and Bauckham, "Luke's Infancy Narrative."

David" is portrayed not only through Joseph (2:4), but just as substantially through his mother Mary.[10] The temple in Jerusalem features in three of Luke's infancy scenes; details of its liturgical cult set the stage for the priest Zechariah's encounter with Gabriel before the altar of incense. Mary and Joseph are shown to be faithfully observant of Jewish laws and customs, including circumcising their son, performing acts of purification, sacrifice, and consecration after childbirth, and making the pilgrimage to Jerusalem for the Passover feast.[11]

While Luke does not employ Matthew's method of using "fulfillment quotations," his infancy account similarly resounds with Jewish Scripture, and other Jewish modes of writing in the Second Temple period. This is perhaps most clearly exhibited in the four canticles interspersed throughout the infancy narrative that have come to be part of the church's worship through the ages: Mary's Magnificat (1:46–55), Zechariah's Benedictus (1:67–79), the angelic multitude's Gloria in Excelsis (2:14), and Simeon's Nunc Dimittis (2:29–32). In the Annunciation to Mary, we find further tantalizing resonance with Qumran; specifically, 4Q246, in its prophecy of a future royal figure, shares several parallels with Gabriel's announcement of Jesus' greatness, eternal kingdom, and divine sonship.[12] While claims about contact between the Lukan and Qumranic texts may be taking things too far, the striking resemblances nevertheless invite the possibility that both texts arise out of a similar Jewish milieu of messianic expectation.

Another important christological aspect of the Annunciation echoes an assertion of Matthew's infancy narrative: Mary's conception of the child through the Holy Spirit. Luke elaborates on Matthew's somewhat sparser version, with Gabriel's answer to Mary's questioning: "The Holy Spirit will come upon you, and the power of the Most High will overshadow you; and therefore the one born will be called holy, the son of God" (1:35). Other christological details emerge in the responses of characters throughout the infancy narrative. Both Elizabeth and Zechariah refer to the son in Mary's womb as the "Lord" (1:43, 76), terminology that overlaps with that of God himself (e.g., 1:68). The angel who appears to the shepherds adds two more titles: the child is "a Savior, who is the Messiah, the Lord" (2:11). Later, the Holy Family encounters Simeon in Jerusalem, a man waiting for "the consolation of Israel" (2:25), as well as to behold "the Lord's Messiah" (2:26).

---

10. Bockmuehl, "The Son of David and His Mother."
11. See further Kozitza, "Legal Exegesis."
12. Brooke, *Dead Sea Scrolls*, 263–64.

When Simeon takes the infant Jesus in his arms, he addresses God in his canticle, the Nunc Dimittis: "My eyes have seen your salvation, which you have prepared before the face of all peoples, light for the revelation of the nations and the glory of your people Israel" (2:30–32). At the age of twelve, Jesus astonishes Jerusalem rabbis with his religious understanding, and Mary and Joseph with his devotion to the affairs of "my Father" (2:49). Each of these details lends a layer of color to Luke's portrait of the child's identity and mission. The various titles present a complex mix of salvific, messianic, and divine attributes. Simeon's pronouncement on the significance of Jesus' birth strikes a balance between the child's importance within his native Judaism and his impact on a more global scale. The final scene of Jesus' childhood gestures forward, toward his adult teaching ministry and his personal focus on a divinely appointed task understood by few.

Because of Luke's emphasis on Mary's role in the birth of Jesus, his narrative also contains seeds of Mariological reflection that continue to develop in later apocryphal narrative (especially the second-century *Protevangelium of James*) and early doctrinal debates. Luke's portrait of Mary foregrounds her virginity (1:27, 34), and associates her with the "grace" or "favor" of the Lord (1:28, 30). The Annunciation is presented as a dialogue, in which Mary freely interrogates Gabriel's message before offering her consent: "Behold, the handmaiden of the Lord; let it be for me according to your word" (1:38). During her pregnancy, Mary is hailed by Elizabeth as "blessed among women" and "the mother of my Lord" (1:42–43)—epithets that anticipate what Mary herself prophesies in her Magnificat: "from now on all generations will call me blessed" (1:48).

Before concluding this section, it is perhaps worth noting that the book of Acts—another New Testament writing widely attributed to Luke, which recounts the early history of the apostles and Christian mission following the ascension of Jesus—is strikingly silent about Christ's childhood or how he came to be in the world. Mary "the mother of Jesus" and his siblings are mentioned briefly in 1:14, and Peter and Paul allude to Jesus' Davidic lineage in their speeches to Jewish audiences in 2:30 and 13:23, respectively. For the most part, the narrative of Jesus' life in Acts (notably in the Petrine gospel summary of 10:34–43) looks more like that of Mark than that of Luke: beginning with his baptism, not birth. Still: on the substantive conviction that Jesus of Nazareth was both Son of David and Son of God, Acts is at one with the Gospels.

Scripture on the Birth and Infancy of Jesus

This puzzle in Acts notwithstanding, Luke's overall contribution to our understanding of the infant and child Jesus cannot be overestimated. Uniquely within the New Testament he offers the extended perspective of Jesus' mother, Mary, as well as miniature portraits of Zechariah and Elizabeth, the manger in Bethlehem, angels and shepherds, Simeon at the presentation of the infant in the temple, and finally Jesus at the age of twelve. Theologically, his complex portrayal holds the exalted identity of the newborn child ("Lord," "Messiah," "Son of God," etc.) together with the modest circumstances of his birth in the city of David. His account vividly highlights the child's Jewish identity, while hinting at his broader significance "for all people."

Readers of both infancy narratives have long been curious about historical questions surrounding the events they contain, as well as the process of their respective stories' composition. For modern readers, such questions have become more persistent, and answers more skeptical. How much of what Matthew and Luke relate really happened? How can we reconcile the two accounts historically, when they differ so strikingly? There remains a spectrum of scholarly reflections on these issues. For some, only the barest of overlapping details qualify as historical fact—Jesus' name, perhaps the names of his parents, Mary and Joseph—and the rest is pure invention. There are also a range of approaches to the distinction between historical fact and theological truth. For some, various scenes might express a theological truth while remaining unhistorical in terms of factual events.[13] Still others defend the historical value of additional details (e.g., Kozitza on the Jewish customs cited in Luke's presentation scene),[14] or even of the narratives more broadly (e.g., the more popular though intellectually thoughtful treatment of Benedict XVI).[15] However one might be inclined to approach such questions, if the infancy narratives are understood in the way described here—as accounts that seek to paint in words the paradox of the divine entering history—then the narratives themselves resist facile answers to issues of history and theology. Rather, their purpose is to invite all readers to grapple with these questions for themselves.

---

13. See this approach in, for example, Brown, *Birth of the Messiah*.
14. Kozitza, "Legal Exegesis."
15. Benedict XVI, *Jesus of Nazareth*.

An Introduction to Child Theology

John's Gospel on How the Word Became Jesus

Like the Gospel of Mark, John has no narrative of the birth or infancy of Jesus matching those of Matthew and Luke. And yet Mark's silence contrasts starkly with this fourth evangelist's lavish and ubiquitous celebration of the Son who has become Jesus.

Although modern critical scholarship long assumed this evangelist to be uninterested in history and historical narrative, John in fact shows a surprisingly keen concern for certain historical and geographical aspects of the last days of Jesus in Jerusalem. Throughout his Gospel his narrative style characteristically telescopes history and significance into one. Matthew, Mark, and Luke tend to unfold a presentation of Christ that ultimately amounts to rather more than perhaps first meets the eye. For John, by contrast, Christology bursts onto the scene fully-fledged from the start: the Word that "became flesh" is the same that was "in the beginning" and that "was God." From then on, each narrative part or discourse invariably radiates the whole. Beginning with the opening lines, we are in no doubt that in the birth of Jesus the Eternal Word, the light of humanity, came into the world (1:4–14). That entrance "into the world" as a human being enables him to "exegete" who God is (1:18). Jesus coming as a child and taking fleshly residence "among us" here attracts no birth narrative—and yet it clearly marks the point at which he was "sent into the world" by the Father "from above" and "came down from heaven" (3:17; 6:41, 51; cf. 8:23; 10:36; 12:46; 17:18; 18:37, etc.). That striking assertion of his identity evokes analogous incredulity in John 6:42 as it does in Mark 6:2–3 at Nazareth.

By stressing this heavenly origin, John admittedly sidelines explicit interest in the birth of Jesus. His eternal, timeless identity makes him superior to his contemporaries and ancestors, even Abraham: "Before Abraham was, I am" (8:58). Nevertheless, at another level his birth is explicitly essential to his ability to serve his mission "among us": the evangelist has Jesus affirm about himself, "I was *born* and *came into the world* to testify to the truth" (18:37).

And finally, that divine birth of Jesus also makes possible the fourth Gospel's powerful claim that redemption is achieved specifically through union with him. This is most fully affirmed in Jesus' teaching about the Bread of Life (6:35–58) or the fruit-bearing branches connected to the vine (15:1–11), and also in his ("high-priestly") intercession for the disciples at the end of the Farewell Discourses (17:21, 23, 26). The same theme of a saving union with Christ also accounts for the way in which believers can be "born from above" in the Son of Man who is himself 'from above . . . from heaven" (3:3, 5, 7, 13, 17, 31; cf. 8:23).

God Manifest in Flesh in the New Testament Letters and Revelation

Outside the Gospels we find no sustained consideration of the birth and infancy of Jesus. But as we have seen in Mark and especially in John, this lack of narrative by no means eliminates a keen commitment to the Son of God being born a child and becoming a man. This is true for the remaining New Testament writers as much as for other early Christian writers from Ignatius to Athanasius and the Creeds.

St. Paul's letters include the earliest surviving Christian documents. Although called to be an apostle when he met and saw the risen Lord (1 Cor 9:1; 15:8-10), it appears that Paul never knew Jesus of Nazareth and did not personally witness his life and teaching. When, for example, he teaches the Corinthian church about the earthly Jesus, Paul draws on preformed tissues of teaching and narrative that he had himself received and now passes on. These concern most notably Jesus' Last Supper as well as his crucifixion, burial, death ,and resurrection (1 Cor 11:23-25; 15:3-8; cf. 7:10; 9:14). Elsewhere he shows himself familiar with additional teaching concerning the moral instruction and example of Jesus (e.g., Rom 12:14-21; 13:7-10; 14:14) or his future return in glory (1 Thess 4:15-17; 5:1-7).

That said, it is true that the story of the human Jesus is for Paul very largely the story of his passion, death, and resurrection. Like Mark and John, Paul is virtually silent about Jesus' birth and childhood. There are no traditions pertinent to either Nazareth or Bethlehem, and of the Gospel references to the mother, brothers, and sisters of Jesus the only hint is his apparently fleeting personal encounter with "the Lord's brother" James (Gal 1:19; cf. 2:9, 12; 1 Cor 15:7).

Again like John, however, Paul affirms the incarnation consistently at the heart of his gospel and message of Christ. To be in the form of God meant for Jesus that he made himself nothing, being born human and taking on a slave's form in humble obedience all the way to the cross (Phil 2:6-8). Being wealthy beyond all imagining, Jesus chose to become a poor man to make his people rich (2 Cor 8:9). Paul conceived of his task as above all taking the mission of the gospel to the Gentiles (Gal 2:9), and the primary addressees of his letters were non-Jewish Christians. Despite this overwhelmingly Gentile readership, Paul somewhat surprisingly insists that Jesus was born to a Jewish mother and that his earthly calling was a messianic mission to Israel (e.g., Gal 4:4–5; Rom 9:5). In this respect Paul's take on the origin of Jesus is not fundamentally different from Matthew's. At two or three key moments Paul even stresses this Messiah's descent from David, just as Matthew and Luke do—and as Luke has him preaching to the synagogue at Pisidian Antioch (Acts 13:23, cited earlier: cf. Rom 1:3; 2 Tim 2:8).

Later parts of the Pauline letter collection find the incarnation as the moment when the fullness of God came to dwell in Jesus, the saving divine "epiphany" when he became "manifested in flesh" (Col 1:19; 2 Tim 1:10; Titus 2:11; 3:4; 1 Tim 3:16).

Hebrews, too, was almost universally regarded as Pauline from antiquity (including by Origen[16]) to the editors of the original King James Version of the Bible. It comments in passing on the incarnation as a theophany: in a scene reminiscent of Luke, the angels are to worship the Son at his birth (1:6).

Similar themes are less fully developed elsewhere, but 1 Peter stresses that Jesus was revealed or "manifested" (1:20) at his incarnation. In 1 John Jesus' dispatch into the world as God's only Son is the Word of Life "made manifest" to take away our sins and to destroy the devil (4:9, 14; 1:2; 3:5, 8). That moment is his "coming in the flesh" (1 John 4:2; 2 John 7).

The book of Revelation, the final book of the New Testament, offers a grand view of "what must soon take place" (1:1) in the context of Christ's future coming to earth in glory rather than on his first coming as a human infant (1:7; 3:11, 20; 12:10; 16:15; 22:7, 12, 20). Revelation nevertheless knows and affirms as important that Jesus is descended from David (3:7; 5:5; 22:16). Clearly both "comings"—Jesus the Davidic child and Jesus the supreme Judge and Redeemer of the world—belong together in summing up and embracing between them the New Testament's message of the Jesus who came and comes as "God with us'": "Look! God's dwelling place is now among the people, and he will dwell with them. They will be his people, and God himself will be with them and be their God. He will wipe every tear from their eyes" (21:3–4 NIV).

---

16. Note Thomas, "Origen on Paul's Authorship of Hebrews."

Scripture on the Birth and Infancy of Jesus

The Infant Jesus Among the New Testament's First Readers

This multifaceted witness to the birth and origins of Jesus resonated in different ways with the readers of the New Testament writings in the early centuries. Some of these responses were apologetic, strengthening key christological dimensions and supporting Christian beliefs about Jesus in the face of increasingly vocal pagan or Jewish detractors. Justin Martyr (100–165), for example, defended the virginal conception and birth of Jesus on both fronts, against the comparison with Graeco-Roman myths in his *Apology* and against Jewish challenges about Jesus' fulfillment of prophetic Scripture in his *Dialogue with Trypho the Jew*. Later in the same century, Irenaeus of Lyons (c. 130–200) articulated his defense of the incarnation in his five-volume work *Against Heresies*, in conversation with external as well as inner-Christian (Gnostic) challenges. Origen of Alexandria (c. 185–254) takes on the pagan and Jewish polemics about the birth of Jesus developed by second-century writer Celsus.

Aside from such apologetic reception of the New Testament texts, the early centuries also witnessed a rich blossoming of associated narrative motifs that came to be developed as standard Christian traditions about the nativity of Jesus. One particularly influential document was the second-century apocryphal *Protevangelium of James*. Here we first encounter such popular narrative motifs as Mary riding a donkey into Bethlehem or Jesus being born in a cave.[17] Texts like these sought to fill gaps in the New Testament birth narrative. The *Protevangelium* focuses on the background of Mary's biography from before her birth through her childhood up to and including the events recorded in Matthew and Luke, including her betrothal to Joseph as a widower with children from an earlier marriage.[18] On a very different and rather less influential note, the *Infancy Gospel of Thomas* is another text with relatively early origins that offers a fuller but sometimes alarming account of episodes from Jesus' early childhood, between his birth and his pilgrimage to the temple aged twelve (cf. Luke 2:41–50). He appears here as a precocious and uncontrollable young miracle worker reminiscent of a child on the autistic spectrum. In addition to these gap-filling techniques of early apocryphal narratives, other well-known motifs—such as the ox and ass at Jesus' manger, and the magi as a trio—begin before long to appear in Christian art.

---

17. There are many more examples; see Bockmuehl, "Scriptural Completion."
18. Cf. Bockmuehl, *Ancient Apocryphal Gospels*, 58–71.

The New Testament narratives of the infant Jesus also came to exercise a strong devotional and liturgical appeal to readers and pilgrims in antiquity. A widely attested early tradition (found already in the *Protevangelium* and Justin Martyr) located the Lukan "manger" in a particular cave in Bethlehem—a site that attracted pilgrims from at least the third century (cf. Origen, *Against Celsus* 1.51; also the pilgrim Egeria's *Itinerarium* 42; Jerome, *Epistles* 46.11; 58.3; 108.10). It is this cave over which Constantine erected the Basilica of the Nativity in the fourth century. Additionally, the four canticles of Luke's infancy narrative came to be widely incorporated into the church's prayers by the fourth century. No fewer than three important ancient feasts in the Christian calendar aided in liturgical reflection and participation in the narratives of the birth and infancy: Epiphany, Candlemas, and Christmas.

Conclusion: Scripture on the Birth and Infancy of Jesus

We have encountered several distinct strands in the New Testament's tapestry of reflection on the birth and childhood of Jesus. We noted the mysterious silence of Mark; the strikingly different infancy narratives of Matthew and Luke; John's assertion without narration of the Word's heavenly origin throughout his Gospel; and, in the Letters and Revelation, the emphatic but similarly nonnarrative interpretations of Jesus' incarnation.

The accounts of how "Jesus became Jesus" are thus handled in sometimes surprising ways in the New Testament. What may be synthesized and liberally expanded in popular conceptions of Christmas is either consigned to very different birth narratives in the New Testament, or may in fact owe more to the ways those stories were devoutly read and supplemented in the second and third centuries. This is demonstrated through untangling the original sources for features like the shepherds, magi, Christmas star, and manger, but equally for Mary's donkey or indeed the idea that the magi were three in number. As we have observed, the different New Testament authors may have very different conceptions of Jesus' birth and infancy. But they widely agree on certain key motifs like the infant's Davidic and divine descent, his messianic mission to Israel and yet his importance for all nations. That meaning of the incarnation, "God made flesh"—and indeed we might press further, childish flesh—is part of the shared story from Matthew to Revelation. This point is well captured by the poet summing up "this most tremendous tale of all . . . / The Maker of the stars and sea / Become a Child on earth for me" (John Betjeman, "Christmas").

We began by musing on the seeming dissonance between the New Testament's relatively economic accounts of the child Jesus and the extent to which in popular imagination they are in danger of being submerged under billows of Victorian religious kitsch. And yet the popular theme of that child's birth into the very ordinariness of deprivation and vulnerability turns out to articulate something at the heart of the New Testament's diverse and complex accounts of the incarnation—both the power of divinity and the lowliness of humanity. "God with us" was born for the world as a child, and grew up to deliver it.

Chapter Nine

Childhood in Islam and the Heritage of Shame

MARK ROBERT ANDERSON

SINCE MOST NON-WESTERN CULTURES are honor-shame cultures, it goes without saying that there is nothing intrinsically Islamic about honor-shame cultures. Hence, my title is not meant to suggest that either Islam's three foundational sources—the Qur'an, the hadith, and the sharia—or all Muslims are responsible for the problems of the honor-shame matrix. Neither do I view honor-shame culture as morally deficient per se: it all depends on how we operate within that matrix. However, children in Muslim cultures and subcultures inherit not just many blessings, but also many challenges, the latter often magnified greatly by their culture's adherence to its honor-shame matrix. And we are right to consider how Islam's foundational sources contribute to those challenges in the lives of both children and their parents.[1]

With over 1.8 billion Muslims in the world today,[2] it could not possibly be that all Muslims adhere to one approach to children and parenting. But despite their many differences, the vast majority of Muslims—even those who are largely Westernized—wrestle with challenges derived from their honor-shame orientation.

---

1. I am grateful to Linda Darwish for critiquing an earlier draft of this chapter. While her suggestions improved my treatment of the subject immensely, any errors that remain are mine alone.

2. Lipka and Hackett, "Why Muslims."

Childhood in Islam and the Heritage of Shame

It is arguable that the different parenting approaches Muslims take relate primarily to their different approaches to Islam's foundational sources. For from Islam's formative period onward Muslims have

1. Been divided over which hadith are authentic
2. Had multiple schools of Islamic law
3. Taken different approaches to interpreting the Qur'an

Qur'an interpretation has historically proven controversial and continues to divide Muslims today. Ismailis, for example, have always spiritualized the Qur'an. And modern interpretative approaches seek to modernize the Qur'an by taking the seventh-century "bite" out of it.

Taking the Qur'an at face value, however, most Muslim communities find themselves bound to a Scripture that strongly emphasizes the community over the individual. It also emphasizes external morality over the sins and virtues of the heart and accommodates the honor-shame matrix.[3] External morality focuses on "watershed sins" and those factors that define a good Muslim, like prohibitions against adultery and apostasy and the need to demonstrate undying loyalty to the Muslim cause.[4]

This relates closely to the honor-shame matrix, which binds individuals to maintain and defend the honor of their community, tribe, and family, and to avoid at all costs anything that seriously detracts from the group's collective honor. In an honor-shame matrix

1. The group is indispensable, the individual often expendable
2. A single member's shame[5] contaminates the entire group
3. The group's patriarchs are its final arbiters of honor and guardians against shame

---

3. In many respects, the New Testament—e.g., the Sermon on the Mount—challenged the honor-shame thinking of Middle Eastern societies. By contrast, the Qur'an did not challenge the honor-shame matrix to the same degree. On this, see Anderson, *The Qur'an in Context*, 121–25, 179–80, 202, 284–86.

Not surprisingly, traditional Islam has primarily spread in honor-shame cultures and proselytizes Westerners largely by obscuring its strong honor-shame component.

4. On the percentages of Muslims that take traditional approaches to such issues as adultery and apostasy, see Pew Forum, "The World's Muslims."

5. M. F. El-Islam describes shame as a self-conscious emotion that includes "a powerful urge to hide—to hide the trigger of the emotion, to hide oneself during the experience of the emotion, to hide the existence of the emotion, and even to hide the fact that one has something hidden." El-Islam, "Cultural aspects," 139.

An Introduction to Child Theology

From my Western Christian perspective, many aspects of the honor-shame matrix as seen in most traditional cultures undermine the gender equality I see taught by the New Testament. Apart from social media platforms, Western culture makes the individual primary and counts shame an individual matter, confined to relatively few issues in life.[6] In honor-shame cultures, by contrast, everything one does amounts to a social credit or debit, accrued to one's family and tribe. Shame is never just an individual matter that sometimes wrongly "spills over" onto one's group. It always relates primarily to the group's identity.[7]

In this essay, we will consider seven elements in traditional Muslim approaches to child-rearing and children. These are Islam's emphasis on 1) the value of children, 2) the child's natural inclination toward God, 3) the importance of family, 4) the need for moral action and discipline, and 5) the necessity of wise and just parenting, as well as the ways in which Islam's foundational sources entrench honor-shame's patriarchal values by 6) making girls inferior to boys, and 7) stressing the modesty/chastity of girls far beyond that of boys. Since there are so many Muslim approaches to parenting, we will focus on points deriving specifically from Islam's foundational sources and, hence, relevant to the majority of Muslims worldwide.

The Value of Children

Muslims typically value children highly. We see this both in their love for their children and in Islam's emphasis on the sanctity of life. Regarding the former, I have seen countless examples of parents whose love for their children was as inspiring as it was exemplary. Many Muslim parents dote on their children, and many would gladly give their lives for them. Two friends, in particular, come to mind: an Egyptian mother whose little girl died of cancer and a Syrian father whose daughter was seriously injured in an air raid. Each of these parents put caring for their girl before their own needs and gave everything they could for their daughter's sake. While Muslims battle the imperfections common to us all, the vast majority of

---

6. This does not mean honor and shame are of no import in Western cultures, but they function very differently.

7. In the case of girls, much of their interaction with males relates to perceptions of the former's sexual purity. This can lead to extreme behavior on the part of a girl's guardians if she appears immodest or unchaste. See further Georges and Baker, *Ministering in Honor-Shame Cultures*, 35–38.

Childhood in Islam and the Heritage of Shame

them love their children dearly and seek to raise them well. In this, they offer a real example to many in the West who are too driven and distracted to appreciate the value of their children as they ought to.

Muslim approaches to the sanctity of life also evidence the value Muslims place on children. One sin roundly condemned by the early Qur'anic suras is that of female infanticide. The pagan Arabs frequently disposed of unwanted newborn daughters to avoid the shame of having a girl and the complications involved in raising one. In response, Q 16:58–59 says:

> When any of them is given news of a female child, his face darkens and he chokes with disappointment. He hides himself from people because of the evil of the good news he has been given. Shall he keep the child in shame or bury her in the ground? Truly, their judgment is evil.

The Qur'an forbade infanticide of all kinds, including for reason of physical want: "Do not kill your children out of fear of poverty" (Q 17:31).

Muslims often apply such stipulations to abortion as well, prohibiting it beyond seven or sixteen weeks—depending on the school of law—except to save the mother's life. Many justify early abortions only in cases of rape or genetic defect. The different time ranges relate largely to different views concerning when the soul enters the fetus. One relevant hadith says:

> God's Messenger, the true and truly inspired said, "Every one of you is carried in his mother's womb for the first forty days, and then he becomes a clot for another forty days, and then a piece of flesh for another forty days. Then God sends an angel to write four things: he writes his deeds, time of his death, means of his livelihood, and whether he will be wretched or blessed [in religion]. Then the soul is breathed into his body..."[8]

However, there is no one view on when abortion becomes illegal. Some Muslims prohibit it right from the moment of conception, regardless of any other considerations, while others make other considerations primary. For example, Grand Ayatollah Yusuf Saanei even permits abortion to avoid poverty or protect an adulterer's reputation and spare her hardship.[9]

But while the Qur'an, hadith, and sharia all make female infanticide—and implicitly, gender-selective abortion—a crime, as we shall see, allowing girls to live does not guarantee that they will be allowed to flourish. If they

---

8. *Sahih al-Bukhari*, vol. 4, bk. 55, no. 549.
9. Wright, "Iran Now a Hotbed."

live crippled by shame over their not having been born male, their culture's honor-shame matrix can rob them of life while requiring them to live.

The Child's Natural Inclination toward God

The Qur'an speaks of the *fitra* or innate nature God has created us all with (Q 30:30). Most Muslims think this refers to the child's natural inclination toward pleasing God and belief in God's oneness. Though the verse has given rise to a broad range of Muslim understandings, it seems to relate to a child's awareness of God, much like Calvin's *sensus divinatus*. Many Muslims take the *fitra* to mean that the child's innocence and purity before God disallows the Christian notion of original sin—that is, that children lean toward selfishness, not just toward God. One well-known hadith suggests that the *fitra* means all children are Muslim at birth, though later they may be made Jews or Christians by their parents.[10] In any case, young children are viewed as innocent before God and naturally inclined toward submission to him.

The Importance of Family

The institution of family is of central importance in traditional Muslim societies. Men and women are expected to marry, have children (if possible), and nurture and protect them. Individuals are members of not just isolated nuclear families, but of functioning extended families. Adultery is forbidden, meaning that children are to be raised within stable marriages.

Since the health of every society depends on family stability, any society that trivializes marriage or divorce fosters social instability. We in the West—with our declining marriage rates and generally higher divorce rates—thus have much to learn from our Muslim friends in terms of their emphasis on marriage and family. But traditional Muslims often so stress marriage that they cannot see singleness as a life choice equally valid to marriage. Also, some Muslim cultures allow the family's need to see its girls marry to trump their need of education and virtually all else.[11]

---

10. *Sahih Muslim bisharh al-Nawawi*, 207.

11. The sharia does not fix the minimum age for marriage. Levy, *The Social Structure of Islam*, 135–49. Hence, it is not surprising that four of the world's six countries with no age requirement for marriage are Muslim: Saudi Arabia, Somalia, Yemen, and Gambia. And according to the State Department, despite prohibitions, forced marriages are

Childhood in Islam and the Heritage of Shame

The extended family structure within an honor-shame matrix contributes much to the strength and stability of marriage in Muslim countries. But Islam's foundational sources support three features of family life that diminish marriage's sanctity and undermine its stability:

1. Permission of limited polygyny, concubinage, and sexual relations with female slaves[12]
2. Legitimization of wife beating in some cases[13]
3. Making a husband's divorcing his wife relatively easy[14]

The Qur'an, hadith, and sharia support all these patriarchal concessions, and where they do try to mitigate them, it is a case of too little too late. For every hadith restraining wife beating, another encourages it. For every legal opinion discouraging polygyny,[15] another upholds it.

Reacting to this, many Westernized Muslims now reject polygyny altogether. Those who do so find interpretive loopholes in the relevant Qur'anic verses[16] and may entirely disregard the hadith and sharia's teachings on

---

common for many children in Pakistan. Sandstrom and Theodorou, "Many Countires Allow."

12. Q 4:3, 24–25 limits husbands to four wives concurrently, provided the husbands have sufficient means to provide for them. Recognizing this, all four Sunni legal schools permit polygyny. Among Shia Muslims, some authorities also permit temporary marriages (*nika al-mutca*, lit. "pleasure marriage"), which by some interpretations can be contracted for just a few hours.

13. Q 4:34 permits a husband to beat his wife as a last resort, when other options have failed to set his heart at rest about her behavior. For more on this, see the discussion in Anderson, *The Qur'an in Context*, 175–76.

14. See the discussion in Anderson, *The Qur'an in Context*, 176.

15. For example, while the Shaafi'i legal school does not forbid polygyny, it discourages it except in cases where a husband can treat all of his wives equally.

16. For example, reformist Muslims dismiss the traditional interpretation of Q 4:3, which allows men to marry up to four wives and takes the expression "what their right hands own" to refer to the female slaves they can marry at will. It is understandable that Westernized Muslims want to make the Qur'an fit the modern world, which condemns slavery and praises gender parity. But the seventh-century world to which the qur'anic messages were first given was both proslavery and highly patriarchal. Hence, anyone dismissing the traditional reading must answer two questions. First, how could the Qur'an have hoped to challenge the Arabs' entrenched misogyny and acceptance of slavery effectively without ever clearly stating that fact? Second, how could Muslims have been expected to grasp that when his earliest biographer says Muhammad had both multiple wives and female slaves taken in battle? I would argue that those who throw out the traditional figure of Muhammad essentially recreate Islam in their own likeness.

polygyny. But to date only Tunisia and Turkey have made polygyny illegal, although several other Muslim-majority countries restrict it in various ways.[17] Despite the partial devaluation of marriage by Islam's foundational sources, most Muslim children grow up in relatively stable families, thanks to the constraints of their traditional honor-shame-oriented cultures.

Moral Action and Discipline

The Qur'an, hadith, and sharia all focus on the need for believers to live a disciplined and moral life. Belief without corresponding action is insufficient in the eyes of God and the Muslim community. Q 9:105 says,

> Take action. God will see your action, as will his Messenger and the believers, and then you will be returned to him who knows what is hidden and what is seen, and he will tell you what you have been doing.

Likewise, Q 61:2–3 says, "O you who believe, why do you say things and then do not do them? It is most hateful to God that you say things and then do not do them." And one of the most important actions, from early childhood, right on into adulthood, is to honor and obey parents. Q 17:23 says,

> And your Lord has decreed that you . . . be dutiful to your parents. If one of them or both of them attain old age in your lifetime, do not say a word of disrespect to them, nor shout at them, but address them in terms of honor.

With this emphasis on praxis, children grow up aware that one becomes a good person by one's moral discipline. Practically, this emphasis is often weakened by an excessive reliance on community, with some seeming to believe that mere membership in the Muslim community, or *umma*, is enough to make them good. However, the Qur'an, hadith, and sharia all emphasize action as the essential test of one's loyalty to the community.

---

17. For example, Iran, Iraq, Bangladesh, Algeria, Lebanon, Morocco, Jordan, Malaysia, and Kuwait either allow a wife to include the prohibition of polygyny in the marriage contract or else give her veto power over her husband's taking another wife. In most Muslim countries, however, women have no such rights.

The Necessity of Careful Parenting

The hadith make parents responsible to care for their families and instill true values in their children. In one hadith, Muhammad is quoted as saying,

> Each of you is a shepherd and is responsible for his flock... The man is the shepherd of his family and he is responsible for his flock. The woman is the shepherd of her husband's household and is responsible for her flock.[18]

This shepherding takes place within the context of parenting as a test of one's devotion to God. Q 64:15 says, "Your wealth and your children are only a test, whereas God, with him is a great reward." And Q 66:6 urges believers to protect themselves and their families from hell.

The Inferiority of Girls to Boys

The Qur'an has relatively little teaching specifically about girls. But in one sense, everything it says about women pertains to girls also since they are women in the making and since the Qur'an establishes a woman's place in society. If the Qur'an and the sharia permit a girl's father to beat her mother, this directly affects the way the girl views her own worth, since she may suffer the same fate someday. Hence, we cannot limit our discussion here to what Islam's authoritative sources say explicitly of girls.

The culture the Qur'an fosters marginalizes women and girls in many respects, and that has profound implications in terms of how they are valued and raised. The hadith have other relevant teachings. But Muslims are divided today over the value of the hadith on girls and women[19] between those holding traditional (patriarchal) views and those with a twenty-first century agenda. And as Muslims typically do, each group here highlights those hadith that support its position. But this tells us only that the Muslim community was divided on the place of females during the classical period, when the hadith were recorded, even as it is today.

The relative inferiority of Muslim girls to boys is often blamed on the cultures of the various Muslim peoples. But as we have seen, that inferiority

---

18. *Sahih al-Bukhari*, 853.

19. As all Muslims know, many hadith are inauthentic. The classical scholars assessing the authenticity of the hadith did so primarily on the basis of the chain of hadith sources, considering a hadith's contents of secondary importance. Most Western scholars view this approach as highly flawed.

has a basis in the Qur'an and Islam's other source texts, even though they also evidence a concern to limit the imbalance. Q 16:58–59, quoted above, suggests that girls are equal in value to boys. Muslims promoting Islam in the West use such passages to support their claim that Islam is not misogynistic. The passage does establish that infant girls have no less right to life than boys because girls are equally gifts from God. Another verse used to establish the equality of women is Q 2:228, which says of wives in cases of divorce, "Women have the same rights and obligations in what is recognized as proper." But the verse goes on to say, "but men have a rank above them."

By contrast, one hadith has Muhammad describing women as "the twin halves of men"[20] and another admonishing that "The best of you are those who are best to their wives, and I am the best of you to my wives."[21] Another hadith promises paradise to men who care for their sisters and daughters.[22] Some Muslims even argue that the hadith value women over men since one hadith puts paradise "at the feet of mothers." Another hadith likewise seems to value mothers above fathers:

> A man came to the Messenger of God (peace and blessings of God be upon him) and said, "Messenger of God, who among people is most deserving of my good company?" He said, "Your mother." He asked, "Then who?" He said, "Your mother." He asked, "Then who?" He said, "Your mother." He asked, "Then who?" He said, "Then your father."[23]

Regardless of whether or not such anecdotes are authentic representations of Muhammad's thinking, they were clearly meant to correct the more extreme defects of patriarchal misogyny. And in many Muslim homes, they undoubtedly do just that. In addition, the Qur'an grants women the right to both inherit property and testify in court. Muslims often present this as a major improvement over the situation of women in pre-Islamic Arabia, despite their belief in the widowed Khadijah's wealth and independence prior to Muhammad's prophetic call.

But how could a few Qur'anic verses and hadith possibly overturn millennia of Middle Eastern misogyny—especially when the improvements they brought women were undercut by other teachings? For example, the

20. *Sunan Abi Dawud*, 236.
21. *Jami al-Tirmidhi*, 3895
22. *Sahih Muslim*, 2/190.
23. *Sahih al-Bukhari*, 5626.

Qur'an ordains that a woman inherit only half of what her brother inherits, although it assumes that a married woman will benefit from her husband's double share. However, it also makes her legal testimony worth only half that of a man (Q 4:11, 2:282). In some cases, the Qur'an commands husbands to beat their wives even when they just suspect them of disobedience (Q 4:34).[24] And due to its legitimization by God in both the Qur'an and sharia, this threat of domestic violence comes with relatively scant legal recourse.

In cases of divorce, older children always go to the father, who is required to care for his ex-wife only till the children are old enough to leave her—usually at about eight years of age. If there are no children yet, he must care for her until it becomes clear that she is not carrying his child (Q 65:1). In either case, this means the children are literally his and not hers. Furthermore, the Qur'an gives men the right to have sex with their female slaves and to consummate marriages to prepubescent girls (Q 4:24, 65:4). According to the hadith and the traditional biography of Muhammad (*sira*), he took advantage of both those rights. And the fact that he is deemed the perfect example for all Muslim men to follow makes those rights relevant not only to earlier times.[25] Such norms inevitably entrench patriarchy, by making females inferior to males.

In addition, the Qur'an never recognizes a single female prophet or communal leader and, in fact, includes the proper name of only one female—namely, Mary, the mother of Jesus—compared with the names of numerous male prophets. And so chauvinistic is its description of paradise that one wonders exactly what sort of eternal bliss it offers female believers.[26]

The hadith, likewise, present a very mixed view of women. For example, one suggests that women are more prone to evil than men since the majority of those sent to hell are women.[27] As we will see, other hadith speak of women as morally inferior to men and representing a great temptation to them. Another has Muhammad explain that a woman's testimony is only equal to half that of a man "because of the deficiency of her mind."[28]

---

24. See note 9 above.

25. Reformist Muslims often argue that Muhammad was allowed to do so only because he was a prophet.

26. To the patriarchal mind, the Qur'an's teaching that God will give believing men multiple female sex partners in paradise is very reasonable. On this, see Anderson, "What Does the Qur'an Teach About Heaven?"

27. *Sahih al-Bukhari*, 1.6.301.

28. *Sahih al-Bukhari*, no. 2658.

Two other well-known hadiths credit Muhammad with saying, "I have left behind no greater temptation (*fitna*) for men than women,"[29] and comparing women—specifically in relation to their sexual charms—to devils.[30]

The best we can say of the hadith here is that they clearly show that the early Muslim community was divided on women's status and rights during the classical period when the hadith were recorded. That being so, both groups of Muslims—patriarchal and liberal—have always simply highlighted those Qur'anic verses and hadith that support their respective positions (or the positions they want others to believe are representative of Islam) and have minimized or ignored those that do not. Regarding the sharia, the balance shifts even more markedly toward patriarchy.

To sum up, the Qur'an seems to have challenged Arab patriarchal culture on several points. From the classical period onward, we know that there have always been more liberal Muslims who wanted to improve the lot of women. And patriarchy preexisted Islam in most of the cultures that embraced it. But on the other hand, the Qur'an clearly did not overthrow Arab patriarchy. At most, it adjusted it. The hadith only compounded the problem, its more liberal anecdotes being insufficient to correct its misogynistic ones. And the sharia did little more to advance the equality of women and girls. Thus, in a number of respects, all three of Islam's foundational sources entrenched patriarchy by granting it religious legitimacy.

That is why Muslims have made so little progress in seeking gender parity. It is why Islamist extremist groups are on the rise. It is why liberal Muslims have always been vastly outnumbered outside of the West and will remain so for the foreseeable future. It is why fully nineteen of the twenty worst countries listed in the Global Gender Gap Index of the World Economic Forum (WEF) are Muslim nations and only two Muslim countries made it into the list's top half. Most Muslim countries seriously lag behind other countries in every dimension of gender parity—from health and education to economic opportunity and political empowerment.[31]

There are doubtless millions of healthy, well-adjusted Muslim girls and women in the world who have developed confidence that their worth is equal to that of their male counterparts. When that does occur, however, it is because their families of origin have somehow mitigated the patriarchy

---

29. *Sahih al-Bukhari*, 7.62.33.
30. *Sahih Muslim*, 8:3240.
31. Kazakhstan and Bangladesh ranked fifty-one and seventy-two, respectively, out of the 144 countries studied. World Economic Forum, "Global Gender Gap."

CHILDHOOD IN ISLAM AND THE HERITAGE OF SHAME

that generally prevails in Muslim countries today, in keeping with Islam's source documents. It seems unlikely that for every Muslim family repressing its girls, another supports theirs well. On the whole, Muslim girls worldwide face many handicaps and hindrances to flourishing that their brothers do not face. Nothing else explains the WEF gender gap rankings.

As one Palestinian American woman laments,

> From the time they are born, girls are looked at differently. Boys act superior and they grow up that way . . . Girls have to have a good reason to do anything, but the boys do what they want. Girls' mistakes are taken very seriously and punishment is often severe.[32]

In the most extreme cases, some Muslim mothers essentially shun their daughters at birth, as major disappointments, and this leaves them to suffer from something akin to post-traumatic stress disorder for the rest of their lives, unless they are fortunate enough to receive professional help.[33] One Iranian Canadian recounted how her father's response to her asking a very

---

32. Cainkar, "Immigrant Palestinian Women Evaluate Their Lives," 48.

33. Most Muslim cultures noticeably value boys over girls. And the effects of this distortion on both girls and boys—not to mention the women and men they become—cannot be overstated. For example, on producing daughters, instead of more highly valued sons, birthing mothers may unconsciously reflect disappointment to their daughters from their babies' birth onward. They do so in their reciprocal gaze behavior, which is a key element in an infant's proto-conversation and the most intense form of interpersonal communication. A mother may do this by so simple an action as withdrawing or hardening her gaze when her daughter seeks to connect with her through eye-to-eye contact. This immediately triggers in her infant daughter a nonverbal, acutely painful and stress-related affect of infant shame, producing "a rapid and unexpected contraction of the self." It also results in the kind of parasympathetic arousal that occurs in extremely stressful situations—e.g., shallow breathing, increased heart rate, indigestion. If this unhealthy reciprocal gaze behavior becomes chronic, the child's internal distress and arousal become prolonged, permanently reducing her capacity to autoregulate or interactively regulate shame. And since "shame generally inhibits the expression of emotion *per se*," this may permanently limit a girl's ability to express emotion.

If a mother goes on to ridicule or humiliate her daughter or reject her requests for comfort in stressful situations, the daughter comes to see herself as fundamentally unworthy. This in turn teaches her to accept the mistreatment she can expect in a patriarchal society. If the socialization a girl experiences during the second year of her life consistently reinforces her relative worthlessness in relation to the family's boys, this affects the development of her brain's orbitofrontal cortex. And that can affect all her future interpersonal interactions since the orbitofrontal cortex plays a major role in calibrating the emotional responses—both internal and external—vital to human relationships. Schore, "Early Shame Experiences," 65–72.

innocent question about religion was simply to slap her. Whether or not he could answer her question, to his mind, she clearly did not know her place.[34]

While the situation varies greatly from one Muslim home to the next, many Muslim girls, like their mothers, aspire to no career outside the home and exist only on the periphery of public religious life, confined to the back of the mosque or excluded from it altogether. This devaluation of girls is complemented by an equivalent overvaluation of boys, which leaves most boys—and the men they grow into—suffering from serious entitlement issues. These issues are very damaging to male-female relationships within Muslim families and within society as a whole. Hence, girls raised in Muslim cultures are at a real disadvantage.

An Unequal Emphasis on the Modesty and Chastity of Girls

The Qur'an limits sexual expression to marriage in its various forms,[35] as well as to males and their female slaves. In that context, it demands chastity and—closely related to it—modesty of all Muslims, male or female (Q 23:1-7, 24:30-31). Men, not just women, are commanded to lower their gaze modestly in the presence of the opposite sex. However, in keeping with Islam's patriarchal framework, the hadith and the sharia stress the modesty/chastity of females to an extent that they do not stress that of males.

One basic difference between Muslim boys and girls is the double standard by which the onus for sexual impropriety is far more on females than males. This leads Muslim societies to make sexual experimentation far more forgivable for boys than girls. Hence, some American Muslim girls "see their brothers allowed to date and resent what they see as inequity." If they complain against these strictures, their families typically respond by ostracizing them.[36] Such patriarchal thinking often functions as the warp by which the woof of religion is interpreted. The result is that the primary responsibility on families here is to keep their girls pure, the unspoken reason being the protection of family lineage. Again, their boys' chastity is of far less consequence than that of their girls since a boy's proverbial sowing of "wild oats" does not endanger his family's lineage or marriageability as

---

34. Missions Fest Vancouver, "Seminar on Women in Islam."
35. See section 3 above.
36. Haddad and Smith, "Islamic Values Among American Muslims," 23.

does his sister's sexual impropriety. This can put immense pressure on girls from an early age.

Three expressions of this drive to preserve female chastity are Muslim veiling, seclusion, and female genital mutilation. The obscurity of the Qur'an passages relevant to veiling (Q 24:31; 33:53) leaves the question open, although a loose cloak or coat covering the female body may be more in mind than veiling per se (Q 33:60). This prompts Muslims to seek clarity in the hadith and sharia. But of the thousands of hadith in the great canonical Sunni collections, only one relates directly to the requirements of the veil. And all Sunni scholars deem that hadith unreliable due to its weak chain of transmission. Hence, they could not use it in legal formulation.[37]

Some Reformist Muslims interpret the relevant Qur'anic references as consistent with many of the freedoms girls enjoy in the West and altogether dismiss the hadith and sharia on these topics. But despite the legal weakness of the sources on this, the past couple of decades have seen a significant increase in the number of Muslim women and girls everywhere veiling. In fact, many Muslims seem to view it as the visible sign of a woman's Islamic devotion and that of her family. For it serves as a prophylactic against the threat of Western immorality and a shibboleth-like declaration that traditional Muslim values are best.

Some argue that veiling derives more from the patriarchal system than from Islam's authoritative sources per se. However, Islam's authoritative sources do entrench a system that puts the onus squarely on the girl (and her family) to protect her/their honor by her veiling. Many Muslim girls in the West freely choose to wear hijab, even contrary to their parents' wishes. But in the most patriarchal Muslim cultures—e.g., Yemen, Saudi Arabia, tribal Afghanistan and Pakistan—girls are made to wear bulky clothing and full-face coverings (*burqa*) in public from age ten or younger, even in extreme heat.[38] Female modesty there may even require a level of seclusion that forbids female education and promotes prepubescent marriages,

---

37. It says, "Asma, daughter of Abu Bakr, entered upon the Messenger of God (peace be upon him) wearing thin clothes. The Messenger of God (peace be upon him) turned his attention from her. He said, Asma, when a woman reaches the age of menstruation, it does not suit her that she displays her body parts, except this and this, and he pointed to her face and hands." Not only is this hadith considered weak—it appears in only one canonical Sunni collection, that of Abu Dawud (32:4092).

38. The question of whether this involves coercion on the part of her parents is moot. For how can a child of nine or ten make a truly free choice in a culture that punishes breaking the rules on modesty with public shunning?

lest anything less lead to a loss of chastity. While Muslims vary greatly in their understanding of what female modesty demands, Islam's authoritative sources are always used to justify and enforce the rules.

Such honor-shame thinking leads some Muslim families who feel their daughters have irreparably damaged their honor by deviating from sexual mores to dispose of them by so-called honor killing. Thus, a girl's failure to abide by the community's rules of modesty or chastity may lead to her death. Muslims who engage in honor killing invariably do so in the name of Islam, believing their faith demands it of them. In fact, none of Islam's three foundational sources explicitly prescribe honor killing. However, do those sources not support the practice to the degree that they maintain the patriarchal system and honor-shame matrix which produce it?

Depending on the legal school, the sharia also either encourages or makes obligatory the highly controversial cutting of girls' external genitals, known as female genital mutilation (FGM), often before the age of five. In 2016, UNICEF estimated that over 200 million women and girls had undergone FGM, many of them Muslims.[39] Sometimes FGM amounts to the equivalent of male circumcision. But it is often more radical, involving removal of the labia and sometimes even clitorectomy and stitching the edges of the vulva closed. Depending on the procedure, the operation can lead to serious health problems, including difficulty urinating and passing menstrual flow, recurrent infections, chronic pain, an inability to conceive, plus complications and fatal bleeding in childbirth. It has no known health benefits.[40]

Defenders of Islam argue that FGM is not Islamic, but derives from the cultures of those who embraced Islam. While the great majority of those who practice it are Muslim, some Christian and animistic Africans practice it also. So in one sense, the Muslim apologists are right. There is also a recognition on the part of many Muslims that the practice is not good. In an effort to eradicate it, the al-Azhar Supreme Council of Islamic Research in Cairo ruled in 2007 that FGM has "no basis in core Islamic law or any of its partial provisions."[41] In support of their position, the Qur'an does not mention it, and only a few weak hadith praise it.

---

39. Cappa et al., *Female Genital Mutilation/Cutting.*

40. Abdul Abdulcadir et al., "Care of women with female genital mutilation/cutting."

41. UNICEF, "Fresh progress toward the elimination of female genital mutilation and cutting in Egypt."

However, the Supreme Council's public relations concerns become clear when we realize that the Shafici legal school, one of Sunni Islam's four great legal schools, requires FGM.[42] It is no coincidence, then, that there is so much overlap between Shafici adherence and the countries where FGM is practiced. This doubtless explains why surveys show that Muslims in several African countries widely believe that their faith requires FGM.[43] So, while the practice most likely predated Islam in northeastern Africa, Shafici Islam subsumed it, then carrying it to Iraq, Yemen, Malaysia, and Indonesia.

Thus, it is like the breast ironing practiced by some African Muslims[44] since it aims to preserve modesty, seclusion, female purity, family honor, virginity, and fidelity—all major concerns of patriarchal systems. However, FGM is unlike breast ironing in that the former has an Islamic basis in the sharia, whereas breast ironing has none at all.

Conclusion

While views of childhood and child-rearing practices vary widely among Muslims, there are many points on which nearly all Muslims agree. They consider all children a gift from God and, so, subscribe to the sanctity of life. They view children as naturally inclined toward God and his path. They place great importance on having stable families, even though they make it easy for husbands to divorce their wives. They value moral action and disciplined living and stress the necessity of wise parenting. Together, these beliefs and practices produce relatively healthy marriages and strong families, especially when supported by stable extended families.

Other child-rearing features are rooted in the Islamic worldview's honor-shame matrix. For example, though baby girls must be kept alive, they may have to live out their days crippled by shame because they are not boys. Likewise, sometimes the family's importance is so entwined with family honor that nothing matters more than its public appearance vis-à-vis the Muslim community's prescribed sexual mores. This is the origin of

---

42. Ahmad Ibn Naqib al-Misri's (d. 1368) exposition of Shafici, *Umdat al-Salik*, on FGM explains that Shafici requires the excision of the clitoris. However, Nun Ha Mim Keller's translation of al-Misri distorts his meaning for Western consumption. See al-Misri, *Reliance of the Traveler*, 59.

43. Cappa et al., *Female Genital Mutilation/Cutting*.

44. Lazareva, "Revealed."

so-called honor killings, by which families dispose of their children to clear the family's name. Though we find no explicit support for this practice in Islam's source documents, they do support some patriarchal systems that require it (not to mention the honor killing of apostates). They thus sacrifice the child on the altar of extreme parental or familial authority. And all this is inextricably bound to the ways Islam's foundational sources make girls inferior to boys and stress girls' modesty/chastity far beyond that of boys'.

In view of all this, optimism about the brightening future of the Muslim child is likely unwarranted. It might be warranted if Muslims were generally becoming more aware of the patriarchal nature of their faith's foundational sources. But the vast majority of Muslims worldwide are traditional Muslims, who defend such patriarchal thinking. Others who are openly critical of patriarchy give cover to Islam's patriarchal standards by refusing to acknowledge their básis in its foundational documents. All such Muslims fear implicitly denying Islam's perfection and dishonoring the Muslim community. The Qur'an's polemical emphasis makes the situation more problematic for them by stressing Islam's necessary triumph over every other religion.

Muslims in the West both appreciate and fear Western freedoms. Many of those freedoms drew them to the West. However, they also fear Western freedoms because secular societies now promote them unmoored from a clear moral vision and a balanced understanding of family, child, and community. The recent increase in the practice of Muslim veiling in the West aims visibly to help counteract Western looseness among Muslims. Reflecting Islam's worldwide resurgence, this increase in veiling suggests that Islam's reform is likely to proceed very slowly and reluctantly, in spite of itself.

Nevertheless, we can hope that, through interfaith friendship and dialogue, Muslims and Christians may learn and grow together in an understanding of family, child, and community—an understanding that honors God, primarily, and the children he has entrusted us with, secondarily. For the sake of all our children, may it be so.

Chapter Ten

Memory and Character Formation
The Ark in Hugh of Saint Victor

Hans Boersma

Introduction

"My child, knowledge is a treasury and your heart is its strongbox."[1] These are the opening words with which around the year 1130 Hugh of St. Victor (ca. 1096–1141) addressed the novices of the cathedral school of St. Victor in a book detailing noteworthy biblical facts, entitled *Chronicle*. The metaphor of a strongbox—Hugh uses the Latin term *archa*, so that we may simply translate "ark"—was an important one to the Parisian teacher.[2] As we will see, he uses it in at least three of his works, with a variety of meanings, but each time his use centers on the functioning of memory.

---

1. Carruthers, "Hugh of St. Victor," 339. Hereafter referred to as TBMA. For the Latin text, see Green, "Hugo of St Victor."

2. Hugh's imagery of a strongbox is part of a tradition going back at least to Saint Augustine. His reflections on memory in Book 10 of the *Confessions* do not include the term "strongbox" (*arca*), but Augustine does refer to images derived from sense perception as treasures (*thesauri*) kept in "vast palaces of memory" (*lata praetoria memoriae*) (*Conf.* 10.8.12), in a "vast hall of memory" (*aula ingens memoriae*) (*Conf.* 10.8.14), or in a "treasure-house of memory" (*thesaurus memoriae*) (*Conf.* 10.8.14).

An Introduction to Child Theology

Hugh was heir to a rich tradition of reflection on the role of memory. Before entering into a deeper discussion of his views on it—and of his use of the ark metaphor—I will trace some of the key moments of the tradition on which he drew, both classical and Christian. My purpose in this essay is to show that Hugh of Saint Victor closely links memory to character formation. Hugh was no exception: Throughout the classical and medieval world, memory was considered indispensable to the development of human identity. It is the contents of the mind "stored" (*recondere*) in the memory and "gathered" (*colligere*) in the act of reminiscence that provides the requisite stability that we long for as human beings. It is, therefore, the proper ordering of the contents of the mind that determines what kind of person we become. Memorizing some things rather than others—say, the contents of the Psalms or the outlines of biblical narratives rather than, perhaps, the latest NFL heroes or Hollywood stars—shapes us in a particular fashion. Memorization, which for Hugh is closely linked to meditation, feeds either virtue or vice. Memory shapes character.

Memory in Classical Rhetoric

In the classical period, memory was a topic typically discussed in the context of rhetoric, both among the followers of Cicero and among the adherents of Quintilian's thought, the philosophers who formed the two most influential schools of thought in later tradition. In the first century BC, the Roman philosopher Cicero (106–43 BC) wrote some of the most significant works on rhetoric: his youthful work *On Invention* (*De inventione*) (ca. 87 BC) and his mature book *On the Orator* (*De oratore*) (55 BC). An anonymous work on rhetoric, entitled *Rhetorica ad Herennium* (ca. 86 BC), was also influential, both in the ancient world and in later Christian tradition, in part because it was commonly (though erroneously) thought also to have been written by Cicero. Each of these works discussed five so-called canons of rhetoric: invention (*inventio*, the search for arguments); arrangement (*dispositio*, the structure or outline of a text); style (*elocutio*, dealing with word choice, syntax, and figures of speech); memory (*memoria*); and delivery (*actio*, the use of voice and gestures).[3] The topic of memory was discussed, therefore, as an element of rhetoric, and as a result memorization was treated as a skill to be mastered for purposes of public speech.

---

3. Cicero, *On Invention* (hereafter *Inv.*), 1.7.9; Cicero, *On the Orator: Books I–II*, 1.142; *Rhetorica ad Herennium* (hereafter *Rhet. Her.*), 3.1.1.

Memory and Character Formation

Memory was considered an art—*ars memorativa*—that one could learn and develop. Scholars speak of mnemotechnics to describe the acquisition of this skill, though this term may have a derogatory connotation (similar to the negative undertone often associated with phrase "rote memorization"). In the *ars memorativa*, the student had to master certain memorizing skills, for the sake of efficiency in public speech and argument.

The *Ad Herennium* illustrates well how the memorative art functioned. The book speaks of memory as a "treasure-house of the ideas supplied by Invention" (*thesaurum inventorum*) (*Rhet. Her.* 3.16.28). In discussing "artificial memory," that is, memory with which we are not born but in which instead we can be trained, *Ad Herennium* explains the importance of places or backgrounds (*loci*) for the task of memorizing:

> The artificial memory includes backgrounds and images (*locis et imaginibus*). By backgrounds I mean such scenes as are naturally or artificially set off on a small scale, complete and conspicuous, so that we can grasp and embrace them easily by the natural memory—for example, a house, an intercolumnar space, a recess, an arch, or the like. An image is, as it were, a figure, mark, or portrait of the object we wish to remember; for example, if we wish to recall a horse, a lion, or an eagle, we must place its image in a definite background. (3.16.29–30)

In the *loci et imagines* approach, places or backgrounds served as compartments (such as a house, a set of columns, a recess, an arch, and the like) within which the student was supposed to place images (such as a horse, a lion, or an eagle) for the sake of memorization.

Ad Herennium suggests that when our minds link the image with the correct background, we can then recall where the topic, indicated by the image, fits within the overall account that we're trying to commit to memory. Once we have memorized the entire architectural framework along with the correct placement of the images, we can then access any given section of the account by recalling which image (*imago*) was associated with that particular place (*locus*) within the architectural framework. If we have memorized well, it no longer matters where in the structure of places we start out in our mind; so long as we know which place (*locus*) goes with which image (*imago*), we will be able to recall its contents: "If these [*loci*] have been arranged in order, the result will be that, reminded by the images, we can repeat orally what we have committed to the backgrounds, proceeding in either direction from any background we please" (3.17.30).

Ad Herennium suggests that in our mind we should try to make each of the backgrounds or *loci* unique by adding all kinds of detailed characteristics in our mind, which will make them stand out, so that memorizing them will be easier.[4]

With regard to the images, the author distinguishes two kinds, one for topics (*res*) and one for words (*verba*) (3.20.33). It is relatively easy to recall a topic or argument (*res*) by means of a picture. *Ad Herennium* suggests simply conjuring up a picture that will represent the topic to be memorized. For example, if I am a lawyer defending an accused of poisoning someone, I might try to remember the accusation by filling the first memory *locus* with an image of a man lying ill in bed, holding a cup in his hand.[5] Representing topics (*res*) through images is thus a fairly straightforward matter.

Using pictures to represent every one of the words (*verba*) of a given account would seem to be much trickier. The author of *Ad Herennium* recognizes this, but he suggests that it is nonetheless possible to find an image for whatever word one wants to represent (3.21.34). Since the images have to stick, the author recommends using extremely vivid images, "images that act" (*imagines agentes*). We will succeed in setting up images that stick in our memory

> if we assign to them exceptional beauty or singular ugliness; if we dress some of them with crowns or purple cloaks, for example, so that the likeness may be more distinct to us; or if we somehow disfigure them, as by introducing one stained with blood or soiled with mud or smeared with red paint, so that its form is

---

4. *Ad Herennium* suggests the following: marking each fifth background with an identifier; using for a *locus* a deserted rather than a populous place; choosing *loci* that differ in size and nature; avoiding excessively large and small structures; ensuring that the *loci* are neither too bright nor too dim; and placing some space between various *loci* (e.g., between columns) (*Rhet. Her.* 3.18.31–3.19.32).

5. The example comes from *Rhet. Her.* 3.20.33–34: "We shall picture the man in question as lying ill in bed, if we know his person. If we do not know him, we shall yet take some one to be our invalid, but not a man of the lowest class, so that he may come to mind at once. And we shall place the defendant at the bedside, holding in his right hand a cup, and in his left tablets, and on the fourth finger a ram's testicles. In this way we can record the man who was poisoned, the inheritance, and the witnesses." A translator's note clarifies that "anatomists spoke of a nerve which extends from the heart to the fourth finger of the left hand (the *digitus medicinalis*), where it interlaces into the other nerves of that finger; the finger was therefore ringed, as with a crown. *Testiculi* suggests *testes* (witnesses). Of the scrotum of the ram purses were made; thus the money used for bribing the witnesses may perhaps also be suggested."

more striking, or by assigning certain comic effects to our images, for that, too, will ensure our remembering them more readily. (3.22.37)

Frances Yates, in her classic book *The Art of Memory*, comments that at this point in the treatise "we have moved into an extraordinary world as we run over his [i.e., the author's] places with the rhetoric student, imagining on the places such very peculiar images."[6] The Ciceronian model of memorizing encouraged, therefore, the use of lively pictures, particularly of a violent or erotic nature.

The Spanish rhetorician Quintilian (ca. 35–ca. 100) was at least as influential as Cicero, with a twelve-volume book on rhetoric that he wrote toward the end of the first century (ca. AD 95), entitled *The Orator's Education (Institutio oratoria)*. Here Quintilian outlines his own distinctive approach to memory, which, as Grover Zinn points out, was critical of the *loci et imagines* method of the earlier classical tradition.[7] While Quintilian acknowledges that images can be useful for memorizing topics (*res*), he is less than confident that we are able to memorize individual words (*verba*) by using a picture for each word: "Will not the run of our speech actually be held up by this double effort of memorizing? How can we produce a continuous flow of words if we have to refer to a distinct Symbol for every individual word?" (*Inst.* 11.2.26).[8] Put differently, Quintilian worried that with the Ciceronian method we are forced to remember not only the words, but also the images: Memorization has become, not easier, but more difficult.

Quintilian, therefore, suggests what he calls something "simpler" (11.2.26), namely, to cut down a section of text into shorter pieces, which simply must be learned by heart (11.2.27–31). To facilitate such textual memorizing, he recommends using the same wax tablet each time we turn to a particular text. Switching tablets between readings causes undue confusion: "Something that every student will find useful is to learn by heart from the same tablets on which he wrote the speech. He thus pursues his memory along a trail, as it were, and sees in his mind's eye not only the pages but almost the actual lines: and so, when he speaks, he is almost in the position of a person reading aloud" (11.2.32). In short, Quintilian focuses on the text itself rather than on associating topics and words with pictures.

6. Yates, *The Art of Memory*, 26.

7. Zinn, "Hugh of Saint Victor and the Art of Memory," 212–13; cf. Carruthers, *Book of Memory*, 92–93; Arvay, "Private Passions," 39–40.

8. I am using the Russell edition of Quintilian, *The Orator's Education: Books 11–12*.

In some sense, all memorizing uses images, because it always depends on sense perception, which produces images in the mind. Even Quintilian's slimmed-down approach makes use of them; this is why he recommends not switching tablets if we want to memorize a certain passage. We have an image in our mind of how the lines of the text run, where the words carved in wax are perhaps somewhat uneven, where the letters were maybe unduly small, and so on. Even in the age of printing, which introduced far more homogeneous pages of text, the position of a piece of text, especially of tables or bulleted lists, often fixes itself as a picture in our mind. (One serious drawback of digital texts is its decontextualized character: Changing font and size, and scrolling up and down the page, inhibit memorization and encourage distraction.)

Ark of Treasures: The Threefold Method of Hugh's Chronicle

Christians in the early Middle Ages mostly followed Quintilian rather than Cicero. Many were apprehensive of the fanciful architectonics of the *loci et imagines* tradition. Susan Arvay comments that Christian teachers and rhetoricians of this period tended to focus on dividing texts (*divisio*) into manageable portions that could be memorized and subsequently put back together (*compositio*).[9] This approach hardly constituted an "art of memory," argues Arvay. Authors of this period did not use "*imagines agentes* [vivid pictures], but static visual markers to aid in the remembrance of blocks of text. During the early medieval period, memory was treated as a skill honed by repetition of reading and writing, not as an art."[10] Arvay does not discuss the logic behind this austere approach of the early Middle Ages. Presumably it has to do at least in part with Quintilian's observation: Memorizing individual words by means of images is cumbersome—particularly when in a monastic context, one has to commit large blocks of text (even the entire Psalter) to memory. In some circles, the desire to simplify may also have been linked with an iconoclastic fear of images in general.[11]

---

9. Arvay, "Private Passions," 40.

10. Arvay, "Private Passions," 41.

11. Mary Carruthers argues that the twelfth-century Cistercians were not opposed to images per se: Bernard of Clairvaux's sermons often deliberately evoke mental pictures. Bernard, according to Carruthers, wanted people to arrive at *their own* images rather than simply to adopt those presented by others: "Bernard's is not the iconoclasm of a

Memory and Character Formation

Hugh of Saint Victor, for the most part, followed the early Middle Ages in using Quintilian's "simpler" method. His work entitled *Chronicle* consists of some thirty-seven lengthy folios of tables and diagrams outlining biblical and church historical events. To help his students in their daunting task of committing the numerous persons, places, and dates to memory, Hugh provides some practical advice in his Preface. He elaborates on the metaphor of the heart as an ark or strongbox by commenting:

> As you study all of knowledge, you store up for yourselves good treasures (*thesauros*), immortal treasures (*thesauros*), incorruptible treasures (*thesauros*), which never decay nor lose the beauty of their brightness. In the treasure-house (*thesauris*) of wisdom are various sorts of wealth, and many filing-places in the store-house (*archa*) of your heart. In one place is put gold, in another silver, in another precious jewels. Their orderly arrangement (*Dispositio ordinis*) is clarity of knowledge. Dispose and separate each single thing into its own place (*locis suis*), this into its and that into its, so that you may know what has been placed here and what there. Confusion is the mother of ignorance and forgetfulness, but orderly arrangement (*discretio*) illuminates the intelligence and secures memory (*memoriam*). (*TBMA* 339)

For Hugh, the heart is a strongbox with multiple compartments or places (*loci*), each of which has its own treasure. Gold, silver, and precious jewels are all stored in their own proper place, so that an orderly arrangement (*dispositio* or *discretio*) results. The purpose of this careful arrangement of treasures is to illumine the understanding and to secure memory.

John Cassian or an Origen, worried about the perpetuation of old mental habits attached to sets of pagan images, but is more like the concern that leads parents to forbid their children to watch television or play video games lest their imagination and attention span remain undeveloped, ineffectual, and 'torpid.'" Carruthers, *The Craft of Thought*, 87. I am not quite convinced that this is actually Bernard's argument, but Carruthers's observation is important in terms of what images do to the imagination.

Frances A. Yates draws attention to the importance of Ramist logic in Protestant attitudes toward memory. Ramus abolished memory as one of the five canons of rhetoric, because his well-known bifurcated classifications (descending from the general to the particular) did not need the *loci et imagines* approach. Yates, *The Art of Memory*, 229. Yates suggests that Ramus's preference for Quintilian over Cicero had to do with his anti-Roman iconoclastic attitudes (233). Seth Long points out that in sixteenth- and seventeenth-century Protestant England, the number of memory treatises declined, while those that were written tended to move away from mental images to an imageless system grounded in a more abstract Ramist logic. Long, "Excavating the Memory Palace," 126, 135.

Hugh's Preface to the *Chronicle* offers a rather straightforward method for classifying memory items. Though he does use memory *loci*, he does not encourage his students to conjure up images in the mind. Instead, he writes: "Matters that are learned are classified in the memory in three ways; by number, location, and occasion. Thus all the things which you may have heard you will both readily capture in your intellect and retain for a long time in your memory, if you have learned to classify them according to these three categories" (*TBMA* 340).[12] With regard to number (*numerus*), Hugh recommends visualizing a sequence of numbers beginning with 1. Taking the psalms as an example, he suggests associating the first line of each psalm—the incipit—with a number: "'Blessed is the man,' with respect to the first Psalm; 'Why have the gentiles raged,' with respect to the second; 'Why, O Lord, are they multiplied,' with respect to the third; this [much] is kept in the first, second, and third compartments" (*TBMA* 341; brackets original). Once the 150 first lines have been linked to a number in one's memory, Hugh suggests creating a similar numbered list for each separate psalm, and linking the numbers with the opening words of each verse of the psalm. The upshot is, says Hugh, "I can thereafter easily retain in my heart the whole series one verse at a time; first by dividing and marking off the book by [whole] Psalms and then each Psalm by verses, I have reduced a large amount of material to such conciseness and brevity" (*TBMA* 341; brackets original).[13]

The second category is that of location (*locus*). Here Hugh recommends making a mental picture of any given section of a page. He uses the same example as Quintilian: When a boy changes copies of a text between readings, this renders it more difficult for him to memorize it. We remember a text more easily when we impress upon our minds the particulars of the writing: "the color, shape, position, and placement of the letters, where we have seen this or that written, in what part, in what location (at the top, the middle, or the bottom) we saw it positioned, in what color we observed the trace of the letter or the ornamented surface of the parchment" (*TBMA* 342).[14] The shape, color, and position of the letters assist in committing the text to memory.

12. For discussion of the Preface to the *Chronicle*, see Zinn, "Hugh of Saint Victor," 221–24.

13. Zinn suggests that Hugh's recommendation of dividing the text into shorter sections may show his dependence on Quintilian ("Hugh of Saint Victor," 223).

14. Cf. Zinn, "Hugh of Saint Victor," 223.

Finally, Hugh mentions the category of occasion (*tempus*). Here he encourages the student to remember at what point in time he first read something: "At a later time we may be able to recall to our mind a memory of the content, as we remember that one occasion was at night and another by day, one in winter, another in summer, one in cloudy weather, another in sunshine" (*TBMA* 342). Remembering the circumstances of one's reading may help trigger the mind to recall what one has read. In sum, by systematically applying the categories of number, location, and occasion, one facilitates the process of memorizing a particular text. In this way, it becomes possible not just to understand what one has read, but also to retrieve it, so as to make it useful. "Indeed," comments Hugh, "the whole usefulness of education consists only in the memory of it, for just as having heard something does not profit one who cannot understand, likewise having understood is not valuable to one who either will not or cannot remember" (*TBMA* 342–43). Understanding and remembering are not one and the same.

Hugh's *Chronicle* employ an architectural system of columns similar to that suggested by *Ad Herennium*. Hugh fills these *loci*, however, not with images but with biblical data. In other words, he avoids the problem of having to memorize both images and actual topics or words. Hugh directly enters the topics or words—numerous scriptural persons, places, and dates—into the columns, thus avoiding images altogether. It was Hugh's hope that with the help of this architectural framework—along with the advice he has given regarding number, location, and occasion—the treasures of Scripture would be transferred to his students' minds, and the *archa* of the page transformed into the *archa* of the heart.

Ark of the Mind: Reading and Meditation in Hugh's Curriculum

Hugh uses the imagery of a box or chest also in his broad-ranging curricular guide entitled *Didascalicon*, written in the late 1130s. Here Hugh describes the main function of memory as that of "gathering" (*colligere*), which he defines as "reducing to a brief and compendious outline (*summam*) things which have been written or discussed at some length" (*Did.* 3.11).[15] Hugh refers to the outline also as an "epilogue" (*epilogus*), a "short

---

15. I am using the Taylor edition, Hugh of St. Victor, *The Didascalicon of Hugh of Saint Victor*.

restatement" (*recapitulatio*), or a "principle" (*principium*) on which the entire subject matter is based (3.11). Rather than follow the winding paths of various streams—all manner of individual details—Hugh recommends instead: "Lay hold upon the source and you have the whole thing" (3.11). The reason for this recommendation has to do with the way memory functions:

> I say this because the memory (*memoria*) of man is dull and likes brevity, and, if it is dissipated upon many things, it has less to bestow upon each of them. We ought, therefore, in all that we learn, to gather (*colligere*) brief and dependable abstracts to be stored (*recondatur*) in the little chest of the memory (*arcula memoriae*), so that later on, when need arises, we can derive everything else from them. These one must often turn over in the mind and regurgitate from the stomach of one's memory (*de ventre memoriae*) to taste them, lest by long inattention to them, they disappear. (3.11)

Hugh uses the diminutive *arcula*—little chest—rather than the word *arca*, perhaps underlining the precious character of a strongbox and its contents. He recommends that after reading (*legere*), his students "gather" (*colligere*) the many, disparate elements, classifying them by means of the various compartments of the memory chest. Whereas memorizing reduces the many (facts) to the one (principle), in subsequent restatement the one (principle) reproduces the many (facts). Hugh then adds a second metaphor: The memory is not only a chest (*arcula*) but also a stomach (*venter memoriae*). Hugh uses this image to talk about the power of recall, which memory affords. Just as certain animals bring up food from the stomach so as to chew the cud, so the mind can bring up items from the stomach of one's memory.

One of the intriguing aspects of Hugh's approach (as well as that of other medieval authors) is his lack of interest in questions of rhetoric, which had served as the primary context for the discussion of memory among classical authors. Hugh's *Didascalicon* instead gives memory a place within the overall functioning of the liberal arts curriculum and in particular within the topic of reading (*lectio*) and meditating (*meditatio*) on Scripture. He is interested in the broader formation of his students. Memory, for Hugh, serves meditation. Reading something repeatedly anchors the contents in the student's mind and thus facilitates meditation and ultimately the student's Christian growth and character.

Hugh did not isolate this practice of biblical *lectio* and *meditatio* from the broader curricular program. For Hugh, the arts as a whole (not just meditation on Scripture) had as their aim the student's restoration to God. While the *Didascalicon* does have a lot to say about the study of Scripture, it deals with every kind of knowledge, with the entire educational spectrum. All memorizing aimed at the beatific vision. "This, then," explains Hugh, "is what the arts are concerned with, this is what they intend, namely, to restore within us the divine likeness, a likeness which to us is a form but to God is his nature. The more we are conformed to the divine nature, the more do we possess Wisdom, for then there begins to shine forth again in us what has forever existed in the divine Idea or Pattern, coming and going in us but standing changeless in God" (2.1). Although it is fair to say that, for Hugh, the reading of Scripture focused directly on salvation, all education, in the end, served this same spiritual goal.

Indeed, the first time Hugh discusses the role of memory and meditation in the *Didascalicon*, he does not deal with Scripture at all. The context is that of reading and meditation in general (3.7). Meditation, explains Hugh, goes beyond mere reading: "For it delights to range along open ground, where it fixes its free gaze upon the contemplation of truth, drawing together now these, now those causes of things.... The start of learning, thus, lies in reading, but its consummation lies in meditation ..." (3.10). It is in this same general context of studying that Hugh makes his comments about memory being a gathering (*colligere*) of things into a "little chest of the memory" (*arcula memoriae*) and about regurgitating material from "the stomach of one's memory" (3.11). These comments are part of a discussion, not of biblical teaching, but of pedagogy in general. Boyd Coolman rightly suggests, therefore, that on Hugh's understanding, "educational formation has a spiritual *telos*. By it, the soul begins to be formed again according to the very Wisdom in whose image it was originally created."[16] God has given us a little chest (*arcula*) to store all manner of things—in order that all knowledge, "secular" as well as "sacred," might aid in restoring the human person.

To be sure, Hugh does draw attention to memory particularly in connection with the *lectio* of Scripture. This becomes clear when in the *Didascalicon* he arrives at his discussion of Scripture. Especially at the literal or historical level of reading the Bible, he insists, the various classical mnemonic tools can prove helpful. Before one moves on from history to investigate allegorical meanings, we need to commit the literal account to memory. The historical foundation must be carefully laid before

---

16. Coolman, *The Theology of Hugh of St. Victor*, 151.

constructing the allegorical and tropological levels: "Just as you see that every building lacking a foundation cannot stand firm, so also is it in learning. The foundation and principle of sacred learning, however, is history, from which, like honey from the honeycomb, the truth of allegory is extracted" (6.3). First and foremost, therefore, the student must "learn history and diligently commit to memory the truth of the deeds that have been performed, reviewing from beginning to end what has been done, when it has been done, where it has been done, and by whom it has been done" (6.3). This recommendation is very much in line with what we have seen in Hugh's Preface to the *Chronicle*. The scriptural account must be committed to memory, and this is where classical (particularly Quintilian) mnemonic tools are helpful.

In some sense, then, memorization and meditation serve a rather pedestrian role for Hugh. What we're dealing with is simply the reading and rereading of the textual material—chewing the cud again and again so as to make it our own. But regardless of the mundane character of chewing the cud, something deeply formative takes place in this activity. Ivan Illich reflects on this in his commentary on Hugh's *Didascalicon*. He explains:

> For the monastic reader, whom Hugh addresses, reading is a much less phantasmagoric and much more carnal activity: the reader understands the lines by moving to their beat, remembers them by recapturing their rhythm, and thinks of them in terms of putting them into his mouth and chewing. No wonder that pre-university monasteries are described to us in various sources as the dwelling places of mumblers and munchers.[17]

The notion of chewing the cud, though it originated with Quintilian in the classical period,[18] took on particular poignancy for Christian readers of Scripture. The imagery reminded them of biblical passages such as Psalm 118(119):103 ("How sweet are thy words to my taste, sweeter than honey to my mouth!"); Ezekiel 3:3 ("'Son of man, eat this scroll that I give you and fill your stomach with it.' Then I ate it; and it was in my mouth as sweet as honey"); and Revelation 10:9–10 ("So I went to the angel and told him to give me the little scroll; and he said to me, 'Take it and eat; it will be bitter

---

17. Illich, *In the Vineyard of the Text*, 54.

18. *Inst.* 11.2.41: "Students of any age who are concerned to improve their memory by study should be willing to swallow the initially wearisome business of repeating over and over again what they have written or read, and as it were chewing (*remandendi*) over the same old food."

Memory and Character Formation

to your stomach, but sweet as honey in your mouth.' And I took the little scroll from the hand of the angel and ate it; it was sweet as honey in my mouth, but when I had eaten it my stomach was made bitter").[19] Though God's words were sweeter than honey—and the prophets delighted in the taste—the effects in their lives were often bitter, especially as God's words confronted people who were unwilling to modify their lives.

Long before Hugh's time, Augustine, in his *Confessions*, had referred to the memory as being like the "stomach of the mind" (*venter animi*), where gladness and sadness are stored like sweet and bitter food (*Conf.* 10.14.21). In *The Trinity*, the North African bishop had explained that the mind can snatch something from a beautiful piece of music and "deposit it in the memory as though swallowing it down into its stomach (*in ventre*), and by recollection it will be able somehow to chew (*ruminare*) this in the cud and transfer what it has learnt into its stock of learning" (*Trin.* 12.14.23).[20] Augustine's depiction of meditating and memorizing as "chewing" what one has read entered deeply into the Western tradition of teaching and biblical reflection.

Hugh repeatedly plays with the metaphors of taste, chewing, and digestion. I already mentioned his comment about summaries, which "one must often turn over in the mind and regurgitate from the stomach of one's memory (*de ventre memoriae*) to taste them, lest by long inattention to them, they disappear" (3.11).[21] Speaking of the threefold meaning of Scripture—history, allegory, and tropology—Hugh compares the exploration of spiritual meanings with searching for honey in the comb: "Thus also is honey more pleasing because enclosed in the comb, and whatever is sought with greater effort is also found with greater desire" (5.2). Comparing the study of Scripture to traveling through a forest, he warns that it is important to take a direct route rather than wander about aimlessly. "What shall I call Scripture if not a wood? Its thoughts, like so many sweetest fruits, we

---

19. Cf. Carruthers, *Book of Memory*, 209. Other biblical passages that speak of digesting the words of God are Ps 18(19):10 and Jer 15:16. For biblical references, I use the RSVCE.

20. I am using the Hill edition, Augustine, *The Trinity*. Medieval theologians often picked up on this theme of meditation as chewing the cud. Speaking of the Eucharist, William of St. Thierry comments: "As your clean beasts, we there regurgitate the sweet things stored within our memory, and chew them in our mouths like cud for the renewed and ceaseless work of our salvation." *Meditations*, 8.5.

21. Carruthers points out that Bernard of Clairvaux uses the *venter memoriae* trope by drawing on Jeremiah 4:19 ("ventrem meum, ventrem meum doleo"), translated in the KJV as "My bowels, my bowels!"

pick as we read and chew as we consider them. Therefore, whoever does not keep to an order and a method in the reading of so great a collection of books wanders as it were into the very thick of the forest and loses the path of the direct route . . ." (5.5). Recognizing the difficulties involved in journeying from study, via meditation, prayer, and performance, to contemplation, Hugh encourages his novices: "As often as we become fatigued by the journey's labor, we are enlightened by the grace of a solicitude from on high, and we 'taste and see that the Lord is sweet' [Ps 33:9(34:8)]" (5.9). And since allegorical interpretation requires "matured mental abilities," Hugh cautions his students: "Such food is solid stuff, and, unless it be well chewed, it cannot be swallowed. You must therefore employ such restraint that, while you are subtle in your seeking, you may not be found rash in what you presume . . ." (6.4). Biblical texts that speak of tasting, eating, and digesting the sweet honey of God's words were important to medieval readers such as Hugh. These texts suggested a process of meditation that opened up deeper levels of meaning. It was only through the pedestrian means of chewing—that is to say, by making the biblical text one's own through the process of memorizing—that one could advance in his spiritual journey.

Chewing the cud was not simply an evocative metaphor for the repetitive regurgitation of the biblical text as a way to ground one's meditative practices—though it was that, too. Hugh's language of chewing also makes clear that he believed memorizing shapes our identity. Just as food is digested and eventually becomes our body, so ruminative reading becomes part of us. Chewing the cud, therefore, was more than a corporeal metaphor for an otherwise strictly mental process. To Hugh and others, the metaphor held appeal in part because they recognized that memorizing is a profoundly physical act, which in turn shapes the mind. Jean Leclercq comments: "For the ancients, to meditate is to read a text and to learn it 'by heart' in the fullest sense of this expression, that is, with one's whole being: with the body, since the mouth pronounced it, with the memory which fixes it, with the intelligence which understands its meaning, and with the will which desires to put it into practice."[22] For Hugh, memorizing was one of a number of elements that involved every aspect of one's being. Hugh's curriculum was grounded in the conviction that by chewing the cud, students would consciously allow the words on the page to give shape to their being and character. Memorization, therefore, was ultimately a matter of character formation.

---

22. Leclercq, *The Love of Learning and the Desire for God*, 17.

Memory and Character Formation

Ark of Noah: A Mnemonic Tool in Hugh's Devotions

The high Middle Ages witnessed a return to the use of architectonics and images, a tendency that both carried dangers and offered pedagogical opportunities.[23] As we have seen, the images of the Ciceronian approach worked only to the extent that they were vivid or shocking. Mary Carruthers points out that medieval memory writers in the *Ad Herennium* tradition (associated with Cicero) "all emphasize that making 'excessive' images for secure remembering (on the observation that we recall what is unusual more readily and precisely than what is common) includes making very bloody, gory, violent *imagines agentes*."[24] The *loci et imagines* tradition was continuously in search of images that one could easily and securely lodge in the memory. It is beyond dispute that the *loci et imagines* tradition amplified the extraordinary, the excessive, and the grotesque. Carruthers, however, wants to draw attention less to the problematic side than to the indispensability of some of these techniques: "Medieval people clearly saw it as necessary to impress memories upon the brain, those all-important, rote-retained 'habitations' and 'pathways' of their culture."[25] Carruthers is right, I think, both about the negative and about the positive aspects of the use of exaggerated images.

Several authors in the high Middle Ages recognized the importance of images for the work of conversion. The well-known turn to the human suffering of Jesus in late-medieval Franciscan devotion included extended meditation on the physical and emotional pain and suffering that Jesus underwent—and we witness around this same time a corresponding interest in the *loci et imagines* tradition. Compunction, a common medieval trope in *lectio divina*, relied on the ability of the text to pierce or puncture (Latin: *pungere*) the reader's heart, so as to elicit grief over one's sin.[26] Identification with the various stages of Jesus' passion was an important means of challenging one's affections and emotions—and so theologians in the late Middle Ages put the classical *loci et imagines* tradition to use by slotting

---

23. For a fascinating inventory, see Carruthers and Ziolkowski, eds., *The Medieval Craft of Memory*.

24. Carruthers, *Craft of Thought*, 101.

25. Carruthers, *Craft of Thought*, 102.

26. Carruthers, *Craft of Thought*, 100. Gregory the Great had spoken not just of a compunction of fear but also of a compunction of love. See McGinn and McGinn, *Early Christian Mystics*, 81–83.

the various moments of Jesus' suffering into architectural or horticultural images.[27]

Hugh, too, despite borrowing from Quintilian in his Preface to the *Chronicle*, explored the use of images (though mostly in the form of symbols), which had its roots in the Ciceronian tradition.[28] He used symbols, for example, to fill the *archa* (strongbox) of the mind or the *arcula memoriae* (chest of memory). Hugh also populated the ark of Noah (*arca Noe*) with symbols that detailed the history of salvation and one's personal pilgrimage.[29] In his treatise *De arca Noe morali*, Hugh describes the ark as being "like a storehouse (*apothecae*) filled with all manner of delightful things. You will look for nothing in it that you will not find, and when you have found one thing, you will see many [things] spread out before your eyes. There all the works of restoration are contained in all their fullness, from the world's beginning to its end . . ." (*Arca Noe* 4.21).[30] For Hugh, the *apotheca* (like our word "apothecary")—a storehouse, warehouse, or cellar—was a useful metaphor because one could easily envision it as made up of many *loci* in which to slot numerous symbols or images to be committed to memory.

Hugh quadruples the numerous rooms of Noah's ark by alluding to the four senses of Scripture. Each of the *loci* of Noah's ark has four different meanings:

> The first is that which Noah made, with hatchets and axes, using wood and pitch as his materials. The second is that which Christ made through His preachers, by gathering the nations into a single confession of faith. The third is that which wisdom builds daily in

---

27. Bonaventure's *The Tree of Life* (*Lignum vitae*) and *The Mystical Vine* (*Vitis mystica*) do exactly this. As such, they serve as a means of memorizing and meditating on the life of Jesus—especially his suffering. See Kimball, "Cultivating Christlikeness in and through Suffering."

28. Hugh used both Quintilian's "simpler" method of memorizing and—though in a carefully calibrated symbolic fashion—elements derived from the mnemotechnics of *Ad Herennium*. Zinn cautions against interpreting Hugh as indebted to the *Ad Herennium* tradition, the reason being that Hugh's symbols are simple figures ("Hugh of Saint Victor," 232). Hugh does indeed avoid overly elaborate and violent images. Nonetheless, his numerous symbols (listed by Zinn, "Hugh of Saint Victor," 229-30) make clear that he employs a *loci et imagines* method of sorts.

29. Mary Carruthers points out that the term *arca* was used also for a storage chest of books—a kind of portable library. Thus, one could say that the mind or the heart served as a portable library (*Book of Memory*, 51).

30. I am using Hugh of Saint Victor, "Noah's Ark: I—*De Arca Noe Morali*."

our hearts through continual meditation on the law of God. The fourth is that which mother grace effects in us by joining together many virtues in a single charity. (*Arca Noe* 1.11)

Noah's ark (*arca Noe*), therefore, not only has a historical meaning but also has various spiritual meanings: It refers to the church (*arca ecclesiae*), to the soul's meditation as an ark of wisdom (*arca sapientiae*), and to one's life of charity as offered to us by mother grace (*arca matris gratiae*). It is through memorizing that we ourselves contribute to the ark's construction. As Carruthers puts it: "Hugh's words make it clear that it is memory he means by this last 'ark'; *meditatio* is the stage at which reading is memorized and changed into personal experience."[31] By meditating on Scripture and memorizing it, we construct an ark of wisdom (the third ark) and so build charity and character (the fourth ark).

Hugh added to his four-part treatise on Noah's ark a fifth part, often referred to as *A Little Book on Constructing Noah's Ark* (*Libellus de formatione Arche*). Here especially, Hugh shows himself an heir to the classical *loci et imagines* tradition. He describes an actual picture of Noah's ark, as a kind of *thesaurus*, a strongbox with numerous levels and rooms that map details both of the history of salvation and of the spiritual life of the believer.[32] Hugh begins by discussing the literal structure of the ark (1.2–2.6). He then moves to a portrayal of the ark as the church, thus turning to an allegorical reading. Here he presents the ark as a Christ-shaped structure,[33] by outlining the history of the church, listing the patriarchs and popes, a genealogy that runs across the length of the ark (3.7–4.10). This same history can also be divided into three periods: natural law, written law, and grace (5.11–5.13). The breadth of the ark can be read as the church consisting of Jews and Gentiles, of men and women (6.14). Next, Hugh moves to a tropological or moral reading of the ark. In this section, he depicts ladders

---

31. Carruthers, *Book of Memory*, 53.

32. The text of the *Libellus* can be found in Hugh of St. Victor, *A Little Book About Constructing Noah's Ark*. For detailed discussion of the *Libellus*, see Carruthers, *Book of Memory*, 293–302.

33. Both in the *Libellus* and in *De arca Noe morali*, Hugh is at pains to point out the Christ-shaped character of the ark. The ark itself is the church (the torso of Christ's body), with Christ's head and limbs reaching beyond the ark (*Arca Noe* 1.10). Noah represents Christ, as does the single cubit at the top of the ark (1.14). The imaginary pillar in the center of the ark is a reference (in part) to Christ as the tree of life (2.11; *Lib.* 2.5). Hugh draws a cross in the ark's innermost square of the ark, and an alpha and an omega above and below it (*Lib.* 1.2).

of spiritual progress that discuss vices and virtues (7.15–10.23), as well as rooms through which God's people have progressed through the history of salvation (11.24–14.27). Hugh concludes by surrounding the ark with a map of the world (14.28–15.30).

Unfortunately, Hugh has not left us with an actual sketch of the ark.[34] His descriptions are detailed and complex—one author comments that "Hugh allows his Ark-diagram to complicate almost endlessly"[35]—but he nonetheless expects the reader to draw the picture in his mind, where it is supposed to function as a mnemonic tool. In a sense, this complexity underscores Quintilian's concern about the *loci et imagines* approach: The use of images may complicate rather than simplify the process of memorization. In fairness to Hugh, he likely expected his readers carefully to meditate on his devotional treatise and its accompanying sketch. By spending time with the intricate details of Hugh's depiction of Noah's ark, the reader would internalize them over time and so commit to memory the various historical, allegorical, and moral meanings of the ark. Undoubtedly, Hugh's purpose with the sketch was to make it easier for Noah's ark and the ark of the reader's mind to become one and the same, namely, an *arca sapientiae*. Hugh's aim was the formation of character.

Ark of Virtue: Hugh on the Purpose of Memory

While the imagery of an *arca* was useful in highlighting the precious character of the contents that were memorized, the metaphor had its limits. In an important sense, for Hugh and others, the mind was much more than a strongbox stored with treasures, for the mind was not like a data bank to be filled with bits of information. The mind had a moral dimension. Mary Carruthers points out that, biblically speaking, to "remember" something is not just an intellectual but also an affective practice. She puts it this way:

> The matters memory presents are used to persuade and motivate, to create emotion and stir the will. And the "accuracy" or

---

34. Several times in *De arca Noe morali*, Hugh refers to a sketch or picture accompanying the treatise (1.7; 1.13; 4.21). Though it is possible that these are simply references to the *Libellus*, the language that Hugh uses seems to indicate the existence of an actual drawing, though, due to a lack of evidence we cannot be sure. For in-depth discussion, see Rudolph, *The Mystic Ark*. See also Rudolph's reconstruction online at mysticark.ucr.edu.

35. Carruthers, *Book of Memory*, 302.

"authenticity" of these memories—their simulation of an actual past—is of far less importance (indeed it is hardly an issue at all) than their use to motivate the present and to affect the future. Though it is certainly a form of knowing, recollecting is also a matter of will, of being *moved*, pre-eminently a moral activity rather than what we think of as intellectual or rational.[36]

I'm not convinced that memorizing is *more* a matter of the will than of the intellect, but still: The will is intimately involved in the functioning of memory. Desire and the imagination play an important role in memorizing. Carruthers points out that people often regarded memory images as composed of two elements, both likeness (*similitudo*) and intention (*intentio*). The "likeness" simply refers to the correspondence between the image in our mind and the thing that we remember. But the "intention" refers to one's inclination or attitude that colors an experience and emotionally shapes one's memory.[37] Memories, then, are far more than bits of information. They carry our attitudes and emotions and powerfully shape the direction of our minds.

The content of one's mind, therefore, is closely linked to the life of virtue. Our memories impact our moral lives—for good or for ill. Again, classical authors such as Cicero, *Ad Herennium*, and Quintilian had already recognized this link between memory and morals. They realized that memorizing was not just a matter of filling a hard drive with extraneous bits of digital data; or, to use a less anachronistic analogy, for classical authors, memorizing was never merely a matter of placing the right objects within the right boxes. From its classical inception, memorizing had a moral component. It was recognized that the content of the mind shapes one's character.

Cicero links memory to prudence, one of the four cardinal virtues. Prudence, he explains, "is the knowledge of what is good, what is bad and what is neither good nor bad. Its parts are memory, intelligence, and foresight. Memory is the faculty by which the mind recalls what has happened. Intelligence is the faculty by which it ascertains what is. Foresight is the faculty by which it is seen that something is going to occur before it occurs" (*Inv.* 2.53.160). Thus, whereas intelligence deals with the present, and foresight with the future, memory recalls things from the past. Although Cicero does not elaborate, his classification of these elements

---

36. Carruthers, *Craft of Thought*, 68.
37. Carruthers, *Craft of Thought*, 14.

under the virtue of prudence is significant. As Susan Arvay puts it, on Cicero's understanding "one can not be prudent without a well-furnished and well-organized memory to supply the mind with lessons from the past that inform both its understanding of the present and its predictions for the future."[38] And the later Ciceronian tradition was no different on this score: *Ad Herennium* draws a similar connection between memory and prudence (*Rhet. Her.* 3.2.3).

In the high Middle Ages, Albert the Great and Thomas Aquinas retrieved this link between memory and prudence. Aquinas's *Summa theologiae* famously deals with memory as part of a broader discussion of prudence, thereby cementing the close link between the two (*ST* II, q.49, a.1).[39] He treats memory as an intellectual virtue belonging to practical reason (II-II, q.47, aa.1-3). As a result, Saint Thomas recognizes that prudence pertains both to the intellect and to desire: "It belongs to prudence . . . to apply right reason to action, and this is not done without a right appetite" (II-II, q.47, a.4; cf. II-II, q.47, a.16). Aquinas links memory to prudence by explaining that prudence deals with contingent matters of action, while our experiences offer us direction in this. "Now experience," explains Aquinas, "is the result of many memories . . . and therefore prudence requires the memory of many things" (II-II, q.49, a.1).

Aquinas's recognition that desire plays a role in prudential judgments—and hence also in memory as an aspect of prudence—goes back to Aristotle. As Susan Arvay observes:

> Building on Aristotle, Aquinas argues that "to use an art aright a person must have moral virtue, which straightens out his loves" and provides him with "rightly disposed affection." Prudence, therefore, needs "rightly disposed affection" as much as it needs a rightly ordered memory, for "the role of prudence . . . is to charge our conduct with right reason, and this cannot be done without rightful desire" [*ST* II-II, q.47, a.4]. It [i.e., memory] straddles the boundary between the intellectual and the moral virtues because it participates in both reason and desire.[40]

---

38. Arvay, "Private Passions," 61.

39. Jörn Müller makes the point that Albert and Aquinas moved the discussion from the area of rhetoric to that of ethics, which was echoed in the Dominican memory treatises in the late Middle Ages. "Memory in Medieval Philosophy," 119.

40. Arvay, "Private Passions," 66-67.

Memory and Character Formation

By treating memory as an aspect of prudence—and so of the practical intellect—Aquinas argues that experiential knowledge (including desire) shapes moral decision-making.

Hugh of Saint Victor was of the same mind. His four books on *Noah's Ark* were a follow-up to a discussion with his fellow monks about the "instability and restlessness of the human heart" (*Arca Noe* 1.1). This instability and restlessness prevents one from attaining rest, and it is caused by disordered desire, which craves the distractions of earthly things and prevents us from focusing on things eternal. Hugh, therefore, explains how to remedy the problem of disordered desire so as to attain stability (1.2). The purpose of Noah's ark is to save us from the storms that rage against the church and the soul. Guiding his church "through the storms of this life, as it were the ark in the flood," Christ "brings her at last to the haven of eternal rest" (1.10).

Memory is not the main topic of *Noah's Ark*; Hugh rarely mentions it explicitly. Still, memory is one of the hidden keys to the book. It is memory, after all, that is the antidote to the mind's endless and aimless wandering, which is led on by the vice of curiosity (*curiositas*). "The great vice of *memoria*," comments Carruthers, "is not forgetting but disorder. This came to be called by some monastic writers *curiositas*."[41] Noah's ark was meant to function, therefore, as a means of reordering the monks' wandering thoughts and so reshaping their memories.

Modern readers are likely to be puzzled by Hugh's intricate allegorical explanations of the numerous details of the ark. The reason is: His interest was not in explaining the narrative of the flood in its literary or historical context. Hugh tried to help his monastic community at redirecting and refocusing their wandering thoughts by suggesting they memorize key aspects of the Christian faith that would enable them to reach peace and stability. The ark, we could say, functioned as a mnemonic device on which Hugh's readers could map the central aspects of the Christian faith and life that would lead them to salvation.

As we saw, Noah's ark has four meanings in Hugh's account: the historical ark of Noah (*arca Noe*), the ark of the church (*arca Ecclesiae*), the ark of wisdom (*arca sapientiae*), and the ark of mother grace (*arca matris gratiae*) (1.11). The first deals with the literal meaning, the second offers an allegorical reading, the third gives a tropological (moral) reading, while

---

41. Carruthers, *Craft of Thought*, 82.

the fourth offers an anagogical reading.⁴² Most of the treatise, beginning with book 2, consists of a discussion of the third ark, the ark of wisdom (*arca sapientiae*). Here Hugh offers a moral reading that is focused on the disciplining of the mind.

Hugh recognizes that for the mind to reach stability—to become an *arca sapientiae*—it needs proper ordering. By constantly moving from one object to the other, our memory loses its way amidst the many distractions offered by the world. Comments Hugh:

> When we let our hearts run after earthly things without restraint, a multitude of vain thoughts arises, so that our mind becomes so divided that even the order (*ordo*) of our native discrimination is disturbed. For, since the worldly things that we desire so unrestrainedly are infinite, the thoughts that we conceive when we remember (*memoria*) them cannot be finite. As from moment to moment they arise one after another in so many different ways, even we ourselves cannot give any account of whence (*quo ordine*) or how they enter or leave the mind.
>
> If, then, we want to have ordered, steady, peaceful thoughts (*ordinatas, et stabiles, ac quietas cogitationes*), let us make it our business to restrain our hearts from this immoderate distraction (*distractione*). (4.4)

Hugh counsels his fellow monks to counter distraction (*distractio*) with ordered thoughts (*cogitationes*). Only when we properly order our thoughts will also our memory (*memoria*) function properly, for the simple reason that our mind will not flit from the one object to the next.

While Hugh may not explicitly discuss memory in any detail in *Noah's Ark*, the topic of "thought" (*cogitatio*) comes to the fore repeatedly. By focusing his thoughts on heavenly things, one trains the mind's memory and so becomes an ordered person.⁴³ We should "keep the sight of earthly things out of our thoughts (*cogitationibus*)," not because the world would be evil in itself, but so as not to corrupt our memory by an undue focus on it: "to prevent our soul, which is weak by its own nature, from being further corrupted by remembering (*recordatione*) them" (4.17). At one point, Hugh

---

42. Hugh only briefly mentions the fourth ark, which he says is made up of the virtues of faith, hope, and love (*Arca Noe* 1.18).

43. In "The Soul's Three Ways of Seeing," Hugh discusses thinking, meditation, and contemplation. Of the first, he comments that it occurs "when the image of some real thing, entering through the senses or rising up out of the memory, is suddenly presented to it" ("The Soul's Three Ways of Seeing," 183).

anagogically interprets the three storeys of the ark as follows: "The first storey is right thought (*cogitatio*), the second is wise meditation (*meditatio*), and the third pure contemplation (*contemplatio*)" (4.20). Ordered thoughts facilitate memory and meditation and so yield spiritual progress.

Ordered thoughts lead to ordered lives. Or, put differently, a properly trained memory is important for the life of virtue. When he discusses the three storeys of the ark, Hugh explains that they "denote three kinds of thoughts, right, profitable, necessary" (2.8). In the first storey, we love meditating on Scripture to "ponder the virtues of the saints" (1.18). By themselves, however, these "right thoughts" do us no good. They are profitable only if we copy them. It is only "if I have taken pains not only to know, but also to perform good and profitable actions" that "my thought is profitable" and I have gone up to the second storey (1.18). Finally, it is when the "works of the virtues" (*opera virtutum*) turn into "virtues themselves" (*ipsas virtutes*)—or, we could say, when the acts of virtue become habits—that I have reached the third story: "that is to say, that I should possess within myself the virtue which I show in outward works" (1.18). And at the very top of the ark, the virtue of charity unites us to Jesus Christ—the single cubit at the very top of the ark (cf. Gen 6:16).[44] The aim of ordered thoughts is good works, which in turn lead to virtues and so to perfection in Christ.

The entire third book of *Noah's Ark* is a digression on the tree of life, located in the middle of the ark.[45] Hugh here discusses the fifteen stages of the tree of wisdom (*arbor sapientiae*)—that is to say, of Christ himself—in the hearts of believers. The exposition elaborates on the various stages of spiritual growth, beginning with the tree being sown in fear, and ending with the saints feeding from it by contemplation. For the topic of virtue, stages eleven, twelve, and thirteen are especially poignant. In the eleventh stage, the tree of wisdom flowers through disciplines. Hugh identifies the flowers as "good works," which offer hope of future fruit, are beautiful to see, and give off a pleasing fragrance (3.11). Next, he arrives at the fruit of virtue, which is the right intention hidden in the outward good work

---

44. Hugh suggests that the tiny nook of a single cubit on top of the ark denotes "Christ, who is the Head of His Church and the goal of our desires. That is why the ark is gathered to one cubit at the top" (*Arca Noe* 1.14).

45. The Genesis account does not mention the pillar that Hugh allegorizes as referring to the tree of life (which in turn is a reference to Jesus Christ). But Hugh is undeterred: "It is of no consequence whether we believe that this pillar thirty cubits in height, which we have set up in the middle of the ark, was actually there or not, so long as we understand that it was a height of that measurement and size from top to bottom" (*Arca Noe* 2.11).

(3.12). And in the thirteenth stage, the tree ripens through patience and perseverance: "Virtue begun is useless, if it be not carried through" (3.13).

For Hugh, a mind that has ordered thoughts is one that leads to good works and to virtuous character. The fifteen stages of growth of the tree of wisdom serve, much like the various levels and compartments of the ark, to provide an ordered focus for the mind. The very process of memorizing the fifteen steps helps the monks move away from the multiple distractions of the world and to focus instead on the one thing that really matters—the cultivation of virtue and, through this process, union with Christ.

Conclusion

Educational trends today do not favor "rote memorization," which too often is still regarded as incompatible with "critical thinking" and "conceptual learning."[46] Hugh's writings may serve as a valuable antidote, which upholds the role of memory as one component within a broader pedagogical strategy.[47] In particular, Hugh allows us to recognize three indispensable benefits of memorization. First, memory contributes to who we are and offers us a sense of identity. The way in which we store and recollect past sense perceptions determines how we make sense of the world today. Our memories are invariably "colored." That is to say, we have positive or negative emotions associated with our memories. The way we evaluate them has to do with our desires and aims, which Mary Carruthers terms "intentions" (*intentiones*).[48] These desires and intentions shape who we are. The interaction, therefore, between sense perceptions and our intellectual and affective evaluations of them is key to how we are formed as human beings. Monitoring sense perceptions—by favoring the intake of what is true, good, and beautiful—as well as deliberately and repeatedly recalling some

---

46. Critical reflections on "rote memorization" are legion. For some examples, see Darling-Hammond, *The Right to Learn*; and Synder and Snyder, "Teaching Critical Thinking and Problem Solving Skills."

47. Carruthers rightly observes that memory is not antithetical to creativity but conducive to it: "The orator's 'art of memory' was not an art of recitation and reiteration but an art of invention, an art that made it possible for a person to act competently within the 'arena' of debate (a favorite commonplace), to respond to interruptions and questions, or to dilate upon the ideas that momentarily occurred to him, without becoming hopelessly distracted, or losing his place in the scheme of his basic speech. That was the elementary good of having an 'artificial memory.'" *Craft of Thought*, 8.

48. Carruthers, *Craft of Thought*, 14–16.

Memory and Character Formation

rather than other things that have been placed in our minds is a way of fostering spiritual development.

All animals have memory. If you hit a dog repeatedly, it instinctively learns to cower when it sees someone's hand. The dog's past experiences of being hit have, as Hugh would call it, been "stored" (*recondere*) in the dog's mind. The dog does not, however, have the capacity deliberately to "recall" or "gather" (*colligere*) what has been learned. It is the ability both to store *and* to recall—what Aristotle refers to as a distinction between memory (*memoria*) and recollection (*reminiscentia*)—that makes for distinctly human identity.[49] All human learning, everything we know, is made up of past memories. Without memories "stored" in the mind, it would be empty; and an empty memory, as we all know, detrimentally affects our identity. Without memories we have no experiences on which to base prudential decisions. The uniquely human ability of recollection makes clear that memory is tied to the will and so to human freedom. Memory is what allows us to aim for the telos or purpose for which we have been made.

We need to recall Mary Carruther's observation that "the great vice of *memoria* is not forgetting but disorder."[50] Her comment echoes Hugh's warning to his fellow monks that distraction (*distractio*) must be opposed by means of ordered thoughts (*cogitationes*). For the most part, it is not forgetting per se that is the human conundrum; it is distraction and disorder. By downplaying or perhaps even disparaging memorization, we fail to uphold what makes us uniquely human, and we render ourselves incapable both of advancing in our own spiritual pilgrimage and of passing on a larger tradition.

Second, because memory has to do both with the past (since it integrates past experiences) and with the future (in that it enables us to direct our aims), it is also connected to character and virtue. Throughout the classical and Christian traditions, scholars have recognized that virtue depends on memory—a link that the medieval theological tradition strengthened by classifying memory under the category of prudence. Hugh's entire curriculum described in the *Didascalicon* aims at character formation. Similarly, as we have seen, he treats the three storeys of the ark of wisdom as a move from right thoughts, via profitable thoughts, to necessary thoughts (2.8). It is a move from thinking about virtues in saints, via copying them in good works, to internalizing them as habits (1.18). None of this should

---

49. Aristotle, "On Memory and Recollection."
50. Carruthers, *Craft of Thought*, 82.

be mistaken for moralism. For Hugh, the entire ark is Christ-shaped. All our actions, from beginning to end, are about participating in Christ. But it is a participation that takes a particular, concrete form. The form is that of people whose very lives (their virtues and characters) are in-formed by Christ. It is by having a Christian memory—a memory grounded in the biblical story and the Christian tradition—that we are being conformed to Christ and so shaped as virtuous people. Education that takes memory seriously is education that takes human character and virtue seriously.

Finally, memorizing and meditating are, for Hugh of Saint Victor, one and the same. The common medieval tropes of "chewing the cud" and of "regurgitating" the content of Scripture were a way of articulating that memorizing is meditation. Or, at the very least, without memory one cannot meditate. It is the repeated recalling of the stored content that constitutes meditation or reflection. This link between memory and meditation reminds us that memory is indispensable to the spiritual aim of meditative reading (*lectio divina*). For Hugh, this was a sustained practice of biblical engagement that consisted of five steps: study, meditation, prayer, performance, and contemplation. Hugh thought of these steps as an ascent to God, with contemplation being a foretaste of our future reward: "You see, then, how perfection comes to those ascending by means of these steps, so that he who has remained below cannot keep ascending . . ." (*Did.* 59). Memorizing (in the liberal arts and especially in biblical teaching) was an essential step in our ascent to God. It is the small, single cubit at the top of the ark—God himself in Jesus Christ—that is memory's aim.

Chapter Eleven

The Child in the Early Middle Ages

James M. Houston

THE ELEVENTH AND TWELFTH centuries were a "hinge period" of Western civilization, for in that period there developed "the rise of the individual."[1] Previous stages of history had a more collective mindset, whether it be that of Greek or Roman cultures, or of the Gothic tribal cultures that invaded and supplanted the Roman Empire.

THE RISE OF THE INDIVIDUAL

The rise of the individual was birthed by intellectual and economic factors, such as the development of monastic communities and of market towns. The ninth-century monastic revival of the study of grammatical and logical texts enabled monks to present the Christian faith in a scholarly way. In turn, this enriched a new anthropology of the soul, so that the combination of both an intellectual and a sensual memory then deepened the spiritual exercise of contemplation.

Economically, "the hoarding/raiding economy" of the Vikings and the Normans, when under pacification, introduced an "exchange economy," with the use of money instead of weapons. This promoted towns on roads, instead of the use of the sea routes of the previous regime. At crossways, market towns evolved, the most prosperous of which could afford to build

---

1. Chenu, *Nature, Man, and Society*.

cathedrals, blending scholarship and wealth. All these new cultural elements, now promoted individual consciousness.

In turn, papal reform was promoted with the new individual context of worship, uncovering the evidence of child abuse. But before we explore this, we have to ask, what then was the view of the child? Philippe Aries, in his classic study of medieval attitudes to the child, has demonstrated that until the Renaissance the child was viewed as a miniature adult, with little sense of the developmental needs of growth.[2] This was retrogressive of the teaching of Jesus in the Gospels, where we all have to be like a child in becoming disciples, following our Lord.

THE DUAL ROLES OF PARENTING

The role of mothering was dominant as the basic natural and spiritual need, as being nurtured as a child.[3] For while the role of the father was following the Gospel's interpretation of Joseph, the medieval role of the father was more like that of a "foster parent," subservient to the dominant Marian role of the mother.[4]

Medieval nativity plays illustrate these two roles of mother and father. A living infant is ritually swaddled, placed in a cradle, and rocked by Joseph at Mary's request:

> Joseph (carrying the cradle): "Mary, I have considered it well and brought you a cradle in which we can lay the little child . . ."
> Mary (sings): "Joseph, my husband mine, help me rock the little one."
> Joseph responds: "Happily, my dear little wife, I'll help you rock the little child."
> Mary says: "Take the cradle in your hands and allow my child to be known and rock him nicely so that he doesn't cry."[5]

Both Mary and Joseph are depicted in medieval iconography as holding lilies in their hands, as expressions of reciprocal sexual purity. Later confraternities depicted Joseph as a uniting force against feuding discord

---

2. Aries, *Centuries of Childhood*.

3. See Alexandre-Bidon, *Children in the Middle Ages*; Bunge, ed., *The Child in Christian Thought*; de Mause, *History of Childhood*; Fass, ed. *The Routledge History of Childhood*.

4. Hale, "Joseph as Mother."

5. Quoted by Hale, "Joseph as Mother," 105.

between the merchant class and the church officials. For Joseph was depicted as an effective household manager, a good husband, and loving father.[6]

PAPAL REFORMERS OF THE ELEVENTH AND TWELFTH CENTURIES

But all this idealistic perspective was not reflective of the state of the medieval papacy.

Peter Damien (1007–1073) was the first papal reformer. He himself as Pope Leo IX, felt called to act like the prophet Jeremiah, as a biblical reformer. Damien bemoans sordid vices and simony (i.e., the purchase of ecclesial office), then a rampant custom. Likewise, Anselm of Bec (1053–1073), was another papal reformer, living in the eastern Italian Alps at Aosta. He has been closely studied by R. W. Southern.[7]

Guibert of Nogent (1060–1125), however, gives us a unique expose, for it is self-revelatory of what he confesses personally, like Augustine before him.[8] He was born in a Norman knightly family, at Clermont in Picardy. At birth, he turned in the womb, and would have died, but his mother prayed incessantly to save him, promising God to give him to the priesthood, as Hannah did at Samuel's birth.

Yet he was an unruly boy, bored by his strict home tutor, so he was sent off to the Benedictine monastery of Saint-Germer (1067–1105). There, he was eventually appointed abbot of Nogent (1104–1125). His mother had followed him, always living close by, until her death (c. 1108).

Then he began to write, among other works, his *Monodiae*, or *Solitary Songs*. In the first part of the book, he tells of the constraining circumstances of his early childhood, the factors that led to becoming a monk. He writes, too, about the monastic life. He is writing at a time when sexuality within marriage is nearly as regulated as the social life of a monk. Such legalism over sexual intimacy, conjoined with celibacy, highlighted "sexual sins," whether masturbation or sexual intercourse.

Along with Bernard of Clairvaux, Guibert condemned the teaching of Abelard at the Council of Sens (1141). Meanwhile, there was the further sexual scandal of Peter Abelard and Heloise. It was an age when sinfulness of the soul was preoccupied with sexual issues.

---

6. Hale, "Joseph as Mother," 110.
7. Southern, *Saint Anselm*.
8. de Nogent, *Monodies and On the Relics*.

CHILDHOOD IN THE CISTERCIAN REFORM

In the light of this sordid monastic life, the family reform of Bernard of Clairvaux and his family are so refreshing, and inspiring for all time!

Bernard of Clairvaux (1090–1153) was born at the castle of Fontaines des Dijon, in Normandy, to Tescalin, a Norman knight, and to his mother Aleth. He had seven brothers—Guy, Gerard, Bernard, Homebeline, Andrew, Bartholomew, and Nivard. He studied at a local school, Chatillon, taught by the Canons of St. Vorles. I have explored elsewhere the remarkable reform Bernard initiated, as part of a knightly family, and yet also a new monastic order.[9] For his seven brothers and his uncle all joined his initial community at Clairvaux in Burgundy.

THE CHILD GOD IN CISTERCIAN THEOLOGY

The disciples of Bernard explored further the wonder of the Child-God. Guerric of Igny (d. 1157), exclaimed that God did not just humble himself to become a man, but came as a little child! Aelred of Rievaulx (d. 1167), adored the boy Jesus and his growth to maturity. As a youth, Aelred had fled from the court life in Scotland, to found his own monastery to the south in Northumbria (appointed Abbot in 1147). There, his love of friends was celebrated in *De Amicitia*, a classic treatise on friendship. His close relation to his sister, an anchoress, and his instructions to her in *De Instit. Inclusiva* all express the sanctity of his personal life.

Indeed, as Susanna Greer Fein has expressed it, "No Cistercian father excelled Aelred in fashioning a life lived within a maternal sensibility . . . Aelred and his sister exemplify one of the first instances in English history of a close spiritual relationship between a prominent man and a devout sister."[10]

THE MEDIEVAL RECLUSE MOVEMENT

In Aelred's treatment, the anchoritic ideal reflects the miracle that took place in the Virgin's womb. The anchoritic cell, as the life of solitude, became the life that may lead to "spiritual fruitfulness." At a personal level, this led to a deepening of desire for God's love, and socially it engendered

---

9. Houston, "Bernard of Clairvaux."
10. Fein, "Maternity in Aelred of Rievaulx's Letter to his Sister," 141.

others to receive God's love. Aelred wrote a treatise, *A Rule of Life for a Recluse*, for the benefit of his sister as a model anchoress.

The Motherhood of Joseph

Meanwhile, while motherhood was so identified with Mary the mother of Jesus, there developed a new reverence for Joseph. Jean Gerson (1363–1429), another conciliar reformer, sought to adulate Joseph. In 1479, Gerson preached and wrote a long poem on the virtues of Joseph, as married to Mary, as being a wise, just man. The maturity of Joseph became iconic of the maturity of the late Middle Ages, no longer "youthful" as the Cistercian reform had been.

Julian of Norwich (c. 1343–c. 1416) is a remarkable example of a woman recluse, because of her highly educated intelligence, her intense suffering, and her interpretation of her own mystical visions. She, like Bernard before her, was living in a period of immense cultural changes, following the pandemic bubonic "Black Plague" of 1347 to 1350.

Pilgrimage was being popularized in Chaucer's *Canterbury Tales*. William Langland was publicizing the need of church reform in his *Piers Plowman*, and John Wycliffe was translating the Bible into the vernacular.[11]

Why, then, was Anchorism so popular? We shall argue that it was because of sexual abuse, which started the age of childhood. The reformer Wycliffe asks: "What cursed spirit stirith prestis to close them in stonys or wallis for all here life?"[12] Julian began writing her *Revealings* on May 13, 1373, at the age of thirty.[13]

Entombed in one's life, the anchorite, male or female, is simultaneously dead and alive, reflecting the life and obedience of the Virgin Mary, in seeking the security of entombment. For her enclosure reflects also her virginity.

Julian's intense suffering within her enclosure reflects too the sufferings of Christ on the cross, while the images of pregnancy and childbirth define the human relationship with God. We are then, "in Christ," as Christ is also "in us," in Pauline language, and this describes the shaping of the Christian life. Now the power of redemption becomes no longer within a

---

11. McCullough, *Julian of Norwich*, 343–44
12. McInerary, "In the Meydens Womb," 157.
13 Watson and Jenkins, eds., *The Writings of Julian of Norwich*, 125.

hermit's cell, but like a hazelnut in the palm of the anchoress herself, contains all things, evoking the Virgin's womb.[14]

Julian then summarizes that the mystery of the divine Trinity that is itself, as well as the created world, enclosed in the body of Christ our Mother:

> Thus in oure fader god almighty we haue oure beying, and in oure moder of mercy we hae oure reforming and our restoring, in whom oure partys to be onyed and all made perfyte man, and yeldyng and gevyng in grace of the holy gost we be fulfyllde. And our substannce is in oure fader god almighty, and oure substance is in oure moder god of all wisdom, and oure substannce is in oure lorde god and the holy gost all goodness, for oure substannce is hole in ech person of the trynyte, whych is one god. And oure sensulltye is only in the seconde person, Christ Jhesu, in whom is the fader and be holy gost.[15]

If this is a profound confession of trinitarian faith, what about the confession of children?

THE CONFESSION OF CHILDREN

Older children were called *pueri*, who were capable of confession and therefore of penance. Canons of confession treat cases of theft, talking in an inadmissible manner, fighting, theft, and several forms of sexual misconduct. These canons were derivative of the Celtic penitential or Cummean, written in Ireland in the seventh century. Evidence that sexual abuse of children was taking place is the existence of a penitential that, even when sexually abused, a boy of ten still had to perform. This suggests that intention was not taken into account, only sexual purity. That is why penance was needed also for talking, as an infringement of the rule of the elders. It helps explain further why the sexual abuse of children was thinly veiled!

Birgitta of Sweden (c. 1303–1373) did not need to hole herself up in a hermitage like Julian of Norwich; just the opposite! As a royal princess, she traveled the world, as a pilgrim to Rome and then to Jerusalem. Canonized in 1391, she was named by Pope John Paul II "a patroness of Europe," a world traveler indeed!

---

14. Watson and Jenkins, eds., *The Writings of Julian of Norwich*, 177.
15. Watson and Jenkins, eds., *The Writings of Julian of Norwich*, 180.

As a youth, she married a nobleman, Ulf Gudmarsson, bearing him eight children. A few years after his death, she moved to Rome in 1349, and then traveled to Palestine.

Like Julian, she experienced "revelations," but not of suffering, rather of inspiration of what to do for God. Like Julian she studied Latin, to ensure the accuracy of her texts recorded by a scribe in her *Revelationes*. She received these from the Virgin Mary, detailing the Virgin Mary's life with Christ as his Mother, like a mother sharing intimate details with another mother, whom she can trust.

Practically, at her home, Birgitta would sew and mend clothes for her servants, as her *famiglia*. In the Bodleian Library at Oxford there is a painting on a document of the Virgin Mary clothing Jesus with the seamless garment he wore on the cross.[16] Yet this is a child's garment, having a mysterious quality of gracing Jesus' body, both as a child and as a grown man.

In Rome, Birgitta met a Franciscan friar, encouraging him not to have an overabundance of clothing, following their founder's example, who removed his cloth of gold raiment which Francis's father had given him. Francis had taken Lady Poverty as his bride.

It was an issue that beset the later Franciscans with many problems of interpretation. The real issue was to wear a simple cloak like Jesus did. The Rule thus states: "Let all the brothers wear poor clothes and, with the blessing of God, they can patch them with sackcloth and other pieces."[17]

Although Birgitta was greatly attracted to the Franciscans, she never renounced her own regal properties, but rather used her palace as a convent, following the devotion of the poor Clares. Her Rule states that the sisters are to wear "a cloak, of gray wool," that is, wearing a tunic like Jesus'.

Legends about the holy tunic depict Jesus making it with his own hands. The Turin garment that has fascinated this generation with the rediscovery of the relic in a Milan cathedral, reflects the continual devotion to the humanity and poverty of Christ.

Birgitta, in her revelations, has the Virgin confiding to her, that she made the garment with her own hands. Reasonably, it was when she was in Palestine when Birgitta had learned that Charlemagne had brought back the holy tunic to Europe. Birgitta herself had been on pilgrimage from the abbey of Saint-Denis in Paris, to Santiago de Compostella, again tracing evidence of the holy garment.

16. Watson and Jenkins, eds., *The Writings of Julian of Norwich*, 225.
17. Watson and Jenkins, eds., *The Writings of Julian of Norwich*, 228.

The Apostle Paul's injunction to "put on the new man" (Eph 4:24), and thereby to "put on Christ" (Gal 3:27), provided Birgitta much rich imagery to meditate upon.

Like Julian, Birgitta too experienced her vision of the passion. While in Jerusalem, she had a vision of Jesus fainting at the foot of the cross, as well as of the intense pain Mary endured in witnessing her son's agony. It reflects the medieval view that Mary's labor pains were not at the birth of Jesus, but at the cross.

In a medieval lyric, and in similar devotional sources, Birgitta voices the co-passion of Mary's heart pierced by the sword that Simeon had prophesied would fall. With the fainting at the cross, these medieval sayings were reiterating that Mary was once more enduring the labor pains of birth. Birgitta then describes how in her Revelations, Mary was embracing her dead son, as she might have fondled her small child. One of the most moving medieval paintings that depicts this, I saw many years ago in the Cathedral of Minorca, in the Balearic Islands; it is unforgettable!

Birgitta then composes a lyric, which translated from Middle English is as follows:

> [O You] of all women who have lived or borne children, abide and see how my son lies before me, upon my knee, taken from the tree. You dangle your children upon your knee, with laughing, kissing, and merry expression. Behold my child, behold now me, for now my dear son, dear, lies dead."[18]

Such meditations brought a conflation of Jesus and his Mother, as a child and mother, and as a son in his manhood, now dead. The babe wrapped in swaddling clothes, placed in a manger, is now in death, is now naked without dignity, as a corpse in his mother's arms.

The famous Franciscan preacher, Bernardino de Siena (d. 1444) likewise depicts Mary's care of Jesus' body, as both the beginning and the end of his life. In a passionate sermon, he states that the sword of sorrow pierced Mary's heart when she witnessed her son's death. Childlike in death, he is taken from the cross into her embrace, as once more he reclines on her breast. The poverty of Christ's birth is like the poverty of his death. Subsequent theologians then speak of "the leaps of Christ," from heaven to the Virgin's womb, to the manger, then to the cross and the sepulcher, and finally back to heaven in the resurrection.

---

18. Birgitta of Sweden, *Birgitta of Sweden*, 242.

Catherine of Siena (1347–1380) was the younger of twins, and twenty-fourth of twenty-five children. Her father was a wool dyer, who fostered her piety, while her mother nurtured her fierce determination. Like Julian of Norwich, she had her visions of Christ, though not in his suffering, but in his glory. She was only six years old when she saw him in papal robes, enthroned above the Church of San Domenico, surrounded by the saints, and he smiled and blessed her. As happens so frequently when one has had a mystical vision—as I, too, have had—it is transformative of all one's future life. For Catherine, it shaped her never-to-be-reversed decision to belong entirely to Christ as a virgin, and in her context, to belong to the Dominican Order.

In her youthful radicalism, she joined a Sienese lay women's order of widows, who did not think it appropriate for her to be a member, so she isolated herself in contemplative solitude for three years, until one day, she felt persuaded by the love of God to reach out to others.[19]

She began to attend to the sick, and took a role as a "mamma" to the disciples drawn to her, many of whom were older and of far higher social rank. But such were her powers of persuasion. For mediation was clearly a strong gift, with her entering into local and ecclesiastical politics.

Barbara Tuchman, in her authoritative analysis of church and state relations in the fourteenth century, called it "a distant mirror of our own times." Similarly, Catharine has a vison to offer our struggles in our own times.[20]

Catharine did her mediation through letters in the last two decades of her life; some 382 letters are still extant. She addresses all conditions of society, from popes to prostitutes, queens to abbesses. But while some letters are intimate, the great majority are homilies. In the intense year of November 1377 to October 1378, she composed what she called "my book," or *Dialogue of Divine Providence*. It was inspired by a mystical experience she had had, written as a long letter to her friend and confessor, Raimondo da Capua, on October 1377.[21] Her voice became distinctive, as an educated woman, writing letters, and interpreting the culture of the times she lived in.

The Dialogue is a remarkable book, impossible to summarize in this short essay. It begins:

19. Noffke, *Catherine of Siena*, 2–3.
20. Tuchman, *A Distant Mirror*.
21. Noffke, *Catherine of Siena*, 3–5.

> A soul rises up, restless with tremendous desire for God's honour and the salvation of souls. She has, for some time exercised herself in virtue and has become accustomed to dwelling in the cell of self-knowledge in order to know better God's goodness toward her, since upon knowledge love follows. And loving, she seeks to pursue truth and clothe herself in it.
>
> But there is no way she can so savour and be enlightened by this truth as in continual humble prayer, grounded in the knowledge of herself and of God. For by such prayer the soul is united with God, following in the steps of Christ crucified, and through desire and affection and the union of love He makes of her another himself. So Christ seems to have meant when He said, "If you follow me and keep my word, I will show you myself to you, and you will be one thing with me and in me."[22]

In contrast to Julian and the hermitage tradition, there is no evidence of childhood abuse with Catherine. Her imagery is then not of the womb, but of the contemplative union with her Beloved. Her key imagery in *The Dialogue* is of a bridge, having three stairs: the first lifts her from her natural affections of this world, stripping her of sin; the second dresses her in love for virtue; and at the third, she has tasted inward peace of soul.[23]

Following the Desert Fathers, she has revealed to her five series of tears, as the source of fear:

1. The tears of damnation, and of this world's evil ones.

2. The tears of fear, of those who weep for fear because they have risen up from the sin out of fear of punishment.

3. The tears of those who have risen up from sin and are beginning to taste God. These weep tenderly and begin to serve me. But because their love is imperfect, so is their weeping.

4. The tears of the saints who have attained "perfection," i.e., maturity, in loving their neighbors and God without self-interest.

5. Here the tears are united with the fourth stage, of sweet tears, shed with great tenderness.

6. Finally, there are the tears of fire, shed without physical weeping, for they burn within the soul.

---

22. Noffke, ed., *Catherine of Siena: The Dialogue*, 25.
23. Noffke, ed., *Catherine of Siena: The Dialogue*, 44–45.

But all these stages rise further as one is freed from fear to love God.[24]

If the poor clothing of the Franciscans symbolized the vow of poverty, for Dominicans like Catherine her clothing was that of truth. It is, to use apostolic language, "to be clothed in righteousness" (2 Pet 5:5).

Clothing, for Catherine, both protects us and expresses who we are, speaking aloud in the outward transparency of our inward selves. Again we hear the Pauline admonition, "Put on the Lord Jesus Christ" (Rom 13:14). So Catherine ends her *Dialogue*: "Clothe me, clothe me with Yourself, Eternal Truth."[25]

While Julian stayed in the cell of security, like a hazelnut Catherine stayed in the Augustinian way, in the cell of self-knowledge, praying:

> Stay in the cell of self-knowledge
> There to keep and spend
> The treasure I have given you:
> A doctrine of truth founded on the rock,
> Christ the sweet Jesus.[26]

While Catherine had no need to hide her childhood innocence as we have argued Julian did, she trusted her Lord, like a child. She was born into an extremely large family of children, and she died as a child of God.

TEACHING THE BIBLE TO CHILDREN

We conclude with the issue, were late medieval children educated in the Scriptures? Yes, they always had been from the beginnings of Christianity.

This is traceable to John Chrysostom, in his treatise *On Vainglory*, where he argues in a homily on Ephesians 6:1–4 that this text speaks to children in a concise manner, since they are not yet of an age to follow lengthy explanations. Teaching biblical stories is the appropriate genre for children to understand and be nurtured morally. Jerome specifies that seven is the age when a child is ready to understand the Bible, because a child can now know the difference between right and wrong, truth and falsehood, and has some sense of shame at being in error.[27]

---

24. Noffke, ed., *Catherine of Siena: The Dialogue*, 161.
25. Fatula, *Catherine of Siena's Way*, 75.
26. See Noffke, ed., *Catherine of Siena: The Dialogue*, 9, 25, 118.
27. Gould, "Childhood in Eastern Patristic Thought."

At the origins of the Celtic Church, there is the evidence of the use of the Psalms to teach small children how to spell. For a child's slate has been discovered in a peat bog in Ireland, using the Psalms as a spelling book. The earliest children's Bible is traceable to Peter Comestor, *Historia scholastica* (1170). A whole succession of Bible stories then follow, one of the most popular being the murder of Sisera by Jael. It still is a gripping story. It seems that the popularity of such a story reflects that it was fathers, rather than mothers, that were the storytellers of the Middle Ages. It is a story repeated for the following centuries, right up to Nicolas Fontaine's version of 1670.[28]

---

28. Bottingheimer, "The Bible for Children."

Chapter Twelve

"Let the Little Children Come to Me"
Evangelicalism as a Young People's Movement[1]

BRUCE HINDMARSH

NINE YEARS AGO I was the speaker for a winter retreat at a twelfth-century castle in Austria, Schloss Mittersill. I flew with my wife Carolyn and three children from Canada, and we had a great week celebrating Christmas with Christians from all over Europe. My sister and her family came down from Poland and joined us. Afterward, we all drove back to Poland to spend time with them at their home in Łodz (pronounced *Woodge*—I always like saying the name of that city somehow; there should be more cities in the world that begin with *Woo*).

---

1. A shortened version of this article was published online on ChristianHistory.net, a web-based publication of *Christianity Today*, posted May 27, 2009, at http://www.christianitytoday.com/ch/byperiod/earlymodern/letthelittlechildrencome.html.

An Introduction to Child Theology

Some weeks before this, I was at work in my basement study in Saskatchewan reading a dense, scholarly account of the evangelical awakening in the North Atlantic world in the eighteenth century. *The Protestant Evangelical Awakening* (Cambridge, 1992) is one of a trilogy of important books written by the English historian Reginald Ward. I have never, before or since, read a book so slowly. I kept coming across towns with unpronounceable names in central Europe, towns I had never heard of but which were key centers for the earliest evangelical revivals in the modern world. I had maps spread out all over the floor of my study, as I tried to figure out the German and Polish names of towns in Silesia that seemed sometimes to have been in German lands, and at other times in Polish or Czech territory. Was Glogau pronounced *Gwog-ov* or *Glog-ow*? And was Breslau really the same place as Wrocław (*Vrawts-wav*) on my Michelin map of Poland? These places were important to get straight, though, since they were the hot spots of a revival in 1708 that began with children, spread to the adults, and soon extended along the length of the Oder River Valley from Germany to Slovakia.

Now I knew all about the revival at Northampton, Massachusetts that began among the young people in Jonathan Edwards's church in 1734 and spread up and down the Connecticut River Valley in New England. But I did not know about this earlier young people's revival in a different river valley in central Europe. I was particularly interested in a town deep in the south of Poland with the German name of Teschen that seemed to become the focus of the revival. On my Michelin map I found a town on the Polish-Czech border that was named Cieszyn on the Polish side, and Český Těšín on the Czech side. I had no idea how to pronounce this, so I phoned my sister in Poland.

Brenda? When I come to Austria and speak at the retreat this Christmas, and then we drive back to Woodge with you, it looks like we cross the border into Poland at a place spelled C-i-e-s-z-y-n. How do you pronounce that?

I heard her say something like *Chesh-in* into the phone, and that was enough to confirm that I had the right place. So, after Christmas I was going to see the place itself on the way to my sister's house. I told Brenda that there was a church I particularly wanted to see with her, if it was still there. It was called the Jesus Church, and it was where the "Uprising of the Children" in 1708 was "baptized into the church."

The Jesus Church became the nerve center of revival for Germans, Poles, Czechs, and Slovaks. This was one of a handful of churches that the ruling Catholic dynasty allowed the Protestants in the region to have, and they had to raise the money for it themselves. A Pietist pastor came in from Germany to oversee the church, but soon the services attracted thousands more than could be accommodated. Some would walk all night to get there. Though the church held 5,000 and had multiple balconies, services had to begin at six on Sunday morning and continue all day in different languages. Great crowds inside and outside the church passed the time in prayers, confessions, and ardent hymn-singing. And revival soon spread to the surrounding towns and villages.

An Introduction to Child Theology

I wanted to see this church. And so I did, with my sister, in the last days of December in 2000. I found out that Teschen (to use the German spelling) was divided down the middle in 1920 between Czechoslovakia and Poland, and that is why it has two names today. The Jesus Church, on the Polish side, is still standing. After all these years and the tumult of war (Auschwitz is only a few minutes away), the church still stands, with its soaring baroque tower, seventy-two meters high. I found a plaque on the church that told the same story I had been reading about weeks earlier in my study in Saskatchewan—of the uprising of the children in 1708 and the revival at Teschen that followed.

"Let the Little Children Come to Me"

I did more research later to follow up on what I had learned. At the Bodleian Library in Oxford I found a forty-one-page tract published in London in 1708 with the long title (typical of the period): *Praise out of the Mouth of Babes, or, a Particular Account of Some Extraordinary Pious Motions and Devout Exercises, Observ'd of Late in Many Children in Silesia.* The form "Particular Account" of "Extraordinary Pious Motions" reminded me of the style of Jonathan Edwards's report on the revival he witnessed in New England with its "Faithful Narrative" of a "Surprising Work of God." Both of these accounts were of the *strange-but-true* genre.

From the account of the Children's Revival in Europe, I learned that the revival began when school-age children of Protestant parents were not willing, like their elders, to be silenced and marginalized by their Catholic rulers. The children at Sprottau (near Glogau) began to meet in the open fields outside the town at daybreak, and then again two or three times a day. They would form a circle and pray—sometimes laying prostrate—and then sing Lutheran hymns, read psalms, devotional texts, and so on, closing with a blessing. One Protestant father was so worried about the children doing this, in defiance of the authorities, that he tried to lock his son and daughter in their bedroom. When he heard that they were going to climb out the window, he relented and let them go.

Soon the adults were gathering and forming a circle around the children. As the children were singing and praying, the adults were weeping. At several of the towns to which this revival spread, there were as many as 300 children, and later one observer reported a thousand. The magistrates issued orders to desist, but the children wouldn't stop. At Frideberg the hangman was sent with a whip to disperse the children who were meeting in the marketplace, but when he saw them at their prayers, he couldn't do it. At Breslau, some of the Roman Catholic children joined the Lutheran young people, despite strict orders from the magistrates for parents to keep their children at home. And still thousands looked on.

This then was the young people's revival that was "baptized into the church" and channeled by Protestant pastors into a regional renewal movement. And this movement was what led, ultimately, to the erection of the Jesus Church at Teschen that I saw in December 2000.

The story does not end here, though. Some Protestants in the neighboring area of Moravia were inspired by the revival at Teschen. They grew weary of religious and economic persecution and fled as refugees to east Saxony in German territory. There they found safe harbor on the estate of the pious nobleman Count Nicolaus von Zinzendorf, who established a village for them on his property. They christened it Herrnhut. A fresh revival among these refugees broke out in 1727 (beginning again with the children), and under Zinzendorf's leadership this movement was molded into the Renewed Moravian Brethren. It was among some of these same Moravian Brethren in London in 1738 that John Wesley's heart was "strangely warmed" at a meeting in Aldersgate Street.

So we can connect the dots. *One*: the children's uprising in Lower Silesia in 1708. *Two*: the revival at Teschen that followed. *Three*: the Renewed Moravian Brethren at Herrnhut in 1727. *Four*: John Wesley's Aldersgate experience in 1738. *Five*: John Wesley reads the *Faithful Narrative* of the revival under Jonathan Edwards in Massachusetts and realizes this is all one great work of God on both sides of the Atlantic.

"Let the Little Children Come to Me"

The story was more complex than this, of course. There were other taproots for the rise of evangelical religion in the North Atlantic in the eighteenth century. There was the fervor of the long communion seasons in Scots-Irish piety that fed into revival in western Scotland and then among immigrants in the middle colonies in America. There was the sort of New England Puritan tradition of community renewal that was the background for the revivals Jonathan Edwards witnessed. And there was the mix of Anglican and Dissenting devotional traditions in England that would contribute to evangelical revival in the 1730s and forties. But, still, the central European taproots of evangelicalism are important too, even though we have only begun to learn the story and pronounce the names.

In May of 2005 I was back at Teschen. This time I was lecturing to a group of Polish, Czech, and Slovakian youth workers. My sister and her husband work for a mission organization named Josiah Venture, which partners with nationals in several central and eastern European countries. There was a banner up in the room I lectured in for the first two days. It announced that these youth workers were united in praying for "a movement of God among the youth of eastern Europe that finds its home in the local church and transforms society." The national leaders I was speaking to—and many of them ran organizations of their own in their countries—were mostly in their twenties. They were children during the Velvet Revolution and the Solidarity movement. But now they were working with young people and seeing a significant spiritual awakening. It was my privilege to tell them that in the very towns and cities where they were working today, evangelical renewal had begun among young people three hundred years earlier. And I could tell them the story of the uprising of the children in the Jesus Church itself. In the group were two youth workers who were running a weekly junior high Bible study on the Czech side of Cieszyn. One of the lectures I gave was in the old Jesus Church itself.

Historians speak of upstate New York in the nineteenth century as a "burned-over district" since revivals seemed to recur so frequently in the region. I was beginning to wonder if Silesia and Moravia were not also burned-over districts.

The year 2009 was the three-hundred-year anniversary of the founding of the Jesus Church at Teschen, and there was an academic conference at the Silesian University in Poland in honor of this. It is a good time for us all to remember the important place of young people in the church, past and present.

Young people were of crucial importance in early America too. During the Great Awakening local revival began first among the young people in Elizabethtown, Boston, Bridgewater, Lyme, New Concord, Philadelphia, Ipswich, Woodstock, Easthampton, and several other places, before it spread to the adults. Many of the preachers at the outset of evangelical revival were also young people themselves, in their twenties, like the Czech leaders I met in 2005. The most famous preacher of all in the eighteenth century, George Whitefield, was called the "boy preacher." And small groups of praying children stimulated revival not just in Silesia, but also among Baptists in Northampton in England, as among Congregationalists in Northampton in New England.

Evangelicalism has always been a dynamic *movement*, with all the energy, restlessness, and idealism that this word suggests. This is in large part because it has been a movement of and for the rising generation. Roman Catholic theologians speak of religious orders as forming round a founding charism—that the Holy Spirit raised up each religious institute for a unique purpose to serve the church. Was there a founding charism in the rise of evangelical religion in the eighteenth century? I think there are many features of evangelical renewal that could be identified, but the story I've been telling here certainly reminds us of one important characteristic, namely, that young people are the life of the church.

A friend of mine who speaks regularly to teenagers likes to tell them: "You are not the church of tomorrow. You are the church of *today*." The neo-evangelical movement in America since at least the 1930s has been

"Let the Little Children Come to Me"

characterized by a tremendous energy for youth work and student organizations. This shows no signs of changing any time soon. And around the world today, where the church is growing most rapidly, it appears that evangelical forms of Christianity are again taking root among the rising generation. As Philip Jenkins reminds us, half the world's population is under twenty-four years of age, and 90 percent of these young people are in Africa, Asia, and Latin America. If the church will thrive in the twenty-first century, it will have to be as a young people's movement—just as it did at Northampton in Massachusetts and at Teschen in Silesia at the beginning of modern evangelicalism.

In Matthew 19 Jesus rebuked the disciples for hindering the children, saying, "Let the little children come to me." Whether in Silesia in 1708 or in Uganda in 2008, Jesus continues, I think, to say this same thing to the church. It has been one of the enduring strengths of the evangelical movement that it has taken this so seriously.

Chapter Thirteen

John Macmurray's Vision of the Personal Based on Child Development

Marty Folsom

INTRODUCTION

Can the study of a child open our eyes to comprehend the nature of all personal being, and maybe even to apprehend the life of God that shapes us? John Macmurray, Scottish philosopher of the personal, serves as our guide in this essay to understand connections he makes between God, the child, and the life of personal relationships. Macmurray thought as a Christian and understood philosophy as theology without dogmatism.[1] This implies that he was getting at the relational actuality of theological life, not just belief systems that remain in the mind. His philosophy pursues an implicit Christian realism that engages all levels of human thought and experience, especially the journey of a child into the world of persons. Macmurray's work pursues a search for reality that engages the fields of science, psychology, education, sociology, theology, and the life of persons in relation at the most everyday level.

---

1. Macmurray, *Persons in Relation*, 224. Hereafter *PR*.

The Personal Universe and the Child

A child is born into the world, but what kind of world is it? Investigating a road less traveled in philosophical study, Macmurray believed that the universe is best understood as being personal in nature rather than viewed as an impersonal expanse. In that the universe has order discernible in our immediate experience, it may be understood as the result of an ordering agent. Thus, we ought not to ask whether God exists, but rather how to best answer the question, "Is what exists personal?"[2] Macmurray says yes. If we pursue this question in our minds as mere theory, we will be without means of verification—the question remains stuck in our heads, left to our mental devices. But if personal existence is explored in the realm of action, he believes we can ascertain whether our beliefs fit the actuality of the world experienced in practical life. Thus, Macmurray's investigation of the personal engages in discerning how it is that meaningful relationships are possible in the world as it exists. He also hopes to create a peaceful future lived in the actual world as the goal of a forward-looking philosophy. His method aims at avoiding all theoretical abstractions of the mind, like those that tend to dominate Western thought.

Macmurray proposes that the primary datum of human understanding is the existence of the universe itself. Humans exist in active relations with what is other[3] than ourselves. The "other" that is the universe is crucial for our own personal existence—it is there and we participate in it. We are authentically selves only in relation to this other—we are persons in relation. And this "other" has a personal character; it is an act of the agent who is the Creator. An agent acts with intention; God is the ultimate agent.

Human "knowing" can mistakenly be conceived as "what is happening in our heads." If a newborn child has no thoughts, are they a person? Alternatively, knowing can be a discovery of the world through active engagement with it. Is the newborn necessarily in active engagement with others? Does "coming to know others" shape the personal life of the baby? This is the road Macmurray will pursue. If knowing is mainly in our heads, we

---

2. PR, 215.

3. "Other" in Macmurray's work can be inclusive of all that exists for a person in the world—the other that is the universe. It can also refer to personal others—all other persons human and divine. It may be referring to objects or acts that imply personal involvement—the world as other with personal ordering. One must consider the context for clarity.

default to a separation between what is in thought and what is in the world outside me. This division sabotages the structure of personal relationships.

Macmurray thoroughly resists any view that separates and isolates the human experience of *thinking* from that of *acting* in the world. Going down that road is a destructive move that loses the value of immediate experience of the world and persons who shape our rationality. "Being personal" can never be reduced to private rationality internal to the self, set against an objectively material world. Persons act and grow with each other—this is personal knowing. A child is personal and needs a caregiver in order to survive; the child dies without a personal other to care for them in fulfilling their personhood.

Personhood is a state of being connected to the world as we find it, starting with infancy. A child comes into this world prepared to attach with it, not to merely contemplate its nature. Thus, from the moment of birth, growing as a person occurs through acting in the world with a nature open to forming safe attachments with other persons.

A child grows in playful interaction within the personal world, and learns through a process of reflecting on acts of intentional involvement with the world. "That hurt; I won't do that again" is reflection after touching a hot stove. Curiosity intends to actively discover. Boredom results from a void of action.

Children desire to know the world in front of them, but they must engage in a practical discovery process to come to know God as the Creator of the world. At the conclusion of *The Self as Agent*, Macmurray proposed, "The argument which starts from the primacy of the practical moves steadily in the direction of a belief in God. To think the world in practical terms is ultimately to think the unity of the world as one action and therefore as informed by a unifying intention."[4] A child will make sense of the world as God's handiwork if that is introduced in the discovery process. This affirms that God's personal universe precedes humanity as one act that prepares the way for personal knowing.

Macmurray implicitly held that God acted to create a personal universe. The corresponding reality is that humans are created as agents to act in relation to this personal world. Thus, the fabric of reality is made by a personal agent whose action provides the basis of understanding. The human is intended to mature to fulfillment within this personal context, not just biologically, but in meaningful relationships. This process begins at

---

4. *The Self as Agent*, 221. Hereafter SA.

John Macmurray's Vision of the Personal

birth and proceeds to the creation of community. This progression is where Macmurray takes the discussion as he continues *The Form of the Personal* in chapter 2 of *Persons in Relation*, titled "Mother and Child."[5]

Macmurray interprets the world as one act progressing toward meaningful connection. This describes a personal universe. Macmurray's quest is to find the best explanation of the world as the context for human being. He held, "To conceive the world thus is to conceive it as the act of God, the Creator of the world, and ourselves as created agents, with a limited and dependent freedom, to determine the future which can be realized only on the condition that our intentions are in harmony with His intention and which must frustrate itself if they are not."[6] God's intention was to create the world and enable us to become the children of God. Anything less is a hollow existence.

Although the universe is there, at birth the infant's mind does not have the ability to reflect on where it came from. The infant lives helplessly as it receives nurturing care to sustain it. The intention of the caregiver fulfills the personal needs of the child who as yet has no intentions of its own. The God of the universe has ordered events so that the infant emerges into this world in an act of receiving grace. The infant comes into a world that is entirely personal; but the specific experience of the personal is with the mother (or another caregiver) who intends to act on behalf of the infant until the infant is able to act in response to other persons with an appropriate response-ability. The first day is its whole length of life; the caregiver is its whole experience of the personal world.

Likewise, the personal universe depicts a meaningful context for an interactive life with other persons, especially God. In an alternative worldview that prefers the material and dismisses the spiritual, a child can miss knowing the God that creates them. But as developing persons, we wonder how we became as we are. The question, "Where did I come from?" can be specific to a child or refer to humanity as a whole. This is where personal meaning is introduced or diverted. For the moment, the most important element of personal knowing is to grow in knowing and being known in love. But in our secular society, God has been relegated to the world of beliefs and ideas, out of sight and, for many, out of mind. The personal world is a private world not to be discussed. God is relegated to a product of the

---

5. PR, 44–63. *The Form of the Personal* is the name for the two volumes *The Self as Agent* and *Persons in Relation* that were Macmurray's Gifford lectures.

6. PR, 222.

mind. As Julian Stern depicts, "If a pupil asks a teacher 'why do Christians say they know that there is a God?', a teacher might, following Macmurray's lead, refer the pupil to Christian arguments for, and purported evidence for, the existence of God. What Macmurray seems to be rejecting is an answer of the form 'nobody really knows; those who believe in the existence of God simply make a leap of faith.'"[7] For Macmurray, the adventure of childhood is to see the wonder of all the world, and especially the value of friendships, and know that this is all intentionally created by God, who is still present and acting, as evidenced by personal being in relationships.

The Field of the Personal and the Child

With insight similar to Einstein, who saw the unity of the space-time field, Macmurray proposed the field of the personal. We can see neither, but both shape our experience of the world. We dwell in a nexus of personal beings who are material in nature, but exist as a personally connected network. Humans are biological in nature, and each biological being is growing toward its own maturity and dying. But beyond biology is personal interconnectedness. Even those who have died are part of the field of significant relations that still shape and sustain us. Humans are much more than mere biological beings. We are persons who are capable of knowing and being known by other beings who uniquely respond and correspond to each other. This is the field into which we are all introduced as infants; some respond better than others.

The field of the personal is constituted through a network of interactions and reflections facilitated by our unique ability for personal communication. The complex of interactions become a shared field of remembering, interfacing, and anticipating. Each human lives within humanity, a person within fields of personal relations. Hopefully, a child is born into a context of positive caregiving, the first strata of many layers experienced within the field of the personal. This field also includes the personal God who made humans as persons in this life of interrelatedness. In this manner, we are made in the image of God as personal beings nurtured by the love and acceptance of others.

For Macmurray, much of the order and relatedness in the field of the personal is not obvious to the naked eye. It was not understood by humanity until the "discovery" of the personal as the clue to history. Jesus is the

---

7. Stern, "John Macmurray," 28.

one who made clear what it meant to exist as personal beings.[8] For Macmurray as a Christian, God is the Creator of the field of personal beings, Jesus gave us insight into what God has made, and in the present we are being called back to God's original intention of communion in relationships. What we currently call Christianity has not followed well in corresponding to the intention of God, as we instead pursue lives of self-improvement, self-protection, or internalized inspiration.

The current secular world has missed understanding the personal, preferring scientific beliefs that can study the world only as object. Macmurray rejects the underlying Kantian worldview that sees world as object—which is by definition impersonal. A child is not merely an object; they are a person with other persons. When we believe that each person lives as a subject separated from others, observing the objective world, the field of the personal becomes lost. Each individual, egocentric human is conceived as an island. Macmurray sees this dualistic formulation as essentially disconnected from reality. The field of the personal is still actually there, but each individual becomes the curator of their own mental world. Acting as though they live in a seat at the theater, life becomes theoretical, a set of ideas through which to observe and reason about the world. Everything is reduced to categories that serve the managing mind. Knowledge becomes power. The field of humanity becomes a battleground of competing selves, each with protective walls and masks. This is life as an illusion and Macmurray hoped to disillusion people from this mess.[9]

The state of the modern world is disintegrating the field of the personal. Rather than creating a safe place of nurture and interrelatedness into which a child is born, the dominant Western model is a sea where each person is their own island, alone unto themselves. God is perceived as unnecessary for the most part, and distant at best. The child is encouraged to fortify and maximize their own island, with the unintended result of lonely disconnectedness in a sea of society whose contacts are occasional and not developmentally interwoven.

It all begins well. From birth, the child is oriented to the other. As they grow, their world expands in relation to others: "They are especially attracted to events that distinguish a person who is displaying an affectionate interest in them, and a readiness for interaction and play, and these

---

8. Macmurray, *The Clue to History*, 55–57. Hereafter *CH*.
9. Macmurray, *Reason and Emotion*, 22. Hereafter *RE*.

preferences are ruled by the principles of dynamic emotion."[10] Trust and friendship are the blissful fuel of a developing child. However, the emotional brakes go into action when the fear of rejection sets in. Masks go up, defense mechanisms are developed, and addictive processes of lying and hiding begin their choking grip. Where is a child to turn for relief? Too often, the family is trying to launch them to go elsewhere. Even the church can be another impersonal opportunity to look good, while the heart and honesty of a child is disregarded in pursuit of indoctrination and moral training.

For Macmurray, religion properly conceived is the field of the personal. Most religious organizations are not built on this vision. But Macmurray does not want to lose the original intent of humanity's life of connection as revealed by Jesus. For Macmurray, the essence of religion is found in the proper facilitation of human relations developed through communities that provide love, care, and growth. He favored no particular form of religion and saw failure in most religious organizations.

Focusing in, we must note that the field of the personal takes on a particular form in the life of a family. For Macmurray, the family is the human community *par excellence*—when it lives with a love that intends its shared interactions. Macmurray notes that it is not strange that the language of the development of the child is a language that corresponds with religion—love, community, etc.[11] Macmurray argues, "The adult who endeavours to create or to discover, in the context of mature experience, the form of positive personal relationship which he experienced as a child, is not indulging in phantasy, but seeking to realize his own nature as a person."[12] The family is the birthplace of the personal with all its relational potential. There are no guarantees that the process will be perfect, but the potential is ever present for healthy persons to grow.

The foundational role of the family is that it provides the ground-level experience of committed care. It is the personal space where a child enters the world as a new creation, acclimatizes to the world outside the womb, and begins to learn the customs of their particular field of the personal, hopefully with loving attention.[13] Unfortunately, a family may create either

10. Trevarthen, "Proof of Sympathy," 81.

11. *PR*, 154.

12. *PR*, 154.

13. See Folsom, *Face to Face, Volume 3*, chapter 1, for a discussion of becoming a knowing person.

a safe and loving environment or a traumatic experience that requires a life of recovery. The family's formative role in shaping emotional connections makes it significant for influencing all subsequent life connections, including with God, community, future family, and even the sense of self as a functioning person. "The family is the original human community and the basis as well as the origin of all subsequent communities. It is therefore the norm of all community so that any community is a brotherhood. So far, then, as religion is a 'projection' of the family ideal upon the larger societies of adult life or even upon human society as a whole, there is nothing illusory or fantastical about it."[14] A family is the original blueprint that may or may not be followed, but its impact will follow a child throughout life.

The study of the field of the personal in the direct relation of persons begins in infancy. The newborn child has no reflective capacity, only the immediate experience of a personal other. Thus, Macmurray claims "all human experience begins in infancy. In this way, we may hope to discover the original structure of the personal, and the pattern of its personal development."[15] The child is never a child alone. The mother must come to be known in a mutual manner for the fulfillment of the personal for the child. Nine months of bonding leads to the act of delivery, but that only begins the many differing modes of discovery to follow in forming the infant into a mature person. That process is the lifelong experience of expanding into the field of the personal initiated with mother and child.

Mother and Child

The birth of an infant presupposes a field of personal existence in the form of a family, as just discussed.[16] Macmurray specifically focuses on the role of a mother (many refer to this role as caregiver). While the infant is newly introduced to the world, he/she is dependent on the other/mother to fulfill the initial intentional acts of personal being. The personal intentions of the caregiver are to fulfill intentional acts that the infant cannot yet fulfill, such

14. PR, 155. What follows in this section is a discussion of the essential nature of religion as universal to all human cultures, unique to humans in distinction from animals, the matrix that has allowed civilizations to develop, and is inclusive of all members of a society to belong (unlike art or science). Religion, as the field of the personal, has provided the elements that have allowed generation after generation to find coherent, meaningful existence.

15. PR, 43.

16. Macmurray does not debate the tragic exceptions.

as eating, cleaning, and putting to bed. This continues until the child matures as a personal agent to fulfill its own intentions in relation to others. The motive of the child causes it to cry, but the intention of the caregiver acts to meet the need expressed. The child does not grow to replace the other, but to interface with them—we are not merely selves as agents; we are persons in relation.

At the point of birthing, the child cannot reflect or think about what might be perceived—Macmurray proposes the world is entirely personal for the infant throughout this stage, in the form of an undifferentiated other who fills their world without their comprehension. Their experience is one of a warm and embracing other who feeds, but the child cannot think that—the immediate experience precedes reflecting on what is happening. The personal interactions of mother and child become the basis for learning to think about what happens. Initially, the reality of a field of the personal is not thought—only experienced. So too with God, we experience the provision of God before we come to realize God's personal involvement with us and for us.

Later on the child begins the act of discernment, to "think" as a reflection.[17] Having been held, one comes to realize that there is an "other who may hold me." As the child grows, other persons enter their experience. They learn to recognize differences, remembering mother, father, and so on. The child's mind learns to reflect on experience. These steps do not create a new reality; they refer to active involvement through experience with personal others. Thinking functions as an internal reflection based on external relations, and for the purpose of further interactions. The child is developing the tools to connect to the reality of the field of the personal. This is a fulfillment of its original capabilities as a person created for this purpose.

With reflection comes choice. Based on developed preferences or experiences to resist, the child develops a unique interactivity with the other. Their distinctive choices form the particular character of each person, what might be called their personality—their distinguished way of being within the field of the personal. They are not separate, only distinct as a complex person in their diverse relations with others.

The reflective capacity births the process of reasoning. Reflective thought, like the negative of a film camera, is gathered data. It contains images and emotional responses of interactions with the other. These

---

17. *PR*, chapter 3.

memories and reflections may either bring desire for connection or a resistance to some unpleasant interaction. Meaningful reflections will move us towards actions that build friendships, as well as a growing understanding of all that is other than ourselves. Reason is a growing relation to the actual world based on intentional interactions.

It is important to note that human reasoning develops from experiences and the emotions that accompany them. Thus, all thoughts are emotive and responsive. These become a library that takes on a life of its own. We may end up referring to our thoughts instead of conversing with persons—these are mere opinion, uninformed by the other. We may give preference to our internal "thought world" to avoid the fears associated with particular actions. Fear of rejection, judgment, pain, or loss may detach us from living out loud in the field of the personal.

The unfiltered emotions of a child that give zest to life can be lost in a prison of self-protection. The developed emotions may form a reasonable interpretation of the world as threat. Thinking about the world may replace acting within its field of experience, especially with other unsafe persons. These children become the lonely, the detached, the shy, the reclusive, and those who suffer mental illnesses.

The quest to explore is often dismissed as childish. We are forced to grow up too quickly. Unfortunately, that diminishes the learned wisdom of children who are motivated to explore the physical and the personal nature of the world.[18] Macmurray would incline us to believe that the reflective activities of science, art, and religion are best engaged in childhood as wonder and curiosity, nurtured in the life of playful interaction. Being fully alive occurs when one is without fear and full of love for what is other. The image of God is a child fearlessly at play with good friends.

A child is born meeting the face of another, "almost immediately . . . craving intimacy"[19] with a caregiver who hopefully greets the newborn with a face of approval and delight. Is this a personal or biological need? In Macmurray's interpretation, the child sees the mother smiling and seeks connection. There is little doubt that the mother is the presence of the

18. This is referred to as objectivity by Macmurray and is picked up by Thomas Torrance, *Theological Science*, as the appropriate means of doing science. To study what is other in a manner appropriate to the nature of what is known is objectivity, rather than trying to fit the other into preexisting categories. To see a body as a friend is more objective; it engages more of what and who is there to be discovered. Torrance credits Macmurray with insight into this understanding.

19. McIntosh, *John Macmurray's Religious Philosophy*, 68–69.

personal, whose love offers what is yet to be nurtured with the child. What begins with a caring touch or gaze becomes a personal integration into a shared life of family, friends, and acquaintances extending into the nexus of relations.

But does the child desire the face? Trevarthen argues that the child actually prefers the voice over the sight of the mother.[20] This connects well with Macmurray's work where he affirms *hearing* the other as the mode of the personal over *seeing* or observing the other. While this may seem insignificant, *seeing* the *other* provides the basis of the split that undergirds Western dualism—I am here, it is there. In hearing, we personally connect with the other. But in observing, we become a subject set over against the world. This gives rise to theory/practice, spiritual/material, and all the other dualistic divisions that fracture our experience of the unitary world. The implication for Macmurray is that we are unwisely trained to prefer the world of thought and diminish the world of relating. And the voice of God becomes lost to humans beneath the dunes of human philosophy and reasoning.

Macmurray desires the restoration of the world, going back to where we got off track. In their beginning, an infant experiences only a unitary world of personal connection—skin on skin, breast, and being held, for example. Connection was God's loving intent for humanity. Over time, things changed. A face *may* continue to nurture a sense of connection and valuing. However, the face of the caregiver may also be interpreted by the child to brood with storms of frustration and anger at times. Thus enters the possibility of fear in the emotional life of the child. If this continues, a long process of defensive strategies will develop and the relationship will suffer.

The possibility of increased connection develops with improved communication. One can approach the other with such basic questions as "Are you my friend?" These habits of friendship work to fulfill the life of the personal. The child learns to trust particular others who meet for daily interaction. But each day adds varied interpretations to the apprehended moments. Both positive and negative interactions create moments of self-definition, seminal in choosing who to accept and who to avoid.

---

20. Trevarthen, "Proof of Sympathy," 85. For Macmurray, the Hebrew people *heard* God as their primary personal relation. Compare this with the Greco-Roman *observational* modes of theoretical and practical relations, thinking and organizing the world for human purposes. One focuses on relating to the personal, the other on relating to the world as impersonal.

John Macmurray's Vision of the Personal

The immediate experience of positive or negative interactions shapes one's emotional relation to the world. In time, the field of the personal subconsciously develops into a landscape of threats alongside safe persons and places. "Our survival and development take shape as a relation of dependence inscribed by individual and collective intentions. This relation of dependence is most evident in infancy and early childhood. Infants are dependent on a mother or other caregiver who creates a shared existence in the effort to sustain them."[21] But when the caregiver is absent, we are thrust into traumatic moments that format us for future times of crisis. Most tragically, some life crises lead people to believe that God is judging them. This results in a traumatic fear that creates a devastating distance filled with shame, guilt, or unworthiness.

The developing course of the child's emotional life forms into their reasonable life.[22] But each person has different reasoning. Each day holds forth questions for every person as to what is wise or pleasurable, as well as what or who is to be avoided or disengaged. Where love exists, it creates conversations that connect our reasonings. On the other hand, fear creates reasonable defenses and our relationships fracture.

For Macmurray, the life of emotion—based on acting in the world we live in—shapes our rational assessment of it. The personal gives way to rational reclusion when it is not safe—we become the child not heard. On the other hand, when the other is met with love, the personal blossoms into a recursive knowing and being known.[23] Knowledge becomes a "shared knowing," the fulfillment of relational being, rather than the "private" world of an individual. "Essentially, therefore, from the start, the child is being groomed in the ways of cooperation rather than being equipped for self-sufficiency in nature."[24] With safe others we find our completion as persons. This companionship process develops with a rationality that includes emotional connection, playfulness, and desire for a shared future together. One could say that the fruit of the Spirit is at work in this stage where love, joy, peace, and so on express core connections, developing friendships and allowing children to work through challenges.

21. Jeff Sugarman, "John Macmurray's Philosophy," 177.

22. *RE*—this is the thrust of that book.

23. See Folsom, *Face to Face, Volume 2: Discovering Relational*, chapter 4, "Discovering through the Mirrors." Recursion is a term to describe deep mutual knowing in a manner that reflects two facing mirrors that creates a corridor extending into the distance. When we know and know that we are known, we feel increasing levels of connection.

24. McIntosh, *John Macmurray's Religious Philosophy*, 73.

The caregiver-child relation takes the initial form of a developing "other-awareness" that is a "human sense" leading to maturity.[25] It is fulfilled in a life of mutual knowing that is grounded in a shared life. This could be referred to as the image of God, although Macmurray did not use this language. The intimacy of humans, within our embodied connectedness, blossoms when pursued in love and connection. As we can see, the mother and child relationship bears the imprint of human contingency, dependent on God's personal nature and creativity for human fulfillment.[26]

Emotion and the Life of Personal Development

The emotional life of the child is developed in relation to the world. Macmurray explains that what surrounds us exists both physically and emotionally as "resistance." Where there is resistance there will be a formative emotional response. Objects such as walls and fences are obvious resistance—they stop us. The floor may be conceived as supportive resistance that allows the act of walking. In either case, the child must learn to act in light of reality in a manner that is appropriate to what is other. With persons, there are some who cause caution and concern, and others who are accepting and invitational. This develops as a spectrum of emotions, a polarity ranging between love and fear in the child. Discernment guides whether to proceed or retreat. But the development of discernment cannot reside exclusively in the thinking mind. If we depend on our thoughts about others, these are likely prejudiced, prejudgments that have not engaged real relations. However, when love guides our judgment to be for the other, we act to form connections with honest openness.

In a loving, supportive environment, love will bring appropriate wisdom to face fearful situations. But when fear dominates, it will cast out love. Negative attachment issues will likely ensue in those relations. Fear's fight-or-flight mechanisms will possibly create familial or societal forms of dysfunction. Fearful situations usually traumatize us. Thus, according to Macmurray, Jesus' call was to save from fear, not from sin.[27] Children need a life not dominated by fear. Fear creates the essential break in relationships, acting from a concern for self at the expense of the other. Love creates

---

25. Trevarthen, "Proof of Sympathy," 95.
26. Which connects with Thomas Torrance's *Divine and Contingent Order*.
27. Macmurray, *To Save From Fear*.

emotionally healthy children with a concern for the other that connects and nurtures in the face of life's challenges.

If a church is experienced as threatening and judgmental, it is likely that the child will construe God as needing to be avoided. Children will miss the discovery of Jesus who came to save us from fear and to love as communities who act as friends. The teachers of a church or family are not always aware of the emotional "resistance" that a child feels. A child needs confidence that they are loved and accepted. The implications of this for attachment theory are huge. Health only happens in safe places.

In the transition from being an infant to becoming a child, Macmurray proposes that the child goes through critical emotional alterations. Having begun by feeling cared for, the day comes when the mother begins to expect the child to take care of themselves. This can feel like rejection. The fear of loss and the pain of "perceived rejection" can begin an emotional shift. Hopefully, the child will come to understand that the caregiver is acting for their good, so they will develop as a capable person. But if the child's conclusion is that the caregiver is not for them, their fear will cause them to protect or defend themselves from such threats. The protection takes on the classic forms of fight (control and rebel) or flight (withdraw). The withdrawing may be into the head or into the bedroom or the woods. The controlling may be expressed as yelling, hitting, and inviting friends who are not approved. Ultimately, these self-control strategies diminish the quality of the relationship.

Children easily get stuck in negative emotional patterns. A teen who has quietly withdrawn in compliance for years may suddenly start acting out. Often, the core love attachment was missing all along. The actions of resistance are expressions of unleashed emotions employing different strategies towards what feels oppressive. Christian homes are particularly vulnerable to this dynamic of a compliant angel transforming to a rebellious demon, especially when their relationships expand outside the immediate family.

God can become the focus of resistance. If God is used as part of a strategy of control by the parent, the parent's God will be expelled in the same exiting strategy. If there is no sense of a loving God, the faint emotional attachment of childhood will be rejected.

Organized religion can feel emotionally controlling and cause children to lose belief in an abstract God. Macmurray suggests that the field of the personal is often heartbreakingly lost or replaced by religion that has little to do with relationships. True religion, for him, engenders a community of love. The discovery of a loving God can provide an authentic emotional life grounded in the reality of this world. Macmurray's search for reality in religion seeks personal relating that is not based in human systems of control. Compliance with God is easier when the Creator God is loving and creates space for meaningful relationships instead of habitual, boring Sunday services. We must never forget that children will not lose the need for the loving field of the personal—only that context creates the possibility of healthy human development.

What is the goal of child development? Macmurray's proposal is to grow persons in relations in a life of action, not a constrained life of an abstract and idealistic mind. The child who has been schooled in the life of the mind, abstract subjects, and knowledge as a means to power will miss the primary task of connecting in a life of mutually invested relationships of knowing and being known. For Macmurray, the field of the personal, as God intended it, is not a self-serving life; it is a life of friendship with others.

The Apperceptions—Cultures in the Cradle

Macmurray saw the emotionally developing life of the child being paralleled and extended in the development of human cultures. In the same way that a child may connect in love or react in fear, so a whole culture may have a shared response to the world. A culture based in *love* will create a community of friendship. A society based in *flight* mode will withdraw to the hills, into the mind, or become conflict avoidant. A society based on *fight* will organize to win and develop military might, powerful organizational structures, and be conflict-inclined to conquer and control. Thus, the emotional life that develops in the cradle becomes the emotional life of a whole culture.

The lenses through which we emotionally view our context is called our *apperception*. It is a way of looking at the world. Apperceptions describe the way that a group interprets its context. "It is a vantage point that gives us perspective. When we look from our cultural crow's nest—for example, from within a scientific point of view, through a religious lens, or with the eyes of an artist—we 'stand under' the wisdom of one way to view and understand our world."[28] If we understand the world as safe, we connect. If the world is threatening, we withdraw or stand up to the threat.

28. Folsom, *Face to Face, Volume 3: Sharing God's Life*, 16.

John Macmurray's Vision of the Personal

Macmurray identified three ancient cultures that manifested these basic apperceptions in Western culture.[29] The *Roman* mindset or apperception was inclined to control the world with organization, military might, and structures of government; and it established an empire. The Romans focused on this material world and devalued the place of the mind. The *Greek* apperception developed an exceptional withdrawal into the life of the mind, which developed philosophy, mathematics, and, literature. This viewpoint created a thinking orientation to the challenges of the world. The Greeks valued the world of ideas and downplayed the material world. The *Hebrew* apperception was different. It found God's personal presence and oversight in the world as God's unifying act of love that produced a meaningful life. The People of God were beloved by God and created a life of loving response—the connecting apperception. These three apperceptions explore the far-reaching implications of the developmental process of the child in response to love and fear. According to Macmurray, these basic motivational orientations of a child have expanded to shape the development of civilization. But they also shaped the development of Christianity.

When Christianity interfaced with *Roman Culture*, the outcome was Roman Catholicism, a highly organized form of Christianity that feared losing control—a managed conformity within a unified system. When Christianity engaged *Greek culture*, it produced Greek Orthodoxy—a thoughtful, abstract form of Christianity engaged in the life of the mind, with worship that transcends this world.[30] Protestants were also unable to find the Hebrew way. For Macmurray, a Christianity that reflects *Hebrew* culture, emulating a child growing up in a loving home, has yet to be seen.

Macmurray's work builds on the formational development of a child in a family. His insight sheds light not only on a child's development but also on the formation of modern culture and contemporary forms of the church. Behind his whole discussion is the God who creates a personal universe and sustains the field of the personal for human fulfillment. This provides the basis for a valuable critique of what is missing. It all begins with the emotional life of a child created to be a person in relation.

---

29. Macmurray, *Freedom in the Modern World*, 74–75. See also Macmurray, *The Clue to History*, 20–21; and Macmurray, *Reason and Emotion*, 168.

30. *CH*, 131–32.

An Introduction to Child Theology

Theology and the Future of the Child

Macmurray provided insight to the field of the personal by means of the experience of the developing life of the child. He refocused the task of theological thinking from a set of beliefs or an organizational structure, to facilitating the active life of a community of persons. This envisioned community must be guided by a practical love that is a mutual form of knowing and being known. The personal character of a community must have friendship at its core, a playfulness that invites growing together, and a safety that creates connection and an acceptance of vulnerability that we call childlikeness. It must be a place where the friendship of children sets the tone for its community life, exuberant with wonder. It must encourage questioning and an engagement with stories. A constant awakening to participate in real life must echo from the simple love of Christ.

Macmurray delved back into the very heart of the Christian God to reenvision the world as the personal field of God's hospitable play for humans to find friendship again. He reintroduced Jesus as the fullness of personal life in childlikeness, resisting religion, and learning to be friends. The age of the personal is yet to come, and must be approached in the dynamic of a loving family and the nurture of children to a joyful maturity. It was Macmurray's opinion that "in the public discussions of important issues, it is apt to be theologians, rather than scientists or even philosophers, who impress one by the depth of their insight."[31]

One might say Macmurray was an idealist, but it is possible to say that his life was one of being a disciple of Jesus and a student of the Bible.[32] His philosophical task was to strip away foolish forms of "maturity" that create cultures of fear. With the discovery of the nature and development of the child he provided a paradigm that is a critical key for the future of theological thinking—and acting in friendship.

I suggest that Macmurray lived with a biblical consciousness. He unveiled the field of the personal expressed in the Bible as the overarching structure of the divine-human relation. All the families of the earth are to be blessed by the biblical God. Macmurray did not collapse into an abstract theological perspective, but assumed that this personal God created the universe and now attunes the field of the personal to be the domain of actual relating. The child is the touchstone of reality in a life of dependence

---

31. Macmurray, quoted in McIntosh, "Science and Objectivity," 23.
32. Costello, *John Macmurray*, 363.

on God's provision and presence. We all must be born again into God's personal life, as infants delight in their mother. Together we grow to maturity in the life of personal relating that was the plan all along. Macmurray functions as prophetic philosopher who facilitates theological cohesiveness that informs everyday life. He believed human relating is irreducibly grounded in the life of God. We have only to awaken to the field of God's attentive care and act from that reality—especially beginning with the life of a child.

Chapter Fourteen

Child Resilience Despite Extreme Trauma/Deprivation

ROBERT AND SUZANNE TAYLOR

Introduction

In the Prologue and Introduction of this book, one purpose is stated as "to expose child abuse as systemic to the human condition and to reveal the creative resources of childhood to overcome evil with good." The statement is also made that "child potential is fragile." Indeed, a child is very vulnerable to various forms of trauma or deprivation that can impede, disrupt, or even arrest a child's development. In their book *The Boy Who Was Raised As A Dog*, Bruce Perry and Maia Szalavitz present a well-written account, both academic and clinical, about brain development from birth to early adulthood, documenting the impact of trauma or deprivation on this development.[1] We shall refer to this book again to help underscore the tenacious reality of the creative, God-embedded resources for resilience in children when given an opportunity.

All children experience some degree of trauma during their development and the impact will vary from none to significant, depending on multiple factors. But what happens when the trauma, arising out of abuse or deprivation, is extreme? Is there still hope that good can overcome evil?

---

1. Perry and Szalavitz, *The Boy Who Was Raised as a Dog*.

In this essay, we will provide a number of examples of such extremes, examples that we have encountered during our careers as health care professionals in settings such as war zones, regions where the impact of terrorist activity was a daily occurrence, detention camps, natural disaster settings, and communities of marked poverty and marginalization. We will also draw on examples from close friends who have worked in post-genocide settings and others who serve victims of childhood sexual trafficking. It will be seen that, even in such extremes, the childhood resilience that has been ordained in creation is still viable if compassionately nurtured.

What we hope to support in this essay, in keeping with the tenor of this book on child theology, is that the *imago Dei* is not reserved only for the spiritually mature, analytical adult but rather is divinely built into (created), and is viable in the child from the onset of life. We see this as the explanation for childhood resilience.

Before embarking on the examples, one comment should be made. In the examples actual locations, individuals, and organizations will often be identified. In some, however, for politically sensitive reasons, locations and individuals/organizations will not be specifically identified.

Child Soldiers in Settings of War and Terrorism

One of our international deployments was to a war hospital in a region of uncontrolled terrorist activity. It was a neutral hospital, and casualties of armed conflict were received daily, whether civilian or military, from all sides of the conflict. This meant that we had some patients who were young men from terrorist units. Very early on it became obvious to us, by facial expressions and nonverbal conduct, that these soldiers bore a deep hatred and hostility toward those of us who were expatriates, even though we were caring for them. When we discussed this fact with our national colleagues at the hospital we learned that these soldiers had been taken from their homes as children, even as young as five, and had been raised to hate and fight and kill any and all who were of a different ideology from their own. This was mental trauma and deprivation at its worst. When we realized this the two of us made a point of daily praying that God would give us, on top of our own training and attitude, a special disposition of compassion and friendliness during our care activity. Some of these young men were badly injured and had to be hospitalized for weeks or months, requiring surgical procedures and frequent bedside care. As time went by and days turned into weeks and then months, their hatred and blatant hostility often gave way to a tolerance that then gave way to a kind of acceptance and finally to outright friendliness. Remembering the times of walking up to patients' beds and being greeted by an enthusiastic wave and a broad smile in place of a countenance full of hate causes thanksgiving to well up in us. Here was evidence of an innate, God-breathed resilience that had been suppressed for years now coming forth in response to unexpected compassion and caring.

In his *A Long Way Gone*, Ishmael Beah vividly recounts a portion of his childhood years in Sierra Leone during the civil war.[2] As a preteen, after being thrown into months of fleeing, frequently witnessing barrages of merciless killings and community destruction including the horrific loss of his whole family, he finally made it to a semblance of safety. This safety was short lived, however, and he was coerced into becoming a child soldier. Societal dissolution and violent conflict became his daily diet. Soon he became the very thing that so terrorized him just months previously. He became emotionally attached to his own machine gun, his grenades, and his knife. Killing his enemy, whether soldiers or civilians, adults or children, became his pleasure. And these escapades were often accompanied by being high on marijuana. It is difficult to imagine the level of mental trauma in this young lad. After three years he was removed from his military unit by a program initiated through UNICEF and transferred to a rehabilitation center. Despite his initial belligerence, through the help of caring staff, over time he learned how to forgive himself and to regain his lost humanity. Through the help of the UN he was able to finish his schooling. He then went on to become a member of the UN Human Rights Watch Children's Rights Division. Subsequently he established the Ishmael Beah Foundation, which is dedicated to helping child soldiers reintegrate into society. More recently he was named UNICEF's first Advocate for Children Affected by War. Such a metamorphosis could only occur if a child had divine resilience built into him.

Victims of Child Sexual Trafficking

Sadly, we live in an era when sexual exploitation and trafficking is widespread globally, including in our own country of Canada. Not surprisingly, this is particularly present in communities struggling with poverty and a

2. Beah, *A Long Way Gone*.

Child Resilience Despite Extreme Trauma/Deprivation

lack of societal resources, i.e., a double burden of sexual exploitation on societal impoverishment. Adding to this sadness is the fact that many of these victims are children, even young ones. We have a close friend who for the past thirty years has been working with partners in Cambodia for seeking out and connecting with victims of such exploitation and trafficking. Through Ratanak International, programs of nurturing in safe environments have seen lives changed and hope restored.[3] Our friend is filled with deeply sensitive stories. There are stories such as that of the nine-year-old girl who was sold for sex nearly every night by her surrogate parents; who, after being rescued and rehabilitated through Ratanak, looked back and said (to the surprise of those nurturing her), "I know that Jesus never left me during those horrible times. I knew that what was happening to me did not define who I really was." Again, there is the story of the young girl who was sold by an impoverished family to a deceitful marriage broker who had promised her a good life but, instead, exported her to China where she was a sex slave for six years. After multiple attempts at escape she finally managed to hear of Ratanak's work through an online site, successfully escaped, and found her way to the Cambodian Consulate where contact with Ratanak and her transportation back to Cambodia was arranged. Gradually, she is now on a journey toward healing.

Our friend is constantly being amazed by the level of resilience in these young folk. How could a young girl while being raped possibly hold on to the truth that, despite this horrific victimization, Jesus was with her? How could a young woman, despite having been sexually exploited hundreds of times, love teaching the Bible to other victims who are weighed down by shame? Is that possible without a deeply embedded God consciousness, a divine presence, present from birth, present from creation? Not all stories of extreme sexual abuse have happy endings, not by any means, but the potential is there; the God-given resources are in the child and can respond to God-ordained nurturing to bring good out of evil.

It is a sobering fact that human trafficking is a growing global crime. In 2012 the International Labour Organization estimated that there were more than four million sex-trafficked persons worldwide.[4] For many reasons it is difficult to know the numbers of children involved, but in 2018 UNICEF stated that children make up almost one-third of all trafficked

---

3. See Ratanak International.
4. International Labour Organization, "Global estimate."

victims worldwide, many of these for sexual exploitation.[5] Ratanak International, and other organizations like it, are attempting to address this misery at different levels: prevention, education, political advocacy, rescue, rehabilitation—and all of these efforts are tied to the truth of childhood resilience and hope.

Child-Led Households Emerging from Genocide and the AIDS Epidemic

Although few readers of this essay will have had direct contact with genocide, the term is still shocking. There have been multiple examples of this extreme of mass murder during the past century and so most will have some understanding of its dreadful impact. Because we have worked many times in central sub-Saharan Africa, the 1994 genocide in Rwanda is particularly poignant to us. Previously we mentioned the concept of "double burden"; here, in the Rwanda of the 1990s, one could say "triple burden," because as well as the background of mass impoverishment and genocide there was also the significant loss of life and of family support from the AIDS epidemic. Child orphans, with either no support or in exploitive situations, numbered in the hundreds of thousands. This scenario led to the formation of some 60,000 child-led households in the country.

In the early 2000s, a group from Canadian Baptist Ministries (CBM) began a mission in Rwanda. Soon after arrival they met a pastor from a rural area who invited them to his church and to the communities he served. The group encountered a staggering number of child-led households that faced issues of grief, isolation, vulnerability, abuse, undernutrition, lack of education, and extreme poverty. A Rwandan-CBM partnership was begun and after discussions, much prayer, and robust research that included the voices of the children themselves, plans were laid through a community-based and household approach to address the real needs.[6] Emphasis was not only on material support such as shelter, school education, and social skills training but also on spiritual and psychosocial support and compassionate mentorship. The project started as a mustard seed and grew into a tree. Although the initial name of the venture was Orphans and Vulnerable Children, two years into the program the children themselves asked that the name be changed to Children of Hope, because they were convinced

5. UNICEF, "Children."
6. Lee, "Youths navigating."

that "God had given them capacities to live full and meaningful lives." And, indeed, God did because many of these children became mentors to other households, and educated citizens contributing to Rwanda and active participants in local churches.

The published article by Laura May Lee on child-led households in Rwanda represents the robust research that was integral to the described Rwanda-CBM initiative.[7] The qualitative study reveals that in youth-headed households, despite marked constraints on them, youths demonstrate a real resilience toward desiring a betterment for themselves and their fellow youths, and that it is critical to recognize the essential importance of mentoring social relationships that enhance this resilience. In this case, those mentoring relationships were provided by the Christian community around them. Surely, this highlights the value of the church recognizing the God-given resources created within the child.

"A Child in the Midst"

One of the most radical statements that Jesus made during his ministry was to put a child in the midst of his hearers and say, "Unless you become like little children you will not enter the kingdom of heaven." There is something profoundly unique about the "child" which quietly grasps both our emotions and our intellect. When a child is front and center, any shocking scenario before us plumbs the depths of our being in a very palpable way. The cruelties of war and the atrocities of terrorism become even more horrific when our focus is drawn to a child soldier. Sexual trafficking is humanity at its most depraved but when the victim is a child our revulsion is multiplied. Genocide and epidemics are heartbreaking but when a terrified orphaned child stands alone in the aftermath our grief is inconsolable. Many of us will remember the gripping photograph that was seen around the world in 1972, of the little Vietnamese girl, naked and crying from burn pain, running away from a site that was just napalm-bombed by American forces. That photograph may have shifted the course of the war, leading to the gradual withdrawal of the American troops. A "child in the midst"!

A thoughtful exposition of the "child in the midst" as portrayed in the biblical account of Matthew 18 is found in an article by Keith White.[8] White leads Mill Grove in London, which is a Christian home of a unique

7. Lee, "Youths navigating."
8. White, "Child Theology."

extended family and residential community that began as an informal foster family in 1899 and remains a place of love and care where children and young people who cannot live with their own families are cared for in a homely atmosphere. Some of them are persons with disabilities. One of White's points is that the child possesses a special humility, one that both looks forward at the entry point of life and looks upward to the Father in heaven. This is so because of the divinely embedded resources, including resilience, given from the beginning of creation to the child by the Father.

Final Comments

During the writing of this essay our focus often returned to the statement previously quoted, that "child abuse is systemic to the human condition." While reflecting on our own experiences, we came to realize just how commonly we encountered it. Apart from the examples we have already recounted, we also witnessed it when working in post-conflict detention camps with 50,000 displaced persons enclosed behind barbed wire and where single women and children are vulnerable to exploitation; and when welcoming and supporting refugees who have been wrenched from their homeland through political persecution and the children feel all the anxiety borne by their families; and when engaging with Indigenous families who are survivors of the North American residential school system with its consequent intergenerational trauma. Yet, in all of these examples there are stories of a God-gifted resilience.

Turning attention again to the book referred to in the introduction of this essay, by Perry and Szalavitz, the subtitle of the book is *What Traumatized Children Can Teach Us about Loss, Love and Healing*. Perry has been instrumental in developing the validated neurosequential models for treating traumatized children. At the same time he makes the statement that "trauma and our responses to it cannot be understood outside the context of human relationships."[9] And these relationships involve rebuilding trust, regaining confidence, returning to a sense of security, and reconnecting to love. Perry states that what these children need most is a social environment where they can belong and be loved. This is the soil in which resilience can come to fruition. Resilience is there, but it needs to be nurtured.

We had an opportunity to meet the Vietnamese girl mentioned previously, some twenty years after that iconic photograph, at a prayer breakfast

9. Perry and Szalavitz, *The Boy Who Was Raised as a Dog*, 259.

Child Resilience Despite Extreme Trauma/Deprivation

in Vancouver. Some of the scars were still visibly present but clearly she radiated hope and peace. For years her life had been dominated by anger, hatred, and a lack of hope. Yet, she always felt deep within her a conviction that "there had to be a God, but where was he?" She read voraciously for answers and one day came across a Bible. Everything changed. She learned to forgive, to love her enemies, and she became an itinerant advocate for justice. She helped to found the Kim Foundation International, which assists children who are victims of war or are severely underprivileged. Where did that deep conviction, in her child's mind, come from that "there was a God and where was he"? Surely it was built into her, from creation, from birth, by God's compassionate will. Thus, we believe that herein lies the basis of a resilience within the child, a God-embedded imago Dei, even in the face of extreme trauma, that can bring good out of evil.

Chapter Fifteen

My Childhood Theology
For The God of My Life

Leighton Ford

An image: God is like the potter in Jeremiah's prophecy. The potter takes the clay to make a vessel, which is spoiled. He doesn't throw it out but reworks it as seems good. So God the potter takes the humus, our earthly clay, with all its potential and imperfections, and shapes and shapes us until we become something useful and beautiful in his sight.

A photo: among our family photos I have kept one of myself and my mother Ford walking together down busy Yonge Street in Toronto when I was about twelve. She is quite short and fairly stout, dressed in a fashionable coat with fur collar and feathered hat. She walks with a stern and determined look. I am tall, slim, wearing a short jacket, carrying a large book under my arm, a disgruntled look on my face.

Circa 1943, Twelve Years Old

MOTHER AND I WERE on one of our periodic shopping trips to the big city. It was not a fun trip for a boy, especially when I had to sit for hours while she had her hair done at Simpson's department store. I usually passed the time reading, and the book I carried in the photo was the latest edition of

My Childhood Theology

Chums, the Boys Own Annual. I had wanted another book but she would only let me have one. Hence my sour look.

This photo captures many facets of my early years. The oversized influence Mother had in my life. The difference in stature hinting at biological variance. The importance of reading, especially adventure stories, in my mind and imagination. The aloneness I experienced as the only son of a couple who tolerated one another and lived with very different values.

Toronto played a large part at special moments of my life. I was born there. There I was given up for adoption by my birth mother. I was dedicated to the Lord there. And there when I was twelve I first learned I was adopted.

On an autumn afternoon (and on another trip) my mother Olive took me for a walk among the leaves fallen in High Park. As we walked she told me that there had been an accident, and she and my dad had adopted me. I assumed there had been an accident that killed my birth parents. Later I realized that I was the accident!

Why she waited so long to tell me I do not know. Nor why my dad was not along when she did. "We chose to adopt you," she said. "We did not have to. But we loved you and chose you. We wanted you as our son." For some reason I was not troubled but felt very much loved.

Olive was brought up in St. George's, an evangelical Anglican church in Hamilton. In early years she also lived in Buffalo and had heard the evangelist R. A. Torrey there and remembered singing his signature "Glory Song" with crowds packing the street cars as they returned from his rallies.

At some early point she wanted to be a missionary and remembered as a girl sitting and swinging her legs and singing "I'm Going to the Congo." She never did, of course, and was not fitted for missionary life. But she did pray to have a son who would be a preacher.

When I came into her life she took me to be dedicated by Henry Frost, a Toronto-based leader of the China Inland Mission. "Dr. Frost held you," she often reminded me, "and told me that God had given you to me for a purpose." Implicit in that was the hope that I would fulfill not only my calling but hers.

In the 1920s my parents had moved to the small southwestern Ontario city of Chatham where they had purchased a jewelry business. Dad was a skilled watchmaker. Mom was the buyer with a sense of what would sell well to the local clientele.

They apparently could not or would not have children of their own. Olive very much wanted to have a son who she could dedicate to the Lord and hopefully shape as a preacher. But the early 1930s could not have been the ideal time to start a family, in the midst of the Great Depression.

In any case the adoption was privately arranged and in the fall of 1931 they took me to live in a respectable two-story frame house on the maple tree-lined Victoria Avenue.

I have very few memories of my first five years. I do have some photos that show her holding me as a baby, or later posed on a couch with a stuffed animal and curly blond hair, or in a swimsuit on some nearby beach. They were, I think, a bit too "precious." Otherwise I draw a blank.

I do know that in that first house Mother began my Christian formation. On the second floor, just above the stairs, was an alcove with a kind of prayer cabinet and bench where she would have me kneel to pray with her at my side. There she would read the Bible to me, instruct me to memorize portions, and have me repeat prayers after her, word by word. These were often tiresome times when I wanted to be outside playing, but Olive had a steely determination to give me basic spiritual training.

She would also hold up for me biographies of famous Christian preachers and missionaries and evangelists—like Dwight L. Moody, Charles Spurgeon, David Livingstone, and Charles Finney. "Leighton," she would admonish me, "God needs other leaders like that." She clearly expected me to be one of them.

Chatham was too small for her, both socially and church-wise. In spite of, or perhaps in part to compensate for her short stature (she barely reached four feet, eleven inches even in platform shoes), she always felt she was better than the farmers and small townspeople who patronized the store. I can't remember her ever having friends in Chatham except for an Anglican deaconess, Lucy Sandys, after whom I was in part named. We seldom ate at home and had most of our lunches and dinners at the Rankin Hotel.

Her sense of being "better than" others fed into my own psyche, I am sure, along with her conviction that I was special. It certainly helped to develop a perfectionist streak that made me (and those I worked with) need a lot of grace in later years!

The Anglican churches in Chatham did not appeal to her, so she decided we would go to First Presbyterian. Dad was not religious and I can't remember him ever going to church with us. But I liked the tall and

My Childhood Theology

warm-hearted Presbyterian minister and also went to afternoon Sunday school where I learned to sing "Dare to be a Daniel, and dare to make it known." The seeds of a calling were being planted.

During these years tensions were growing at home. Dad had gambled on the stock market, buying shares on margin. When the 1929 financial crash came most of their savings were lost. I don't think Mother ever really forgave him, and the loss amplified fears that had been rumbling in her since she was young.

She began to accuse my dad of spending money on other women, drinking, and stealing money from her. Eventually, by the time I got to high school, I would lie in bed trying to shut out her screams at Dad in the middle of the night. I was too young to understand that she was suffering from classic paranoia.

Whether from frustration or fear, trips to Toronto became her escape from Chatham, and eventually from Dad. When I left after high school to attend Wheaton College she followed me there for some months, and then left Chatham and went to live in Toronto and later Ottawa for the rest of her life.

"Toronto the Good" as it was then known drew her not only as a cosmopolitan city but also a center of the evangelical Christianity of that era. We bought books at the Evangelical Book Store not far from city hall. We subscribed to *The Evangelical Christian Magazine* and were thrilled when one issue featured a boy (me!) who had donated his allowance to pay for free subscriptions for missionaries. We would occasionally visit Knox Presbyterian Church, known for its biblical preaching. Once we went to St. Paul's Cathedral to hear Bishop Taylor Smith, chief of chaplains for the British Army. "Sit up and listen to him," Mother hissed, poking my side. "That's a great man!"

One of the key evangelical influencers in that era was Rowland Bingham, who was also one of the pioneer founders of SIM, then known as the Sudan Interior Mission. Bingham was instrumental in starting the Canadian Keswick Bible Conference. Modeled on the British "deeper life" conferences, the Canadian sessions were held each summer on Lake Rosseau in the Muskoka Lakes region.

Each summer from the time I was five Mom and I would go by train through Toronto to Muskoka and then by lake steamer to the rock-rimmed Keswick shore. That first year I went dutifully to children's sessions led by a returned missionary woman and a college student. At the end of the week they asked who wanted to follow Jesus. I raised my hand. They said I was too young. After this happened three times the leaders agreed that I meant it!

Three years later I was not sure I had meant it. "I was only six," I protested to Mom. "Did I really mean it?" She was wise enough to tell me to tell God. So I did. "Jesus, I think I accepted you when I was six. If I didn't, now that I'm nine I do mean it. I do trust you." So there I was.

Summer after summer Keswick was in our plans. Sometimes Mom and I would stay for weeks, sleeping in a "canvas cabin." In the mornings we would go to hear some well-known Bible teachers, and even if I was bored my mind was well stocked with Bible. Afternoons I could play croquet or swim. After supper each evening we would sit on rough lakeside seats and hear missionaries on home leave recount stories from their fields. Those were the years when the world was enflamed in World War II. For me they were the years when the fire of the gospel was also at work around the world.

Meanwhile—and it was a long meanwhile through those years—my father was never very close, emotionally or physically, but also never very far away. My most lasting image is of him hunched over his workbench, eyeglass in place, fixing the parts of a watch.

If "all the world's a stage," then Mom and I were the actors up front. Dad was a stagehand off in the wings, part of the behind-the-scenes crew who set the stage and keep the lights and sound on.

He and Mom were mostly business partners, with some small affections, but a very troubled relationship. How he put up with her baseless accusations for so long I have no idea. He was not religious but he must have had some saintly quota of patience.

In his youth he had been an altar boy in a high Anglican congregation. In Chatham he was never a churchgoer. My guess is that he relished Sunday mornings by himself while Olive took me to church. Apart from lawn bowling in the warmer months, and taking me to an occasional hockey or baseball game in Detroit, he had no diversions (or friends) that I was aware of.

In spite of Mom's suspicions, he took care of us. I always had a safe home to live in, enough to eat, and fine clothes to wear that Olive chose. Dad paid for the shopping trips to Toronto and the summer Bible conference vacations in Muskoka. Later, when I became involved in Youth for

Christ, he paid for my friend Danny and me to go to out-of-town youth rallies.

When our Wheaton College gospel team did a spring tour in Florida he flew down to hear me preach and at the end of one of my messages raised his hand to indicate he wanted Jesus, as I had raised my own hand at Keswick as a child. When Jeanie and I got married he was there; Mom wouldn't come. And the night before he died of a heart attack he sat unwell in the hall of an Ontario church to hear me preach.

I was a grown man before I realized how much I missed having a close father relationship. Once in a creative writing course we were asked to imagine an event from childhood. My memory went back to a costume party in grade school, where I went dressed in a Canadian Mountie outfit Mom rented for me. It needed to be cleaned and a residue of the cleaning fluid was left on the collar. During the party my neck began to itch and burn so badly that I left school and went home in tears.

As I wrote about that scene I tried to imagine how I must have felt. For a moment in my mind I was that small boy again, and when I got home my dad was there, put his arms around me, and said, "It's okay, son, it's all right. Let's go fishing."

Forty-Eight Years Later, Fifty Years Old

I am driving north from Toronto to the small lakeside city of Orillia to meet my birth mother for the first time.

After my mother Ford told me I was adopted she shared with me only two things about my biological parents. My mother, she said, was the daughter of an Anglican bishop, which proved not to be quite true, and my father was a Harris, which did turn out to be accurate.

Being adopted was not the problem for me as I know it is for some adopted children. As I said, I felt loved and chosen, adopted in God's family too. I was never aware of any deep need to find my birth family. But then watching *Roots* on television, and learning how the descendants of African slaves found their families of origin, made me at least curious to see if my other parents were still alive.

With the help of a friend I did find and connect with Dorothy and was now on the way to meet her. The story of that first meeting, and later with my birth father Tom, I have told at length in my memoir *A Life of Listening*.

What is of interest here is what I learned from them about my roots.

An Introduction to Child Theology

Dorothy was the sixteen-year-old daughter of a Presbyterian minister when she met a handsome young man at a summer resort. Tom Harris was an engineering student at Queens University. They had a brief fling which resulted in me! I was that "accident."

My birth certificate shows that I was first named Peter Morgan Mahaffy... Mahaffy for her family... Morgan a name from Tom's family... Peter for an odd reason. When I asked her why that name, she said, "Peter denied Jesus. Your father denied you." That seems a strange connection but surely reflects the hurt she felt.

She and Tom were in contact only once after that. Dorothy's preacher father never mentioned to her about her having a child. And although she later married a hard-drinking doctor, and had three other sons, she had separated from her husband and for years lived alone.

Tom, I learned, was descended from a quite well-known Ontario family. One of the early Harrises was a farmer/preacher who on the side invented farm machinery and whose engineering son then founded what eventually became the Massey-Harris-Ferguson company. Another was a prominent Baptist preacher who started a Bible college in Toronto that has now become Tyndale University College and Seminary. A distant cousin, Lawren Harris, was a celebrated artist, founder of the renowned Canadian Group of Seven.

So although Dorothy and Tom were not part of my childhood their genes were certainly part of me.

The fact of my adoption, and the discovery of my biological roots makes me reflect on the oft-debated question: what most forms our character and identify—is it nurture? Or nature? The genes we inherit? Or the environment in which we are raised?

And how does this affect the way we think about a "childhood theology"?

A quick biblical reflection suggests that God forms us through both. Family is a central biblical theme, as children either benefit from a godly heritage, or are devastated by human selfishness. Children may be the fruit and glory passed on through parents. Others are spoiled, because "the parents ate sour grapes and the children's teeth are set on edge" (Jer 31:29).

From Adam to the second Adam to the "new name" forecast in Revelation, God's thread runs through the story of Scripture on the way to the new family of God's children, adopted through Jesus. And Jesus is not ashamed to call us brothers and sisters. "Here am I," he says, "and the children whom God has given me" (Heb 2:13).

The "potter," it seems, works through both nature and nurture.

2020, Eighty-Eight Years Old

How does this relate to my childhood theology?
It would be an anachronism to look back and try to interpret my childhood faith through the filter of eight decades of life. But now and here, perhaps, I can say what I might have said then:

- I am loved and adopted
- Jesus is real and I can know him
- This is serious—I better be sure about it
- Prayer is important—I should pay attention to the words I pray
- So is the Bible—that's where God tells us what to do
- I can do bad things—but God still loves me
- Life is often lonely—but I am never alone
- The world is a big place—I can explore it—my life can be an adventure
- God has a purpose for me—I want to find out what that is

And, come to think about it, I might add to all that, but it's still a good starting place.

PS I should add that by the time I got to college I was no longer a "momma's boy."

Chapter Sixteen

And That Is What We Are
Embracing the Child

Mike Mason

I'VE LONG BEEN INTRIGUED by the notion of the garden of Eden as a geographical place that still exists on this earth and which, were it not for sin, we could go to. I think of childhood in much the same way. I picture it as a country, a lost parkland, like Atlantis except rural, sunk beneath the waves of adult consciousness, guarded by the cherubim of lost time and the flaming sword of innocence.

Is there any way back to this ever-ever land? There must be, for our Master Jesus bids us go there by becoming as little children (Matt 18:3). He declares childlikeness a prerequisite for entering the kingdom of heaven, which is not "out there somewhere" but within us. How could it not be, since we ourselves have lived it? Childhood is, at the deepest level, ourselves. Philip said, "Lord, show us the way to the Father," to which Jesus responded, "Don't you believe that I am in the Father, and that the Father is in me?" (John 14:10). Similarly, the Land of Childhood is within you, and not only do you know the way to it, you *are* the way.

Emmett Kelly, aka Weary Willy, was a sad-faced clown who began his career in the Depression era. A wretched, ill-starred character, he was the tramp who couldn't crack a peanut with a sledge hammer, the janitor who tried but always failed to sweep up the pool of light from a spotlight. He was famous for wearing a perpetual sad face that never smiled. One day during an interview with a reporter, he received a call from the hospital to announce, "Congratulations! You're the father of a baby daughter!"—whereupon the clown broke into a broad smile and the reporter promptly snapped his photo. It was the only photograph ever taken of Weary Willy smiling.

What is it that plasters the smile on a new father? The wonder of a new life, certainly, which one has participated in creating, and the satisfaction of knowing that one's own life will, in a sense, continue in one's offspring. All of this and more. But deepest of all, perhaps, is the invitation one senses to reenter, through the new child, the mystery of one's own childhood, of childhood itself. At birth a door opens, for both baby and parent: for the one into a new world, for the other into a lost world. So hermetic is childhood for an adult that this secret door may remain forever shut, accessible only through the help of another child as guide.

I wrote the story of Emmett Kelly's smile on my daughter's thirtieth birthday card, to tell her how, after all these years, she still puts a smile on her old man's face. Though fully an adult now, she continues to connect me with childhood because I consciously lived hers alongside her, in a way I did not—could not—my own. And this connection will deepen dramatically, I trust, when, God willing, she presents me with grandchildren.

My first trip overseas was to London, where I drank in the sights and sounds, the cobbled laneways and old buildings, the galleries upon galleries, like a man who had just crawled out of the desert. I'll never forget that first walk in Hyde Park when, after flying through the night, in London it was late afternoon and *everything looked so different* that we might have landed on another planet. O brave old world! After only a few days in the city, immediately upon leaving I felt an intense desire to return. I longed just to get back there and imbibe more of that intoxicating culture. It had never occurred to me that the land of my family origin, which I had never even wished to visit, could exercise such a deep tug on my psyche. Paris left me cold but England won my heart. And so we returned the next year and toured the country from top to bottom.

It's not difficult to go to England. But how might a grown-up return to the country of childhood? Is there not something amusing about adult theologians attempting to write a volume of reflections on the theology of the child? Are we not like so many monkeys at computer terminals? We do our best, but the telephone lines to authentic childhood have been cut, the roads flooded, the airports closed.

An Introduction to Child Theology

One need not read all 4,215 pages of Marcel Proust's *In Search of Lost Time* to know that the narrator's taste of a madeleine cake dipped in tea triggers a nostalgic memory from his childhood, which in turn sets in motion the entire seven-volume novel. Here is a writer who knew that the route back to childhood is not intellectual but sensory. My own trigger was not a madeleine cake but a daughter. And not just having a daughter, but having a daughter combined with a midlife crisis. Suddenly the idea of recovering my childhood was not just interesting but a vital necessity. At thirty-five I was, essentially, a man without a childhood, the roots of my depression buried in places I could not access. As I wrote in an early short story, "People who have had no childhoods are old at forty. They have lived their lives, they can see no way forward. There is nothing left for them but to go back, back where they have never been. This prospect is terribly frightening. Imagine being frightened of becoming a child! It's like being afraid of ice cream."

Fear (gelatophobia?) is just one of the monsters blocking our path. Another is the practical difficulty of locating our childhood, which may as well be in the garden of Eden. Where is it, exactly? Where did we leave it? We're like the old woman who lost her glasses and cannot see to find them, when all the time they're perched on top of her head.

Enter Heather, my little daughter. As she grew, each stage of her growth reminded me of certain events—and, less specifically, certain feelings—from a comparable time in my own childhood. At first these flashbacks seemed random and inscrutable, until I began to discern a consistent message in them. I was being invited to reenter, deliberately, my own childhood through the doorway of my daughter. Indeed, if I was to learn to parent her well, it was essential that I embark on this journey, for to be a good parent is first to be a good child.

This was the insight that inspired my book *The Mystery of Children*. What arrogance to presume we can parent from on high, without stooping to our child's level to accompany her on her own turf. Is this not what our heavenly Father did for us, entering our world as a little child? Here is the ultimate compassion: to embrace the weakness of the weak, the pain of the suffering, the littleness of the young.

How can we do this for others if we have not done it for ourselves? To embrace the weakness and littleness of our own childhood we must learn the truth about those years, enter the dark places hidden from our adult selves, confront suppressed traumas. With each foot of ground gained into this secrecy, we make way for the Holy Spirit to shine where he was never before admitted, and in this way—as little children—we enter the kingdom of God.

There was a time in church history when the highest service one could offer the Lord was to be a soldier of Christ. But who are the crusaders and holy warriors of today, if not those who have planted their flag in the ground of childhood, knowing that, like infants, they are "wretched, pitiful, poor, blind, and naked" (Rev 3:17). This "infantry" has healed their midlife crisis by learning to walk in the childlike beatitudes of poverty, meekness, hunger and thirst, purity of heart.

Hear the passion of the Apostle John as he writes, "How great is the love the Father has lavished on us, that we should be called children of God! And that is what we are!" (1 John 3:1). What a shout of acclamation! Boggling enough for God to have one child, his only Son; but for the divine progeny to be astronomically multiplied to all who, merely through faith, grab the coattails of the One . . .

Yet hear also the warning in John's words, as much as to say, *Dear ones, we are not the adults of God but his children.* This note carries into the next verse, surely one of the most intriguing in all of Scripture: "Now we are the children of God, and what we will be has not yet been made known." The very fact that we are now children implies that one day we shall grow up—not in this life, where our focus must be on *growing down* into greater childlikeness, but in the next life when God himself will grow us up into someone the glory of whom we cannot now imagine.

Such glory is not to be grasped prematurely. Our glory for now is in being children. As Goethe put it, "Life is the childhood of our immortality." Or T. S. Eliot: "The way up is the way down." Even the famous passage where Paul writes, "When I was a child, I talked like a child, I thought like a child, I reasoned like a child. When I became a man, I put childish ways behind me" (1 Cor 13:11)—even here, while it may sound as though Paul is exhorting us to grow up, really he is saying the opposite: Now I must rest in being a child, knowing only in part; but later, in heaven, "I shall know fully, even as I am fully known."

Thus even the most mature of believers is still but a child. John's first epistle addresses his readers ten times as "dear children," a phrase Jesus and Paul also use. Yet in our times childhood is disappearing, not only in society but in the church. Following the lead of our fast-paced, overworked culture we take on too much responsibility too soon. We walk before we can crawl and run when we ought to be nursing at the breast. Believers like the idea of being "born again," but who is prepared to be a child again?

The editor of this volume, Dr. James Houston, was ninety-five years young when he invited me to contribute this essay. He was still teaching courses, traveling the world, leading a full social life. When I asked him if he had experienced any diminishment of his energy, he replied, "Yes and no." As long as he slept for ten hours a night, with a further two-hour nap in the afternoon, he was fine! It struck me that he had reverted to the sleep patterns of a child. Here is someone who had accepted that, in order to maintain his energy, he must spend half his time sleeping—to say nothing of more hours in prayer. Many of us have never gotten enough sleep in our entire lives: not as teenagers, nor as middle agers, nor in our elderly years. We don't want to be told to lie down. If we wonder what it might look like to live a childlike faith, we could start by spending more time sleeping, resting, or simply sitting prayerfully on our Daddy's knee.

When my daughter was four years old I caught her standing on a chair and reaching up into the medicine cabinet to get a bottle of pills. Is this a picture of you? Are you always trying to make yourself bigger than you are, reaching too high for strong spiritual medicine that might be dangerous? Do you lust after signs and wonders, mystical experiences, a choice position in leadership? If we do not mature properly in our faith and character, we may be obliged to make up for it later. After years of a high profile, we may find ourselves back to crawling, or having to learn again how to walk. As the author of Hebrews scolded, "Though by this time you ought to be teachers, you need someone to teach you the elementary truths of God's word all over again. You need milk, not solid food!" (5:12).

The best way to reengage with childhood is to love a child, for we take on the likeness of who (or what) we love. In my case, certainly my daughter Heather has been my prime muse, but I've also been graced by a child I never met: my brother Jimmie, who died at age three, before I was born. His premature passing hung like a cloud over my family, the never-resolved grief oppressing my childhood with a mysterious weight I could neither see nor comprehend. Not until my thirties did I begin intentionally to seek Jimmie through stories, photographs, conversation, meditation, prayer. My middle name is William, which was the name of a minister who comforted my parents at the time of Jimmie's death. I never learned about my namesake until I asked, and that other William never came into focus until I visited the church he had pastored and saw his portrait on the wall—the

And That Is What We Are

same church where Jimmie's funeral had been held. Near our old house, I saw a stepped stone wall that my father had described, which Jimmie loved to walk along as Dad held his hand. I know Dad must have done the same with me, though I have no memory of this and he never spoke of it. Thus precious pieces of our childhood may be recovered even through people we never knew.

In my office hangs a picture of myself as a little boy—a boy about three whom I never met. This was the illustration on a calendar for February, my birth month, in the year 1955 when I was three. My mother saved it because she thought it looked like me. What is really remarkable is that this boy, my doppelgänger, is sitting at a typewriter, not typing but gazing off into space with an expression of wistful perplexity, as though searching for his next words—exactly as I do every day at my desk. Naturally my mother had no idea that I would grow up to be a writer, yet somehow, with the intuition of motherhood, she unwittingly prophesied it. Like Jimmie, this little calendar boy whom I never knew, yet whom I've come to know so well, inspires me, even holds my hand as I precariously navigate the stone wall of each day's writing.

If childlikeness were a country, it would have many border crossings. Delving into one's past, loving an actual child, reading old books—especially books we read and loved, or that were read to us, as children: these are just a few of the portals into the lost country. Another way is to revisit—in imagination—the garden of Eden before the fall. For quite apart from the imputed innocence of Christian justification, all of us carry vestiges of the original innocence of our race. We distantly "remember," as it were, Adam's thoughts as he came to himself on that first morning in Eden, and his feelings upon first setting eyes on Eve. Something of such "memories" lives in those moments when we look upon another person with childlike wonder, or when we seem to see creation as if it had sprung into being just moments ago, the paint still fresh on trembling leaves and grasses, the stars like flaring matches, just lit. As Mary Oliver put it, "Though Eden is lost, its loveliness remains in the heart and the imagination." Think of Van Gogh's "Starry Night," or of the remarkable awakening that inspired the poetry of Walt Whitman, that "chanter of Adamic songs":

> As Adam early in the morning,
> Walking forth from the bower refresh'd with sleep,
> Behold me where I pass, hear my voice, approach,
> Touch me, touch the palm of your hand to my body as I pass.

An Introduction to Child Theology

Was Adam an adult or a child when God breathed life into his nostrils? It matters not, for whoever he was, Adam was *childlike*, and our modern blood retains traces of this Edenic childlikeness. Indeed the New Testament carries hints of a return to Eden through faith: "Today you will be with me in Paradise" (Luke 23:43); "To him who overcomes, I will give the right to eat from the tree of life, which is in the paradise of God" (Rev 2:7).

Just as we retain remnants of the Eden we never knew, so we recall an Eden we did know: our experience of first seeing the light and being born again. Indeed at the time when I became a Christian there was literally a beautiful garden just down the street—the grounds of an experimental farm featuring countless exotic varieties of trees and flowers—where I used to wander for hours, or simply sit and contemplate the glory of creation in the flush of my newfound faith. To this day, I return there in imagination to relive those golden days.

For the writers of the New Testament this time of conversion is another critical door into childlikeness, which they keep calling us back to:

> Think of what you were when you were called. (1 Cor 1:26)

> Remember those earlier days when you had received the light. (Heb 10:32)

> You have forsaken your first love. Remember the height from which you have fallen! Repent and do the things you did at first. (Rev 2:4–5)

Why is our infancy in Christ so vital? We may as well question the significance of Christ's infancy and why we celebrate Christmas! It's because, as Wordsworth put it, "The Child is father of the Man." It's because this original season in our lives had sufficient power to remake us, to recreate our innocence, turning us from darkness to light as we beheld Christ for who he is and laid our hearts at his feet. What once affected us so powerfully retains its power to correct, to admonish, to inspire our present lives and to keep us on course. "Tell my brothers to go to Galilee," said the risen Christ (Matt 28:10)—because Galilee is where they had first believed. Many today make pilgrimages to the Holy Land for this very reason, because there was lived the childhood of our faith.

Currently I'm at work on a novel—a sci-fi/fantasy about angels and aliens—and while writing this essay I noticed that my story actually contains all the gateways to childhood which I have been describing. My protagonist reflects often on his own childhood; he has a significant relationship with a child; he becomes a Christian and so experiences the first glow of faith; the novel's central scene takes place in the garden of Eden; and so on. Moreover I've invented an alien world in which the beings begin as adults and grow downwards into children; another where children are treated with complete equality (for example, being allowed to govern); and still another society comprised entirely of children. While I did not consciously plan this parallelism between my fiction and my nonfiction, it shows that art, too—and the subconscious in general—may be potent means of recovering youth.

Last year my wife and I moved from the west coast of Canada, where we'd lived for thirty-five years, halfway across the country to Ontario where I grew up. While there were other important reasons for this move, one motive was to return to my roots and to reconnect with that physical environment. For life impels one to become a complete human being, and I sensed that the right conditions for further growth were to be found in the place where I was planted.

The title of this essay employs the word *embrace,* meant literally. It is not enough to contemplate childlikeness theologically. What is needed is a warmer, deeper, more vibrant experience: an actual embrace across the years, so real as to be *felt* in the gut. The ancient Hebrews understood three ways of knowing: from the brain, from the heart, and from the bowels. To know in the brain is to know propositionally. To know in the heart is to know by feeling. To know in the gut is to know by unknowing, a state attained when the ties of worldly enculturation are so loosened as to allow the kingdom of God to rush in. Adults possess their own sort of wisdom, but a child *knows,* and somehow adult and child must reach across the vast gulf to join hands and hearts. Does the child reach too? Oh, yes! The child yearns for the acknowledgment, the loving regard of its older self. Will you grant your little boy his heart's desire? Will you cherish your little girl? Consider making Catherine Doherty's favorite prayer your own: "Lord, give me the heart of a child and the awesome courage to live it out as an adult."

On a visit to my aunt and uncle as a teenager, one day I was left to babysit my two young cousins. I happened to be reading a book called *Some Main Problems of Philosophy,* and I figured I'd spend a quiet day reading while my little cousins played. No such luck. The first thing they did was to hide my book, proceeding to lead me on a merry chase for hours as they teased and tormented while I bargained and cajoled—to no avail. Not until just before the adults returned did I finally get my book back, by which time I'd concluded there was at least one main problem of philosophy that the book did not cover—namely, *how to handle little brats*. Of course this is not a philosophical problem at all, and any attempt to approach it philosophically will meet with as much success as I did that day. As Plato put it, "You can discover more about a person in an hour of play than in a year of conversation."

How will you know when you have embraced your alien child? There will be a lightness in your step; you will relax with people; you will sleep more peacefully; you will laugh easily and tears will flow readily; you will take the hand of spontaneity; you will approach work more playfully; gratitude will be your native tongue; you will breathe forgiveness.

These are a few of the blessings and glories of becoming, once more, a child. And that is what we are.

Epilogue

Hardly had I written that last sentence when my doorbell rang, and some concluding lines were handed to me:

> While writing an essay on childhood
> two small boys appear at my door—
> my neighbors—collecting pledges
> for a school walkathon.
>
> I invite them in, find some cash,
> fill out the form, make small talk—
> the whole time keenly aware I'm not
> in the presence of ordinary humans
>
> but of something more mysterious,
> more redolent of Another Place
> than earth. So here I am, brought
> up suddenly, my abstract topic
>
> made flesh in a gentle rebuke.
> You see, it is not so easy to capture
> such a wonder in words, wherefore
> Jesus placed a little child front and center.
>
> Who was that child, I wonder?
> Boy or girl? And did he

And That Is What We Are

or she feel blessed? No doubt.
Yet that was not the point.

The point was all of adult
wisdom and know-how held
up to question in the presence
of littleness, as befell me today.

*I tell you the truth, unless
you change and become like
little children, you will never
enter the kingdom of heaven—*

for back there, not up ahead,
is where the light blazes
and the gate is not
only narrow, it is low.

Chapter Seventeen

To Be a Christian Was to Be a Child to God
Kierkegaard's View

Tetsuya Shimada

In response to childlikeness and childishness described in Kirstin Jeffrey Johnson and Sharon Smith's essay on George MacDonald, I would like to present someone who appeared before MacDonald but demonstrated childlikeness so aptly. He lived not in the United Kingdom where MacDonald was situated, but Denmark where Hans Christian Andersen (1805–1875) resided. Søren Aabye Kierkegaard (1813–1855) was his name. And apparently, Andersen, a well-known author of children's literature, was one of his contenders. They were both part of the Danish Golden Age—a distinguished period in the history of letters.

In this essay, I shall show that why Kierkegaard was an exemplar of the childlikeness described by MacDonald, particularly, the joy of being a child. For Kierkegaard, such childlike aspects were largely absent in his own childhood, but they began to appear later in life. As we look into the details, his childhood was characterized by him striving to survive in the rather harsh environment he lived. And this manifests the qualities of childishness described in MacDonald. Somehow, the life he lived as a child and young adult would bring a tone of murkiness and despondency. It took him his life amidst suffering, intellectual searching, and much emotional turmoil, to finally be planted on a new plateau, where he began to thrive. Such a shift is what I will try to depict in this essay. And this shift is the

To Be a Christian Was to Be a Child to God

transition from childishness to childlikeness as seen in the life of Søren Kierkegaard. The key to such a transformative life was his longing that the biblical message be realized in his real life. Though he had his home in Denmark, he was looking for something more—his true home in God.

In 1813, just a year before the ending of the Napoleonic Wars, Søren Aabye Kierkegaard was born in the heart of the Danish capital Copenhagen. His father Michael was fifty-seven, an affluent businessperson who was astute, and his mother Ane was forty-five, underprivileged and illiterate, the former housemaid of his deceased wife.[1] Søren was the youngest of seven. The family belonged to the nearby Lutheran church, but his father had his part in the Moravian congregation in town. Though self-educated, Michael knew theology and philosophy to a great extent. There was a gap between Michael and Ane—not only their difference in age, but also status—the upstanding citizen and the maidservant, a self-learned scholar and an unlettered wife. So, in matters of education and economics, Ane seemed to not count at all. "Michael did the daily shopping and did not entrust the household accounts to her. Ane was not relied on to educate their sons, and Michael enlisted the assistance of another woman to train up their daughters."[2]

Here, however, I would like to add a few more accounts that may shed a different light on this couple. Peter Munthe Brun (1813–1904) was one of Søren's classmates who described Michael as "the odd, old hosier and the serious, somber"[3] man, which corresponds to how Søren himself reminisced in his journals. He writes: "It is appalling to think even for one single moment about the dark background of my life right from its earliest beginning. The anxiety with which my father filled my soul, his own frightful depression, a lot of which I cannot even write down."[4] Ane was depicted rather differently. Historian Joakim Garff portrayed her as "a pleasant, chubby little woman with an even and cheerful temperament." In her very minimal wedding possessions, there were two books, which I would like to emphasize. For those two books—Hagen's *Historic Hymns and Rhymes for the Instruction of Children*, and Lindberg's *Zion's Harp: A Christmas Present to the Christian Congregation*—could indicate not only her capacity to read, but also her interest in child-rearing, with exposition of pietistic notions

---

1. Garff, *Søren Kierkegaard*, 6.
2. Backhouse, *Kierkegaard*, 49.
3. Kirmmse, ed., *Encounters with Kierkegaard*, 6.
4. Kierkegaard, *Journals and Papers*, vol. 6., 72.

through hymns.⁵ Perhaps we can say that Michael was an intelligent man whose life's concerns were exercised in the form of control and management. Whereas Ane was not academic, but her life seemed more congruent with a sense of lightness and cheerfulness. Between these two parents, Michael's influence seems stronger and more obvious in Søren's life, but as his faith would demonstrate later, it was perhaps more his mother's qualities that he was looking to.

Reflecting on his own childhood, Søren noted one of his dispositions inherited from Michael, from which he later experienced freedom in the form of recovery of childlikeness in Christ. A journal entry from 1843 suggests what was missing from Søren's childhood—joy:

> Why did I not thrive as other children do, why was I not wrapped around in joy, why did I come to look into that region of sighs so early, why was I born with a congenital anxiety which constantly made me look into it, why were nine months in my mother's womb enough to make me old so that I was not born like other children but was born old?⁶

Kierkegaard saw that thriving as a child was to thrive into joy, which is how MacDonald describes childlikeness in the following essay. Kierkegaard did not have this quality when he was a child. And in the following remark, we may detect a clue to his gloomy childhood. He writes:

> My father was an old man; I never knew him otherwise. The fundamental misfortune of my whole life is that I was confused with being an old man, and this appeared also in my clothes. I remember very well how distressed I was, from childhood on, to have to wear such short trousers. I remember, too, my brother-in-law Christian's constant teasing.
>
> Then I became a student, but a youth I never was. I never received a youthful impression of life (that a long life stretches out ahead of one, because for me there literally was never more than half a year, and hardly that), which leads a person to have interest and pleasure in his appearance. I consoled myself in another way. My mind developed prodigiously, and I thought about such things least of all ... I recognized that in suffering I had been an old man

---

5. Amongst the names of the authors, such as Ingemann, Grundtvig, and Lindberg, we find the name of Hans Adolph Brorson, who was, according to Christopher B. Barnett, Danish Pietism's greatest hymn writer. See Garff, *Søren Kierkegaard*, 6. Regarding Brorson and Danish Pietism, see Barnett, "Hans Adolph Brorson."

6. Kierkegaard, *Journals and Papers*, vol. 5, 232–33.

To Be a Christian Was to Be a Child to God

at the age of eight—and that I never had been young; intellectually well-endowed, I elevated myself ironically over everything connected with the animal aspects of being human.[7]

Though he grew intelligent, his intelligence did not seem to make him happy. His rather mournful school years were perceived as joyless. Søren's classmate Frederic Welding points out that such joylessness was not unrelated to his home, which was "shrouded in mysterious shadows of strictness and eccentricity."[8] And in Welding's account, Søren as a lonely boy emerges: "There were surely only a very few classmates who understood [Søren]," and it was because:

> [Søren] did not reveal his character in the way that boys and young people of school age usually do. He went his own way, almost self-contained, never spoke of his home, and neither brought classmates home with him nor visited them in their homes . . . As far as I can remember, he was a not friend with any of the other boys.[9]

Welding continues: "[He was] a stranger and an object of pity, especially because of his clothing, which was always the same, of rough dark tweed fabric with an odd cut, a jacket with short tails, and always with shoes and woolen stockings, never boots, as far as I remember."[10] Søren received his nickname "the Choirboy," or its alternative "Søren Sock," because of his attire. As we come to Kierkegaard's own reflections, we are again hit by an impression of Søren as a joyless lonely schoolboy. One of his journal reads:

> The joy of being a child I have never had. The frightful torments I experienced disturbed the peacefulness which must belong to being a child, to have in one's hands the capacity to be occupied etc., to give his father joy, for my inner unrest had the effect that I was always, always, outside myself.[11]

To be observant was a characteristic that Søren developed, and without which he would not have been so influential later as a philosophical author. But his observational talent—even mania—might have been a curse as far as his personal life as a child was concerned. In any event, Søren's childhood lacked joy because he was fixated on and working hard to give his

---

7. Kierkegaard, *Journals and Papers*, vol. 6, 136-37.
8. Kirmmse, ed., *Encounters with Kierkegaard*, 7.
9. Kirmmse, ed., *Encounters with Kierkegaard*, 7.
10. Kirmmse, ed., *Encounters with Kierkegaard*, 7.
11. Kierkegaard, *Journals and Papers*, vol. 6, 84.

father joy. And in doing so, perhaps he was suppressing his childlike needs and emotions.

As we turn to one of Søren's later works, *Johannes Climacus*—often considered the work in which Kierkegaard's own upbringing was reflected—we see a similar tone:

> What other children obtain through the magic of poetry and the surprise of fairy tales, Johannes [Søren] obtained through quiet intuition and the ramifications of dialectic . . .When Johannes grew older he had no toys to lay aside, for he had learnt to play with that which was to be the serious business of his life. And yet this never lost its attraction. A little girl plays for so long with her doll that at last it is transformed into her beloved, for woman's whole life is love. His life had a similar continuity, for his whole life was thinking.[12]

This account tells us of the boy Søren having no toys to play with, but he had something that he refers to as "the serious business of his life," which later developed into "thinking." When we come to this point, what this little child Kierkegaard was becoming was like his father, particularly in their common temperament of seriousness and intense thought. Seriousness, in other words, is efficaciousness for productivity, but can squeeze out playfulness. According to the Kierkegaard scholar Gregor Malantchuk, such shared traits between Søren and his father were not unrelated to an equally shared propensity to depression, or what he called "closed-upness and melancholy."[13] Though Søren inherited useful skills from his father, with which his authorship would benefit immensely, a good part of his childhood seemed hindered and tainted.[14]

A school report by Professor Nielsen—who was the principal of Borgerdyd School where Søren attended from around age nine—brings further description to how he was brought up by his father. Nielsen writes:

> The root of these virtues is the pure devotion to God that was implanted in his character from the very beginning of his life. Indeed, his father has conducted his business in accordance with the precepts of philosophy, and he has united his business life with

---

12. Kierkegaard, *Johannes Climacus*.

13. Malantschuk spends one whole section of his work building an argument that Kierkegaard learned the depth of human psyche by observing his father's temperament. See his "Anthropological Contemplation" and, for the quotation, 26.

14. Here I refer to Kierkegaard's own descriptions on his childhood and relationship with his father Michael in *Johannes Climacus*.

To Be a Christian Was to Be a Child to God

> the reading of works of theology, philosophy, and literature. His wisdom and goodness can be seen in all of his circumstances, and especially in child rearing, from which he himself derived great benefit in the cultivation of his mind and in intellectual enjoyment. Because his father's home is thus such a model of industriousness, patience, and moderation, and is arranged in conformity with the principles by which children are trained in virtue and in the wisdom which is given by God.[15]

Some of us may be surprised, for Nielsen uses religious expressions to honor the father of the student. But it is a reflection of the Denmark in which Søren spent his life. Since it was root and branch a part of Christendom, being a Christian there was as effortless as breathing. Later in his journals—now Søren was around thirty—he marked this aspect much more negatively: "The tragedy of my childhood, the terrifying, secret elucidation of the religious which a fearful presentiment gave me, which my imagination hammered out, and my offense at the religious."[16] And this "offense at the religious" might have been intensified when he found out something called his family's secret.

Kierkegaard scholar Keiji Ogawa succinctly recapitulates this secret. It was about particular events which had taken place in the life of Michael, the respected father of Kierkegaard's family. There were two: One was him cursing God when he was a child; and the other was his illegitimate marriage. The former took place when he was still a boy. When he was tending his family sheep in Jutland, out of poverty, and harshness of his life as serfdom, he ran up on the rock in the heathland, raised his hands, and cursed God. He said, "If there is God who doesn't even seem to help one lonely destitute child, on top of that, keep putting him agony to this point—I curse the Lord God."[17] And this event took root in his conscience, and never left even at his old age. Instead, it later became a sore point in his line of thought. His illegitimate marriage was another event that would determine his eventual conviction that he never was forgiven by God. In short, when he married Ane, she was already pregnant with their first child, which meant the conception took place while Christiane, his first wife, was still alive—likely in the midst of her affliction—and Ane was Christiane's maidservant. Such was Søren's family secret that was like a millstone weighing down not only

---

15. Kirmmse, ed., *Encounters with Kierkegaard*, 17–18.
16. Kierkegaard, *Journals and Papers*, vol. 5, 243.
17. Ogawa, *Kierkegaard*, 66.

An Introduction to Child Theology

Michael himself but also everyone else in the family. So, when deaths fell upon Søren's family, it was like adding fuel to the fire.[18]

Starting when Søren was six, this family had to face death continually. When Søren was in college, there was at least one death per year in the family. By the time Søren became twenty-one, he had only two family members left: Peter, his brother, and his father. With all of these children dead before age thirty-three, Michael developed an alarming religious conviction. Michael took this turn of events as the judgement of God upon him and his family. Søren wrote in his journal:

> [M]y father's old-age was not a divine blessing, but rather a curse ... [what] I saw in my father [was] an unhappy man who would survive us all, a memorial cross on the grace of all his personal hopes. A guilt must rest upon the entire family, a punishment of God must be upon it: it was supposed to disappear, obliterated by the mighty hand of God, erased like a mistake, and only at times did I find a little relief in the thought that my father had been given the heavy duty of reassuring us all with the consolation of religion, telling us that a better world stands open for us even if we lost this one.[19]

Michael believed all this was the consequence of his unforgivable sins, and expected that none of his children could live beyond thirty-three—the age Jesus Christ died on the cross. And the punishment was for him to witness their deaths as the lone survivor of the family. This must have been a shared notion of his family, for when Søren turned thirty-four—unexpectedly(!)—he went to the municipal office to inquire after his family register and birth certificate to make sure he lived beyond the age of the curse.[20] Thus the Kierkegaard's family secret haunted Søren's childhood and young adulthood. No wonder he later became one of the sharpest critics of Christendom's faith.

Now let us turn for a little while to the gifts Søren had received regardless of such negative and loathsome family influences. Regarding his skill set, we should note at least two talents—both of which came from his

---

18. In 1819 when Søren was six, his second oldest brother Søren Michael died of a head injury following a playground incident. In 1822 the oldest sister Maren died at age twenty-four from convulsions. In 1832 his second oldest sister Nicoline died at age thirty-three after having a stillbirth. In 1833 his third oldest brother Niels died at age twenty-four. And in 1834 his mother Ane died from neurosis. Then in the same year his third oldest sister Petrea died at age thirty-three.

19. Kierkegaard, *Journals and Papers*, vol. 5, 140–41.

20. Kierkegaard, *Journals and Papers*, vol. 5, 90–91.

To Be a Christian Was to Be a Child to God

father: the power of the imagination and dialectic, and I argue that without these we would not have had the Søren Kierkegaard we know of today.

Studying at home was compulsory when Søren was a child. But at Søren's request, Michael often took his little son's hand and began to walk inside their small apartment room. This seemingly intolerably dull play became indescribably fun. Taking Søren for a virtual walk, Michael opened up a whole new world in front of him. It was the power of the imagination.

> Johannes [Søren] was given completely free choice as to where they should go [in their imagination]. They walked out of the city gate to a nearby country castle, or away to the beach, or about the streets, or wherever Johannes wished, for the father was equal to anything. While they walked up and down the room the father would describe everything they saw. They greeted the passers-by; the carriages rattled by them and drowned the father's voice; the cake-woman's wares were more inviting than ever. The father would describe so accurately, so vividly, so faithfully—even down to the most insignificant detail—what was already known to Johannes, and so forthrightly and graphically what was unknown to him, that after half an hour's walking with his father he was as overcome and weary as if he had been out for a whole day.[21]

Accordingly, "Johannes soon learned his father's magic power."[22] This was the first gift Søren received: the nurturing of the imagination.

Another gift given to him from Michael was a particular approach to thought—that is, dialectic. Søren observed his father engaged in scholarly discussion at the Moravian congregation of which his father was an earnest member. Seeing how his father handled the arguments, and integrated other people's viewpoints into his own, Søren was often left in awe. He recalls:

> When on any occasion his father engaged in an argument with somebody, Johannes was all ears . . . His father always allowed his opponent to state his whole case, and then would ask him very carefully whether he had anything more to say before he began his reply . . . Then came the pause, the father's rejoinder would follow, and look!—in a twinkling everything was changed . . . In an instant everything would be inverted; what was clear became obscure, what was certain doubtful, the opposite became self-evident

---

21. Kirmmse, ed., *Encounters with Kierkegaard*, 18.
22. Kirmmse, ed., *Encounters with Kierkegaard*, 18.

An Introduction to Child Theology

> ... He soon forgot what was said, both by his father and the opponent, but this thrill in his soul he never forgot.[23]

Here, we can see how this little Søren was fascinated by his father's dialectical discourses with those who might have often been viewed as more sophisticated than himself, such as those who earned academic degrees or so-called "well-educated" people from society.

Having such a father at home, a lonely boy was being nurtured and equipped. Søren developed the power of imagination, as well as his dialectical skill, with which he quickly responded to his opponents by using their very arguments to debunk their fraudulence. Welding's observation is helpful here; he writes that Søren

> had a good eye for people's weak points, for the incoherent and offensive features of their behavior. He therefore pounced upon tall fellows who were intellectual midgets ... in general upon those who were quick to develop physically but slower intellectually ... I myself belonged to this latter group.[24]

The power of imagination and skillfulness in dialectic were Søren's skill set that accompanied him throughout life, and without which all his inextricable works would not have been produced when he later began writing in his thirties. But back then when periods of "closed-upness and melancholy"[25] occupied Søren, his school days passed quietly and, it seemed, without joy. "He worked more out of fear and compulsion than out of desire or any happy industriousness," Welding recalls.[26]

Let us now turn to another event, which changed the direction of Søren's life. When he was twenty-four, he met Regine Olsen. She was sixteen. This experience determined the course of his faith. The following account reveals the tension and motion of Søren's heart when he visited the Rørdam's, one of his friend's homes. Perhaps listening well to one's own emotions is the most difficult thing for many of us, and I think it was certainly a dreadful thing for Søren. Having been raised under a stern and prosaic father with an illiterate and emotional mother, whose presence seems almost always to have been under the shadow of his father, the emotional aspect of human life might not have been valued in his family culture. So, when Søren found himself moving toward a fondness and loving affection

23. Kirmmse, ed., *Encounters with Kierkegaard*, 20–21.
24. Kirmmse, ed., *Encounters with Kierkegaard*, 8.
25. Malantschuk, "Anthropological Contemplation," 26.
26. Kirmmse, ed., *Encounters with Kierkegaard*, 7.

for Regine, it must have been like being in a foreign land. He was thrown into confusion. In his journal, he writes:

> O God, how easy it is to forget such intentions! Dethroned in my own inner being, I have once again returned to the world in order to prevail there for some time yet. But what good is it to win the whole world and lose one's own soul. Again today (May 8) I tried to forget myself, not in the boisterous tumult (that surrogate does not help) but by going out to Rørdam and by talking with Bolette and by getting (if possible) the devil of my wit to stay home, the angel with the flaming sword (as I have deserved) who places himself between me and every innocent girlish heart—since you overtook me, O God, thank you for not letting me immediately go mad—I have never been so fearful of it—thank you for once again [for] inclining your ear to me.[27]

It seems Søren was torn between God and girls. Both had real gravity. While his mind/theology pulled him back from forming in him an "innocent girlish heart," it is obvious that the other pull was so strong that he almost failed to overcome it. The echo of his petition suggested the poignancy of his helplessness. Here is another example:

> Today the same episode again—but I got out to Rørdam—good God, why should the inclination begin to stir just now—how alone I feel—confound that proud satisfaction in standing alone—everyone will now hold me in contempt—but you, my God, do not let go of me—let me live and reform—[28]

Søren struggled, for "the inclination" was out of his control. Although he did not put her name directly in his journal at this point, it was clear that it was Regine he was smitten by. However, this time his sober mind won over the emotional drive within. Perhaps he did not have space for it. But "[so many] other things [were] going on: spiritually, mentally, and physically" in his life at that moment.[29] If listed, they were: his own ill health; estrangement with his family; an unrecoverable slump in his academic life; and the stranding of his faith. As a result, he withdrew from everything—his father's home as well as his church. "Søren ceases to attend Holy Communion."[30]

During this period as a prodigal, something significant happened, for about a year later, Søren came back to faith, with an almost renewed or

---

27. Kierkegaard, *Journals and Papers*, vol. 5, 97.
28. Kierkegaard, *Journals and Papers*, vol. 5, 97.
29. Backhouse, *Kierkegaard*, 81.
30. Backhouse, *Kierkegaard*, 84.

newborn joy. This newborn joy would later grow deeper in his conviction, but nevertheless, this was its foretaste. Now, the key to his return was the death of a respected and adored teacher and mentor, Poul Møller. Later, in the dedication of Søren's early work, titled *Concept of Anxiety*, in its draft, he wrote: "To the late Professor Poul Martin Møller . . . the mighty trumpet of my awakening . . . my lost friend; my sadly missed reader."[31]

During this time, Søren's journaling faded into irregularity, so we could not see what else happened to him, but there was joy that he was experiencing. In the entry from May 19, 1838, he writes:

> There is an indescribable joy that glows all through us just as inexplicably as the apostle's exclamation breaks forth for no apparent reason: "Rejoice, and again I say, Rejoice." — Not a joy over this or that, but the soul's full outcry with tongue and mouth and from the bottom of the heart.[32]

A month later, the mark of joy was still with him. This was a day of reconciliation between him and his father, Michael—wishing his father greater joy in his son's return to faith.[33] Søren's change was evident in this action. Furthermore, his self-observation explains that it was a shift from the external to the personal. On that day he wrote in his journal: "I am going to work toward a far more inward relation to Christianity, for up until now I have in a way been standing completely outside of it while fighting for its truth; like Simon of Cyrene (Luke 23:26), I have carried Christ's cross in a purely external way."[34] A month later, his father passed away.

Søren mourns his loss in his own way; perhaps Søren's dialectical writing was a substitute for his lost friend and debate companion, Michael. As he claimed in his July 9 journal entry, he started composing an "inward relation to Christianity"[35] against "poseur philosophers . . . who align Christianity with Hegelianism."[36] Throughout all this, Søren did not forget Regine and about two years after their first contact, he made his move.

The sociable relation between Søren and the Olsen family had been growing over those two years, and the inheritance from Michael, plus his

---

31. Backhouse, *Kierkegaard*, 85. Backhouse traces to *Concept of Anxiety*, dated in 1844.
32. Kierkegaard, *Journals and Papers*, vol. 5, 120.
33. Kierkegaard, *Journals and Papers*, vol. 5, 120.
34. Kierkegaard, *Journals and Papers*, vol. 5, 121.
35. Kierkegaard, *Journals and Papers*, vol. 5, 121.
36. Backhouse, *Kierkegaard*, 89.

To Be a Christian Was to Be a Child to God

renewed faith in Christ, were more than enough of a boost for him to take a step forward. For the first time, he sent her a letter that was expressive of his passion and waited.[37] All the exams were done, including a national examination for theology; he traveled to Jutland—his father's homeland. After coming back from the trip, he started visiting the Olsens more often than ever, and got closer to Regine. Then, on September 8, 1840, about a month after his passionate letter, Søren proposed to Regine.

Søren enjoyed writing to Regine daily, and occasional walks and rides with Regine were assuring activities for the lovers.[38] This was their courtship, and it lasted thirteen months. His love for her was real, and it was his first love. Sharing his grief and angst, Søren's heart was opened up to Regine.[39] She supported Søren with all her heart. Their love seemed to be growing strong and taking root. "Like Søren, she too is the youngest of seven. Like Søren, she too knows what it is to live with a melancholic father. Even accounting for differences in their ages and stages in life, Regine's and Søren's temperaments, personalities, and experiences are well matched," and Regine's father was supportive.[40] Everyone saw that they were doing well in tying their cords together slowly but surely, as one was becoming an important part of the other.

Søren started to notice that he was putting his hope in her, and it became an issue for him. He began questioning between marrying and not marrying. Fierce perfectionist as he was, his master's thesis probably put pressure on him and perhaps clashed with his emotions, even though he was in love. Whatever the root cause, his imagination went high above that of Regine's. There was discord. His latent calling to be a sharp-eyed writer for Christianity was conflicted with his imaginable future with Regine's expectations of him to be a good husband and clergy in a state church. Søren's uncertainty produced anxiety over their compatibility and tension between the lovers developed. Søren began to think it could not be right if they were poles apart. Regine tried her best to understand and support her fiancé, and Søren tried his best to seek God's will. The discord was between Regine's affectionate love and Søren's convoluted love.

Søren fell back on his familiar tools—melancholic anxiety as an emotional undercurrent, and imaginative thinking accompanied with the

---

37. Kierkegaard, *Journals and Papers*, vol. 5, 127–28.
38. Backhouse, *Kierkegaard*, 92–95.
39. Backhouse, *Kierkegaard*, 94.
40. Backhouse, *Kierkegaard*, 94.

teachings of the Scriptures as an intellectual scope—to determine his course of action. With that, he broke the engagement. This was a total surprise to Regine and she was devastated. Something new and something beautiful growing between two people was all of a sudden utterly shattered. But in this very moment, something unexpected happened to Søren. A flood of emotions swept over him. Seeing Regine thrown into unfathomable despair, he broke down weeping. There was nothing he could do. Sunk into immense agony, he fled to Berlin and remained there for five months.

Søren's "last hope in life" was now gone; he was left alone—with "so deep a wound," but still with "God."[41] There was no one to talk to. Occasional attendance at the lectures of the cutting-edge German intellectuals, including Friedrich Schelling, brought no satisfaction or comfort—it was not what he was looking for. He was looking for someone like Regine, to whom he could bring all his emotions, all his love. He still loved her and because of that, he suffered—"he could not talk about what he wants to express, to whom he wants to share the most."[42] It was his "suffering of love."[43]

Having lost everything, where did Søren go? Not into thinking, nor philosophical ideas, nor even a church—Søren went to the Lord. There was nothing to hold onto, but it was the Lord holding him ever more assuredly. We can discover what might have been taking place inside Søren in his journal dated five years after the event. Surprisingly, he couples it with the joy, which he could not articulate earlier in his life.

> The joy—that the weaker I become myself
> the stronger God becomes in me.
> The joy—that what I lose temporally
> I gain eternally.
> The joy—that it is not the believer who holds the anchor
> but the author of faith who holds the believer.[44]

One's upbringing, family background and theological training all matter to one's character formation. Nothing is trivial, and that was true with Søren's character formation as well. But perhaps in this particular case, it brought nothing but sadness. Passed down traits of melancholic anxiety and unappreciated emotions in his family dynamics were programed into him made him drift to his default. However, we just saw that such an impossible shift

41. Kierkegaard, *Journals and Papers*, vol. 5, 176.
42. Ogawa, *Kierkegaard*, 133.
43. Ogawa, *Kierkegaard*, 134.
44. Kierkegaard, *Journals and Papers*, vol. 2, 496.

To Be a Christian Was to Be a Child to God

was made possible in his intrapersonal testimony. But it involved him in his own pain and suffering. Highly intellectual as Søren had been, only when his intelligence lost its hold did his emotions cry out loud. There the Lord became his Father, and Søren became his child. Here he found the joy. His journal attests this fundamental shift:

> The joy of being a child I have never had. The frightful torments I experienced disturbed the peacefulness which must belong to being a child, to have in one's hands the capacity to be occupied etc., to give his father joy, for my inner unrest had the effect that I was always, always, outside myself.
>
> But on not rare occasions it seems as if my childhood had come back again, for unhappy as my father made me, it seems as if I now experience being a child in my relationship to God, as if all my early life was misspent so dreadfully in order that I should experience it more truly the second time in my relationship to God.[45]

Isn't this what we all talk about when we say that Christians are children of God? Yes, and I argue that for Søren this was not a mere idea, nor an eschatological concept, but a reality. As lonely a boy as he was, he used his imagination and his dialectical skill to fight against his peers. His upbringing gave him this skill set, and it was what he needed for survival. He thrived in it, for the surroundings were ever severe, though it was Christendom he lived in. In his pains and sufferings, he was not understood and left alone, yet he rejoiced, for that was God his Father, hearing Søren's deepest cry.

An essential quality of being a child is trust, and what precedes it is an acceptance of one's vulnerability. Unless we come to a recognition of our own impotency, we would not see our need of help. For this very notion of our own weakness provides us the potential of appreciation, and therefore reception of the divine grace. Paul wrote in 2 Corinthians:

> [B]ut he [the Lord] said to me, "My grace is sufficient for you, for power is made perfect in weakness." So, I will boast all the more gladly of my weaknesses, so that the power of Christ may dwell in me. Therefore I am content with weaknesses, insults, hardships, persecutions, and calamities for the sake of Christ; for whenever I am weak, then I am strong. (2 Cor 12:9–11 NRSV)

With an increasing awareness of one's frailty and deficiency, self-reliance decreases. This is so critical, particularly as far as our walk with the Lord

---

45. Kierkegaard, *Journals and Papers*, vol. 6, 84.

is concerned—for without such trust we will not be able to enter into relationship with the Father. For without trust in him, how could we call him our Father, how could we live like his children? We develop skills in life—it may often start in our childhood—like sharp counter- and self-defense that Søren equipped himself with in the early part of his life. This would tell of nothing but the harsh environment we live in that required us to develop a variety of survival skills. But those same survival reactions may tell of our insecurity in life. In fact, the fragility of our foothold in life is examined and further discussed in Søren's *The Sickness unto Death*.[46] As long as our skill set in life can keep us going—keep us surviving—we will not come to see our own need of the Savior, for we remain our own saviors.

This was, I argue, what happened in Søren's life. His long-lasting interior discord was finally debunked when his mind and emotion clashed. He chose his calling, and he had to suffer for it. As he became utterly lonely, there was the Lord upholding from beneath. Though he was hardly understood by the people of his time, he kept writing and writing and writing—until he died at age forty-two. The one who upheld Søren's steps was "the author of faith,"[47] in whom he became less and less on his own, but became "more and more a child." [48] For Søren, such was to become a Christian, to become more and more a child to God.

---

46. In *The Sickness unto Death*, human interactions and behaviors are analyzed, all of which draw on the same condition. Considering the true death of humankind through observation of human life, Anti-Climacus concludes that every one of us is on the verge of despair, which is the sickness unto death. Despair without hope is like a human being without a firm foundation. No one but the one who made humankind can really provide a firm foundation, the rock beneath the ever-changing human condition. See Kierkegaard, *The Sickness unto Death*.

47. Kierkegaard, *Journals and Papers*, vol. 2, 496.

48. Kierkegaard, *Journals and Papers*, vol. 1, 122.

Chapter Eighteen

"A Childhood into Which We Have to Grow"

George MacDonald and Childlikeness

SHARON JEBB SMITH AND KIRSTIN JEFFREY JOHNSON

> "The boy should enclose and keep, as his life,
> the old child at the heart of him,
> and never let it go....
> The child is not meant to die,
> but to be forever fresh born.
> — George MacDonald, *The Princess and Curdie*

GEORGE MACDONALD (1824–1905) WARRANTS considered attention in the discussion of child theology. Not least as he was a significant influence both on some of the most popular Christian writers as well as some of the most prominent children's literature authors of the twentieth century (and continuing into the twenty-first). A lecturer and professor of literature for forty years, MacDonald was at the same time a best-selling author of fiction and nonfiction in multiple genres—throughout which one of the key themes is the discipleship of childlikeness. Though only employed as a minister for a brief period in his twenties, MacDonald's pastoral heart infuses his writings, and led C. S. Lewis to claim "I know hardly any other writer who seems . . . closer . . . to the spirit of Christ himself . . . I have never concealed the fact that I regard him as my master."[1] G. K. Chesterton similarly acknowledges mentorship, asserting that a children's book by MacDonald, *The Princess and the Goblin*, "made a difference to my whole existence."[2] MacDonald's writing is quoted extensively by Oswald Chambers, cited as inspiration by Philip Yancey, and translated into German (the *Anthology*) by Hans Urs Von Balthasar. However—somewhat unusually—it is not only those writing explicitly Christian literature who acknowledge MacDonald's formative influence: authors of such culture-shaping children's classics as *Peter Pan*, *Alice's Adventures in Wonderland*, *Black Beauty*, *The Secret Garden*, *The Railway Children*, *The Little White Horse*, *Where the Wild Things Are*, *The Hobbit*, and *A Wrinkle in Time* also pay MacDonald tribute.

In the following pages Sharon Jebb Smith poses some questions to Kirstin Jeffrey Johnson about George MacDonald's unique and significant contribution to an understanding of the "discipleship of childlikeness."

George MacDonald is often cited as an important facilitator in helping people better understand their relationship with God as a loving Father rather than a condemning judge. But the more familiar I become with his work the more aware I am that he writes about us being "childlike" at least as much as he talks about God as parent. Is there an important distinction to be explored here?

Even in the nineteenth century, writers gave George MacDonald credit for popularizing the understanding of God as Father rather than condemning judge.[3] In this love-oriented (rather than judgement-oriented) attitude, MacDonald was reiterating truths he had come to understand

---

1. Lewis read MacDonald as a child, and then rediscovered him in his late teens and from then until his death was an avid reader and promoter. Upon first reading Tolkien's *The Hobbit*, Lewis wrote of his excitement to a lifelong friend of having met a kindred (and colleague) who also grew up on MacDonald. (Above quote from Hooper, ed., *Together*, 449.)

2. Lewis, ed., *George MacDonald*, 9.

3. See Dearborn, *Baptized Imagination*, for a fuller exploration of this theme in MacDonald's writing. Dearborn also gives considered attention to *childlikeness*.

with greater theological clarity through the writings and teachings of his mentors Thomas Erskine and A. J. Scott. Yet to speak only of MacDonald's understanding of God as Father is to miss the very essence of his telos: that his readers might recognize and respond to God's call of his children to *childlikeness*. This theme runs throughout MacDonald's corpus, from beginning to end and in every genre—poems, essays, sermons, short stories, fairy tales, fantasy, realistic novels, even his literary criticism and in the selections he makes for his anthologies.[4] His very first sermon in *Unspoken Sermons I*, "Child in the Midst," addresses the gravity of Christ's dictum: "unless you become as one of these . . ." It is the foundation of all that follows.

MacDonald understands that while learning to view God as loving Father may be countercultural for some of his readers, it is in truth a less significant shift than learning to become childlike. What may seem sufficiently challenging for a goal-focussed, progress-oriented, self-improving twenty-first century reader to comprehend, was even more radical a concept for MacDonald's nineteenth-century readers. At a time when many of his Christian contemporaries were warning parents against "inflaming the imagination" of their children with fanciful literature, lest it lead to a life of disillusionment and disappointment,[5] MacDonald completely shifts the angle: he calls, invites, urges even his adult readers to re-engage in childlike imagination.

It's interesting that MacDonald was often countercultural in this respect. But I wonder about the context in which he wrote. Surely Romanticism was a movement that encouraged a high regard for childlikeness?

At first glance MacDonald's emphasis on childlikeness might seem like a Romantic's reaction against Classicism and the Enlightenment, but MacDonald is hoping to entice readers of all ages into something he believed much more complex and rich than that intellectual movement, rather, into a scriptural, Christ-uttered imperative that he took at face value.[6]

---

4. Gabelman argues that the childlike is inherent "in the very structure and style" of MacDonald's writing: it is integral to MacDonald's whole cast of mind. "Organised Innocence," 70–71.

5. See Gabelman, "Organised Innocence," for discussions on the dangers of "inflaming the imagination."

6. Some have argued that MacDonald merely "Christianizes Romanticism," but this is simplistic and trivializes not only MacDonald's cultural inheritance but also his exegesis of Scripture. There is no room here to address the variances between Continental and

An Introduction to Child Theology

To tease out some of his differences from—rather than commitment to or rejection of—Romanticism, it is helpful to look at a bit of his background. MacDonald tended to have conversations with writers and with movements, rather than either embracing or rejecting them wholeheartedly. He deeply enjoyed some of the Romantic literature he read as a young adult—such as Coleridge, Novalis, LaMotte Fouqué—and for some he had a deep distaste, such as Byron. But it is important to note that standard Romantic emphases such as imagination, emotion, nature, myths, mysticism, and freedom were deeply entrenched in MacDonald's lived Celtic and scriptural upbringing long before he discovered the philosophies of Romanticism. And Romanticism's emphasis on individualism, disdain for rules, and solitude rather than community were antithetical to both the Celtic and scriptural foundations.

Some of this can be traced to MacDonald's own childhood experience. He grew up on a farm near the small Scottish town of Huntly. It was a culture in which children were a fully integrated part of community life, participating in a mix of church, farmwork, family, and fun. Such a culture necessarily clashed with the notion of childhood that was propagated by Romanticism: the "natural childhood" as envisioned by Rousseau (no responsibility, little to no formal education, free of constraint) was not only a class luxury simply not possible in rural Scotland, it also was antithetical to many of the cultural values. In significant contrast to contemporary England, the majority of Scottish children—even in the remote Highlands—not only had access to free education, but education (literacy in particular) was highly valued.[7] This centuries-long emphasis was directly tied to the import placed upon biblical literacy. And perhaps it is not surprising in a

---

English Romanticism, but both Dearborn and Gabelman address this.

7. Even Victorian English readers sometimes wondered at the idealization of farm-boys reading classics out in the fields in MacDonald's novels, but contemporary school inspection reports make very clear that this was not a romanticized notion: studying for school and doing farm chores were not mutually exclusive, and not infrequently inspectors had to go out to find students in the fields to assess their level of education. The surprising reports are of better than average students. In 1864 the English journal *Cornhill* dedicated an article to this topic: "The Scottish Farm Labourer." Scotland's literacy rates at the time exceeded England's by almost 20 percent for both genders—and were even higher in the remote regions. In 1855—the earliest such records are available—Scotland's literacy rate was 89 percent for men and 77 percent for women, compared with a respective 70 percent and 59 percent for England and Wales. In the majority of the Lowland counties, outside of the industrializing areas, male literacy was over 90 percent. (Anderson, *Education and Opportunity*, 1.)

community in which the assistance of able-bodied children was a necessary way of being, for feeding and tending animals, and planting and harvesting food, that the children were then also involved at an early age in family prayers, Bible readings, and Sunday schools. (MacDonald and his brothers led fellow children in Sunday school, and apparently were quite content to do so.)[8] At the age of thirteen MacDonald is recounted as delighting the farm-helps with his memorized performance of a sermon by Scotland's famed preacher Thomas Chalmers. His letters at the time indicate that he is reading such literature on his own—but this is no proof of dour Calvinistic repression, as some biographers argue. Those letters make clear that he is enjoying this reading, as well as many other genres found in his family home: *Arabian Nights*, Bunyan, Shakespeare, Milton. His schoolmaster recalls him telling Scottish fairy tales and local ghost stories to fellow students. With his father he could discuss sermons, theological concepts, or the discoveries reported from Darwin on the *HMS Beagle*. Agricultural science intrigued him as a teen, and was one of his career considerations, along with being either a physician or mathematician. Imagination, reason, faith, and science were matters of import for children as well as adults in the house in which MacDonald was raised, and certainly not antithetical as some Romantics would have them.

Much as MacDonald enjoyed reading Walter Scott and William Wordsworth, his lived experience eschewed simplistic concepts of the "noble rustic" and the geographical sublime; the supposed "wild Highlanders" were his relatives and the "rugged expanse" the tangible land he knew.[9] His was a realistic childhood that contained communal responsibility *and* work *and* playfulness; one that highly valued formal education *and* encouraged free engagement in nature; one that navigated joviality and adventures as well as sickness and death (he lost siblings and his mother to the tubercular bronchitis that he likewise battled); one in which science and business was valued in addition to, rather than instead of, languages and arts. His admittedly dour Federal Calvinist grandmother, who was passionate about education but less comfortable with Celtic "frivolity" (and as such certainly represented a portion of the wider community), was balanced out by relatives on both sides who reveled in music, folklore, poetry, jokes, art,

---

8. For more such biographical details and their primary sources, see Jeffrey Johnson, "Rooted in All Its Story," as well as "The MacDonalds," 41.

9. His novel *What's Mine's Mine* (one of Lewis's favorites) deftly teases out some of the differences between Romanticism and lived Celtic culture, whilst also serving as a social justice condemnation of the yet ongoing Highland Clearances.

and were passionate readers of fiction as well as of expositional texts. As a result, despite losing his birth mother when only six, MacDonald had a rich community-oriented childhood that was thrust into sharp contrast with some of what he saw when he moved to industrial London in the 1840s, where many in the upper class were still enamored with ideas of Romanticism yet many in the lower class were facing the brutalities of child labor, generational illiteracy, and broken communities incurred by the Industrial Revolution. In both of these, as well as in the Federal Calvinism he had been exposed to through his paternal grandmother and others, MacDonald found significant contrast with the more Celtic culture of his own household. An ongoing dialogue between the perspectives swirls around his portrayals of the wide variety of children that then appear in his work.

In MacDonald's young adulthood, the writings and mentorship of A. J. Scott, Thomas Erskine, even the Free Church's Thomas Chalmers, seem to have coalesced some of what he had come to understand about a loving Father-God from his own father and others in his community, as opposed to the judging God that seemed to loom large for his paternal grandmother—as represented perhaps most memorably in *Robert Falconer*. In that novel MacDonald optimistically writes: "When souls have been ill-taught about God, the true God will not let them gaze too long upon the Moloch which men have set up to represent Him. He will turn away their minds from that which men call Him, and fill them with some of his own lovely thoughts or works, such as may by degrees prepare the way for a vision of the Father." MacDonald is fully confident in what he calls "the everlasting Fatherhood."[10] But as indicated, for MacDonald that eternally proffered Father-love was only part of the equation—it could not be divided from Christ's stark insistence in Luke, Mark, and Matthew that nonetheless for the Christian disciple reception of, access to, the kingdom of heaven is conditional on this: becoming childlike. His own childhood experiences forfended against a fully Romanticized notion of what that meant, and perhaps convinced him more fully that what Christ required was indeed achievable by all.

MacDonald is very practical in his explorations of Christ's statement "unless you become like one of these." Can you tell us more about the distinction MacDonald makes between childlikeness and childishness?

---

10. MacDonald, *Unspoken Sermons (Series Three)*, 12.

"A Childhood into Which We Have to Grow"

In his earliest published pieces (literary criticism on Robert Browning [1853] and a poetic drama *Within and Without I* [1855]) MacDonald already discusses the importance of a childlike heart, and in his first realistic novel, *David Elginbrod* (1863), he begins parsing out the difference between *childlikeness* and *childishness*: "There is a childhood into which we have to grow, just as there is a childhood which we must leave behind; a childlikeness which is the highest gain of humanity, and a childishness from which but few of those who are counted the wisest among men, have freed themselves in their imagined progress towards the reality of things."[11] This intentional distinguishing between childlikeness and childishness continues throughout MacDonald's work for the remainder of his life—at times almost belabored, indicating concern that readers would not discern the difference.

It is in his first published "literary" sermon (*Unspoken Sermons I*, 1867) that MacDonald unpacks this differentiation the most clearly, referencing the potentially uncomfortable message as communicated in Mark 10 and Luke 18: that whoever does not receive the kingdom of God as a child shall not enter it. With great deliberation MacDonald explains that a childlike child is an emotionally healthy child, and that a childlike—*not childish*—adult is a mature and wise person. And he argues that Matthew 18 has a significant "enrichment" not found in the other passages, including the call to *change* (στρέφω).[12] MacDonald reminds his readers that as Christ sets a child before these disciples who have already given up so much for him, who have already altered their ways of life for him, who have already committed to his message, Christ says that—even now—unless they *change* and become childlike, they will never enter the kingdom of heaven.

Whilst this sermon is MacDonald's most careful and explicitly scriptural exploration of the call to childlikeness—and exhortation against childishness—there are literally hundreds of references to or direct discussions of the concept of childlikeness throughout his work. He repeatedly uses words such as *childlike*, *childness*, and *childlikeness*, as well as *unchildlike* and *childishness*, and often in conjunction with exegetical comment. A distillation of 150 passages across his corpus helps makes clear what he understands a disciplined change into childlikeness entails. Although a list

---

11. MacDonald, *David Elginbrod*, 50.
12. A synonym of μετάνοια (*metanoia*). "Truly I tell you," Jesus said, "unless you change and become like little children, you will never enter the kingdom of heaven" (Matt 18:3).

of these qualities will not be as compelling as the lives MacDonald sketches of both childlike persons as well as distinctly *un*childlike persons, nonetheless there is merit in a succinct overview.

According to MacDonald, to be *childlike* is to:

1. cultivate an attitude of wonder, imagination, and attentiveness—towards people, nature, etc.
2. both pursue and be willing to receive/apprehend truth, beauty, goodness—be curious about and delight in these things
3. participate/engage in what unfolds around one
4. treat *all* humans (regardless of status) as worthy of equal attention and respect; simply, be friendly and kind—to care more about the person than the reputation
5. delight in both freely giving to, and delighting in freely receiving from, others
6. not affect to be other than who one is; be humble and honest about what one does not know/cannot do—and what one can
7. admire and seek out the noble, the pure
8. exercise a peace and confidence that chooses (to see) the best in others, and is patient when needed
9. be unselfish; loving and forgiving easily
10. be comfortable with imprecision, mystery
11. enact unity in thought and deed
12. be trusting, obedient

According to MacDonald, to be *un*childlike, to be *childish* is to:

1. cease to wonder
2. cease being curious
3. cultivate wariness or worse, cynicism
4. be opposed to or squelch wild imagination and dreaming in others
5. be cruel
6. be keen to point out errors
7. be highly critical

"A Childhood into Which We Have to Grow"

8. put weight on public accolade
9. put "efficacy" ahead of kindness
10. participate in false reverence
11. be greedy
12. be lacking in trust, fearful[13]

So, essentially, *childlikeness* in MacDonald's understanding is what is naturally exhibited by the happy, healthy child at his or her best, before wariness, jadedness, and self-promotion or aggrandizement begins. *Childishness* is the immature inability to control or indeed repudiate those negativities. MacDonald repeatedly recognizes that a number of items in the second list are assumed to be savvy or practical aspects of "growing up," and he acknowledges that they can be very efficacious, especially in the short term. He points to Christ himself as the most perfect fulfillment of the discipleship call to live the first list—the Christ Child who in his perfect human maturation never left behind childlikeness.

MacDonald also recognizes that despite having Christ as the consummate model, facilitating change is not simple: "the childlike are not yet the many."[14] He asserts that those who are learning to live in childlikeness have a responsibility to actively assist others:

> he should seek to make others partakers in his pleasure and profit [. . .] Surely if a man would help his fellow-men, he can do so far more effectually by exhibiting truth than exposing error, by unveiling beauty than by a critical dissection of deformity. From the very nature of the things it must be so. Let the true and good destroy their opposites.[15]

Along with his family MacDonald modeled this not just in word but also in deed, showing how playfulness can assist others into such pleasures and thus profit. The MacDonalds were renowned for enticing adults into games and laughter; theater and dancing; music, costumes, and of course stories. A letter MacDonald wrote to his wife indicates the weight of import MacDonald put upon play: "We romped a good deal at the Forest. I laughed

---

13. Gabelman explores the link between childlikeness and fearlessness, "Organised Innocence," 78–86.
14. MacDonald, *Unspoken Sermons (Series Three)*, 30.
15. MacDonald, "Browning's Christmas Eve," 196.

very much, and was merry, and seemed to have clearer brains for it. I am sure it is good. I understand the Bible better for it, I think."[16]

So MacDonald tried to live out the teaching himself. And it was his choice to communicate this message, when writing, primarily through the medium of fiction. I am aware that his contemporaries claimed that this helped to transform the theological imagination of reading Britons in a manner those Scottish divines had not achieved. Can you explain to us why he uses story and how he does so?

MacDonald knew from his own experience in a story-oriented culture and story-oriented family that narrative was a powerful medium of communication and education. He became convinced by the dominant role of narrative throughout Scripture, and in particular its use by Christ (and within the very narratives that tell of Christ's life), of the transformational nature of story.[17] But then particularly under the tutelage of his mentor A. J. Scott (the first ever full-time English literature professor) MacDonald was brought to consider the power of story—in either its presence or absence—with a whole new level of insight. Scott lectured on the philosophical, theological, and educational role of story. He showed how not just in Scripture but repeatedly throughout human history the transmission of stories shaped identities, fortified movements, rooted communities. Scott also traced the cost of loss or omission of stories. Indeed his life work as a pastor, a facilitator for social justice (education for women and working-class men, voting rights, labor laws), and a public and university lecturer, was propelled by this conviction that God has made his children a storied (and story-needing) people.[18] MacDonald was entirely convinced by Scott's argument for both the necessity and the efficacy of stories. He followed Scott's footsteps in both lecturing on literature to the public as well as teaching literature in the academy.[19] But the majority of what MacDonald taught —and even how he voiced his own social justice concerns—was through

---

16. Sadler, ed., *An Expression of Character*, 62.

17. Not only did Christ repeatedly tell short stories and parables, but he continually references the myriad of stories that are central to what we now call the "Old Testament."

18. For more on this, see Jeffrey Johnson, "Rooted in All Its Story." See also Scott's *Notes of Four Lectures*, and his "On University Education."

19. MacDonald lectured most widely throughout Britain, but also in Ireland, Italy, the USA, and even a little in Canada.

"A Childhood into Which We Have to Grow"

the medium of written story (with, unsurprisingly, Scott's encouragement and blessing).

Within the space of these stories MacDonald drew his readers into considerations theological, political, and social, that they might never have otherwise ventured. In the imaginative experience of watching relationships unfold on a page and being drawn into the adventures and dilemmas and delights of those characters MacDonald knew that he had a platform otherwise not possible. And through his readers' imaginative engagement, he invites them into new realizations—realizations he hoped would thus incur actions. MacDonald writes in "The Fantastic Imagination" that "the best thing you can do for your fellow, next to rousing his conscience, is—not to give him things to think about, but to wake things up that are in him; or say, to make him think things for himself."[20] And this is what he seeks to do by inviting readers into his stories. As ever, MacDonald refuses to hold up imagination as an alternative to reason—rather he argues that true imagination cannot be divided from reason. They are, he says, two sides of the same holy coin. In his seminal essay "The Imagination" he argues that imagination "is aroused by facts, is nourished by facts, seeks for higher and yet higher laws in those facts; but refuses to regard science as the *sole* interpreter of nature, or the laws of science as the *only* region of discovery."[21] MacDonald understands both reason and imagination to be incomplete each without the other; "Poetry is true as Science, and Science is holy as Poetry."[22]

This approach shapes MacDonald's presentation of childlikeness and unchildlikeness in his writings. There is no single stock type of child across the corpus—there are impoverished orphans and children from comfortable families, working children and overprivileged children, academically gifted and mentally handicapped, self-assured and emotionally depressed, suspicious and trusting, cruel and kind, hardworking and lazy, mischievous and boring, streetwise and innocent, confident and timid, rural and urban, those who will live long and those who die young. Yet what is consistent in all their tales is that as their lives unfold, the distinctive traits of *childlikeness* or *childishness* in these children determine their mental, emotional, and spiritual well-being. However—and this is so important—it is to significantly misunderstand MacDonald if one only looks at his child characters

---

20. MacDonald, "The Fantastic Imagination," 319.
21. MacDonald, "The Imagination," 2 (emphasis added).
22. MacDonald, "Individual Development," 51.

to understand his portrayal of childlikeness: because his argument is that the spiritually mature adult, the true disciple, is also childlike.

In order to help us imaginatively lean into this, can you give us some concrete examples of MacDonald's childlike characters?

This is perhaps most easily evidenced in the characters who are followed from childhood through to adulthood. The mute character Gibbie, from *Sir Gibbie* (1879), may seem an ideal example as over the course of two books he is shown from the age of eight through to being a married landowner. He is certainly one of MacDonald's fullest embodiments of childlikeness. However Gibbie is exactly that: an intentional ideal, and MacDonald's exploration of what a truly childlike human might look like. MacDonald had crafted another such character a few years earlier, the boy Diamond in *At the Back of the North Wind* (1871). Diamond's own childlikeness is highlighted by the more typically complex children in the novel, such as the kind but cynical and slightly sly Nan. However Diamond dies whilst still quite young, so is easily cast into the Victorian trope of "too good to live." With Gibbie, MacDonald challenges the notion that such a character must either perish or be tarnished as he or she ages into adulthood. However that tale is incomplete without the relationships that unfold throughout idealized-Gibbie's life. In *At the Back of the North Wind* the somewhat involved adult narrator pontificates on how Diamond has indeed impacted his life, and left him longing to be more childlike as Diamond was. In *Sir Gibbie* the reactions in both the children and the adults around Gibbie—incurred precisely because of his childlikeness—drive the entire tale. There are peers such as Fergus and Ginevra—the former who largely rejects and scorns Gibbie's model, the latter who is sincerely compelled and fortified by it. There are older adults such as Reverend Sclater who are at first repelled, then perplexed, and then transformed by it. There is the kindred soul, elderly Janet, herself a more naturally imperfect yet compelling example of a wisely childlike senior who continues to learn and grow through her engagement with and reflection upon it. But perhaps most importantly there is Donal—who becomes Gibbie's friend and spends an entire lifetime sometimes joyfully and sometimes very painfully seeking how to healthily emulate his childlikeness.

In many other of MacDonald's stories the reader is introduced to characters who struggle through to adulthood, navigating how to do so

"A Childhood into Which We Have to Grow"

without losing—or perhaps needing to find—the traits of childlikeness. This is part of the journey in *Malcolm, Robert Falconer, Alec Forbes, There and Back Again, Heather and Snow*, and others. *The Princess and Curdie* begins with showing Curdie—who readers of the prequel will remember as being musical, playful, mischievous—as being in a very bad way precisely because he's discarded his childlikeness: "On his way to and from the mine he took less and less notice of bees and butterflies, moths and dragonflies, the flowers and the brooks and the clouds. He was gradually changing into a commonplace man."[23] Perhaps one of MacDonald's most unusual explorations of childlikeness is in his penultimate work, *Lilith*. In this adult fantasy the protagonist is on a journey of self-understanding and discovering the necessity of relationship. When he meets the kind, trusting, adventurous, loving "Little Ones," they seem to be a fantastical version of Gibbie or Diamond. Yet, for all their veritable attraction, there is something a little vacuous about them. Eventually the protagonist has to be told: lovely as they are, the Little Ones are unhealthily static. In restricting their curiosity and their intellectual growth, in their being protected from experiencing hardship and pain, they were not growing into mature childlike adults but were rather stuck, inhibited from what they were yet meant to become. In this MacDonald emphasizes that to be a childlike disciple does not mean to stagnate or to avoid some of the trials and difficulties inherent in maturation.

I love the distinction that MacDonald makes for us with the Little Ones. But I still wonder if there remains a whiff of idealism to MacDonald that we now find hard to accept?

Certainly both *Sir Gibbie* and *At the Back of the North Wind* have faced the charge of idealism. And this is why it is important to recognize that MacDonald was intentionally presenting idealized characters in those tales: "I will try to show what we might be, may be, must be, shall be— and something of the struggle to gain it," he writes to a friend.[24] And it must not be overlooked that there are plenty of very unidealized characters in those stories as well. Gibbie and Diamond are aspirational models of what it might look like to never have lost childlikeness. And a fair reading of

---

23. MacDonald, *The Princess and Curdie*, 4.
24. Sadler, ed., *An Expression of Character*, 54.

those texts will acknowledge that the unideal societal depictions—poverty, alcoholism, housing injustice, swindling, abuse, prejudice—are moving cries for social action in MacDonald's contemporary world. The pervasiveness of the Romantic "cult of childhood" certainly meant that MacDonald's readership was more open to reading about "good children" than a readership would be today. But a careful consideration of not only the breadth of MacDonald's many child characters, but also of his continued distinction between childlikeness and childishness, makes evident that he is actually usurping the cult concept. Not just in the variety of personalities he portrays—he is very clear that not all children are embodied innocence, let alone childlike—but in his insistence that childlikeness is not something ever intended solely for children.

Regardless, do Diamond and Gibbie succeed as characters who inspire us to childlikeness? Perhaps the response to that depends as much upon the reader as the author. Both characters—despite MacDonald's defense that they are intended as ideal examples rather than everyday portrayals—have certainly elicited critical contempt, particularly in later twentieth-century criticism. And yet, those books are also two of the most frequently cited as beloved and transformative tales—from the cynical Mark Twain through to the stoical Madeleine L'Engle.[25] Many critics, C. S. Lewis amongst them, point out that MacDonald is one of the few writers who is actually successful at crafting compellingly *good* protagonists. But cultural climate also affects the reception of readers. There is certainly a stronger cynicism about "good characters" now than there was amongst MacDonald's original audience—but perhaps that in itself ends up serving for an argument as to exactly why today's readers need to reconsider what MacDonald was doing, and why. Is that lack of reception indicative of a cultural lack of childlikeness? Of a pervasive cynicism? Of an inertia to see beyond the seeming-surface? The model for MacDonald's ideals is, after all, Christ; he suggests circumspection before scorning the concept:

> To the man who believes in the Son of God, poetry returns in a mighty wave; history unrolls itself in harmony; science shows crowned with its own aureole of holiness. There is no enlivener of the imagination, no enabler of the judgment, no strengthener of the intellect, to compare with the belief in a live Ideal, at the heart of all personality, as of every law. If there be no such live Ideal, then

---

25. Surely one of the most cynical of MacDonald's contemporary readers was his friend Mark Twain—whose family copy of *At The Back of the North Wind* was so worn from rereading that he wrote to ask MacDonald for another.

"A Childhood into Which We Have to Grow"

a falsehood can do more for the race than the facts of its being; then an unreality is needful for the development of the man in all that is real, in all that is in the highest sense true; then falsehood is greater than fact, and an idol necessary for lack of a God. They who deny cannot, in the nature of things, know what they deny. When one sees a chaos begin to put on the shape of an ordered world, he will hardly be persuaded it is by the power of a foolish notion bred in a diseased fancy.[26]

MacDonald argues that ideals are indeed needed—the christological one most certainly—as well as examples of those that struggle along, drawing readers into their learning as they struggle.

Yes, MacDonald's Trinitarian emphasis allows him to hold Christ before us a model for our loving obedience and childlike trust in the Father. But I am struck by one particular image that seems to recur in various forms in Mac-Donald's work. It's that of a child turning from their misery and climbing up stairs to a father or mother figure. In its simplest form we find it in The Diary of an Old Soul, *where MacDonald pictures a child searching in the gutter for "possible things."[27] Nearby is a royal palace where the child's father lives, but although the child does not realize it initially, he subsequently turns round, and climbs the stair to find the father who has been thinking of him. The father clasps the child, kissing him, stroking his hair and holding him in "fold on fold of lovely rest." In that version, the child represents all God's children who are invited to turn and to receive love and rest. We find a very similar but more complex image in* Sir Gibbie, *where Gibbie's pleasure in finding jewels in the gutter is far exceeded by the delight he finds in climbing to the attic to enjoy his earthly father's company. Yet this time, the father figure is presented as flawed and inadequate and greatly in contrast to the constant watchfulness of Father of fathers. And we find MacDonald playing about with the same image elsewhere too, but for me, the simple parable in* Diary of an Old Soul *is the most resonant; we seek wrongly, we turn, we climb to a hidden place to be alone with a loving God.*

Yes, I know many readers for whom such images have been deeply consoling, even healing: Irene in *The Princess and the Goblin* lost and climbing the stairs up to the arms of the ever-wise great-great-grandmother;

---

26. MacDonald, "Sketch of Individual Development," 75.
27. MacDonald, *The Diary of an Old Soul*, September, stanzas 26–27.

An Introduction to Child Theology

Curdie in *The Princess and Curdie* accepting forgiveness and renewed vision when he flies to her in moral despair; Tangle in "The Golden Key" lovingly held by the forest grandmother after a tearful flight of harassment and fear. There are many such. But these each also learn, after their periods of trusting rest and childlike reception of love and beauty, that they are next called into trusting obedient action. Action that will require a mix of playful delight with sacrificial (and sometimes fearsome) service. Their consolation has been in part a fortification, that moves them into a new place in their journeys of childlike maturation.

It is so good to be reminded of MacDonald's emphasis on the healing nature of being childlike in relation to God, and to receiving his love, "and the heart is absorbed in loving."[28] But MacDonald takes it even further in "The Child in the Midst," doesn't he? He argues that not only is Christ childlike, but that God himself is also childlike because of his utter truth and goodness towards us. "He has not two thoughts about us. With him all is simplicity of purpose and meaning and effort and end . . ."[29] The end that he has in mind is to love us into purity, and to bring us to completion in our loveliness.[30] And for MacDonald, that inexorable love has a simplicity of purpose to it, "namely, that we should be as he is, think the same thoughts, mean the same things, possess the same blessedness."[31] There is much emphasis upon our receiving—receiving the love, receiving the child, and as a result then we can receive all humanity in our own childlike love.

Yes, isn't this a beautiful understanding of God's being and attitude towards us? And the relational necessity of "receiving" is key. MacDonald wants his readers to be able to recognize that God never ceases inviting us into a participatory engagement with him. Ever reaching out, ever waiting for our response to his standing invitation, longing for us to participate with him in the life more abundant. Not wanting an audience, but rather playmates, friends, mutual delighters—children designed to be in living, loving relationship with their divine parent. Participation does not negate worship—nor does it negate our need for God's care. MacDonald spends much time exploring how God-with-us walks alongside his children in

28. MacDonald, *Unspoken Sermons, Series One*, 14.
29. MacDonald, *Unspoken Sermons, Series One*, 15.
30. MacDonald, *Unspoken Sermons, Series One*, 18.
31. MacDonald, *Unspoken Sermons, Series One*, 15.

"A Childhood into Which We Have to Grow"

their suffering and trials, but he is careful to ensure his readers know that God also accompanies them in their joys and laughter. And that God wants us to choose to receive his invitation for that to be a relational, mutually engaging accompaniment. MacDonald's seminal essay on the imagination ends with this:

> Thus to be playfellows with God in this game, the little ones may gather their daisies and follow their painted moths; the child of the kingdom may pore upon the lilies of the field, and gather faith as the birds of the air their food from the leafless hawthorn, ruddy with the stores God has laid up for them; and the man of science
>
> "May sit and rightly spell
> Of every star that heaven doth shew,
> And every herb that sips the dew;
> Till old experience do attain
> To something like prophetic strain."[32]

"To be playfellows with God." I think I can trace something of these stories in C. S. Lewis's Till We Have Faces, *when Orual refuses to see the god's castle and instead chooses to live her own life on her own terms in line with what she wants to believe. Her life becomes one of grim, incessant hard work. But the gods bring her to a point of simplicity too, ultimately, leading her back to both her own humanity and a sense of wonder at the divine. Which raises the question,* did MacDonald influence those who came after him with regard to childlikeness?

It is interesting to reflect on just how much MacDonald has influenced broader English-speaking culture (and beyond) by virtue of his influence upon the authors of some of the best-beloved children's novels—and their inheritors. It is arguably in the enduring legacy of some of those texts despite society's pervading cynicism about the sovereignty of goodness, that MacDonald's explorations of childlikeness have most proved a long-term success. Consider the examples of Colin and Mary learning from Dickon how to delight and anticipate in *The Secret Garden*; Susan and Lucy being invited into a game of tag and laughter as Aslan's first act upon resurrection in *The Lion, The Witch and the Wardrobe*; Meg finding the courage to trust and to love despite the danger and uncertainty in *A Wrinkle in Time*. Such iconic inheritors helped foster an understanding of healthy childlikeness.

---

32. MacDonald, "The Imagination," 42.

And in such stories there are adults who are mature and wise (and sometimes even burdened) leaders, but also unabashedly childlike and story-focussed: Aslan who initiates the game and rescues storytellers; Gandalf who brings fireworks and encourages storytelling; even Dumbledore who sings silly songs and reignites stories. Now in the twenty-first century more literate adults unashamedly read and watch and revisit the same stories as their children than perhaps any time since perhaps the Enlightenment. Many years have passed since MacDonald, compelled by the exhortation of Christ himself, began presenting to his readers just how essential childlikeness is to the discipleship of one who desires to follow Christ. But perhaps readers are better primed now, many years after his own arguments have permeated and percolated through the imaginations of key fiction writers, to return to his own carefully sketched explorations of Christ's call.

So what do you think MacDonald would have wanted us to take away from his corpus? Is it possible to summarize it?

In the sermon "Child in Our Midst," MacDonald reminds his reader of the context of Christ's call to childlikeness: his disciples had been wondering who amongst them is "the greatest." It is in response to this that Christ draws an actual child into their midst, for them to see/hear/be, before it. He tells the men that they all need to *change*, and *become like children* . . . that only in becoming humble like this little child will one become "great." Yet even more dramatically, he tells them that only in becoming as a child will they even enter/receive the kingdom of Heaven.

MacDonald makes clear throughout his corpus that as disciples of Christ we are all called to change and become childlike. Matthew, Mark, and Luke do not really present it as an option. Yet it is encouraging that in telling those disciples to change, Christ—the prototype for true childlikeness—is making clear that to do so is indeed possible. MacDonald repeatedly argues that becoming *childlike* will lead to a more joyful, trusting, wonder-filled experience of life generally—"life more abundant." He believes, like Christ, that change *is* possible: that adults actually can increasingly mature into an increasingly wise and brave childlikeness—be "forever fresh-born"; that they have the choice to respond to an ever-proffered invitation to become "playfellows with God," and delight together with him in his creations. MacDonald's writings and stories about this compelled many children's

"A Childhood into Which We Have to Grow"

authors and some notable Christian teachers—and thus his legacy has persisted. This book and its MacDonald-influenced editor are tribute to that.

> ... the very essence of childhood being nearness to the Father
> and the outgoing of his creative love ... For God is not only the father
> of the child, but of the childhood that constitutes him a child,
> therefore the childness is of the divine nature.
> The child may not indeed be capable of looking into the father's method,
> but he can in a measure understand his work, has therefore
> free entrance to his study and workshop both,
> and is welcome to find out what he can,
> with fullest liberty to ask him questions.[33]

> It is as if God spoke to each of us according to our need:
> My son, my daughter, you are growing old and cunning;
> you must grow a child again, with my Son, this blessed birth time.
> You are growing old and selfish; you must become a child.
> You are growing old and careful; you must become a child.
> You are growing old and distrustful; you must become a child.
> You are growing old, and petty, and weak, and foolish; you must become a child
> —my child; like the baby there, that strong sunrise of faith and hope and love,
> lying in his mother's arms in the stable.[34]

---

33. MacDonald, *The Hope of the Gospel*, 56.
34. Christmas sermon in MacDonald, *Adela Cathcart*, 20–21.

Chapter Nineteen

To the Time before Time Began
The Spiritual Vocation of Childhood

Patrick Calvo

The ignorance of a child, the innocence next to which sanctity itself, the purity of the saint is nothing but filth and decay.[1]
—Charles Peguy

I, trusting that the truly sweet
Would still be sweetly found the true,
Sang, darkling, taught by heavenly heat,
Songs which were wiser than I knew.[2]
—Coventry Patmore

The world shall be judged by children.
The spirit of childhood shall judge the world.[3]
—George Bernanos

---

1. Peguy, *The Portal of the Mystery of Hope*, 25.
2. Patmore, "A Retrospect," 439.
3. Bernanos, *The Heroic Face of Innocence*, 23.

To the Time before Time Began

A Tale of Two Cities

From the earliest memories of my childhood, depressiveness remains a visible thread woven into the fabric of my life. William Blake reminds me: *"Joy and Woe are woven fine, a clothing for the soul divine."*[4] Looking back upon my younger life as objectively as one can without minimizing or inflating joy or woe, my life appears an amalgamation of "the best of times and the worst of times:" A tale of two cities bound within my heart.

Each of us are born into a pre-constructed familial subculture created before we ever arrived. I grew up a middle child in a middle-class American family in the sixties. As a newborn, fresh from the womb, I was immediately swept up in the winds of life with a loving, but unpredictable, absentee, alcoholic father, and a loving, but depressive, dependent mother. As a sensitive child, one defining assumption about myself I grew to believe early on was the reason my father didn't want to be with me was because I was not worth being with.

One of my earliest childhood memories was a work party my father organized with his buddies to landscape the front yard shortly after we moved into our new family home. Our front yard pitched steeply toward our suburban street. A large round three-man landscape boulder lay in the center of the yard, at the top of the slope. My father and his friends rolled the boulder down to the toe of the slope and just off the front corner of our property. There this large round field stone sat alone on the property line. I remember as a child occasionally sitting on that stone watching the world go by. The boulder and I shared a kinship: off on the margin, stoic and alone, as we quietly observed life pass by us.

Depression orients towards the past: past trauma, past disappointments and regrets; dead hopes and dreams. Though I reminisce upon many cherished moments infused with vitality and contentment throughout my life; nonetheless, my life has also been marked by trauma and alienation and confusion: A breeding ground for the depressive.

East of Eden

Nearly sixty years ago I was expelled from the warmth and communion of my mother's womb, crash landing head first into the realities of this

---

4. Blake, "Auguries of Innocence," 78.

postlapsarian world order. It was my own kind of personal, historic expulsion, finding myself outside the womb, east of Eden.

The Genesis account of humanity's expulsion from the garden marks the death of sweet dependency: The death of unhindered intimacy before the face of God, where existence was grounded only in knowing the Creator and Sustainer, whose very triune being and essence is Communion.[5] At that moment, the perfection of communion was severed, and with this break the primal core of our image and likeness as the children of God was damaged. And what was always and only the realm of the sacred, transmogrified into the realm of the vulgar and profane.

Many primal cultures possess an ancient mythic story of the breaking of communion between God and humanity. Primal man turned around, looking backward at the golden age of beginnings, before the inception of ugly time: Before Pandora opened her box and sin and suffering piled high a karmic retribution bound up now within a broken cosmic order. This great fall is humanity's ancient primal trauma. It is both a collective and individual wounding, characteristic of an archetype.

Humanity tries to return to this time before profane time began, to fix what is broken beyond repair. This drama plays out in different scenarios. Primal man attempted to give meaning (sacredness) to the profane existence by ritually reproducing mythic primordial acts (archetypes). Traditional man attempts to escape the pain of the fall through returning to the chaos of the formless void, before meaning and order, by reproducing acts of excess and anarchy (Fat Tuesday, Upside-Down Day, Carnival). The chaotic unleashing of social mores and taboos were a precursor to the climactic moment when the priest offered the bloody sacrifice (usually human) on the altar, whereby the sins of the community were propitiated, and the profane was reset to the sacred "Time before time began."[6] For Psychological man it can be through the tacit role-playing of dysfunctional family of origin scenarios into adulthood, sometimes over and over again in order that we may repair the trauma and return to "the Time before time began."

Yes, depression orients me towards the past; a long-forgotten past both within and beyond my personal experiences. The world is just not right. My inner world is just not right. It lingers strangely like muscle memory within

---

5. Our essential nature as one's made in the image and likeness of the Triune God of Grace, is communion/relationality. See: Zizioulas, *Being as Communion*; Macmurray, *Persons in Relation*.

6. Eliade, The *Myth of the Eternal Return*.

the fiber of my very being. Galadriel's Lament in The Lord of the Rings rings true in hearts today, yet many cannot apprehend it:

> The World is changed.
> I feel it in the water
> I smell it in the air
> Much that once was is lost
> For none now live who remember it.
> Some things that should not have been forgotten were lost.[7]

And yet, it was J. R. R. Tolkien who also understood: "Though now long estranged, man is not wholly lost nor wholly changed. Dis-graced he may be, yet is not dethroned, and keeps the rags of lordship once he owned."[8]

Beyond My Immanent Frame

My entrance into this world was wholly dependent upon the care or carelessness of my caregivers, whether intentional or unintentional. I was well cared for in comparison to many; nonetheless, the carelessness of caregivers is part and parcel of my lived experience in the world that surrounds me. It matters little whether rich or poor, the therapeutic revolution affirms that most suffer some degree of childhood trauma.

Though I am not a psychotherapist, I have parsed out some of my past personal psychological history with the help of therapists. I am greatly indebted to the psychotherapeutic tools and templates currently engaging me, uncovering deep things. They put a much finer point on the origins of my personal psychosocial ills: A modern double-edged sword that cuts deep and divides matters of the heart and mind and soul. And yet, with all the insight and work done, I find a distracting by-product of therapeutic theories and constructs and templates: They lure me into a mesmerizing navel gazing quest, inordinately inflating a swollen self. Deep within I find a microcosmic primordial void; a chaos to be filled and ordered, in which modern self-making psychotherapies alone could preoccupy me with forever unfinished business. At times I am lost within the endless interior caverns of my thoughts, feelings, and memories.

---

7. Peter Jackson, dir., *The Lord of the Rings: The Fellowship of the Ring*. Galadriel's Lament in the movie is partially Treebeard's Lament in the book. Tolkien, *The Return of the King*, 981.

8. Tolkien, *The Tolkien Reader*, 54.

Despite this tendency I recognize and celebrate psychotherapies' profound impact upon my life, continuing to take what I am learning as I educate my emotional life, propelling me forward towards living more vitally engaged in the world of persons. Nonetheless, as Kirby Farrell points out: "... *trauma is an injury not just to the central nervous system or to the psyche, but also to the culture which sustains the body and soul.*"[9] I wish to expand this understanding of trauma beyond culture itself, to find meaning and healing within the realm of religion and spirituality; for the social science of psychotherapy has inherent limitations.[10] Valuations of human dignity and what ultimately constitutes mental health (and spiritual health, for that matter) cannot issue forth unitarily or singularly from modern psychotherapy alone, just as a custom home does not issue forth from a hammer, or a fine painting from oil paints alone. In the West, valuations of what it means to be human and how to direct the tools of modern science toward becoming truly whole, originally issued forth and was driven from a Judeo-Christian ontology and ethic of truth and love.[11]

I do not discount the necessary healing of my nervous system and my brain chemistry as neuroscience reveals; however, faith informs me that the cure of my soul lies well beyond chemistry and biology, or even "the talking cure." I am more than an individual ghost trapped in a biological machine. I will spend the rest of my life developing my emotional intelligence, interpersonal communication skills, self-compassion, and healing from attachment wounds, etc.; nonetheless, if I am merely a culture-bound biological machine, then psychological healing terminates within nature-bound, truncated coping mechanisms and I need to adjust my existential expectations, no longer seeking a more expansive, transcendent healing of spirit and soul.

Science-based theories of modern therapies by definition and intent, lack a meta-dimension. Modern social science as a discipline cannot traverse into the transcendent realm of spirituality or ethics; or aesthetics and ontology for that matter.[12] It is an imminent, earthbound outlier. Its sterile

---

9. Farrell, *Post-traumatic Culture*, xii.

10. The word religion gets such a bad reputation in evangelical circles. But I am speaking of religion in the most positive sense of the word: How we are essentially bound to God. Religion etymology, *The Compact Edition of the Oxford English Dictionary*, 2481.

11. Macmurray, *Religion, Art and Science*. The essence of what it means to be human and the development of modern science to "better the estate of mankind" is a vast topic.

12. The etymology of the word modern has to do with the sense of "just now, and only now." There is nothing beyond the now. Modern etymology, *The Compact Edition of*

shears of logic can make it a useful tool for mental health; nonetheless, this stepchild of modern science falls deaf and dumb within the realm of spirituality and religion. As the poet Walter de La Mare so eloquently reminds me:

> So 'tis when Logic peers
> Sand-blind at her bright shears
> Snip-snapping this and this;
> Ay, on my soul, so 'tis,
> Till looking up thou see
> Noonday's immensity,
> And, turning back, see too
> That in a bead of dew.[13]

The inner exploration of the self alone cut off from transcendency, leads me down constricted, self-contained, horizontal pathways. It distracts me from an expectant, expansive horizon where I gaze upward to see "noonday's immensity": A vertical lifting of my eyes to the hills from whence cometh my help.[14] As C. S. Lewis clarifies, one needs "to distinguish between the need for a 'clean window to look through in order to appreciate the view' and secular culture's use of psychoanalysis to look through everything but which ends up seeing nothing."[15] The clinical therapeutic framework that directs and defines my individual coping skills in "the just now and only now" is but one dimension of my cure; for I was created a glorious spiritual and psychological and physical person. I was coined in the image and likeness of the One True Person[16] The Psalmist apprehends this transcendent wonder and profound mystery:

> Thou in the Womb my Form didst shape;
> So marvelously I was made,
> E'en of my self I stand afraid.
> For this my Soul, which knows so well
> Thy wondrous Works, thy Praise shall tell.
> My substance was by thee survey'd,
> When it was first in secret made.

---

the Oxford English Dictionary, 1828.

13. de La Mare, Self to Self.
14. Psalm 121:1, 2 (KJV).
15. Houston, Joyful Exiles, 135.
16. Genesis 1:27. The country parson was: "The true person" by virtue of his/her transformation in the Christian graces, being perfected in the image and likeness of God.

An Introduction to Child Theology

> Thy hand did free, with curious Art,
> From imperfection every part;
> And ev'ry Member, which had yet
> No being, in thy Book was writ.[17]

The melancholic wounded child in me beckons beyond my immanent frame into the realm of a metapsychology, nourished within a transcendent spiritual theology. I therefore chose to move both within, as well as beyond the manufactured framework of a modern scientific mode.[18] As a postmodern *proficiscere* leads the dying beyond this disordered world order into a good death, I to wish to move beyond; to go forth well, both in a good life and a good death:

> Go forth, Christian soul
> Up from this sterile concrete world of steel and glass
> Go forth, Christian soul arise from the foolish lies of biological machines.
> In the name of God, the Father Almighty who created you.
> Go forth, Christian soul, leave this secular place, bereft of meaning.
> In the name of Jesus Christ, Son of the living God, who suffered for you.
> Go forth, Christian soul, beyond the desiccating immanence of the walking dead
> In the name of the Holy Spirit, who was poured out upon you.[19]

There are seasons of the soul when best to rest and not to know too much; to cease from my work. To be still: to "be at leisure, and know that I am God."[20] For it is out from the transcendent depths of my creaturely, immanent frame that my soul cries to thee, O Lord! Lord, hear my voice.[21]

Those whose hearts awaken seek a transcendent place where Deep calls to Deep: A place where the Lover whispers to the Beloved, longing at once for what was, and is, and is to come. Eschewing sterile therapies of the

---

17. Denham et al., *The Psalms in English*, 174–75 (Psalm 139:15–16).

18. The word manufacture is derived from the Latin root *facere*: "to make." From the bits and bytes of facts we each construct/manufacture a meaningful narrative of our lives. See Palmer, *To Know as We are Known*, 22.

19. Adapted from the Proficiscere by author. Lampard, *Go Forth, Christian Soul*.

20. Pieper's translation of Psalm 46:10a in *Leisure*, trans. Gerald Malsbary, 2.

21. Psalm 130: 1–2a, *De Profundis*.

alone with the alone, I wish to grasp this root of life beyond my own "where deep roots are not reached by the frost."²²

Hungering for the Absolute

Though this essay began with my sad tale of woe, in the end, I am grateful for it. I embrace my childhood perspective, stoically sitting upon that large, round rock. The worst of times drive me forward, seeking a grounding; a deep rooting well beyond the vicissitudes of life that toss my heart to and fro. The trauma and the ensuing depressiveness marking my life is exposed through psychotherapies. With this help I can now more fully embark on the healing process of becoming. Though this be true, at its essential core it is also true that ultimate healing, my complete redemption, can only be sated from a deep draught from the dregs from the absolute, where belief and feelings unite. I feel a kindred spirit with the great French Catholic novelist George Bernanos who truly believes: "I am between the Angel of light and the Angel of darkness, looking at them each in turn with the same enraged hunger for the absolute."²³

Bernanos is fierce in his understanding of this vulnerable position of ambiguity and angst. The fire of transcendency is embedded in my soul too. Yet, I am an immanent creature bound by feet of clay. I wish to wrestle with the angel as Jacob did. I wish to ascend and descend his angelic ladder. My journey (all our journeys) involve the embrace of the immanent and the absolute. I am a wannabe pilgrim of the absolute.

I agree with Leon Bloy: "There is only one sorrow: Not to be a saint."²⁴ The Christian mystics were those privileged to live within the absolute; yet I am a mere mortal. Nonetheless, I quest a visceral communion with the absolute. My trauma and ensuing melancholy tasks me to find transcendent meaning between the sacred and the profane. It is my primal wound. No matter how painful and real my localized childhood trauma was, it is a byproduct; an extension; an outworking of this primal wound. This wounding is expressed in the pathos and wonder of childhood within a broken world:

---

22. J.R.R. Tolkien, *The Fellowship of the Ring*, 170.
23. Speaight, *George Bernanos*, 12.
24. Kepler, ed., *The Fellowship of the Saints*, 7.

Naivety/Nativity[25]

Before the ancient wall I wait
Yearning to pass beyond
To the Time before time began
Returning to the warmth of my mother's womb . . .
Before Humpty Dumpty fell
And I stepped on a crack and broke my mother's back;
Before I realized I was naked and ashamed;
Before I understood what a stranger was
And discovered the existence of monsters;
Before Santa died and the Tooth Faerie flew away;
Before the magic of play dissolved into the labor of work
And the idle hands became the devil's workshop;
Before I first gave my heart to her . . . and she filed it with the others;
Before beauty was hijacked by concupiscence
And I learned to be someone other than myself
And yet . . . if you draw Oh so near
And gaze deeply into the crystal eyes of The Infant
You will catch a glimmer from
The Time before time began
'Beyond the walls of the world'[26]

Down the Labyrinth of Years[27]

Andrew Solomon speaks rightly when he points out that "what the depressives are illustrating is not illness, but insight."[28] The problem is: Humpty Dumpty did have a great fall, and all the king's horses and all the king's men couldn't put Humpty Dumpty together again. When my little children each asked me if there were monsters in the world, I had to explain to them that: "Yes, there are!" And I have learned to be someone other than myself. The world has not always been a safe place for me to be myself.

And so it goes. The world is broken and marred. Communion is severed. And all of creation groans to be restored, waiting in eager expectation

---

25. Patrick A. Calvo, "Naivety/Nativity," 32.
26. Tolkien, *The Tolkien Reader*, 68.
27. Thompson, "The Hound of Heaven," 107.
28. Solomon, "Depression," TEDtalk.

for the children of God to be revealed in the consummation of all things in Christ.[29] The realities of surviving let alone thriving among thistles and thorns down the labyrinth of years can turn both rich and poor into hopeless, jaded adults. Like a professional cat burglar in the dead of night, the harsher realities of my personal experience deftly liquidated portions of all that was good and pure from my wide-eyed childhood. Its sacrilegious influence has stolen some of the most holy and precious artifacts from under the sacred canopy of my inner world.[30]

Nonetheless, a glimmering tapir of hope in the night remains upon my inner altar, lighting the days dead sanctities.[31] Peering into the crystal eyes of the Infant, I find my way back beyond. I find a place of vitality and full contentment within the sacred Time, before the chronological start of profane time scarred me down the labyrinth of my years. As Rufus Wainwright was struck by the beauty of his lover, I am undone by the stark, pristine beauty of the Infant in the manger:

> I really do fear that I'm dying
> I really do fear that I'm dead
> I saw it in your eyes what I'm looking for
> I saw it in your eyes what will make me live
> All the sights of Paris
> Pale inside your iris
> Tip the Eiffel Tower with one glance
> Stained glass cathedrals with one glint
> You smashed it with your eyes
> What I'm looking for
> One blink and then my heart wasn't there no more[32]

Little Sister Hope

> Pandora hastened to replace the lid! but, alas! the whole contents of the jar escaped, one thing only excepted, which lay at the bottom, and that was hope.[33]
> —Thomas Bulfinch

29. Romans 8:19, 22
30. Peter Berger, *The Sacred Canopy*.
31. Thompson, "The Hound of Heaven," 109.
32. Rufus Wainwright, "The Tower of Learning," MP3 audio, track 6 on *Poses*, DreamWorks Records, 2001.
33. Bulfinch, *Bulfinch's Mythology*, 14.

As the way into my depressive nature came to me as a little child, I find the way out is to take the hand of the child and be led to the place where the immanent and absolute embrace. My depressive insight bids me, calls me forth, to return; to enter the heart of childhood. The child leads my spirit like Dante's guides, as I seek to ascend from the chaos of the abyss to the communion of celestial bliss. I am convinced the only way in is through the simple, uncluttered way of the child. Like the innocents who naively marched in the Children's Crusade, the world-weary adult I am caged within must follow where they lead me, here and now. For truly, unless I change and become like a little child, I will never enter the kingdom of Heaven.[34]

I dream of taking the hand of Charles Peguy's little sister Hope, as she walks home down the country lane together with her two much older sisters, Faith and Love:

> The little Hope moves forward in between her two older sisters (Faith and Love) and one scarcely notices her . . . Lost in her sister's skirts. And they (we) willingly believe that it's the two older ones who drag the youngest along by the hand . . . They are blind who cannot see otherwise. That it's she (Hope) in the middle who leads her older sisters along. And that without her they wouldn't be anything . . . It's she, the little one, who carries them all . . . On the uphill path, sandy and troublesome . . . in reality it is she who moves the other two. And who carries them, And who moves the whole world.[35]

Little Hope takes my hand and moves my whole world "in the future of time and of eternity."[36] The dear child Hope sees and loves "what has been and what will be."[37] And follow I must.

The Truly Beautiful and the Beautifully True

> Moral conduct is beautiful conduct . . . Nothing that is not inherently beautiful is really good.[38]
> —John Macmurray

---

34. Matthew 18:13
35. Peguy, *The Portal of the Mystery of Hope*, 10–12.
36. Peguy, *The Portal of the Mystery of Hope*, 12.
37. Peguy, *The Portal of the Mystery of Hope*, 11.
38. Macmurray, *Freedom in the Modern World*, 218.

To the Time before Time Began

Since I was a young man, I have been delighted by the essential world of children. Often, I am hushed, aware that I am standing near holy ground when I am in their presence. I never cease to be awe struck by the innocent part of children that has yet to be fully exposed to all the cruel and disappointing traumatic realities of this world order: That sweet, open, naïve trust, that inherently recognizes the truly beautiful as the truly good, well before caution and fear appears. Here I find the nexus of the truly beautiful and the beautifully true. As the years press in on me, I am ever more aware that children see with fresh eyes and can spot the true and the beautiful more directly and clearly than I can.

The intrinsic communion between the truly beautiful and the beautifully true that children so clearly see, fades in our deadening day. I tacitly imbibe so much of my thought and practice from the liquidating essence of my secular age. Being embedded within the sterility of modernity often juices the spiritual pulp out of my personal existence, extracting much that is true from the beautiful and much that is beautiful from the true. As a result, what was truly human and transcendently sacred is shorn away, leaving merely profane, stark mechanical physiology and chemical processes. Dissolved into base elements it resembles the discarded corpse of Black Beauty in a rendering plant, once so virile and full of grace, now nearly unrecognizable, emptied of the vital essence that made it so real and alive. As Ivan Illich explains: "The corruption of the best becomes the worst; For sweetest things turn sourest by their deeds; Lilies that fester smell far worse than weeds."[39]

When I meet someone especially hard and jaded it helps me to look inside for something of the child they once were, before the passage of time educated each in an evolving, affected understanding of good and evil; like the rough leathery skin of a sun worshipper lying on the beach, exposed to too many hot summer seasons. All of us, like trees, have rings inside that connote our years. A ghost of a child though long silenced remains deep inside me. We are all at once, two and three and four and five and six and seven or eight or nine years old, etc., trapped within the skin of serious adults.

The spirit of a carefree childhood is a beautiful mystery, filled with uncluttered essential truth that circumscribes what is most beautiful and true. This is the strength of George Bernanos's fictional Sermon of an

---

39. Illich, *The Rivers North of the Future*, 45.

An Introduction to Child Theology

Agnostic who is invited to preach from the pulpit on the Feast of St. Therese of Lisieux (Sister Therese of the Child Jesus and the Holy Face). The child Therese's simple, pristine faith was an anchor of inspiration amidst the vacuous groundswell of Darwinian scientism and the Great War to come. She felt she was too small to ascend the rude ladder of perfection that the great Christian mystics did: "You know my mother . . . I have always wanted to be a saint, but, alas, I have always found, when I compared myself with the saints, that there was as great a difference between them and me as there is between a mountain and its summit hidden in the sky and an unnoticed grain of sand trodden underfoot by the people who pass by."[40]

Just prior to her death from tuberculosis at age twenty-four she said to her sister Mother Agnes: "'I feel my mission is soon to begin, my mission to teach souls my little way.' Mother Agnes asked: 'What is this little way which you would teach souls?' 'It is the way of spiritual childhood, the way of trust and absolute surrender.'"[41]

And so, Bernanos's agnostic climbs up to the pulpit on this liturgical day of little Therese and prophetically pleads with the jaded congregation as if on her behalf:

> Christian, hurry up and become children again, that we may become children too. It can't be so very difficult. Because you do not live your faith, your faith has ceased to be a living thing. It has become abstract—bodiless. Perhaps we shall find that the disincarnation of the Word of God is the real cause of all our misfortune . . . Become as little children—there lies your refuge.[42]

I must become as a child again! Oh God take from me my flesh-cutting sarcasm and my faithless cynicism and my depressive nature. Re-sacralize the wonder and mystery for me of all creatures great and small! May I live as though every present moment were a deeply meaningful gift, full of the innocence and simplicity of a child! May I intentionally incarnate within this world as a child, innocently present and alive in a world of wonder; though, as a grown-up, I know full well I dance and play upon the precipice of a worldly catastrophe, albeit a eucatastrophe.[43]

---

40. Tugwell, *Ways of Imperfection*, 223.
41. Wakefield, ed., *Dictionary of Christian Spirituality*, 377.
42. Bernanos, *The Heroic Face of Innocence*, 36–37.
43. Eucatastrophe is a Tolkien word meaning: "A joyous catastrophe." The cross and resurrection is the great eucatastrophe upon which I can have the courage to face my own existential, real-time catastrophe(s). Tolkien, *The Tolkien Reader*, 68.

To the Time before Time Began

> Nothing so Beautiful
> He who mocks the Infants Faith
> Shall be mocked in age and death . . .
> He who respects the Infants faith
> Triumphs over Hell and Death[44]
> —William Blake

It was the child (the real Christopher Robin of Winnie the Pooh fame) who truly and regularly talked to God at evening prayers (Vespers) with his beloved nanny. Yet his prim and proper Father, A. A. Milne, coddled within the jaded disbelief of a secular age, discounted his child Christopher as naïve, mocking the genuine childlike faith of the young boy he never knew at a more profound level.[45] It seems his father knew Christopher Robin in an unreal way; chiefly as a muse. He utilized his son as a sweet little tool to spur the imaginary world of a fictitious characterization of a boy: "Not as he was, but as he filled his dream."[46]

The poetry of Charles Peguy corrects A. A. Milne's misconception of his son's prayer life from afar, as Peguy speaks tongue-in-cheek as God:

> Nothing is so beautiful as a child going to sleep while he is saying his prayers, says God. I tell you nothing is so beautiful in the world.—And yet I have seen beautiful sights in the world. And I know something about it. My creation is overflowing with beauty . . . I have seen millions and millions of stars rolling under my feet like the sands of the sea . . . I have seen the deep sea and the deep forest, and the deep heart of man. I have seen hearts devoured by love . . . And I have seen looks of prayers and looks of tenderness, lost in love, which will gleam for all eternity . . . But I tell you, says God, that I know of nothing so beautiful in the whole world as a little child going to sleep while he is saying his prayers.[47]

Our world glosses over such beauty. It is a faint, unnoticed ping. The world has no time for one who is so heavenly minded he's no earthly good. We often bemoan such people as lacking common sense. But what we do

---

44. Blake, "Auguries of Innocence," 75.

45. His famous fiction filled the void of a relationship that never quite happened. Getting to know the real Christopher Robin is a delightful experience. Melrose, ed., *Beyond the World of Pooh*, 25–31.

46. Adapted from the last line of Christina Rossetti's poem castigating her brother's (Dante Gabriel Rossetti) utilitarian and bizarre treatment of his muse and lover Elizabeth Siddal: "In an Artist's Studio." Prose, *The Lives of the Muses*, 110.

47. Peguy, *God Speaks*, 56–58.

not realize is the problem with common sense lies in fact that it is often only what is common to man's senses! Yet, from a transcendent perspective that only faith provides, common sense alone is Machiavellian natural human knowledge, unenlightened and emptied, sterilized of any wonder or revelation. A rationalist may say that detached, bottom-up, empirical human reason is the only authentic source of knowing, and all religious top-down transcendent knowing is irrational. But the pilgrim's way of faith in me holding the hand of the child is not irrational, but *a*-rational (beyond rational). Or better yet we could say the way is *supra*-rational (above anemic human cognitive abilities).

My hope as a pilgrim on a sacred journey following the child, I become so heavenly minded that all I do is earthly good. It is here where the immanent and the transcendent embrace and incarnate, where psychotherapy meets the faith that originally nourished and directed it. It is here where that child sitting on that stone, off on the margins of life watching the world go by, finds healing and redemption, entering into a vital, unfettered spiritual life.

Beyond his father's perspective, it is the adult Christopher (Robin) Milne with a voice of his own, that beckons me. His voice calls to me on the winds of the absolute, as he corrects and affects my corroded attitudes as a depressive, traumatized, world-weary adult, seeking healing and vitality "beyond the walls of the world":

> "There is not much time left. The child is waiting for us, beckoning to us. We must hurry."[48]

---

48. Melrose, ed., *Beyond the World of Pooh*, 286.

Chapter Twenty

The Child in the Midst

Preston Manning

ON THE LAST OCCASION that the disciples of Jesus met with their master before his arrest, trial, and crucifixion, "a dispute arose among them as to which of them was to be considered the greatest" (Luke 22:24). Notwithstanding how consistently Jesus had taught them by word and example the principle and practice of self-sacrificial love, this was not the first time that personal ambition and jockeying for personal position had manifested itself among the twelve. Shortly after James and John had witnessed the transfiguration, they came to Jesus privately seeking the right to sit on his right hand and his left in the future kingdom (Mark 10:35–39; see also Matt 20:20–26). "When the ten heard about this, they became indignant" (Mark 10:41) and again, "an argument started among the disciples as to which of them would be the greatest" (Luke 9:46).

It was an argument prompted by personal ambition for position and influence on the part of the participants. It was an argument, not about how best to serve the interests of the kingdom based on self-sacrificial love, but about which of them would occupy the greatest and most prominent positions in that kingdom. Who would sit on the right hand of the King and on the left? Who would occupy the most important cabinet positions in his administration?

How Jesus' heart must have sank on these occasions. Within a very short time he would be leaving these disciples to carry on his work—the work of the kingdom. But it would be corrupted and misdirected if personal political ambition was the driving motivation of its leadership.

So what to do? What to say? What he did and said on those occasions was unique and memorable, providing valuable instruction to the spiritually and politically ambitious of any and every age. It is the story and the lessons of "the child in the midst."

According to Matthew 18:2-5: "He called a little child to him, and placed the child among them. And he said: 'Truly I tell you, unless you change and become like little children, you will never enter the kingdom of heaven. Therefore, whoever takes the lowly position of this child is the greatest in the kingdom of heaven. And whoever welcomes one such child in my name welcomes me.'"

According to Luke 9:47-48: "Jesus, knowing their thoughts, took a little child and had him stand beside him. Then he said to them, 'Whoever welcomes this little child in my name welcomes me; and whoever welcomes me welcomes the one who sent me. For it is the one who is least among you all who is the greatest.'"

And according to Mark 9:35-37: "Anyone who wants to be first must be the very last, and the servant of all. He took a little child whom he placed among them. Taking the child in his arms, he said to them, 'Whoever welcomes one of these little children in my name welcomes me; and whoever welcomes me does not welcome me but the one who sent me.'"

So what is the threefold instruction in these passages? Jesus uses contrast and comparison with the child in the midst to teach seminal lessons on the necessity of change, humility, and service on the part of his followers and their would-be leaders.

First, the politically ambitious are to change. "You are to change and become as little children." In what respect? To become humble and act in humility—willing to take the lowly position rather than grasping after the higher one. In this respect, Jesus leads by example: "Who being in very nature God, did not consider equality with God something to be grasped, but made himself nothing, taking the very nature of a servant, being made in human likeness. And being found in appearance as a man [as a babe in Bethlehem, as the child in our midst], he humbled himself and became obedient to death—even death on a cross" (Phil 2:5-8).

Second, we are to not only be humble, but welcome the humble—those in the lowly position—into our associations and fellowship. Usually the politically ambitious seek to grasp the higher rung on the ladder, to associate as much and as ingratiatingly as possible with the high and mighty—those in positions to help the ambitious on the upward path. But it is not to be so for the disciples of Jesus. We are to seek and value the company of the lowly and humble, and in doing so we are welcoming him and the one who sent him.

In particular, we are not to ignore, disparage, or mislead children. Once before Jesus severely rebuked his disciples for preventing children from coming to him, saying, "Let the little children come to me, and do not hinder them, for the kingdom of heaven belongs to such as these" (Matt 19:13–14). And he directed one of his harshest rebukes to anyone causing a trusting child to go astray, saying, "it would be better for him to have a large millstone hung around his neck and to be drowned in the depths of the sea" (Matt 18:6).

Third, we are to serve, to be the servant of all. The servant occupies a humble and lowly position in the household and Jesus delivers this commandment to serve while pointing to the humility and lowly position of the child in the midst. Note that Jesus does not directly disparage the ambition of his disciples but endeavors to harness it to the service of others. On another occasion, he in effect put it this way: You want to be chief? Fine! Aspire to be chief. But "whosoever will be chief among you, let him be your servant" (Matt 20:27).

On that very last occasion, at the Last Supper, when again the "dispute arose among them as to which of them was to be considered to be greatest," it was this call to humble, exemplary service that Jesus most strongly emphasized. The ambition of the kings of the Gentiles is to *be* served, but you are not to be like that (Luke 22:25–26). Your ambition must be to serve. "The greatest among you should be like the youngest, and the one who rules like the one who serves" (Luke 22:26). You have been called to follow me, and "I am among you as one who serves" (Luke 22:27).

In a moment we shall look at the application and relevance of these three injunctions from the story of the child in the midst to contemporary situations where ambition is a dominant factor, particularly in the area of politics and governance. But first let us consider the fact that this story has its scriptural precedents which are also instructive.

The last of the great judges of Israel, Samuel, was brought by his mother—"young as he was"—to serve God in the temple at Shiloh (1 Sam 1:24–28). In those days, the priesthood under Eli and his sons had become corrupt. It was to and through Samuel, the child in the midst, that God spoke directly concerning the judgment that he was about to bring on the house of Eli (1 Sam 3), a reminder that God can and does reveal his truth and will to and through children.

Flash forward to a contemporary home occupied by a couple in their twenties or thirties with a precious five-year-old daughter. Somewhere in the parents' backgrounds—one generation back, perhaps two or three—there has been a spiritual tradition, maybe Catholicism, perhaps traditional Judaism, maybe some form of Protestantism or another faith tradition. But it has been largely lost, swamped by modernity, or maybe jettisoned for understandable reasons.

But one day their little one comes home from kindergarten with a simple but profound question: "Who is Jesus?" Mom and Dad love the child and are wise enough to realize that this is a question that cannot be casually dismissed. The simple question starts them on a journey of reflection and spiritual discovery, addressing the all-important questions: What do they themselves believe? And what beliefs do they intend to pass on to their children? They are challenged as never before—challenged spiritually—by the child in their midst.

One of Samuel's final acts as the last of the judges was to anoint David as the king-to-be after God had rejected Saul as king of Israel. Samuel was directed to Bethlehem and the household of Jesse with the instruction that God had chosen one of Jesse's sons to be king. But which one? Eliab the oldest was most impressive, and when Samuel saw him, he thought "Surely the Lord's anointed stands here . . ." But the Lord said to Samuel, "Do not consider his appearance or his height, for I have rejected him. The Lord does not look at the things man looks at. Man looks at the outward appearance, but the Lord looks at the heart" (1 Samuel 16:1–7).

Six more of Jesse's sons are presented, but Samuel says to Jesse, "The Lord has not chosen these . . . Are these all the sons you have?" Jesse answered, "There is still the youngest, but he is tending the sheep." Samuel said, "'Send for him . . .' So he sent and had him [the youngest child] brought in . . . Then the Lord said, 'Rise and anoint him: he is the one'" (1 Sam 16:8–13).

Flash forward to today, and the desperate need for leaders of integrity and ability—academic leaders, business leaders, labor leaders, media leaders, political leaders, spiritual leaders. The tendency today, despite all our vaunted sophistication, is still to search among the most visibly obvious candidates. And in the age of social media and image politics, to

The Child in the Midst

still be fascinated and impressed by outward and carefully manufactured appearances.

This story of the child in the midst of Israel's leadership crisis reminds us to look for character and the inward condition of the hearts of potential candidates for leadership. But it also suggests that any search for purity and integrity of heart should include searching the hearts of the young. If our only criteria for leadership is experience, well-developed skills, and a carefully cultivated outward image, the young will not make the cutoff. But if God himself was willing to look at the heart of the youngest candidate—a heart not yet molded to the fashion of the age or corrupted by the factors that rendered other candidates unacceptable—perhaps we should do likewise.

So Samuel found "a man after God's own heart" (Acts 13:22) as a youth herding sheep on the hills outside Bethlehem. Flash forward another 800 years to the same location to yet another account of a child in the midst, the best known and most instructive of all such accounts.

> And there were shepherds living out in the fields nearby, keeping watch over their flocks at night. An angel of the Lord appeared to them, and the glory of the Lord shone around them, and they were terrified. But the angel said to them, "Do not be afraid. I bring you good news that will cause great joy for all the people. Today in the town of David a Savior has been born to you; he is the Messiah, the Lord. This will be a sign to you: You will find a baby wrapped in cloths and lying in a manger." When the angels had left them and gone into heaven, the shepherds said to one another, "Let's go to Bethlehem and see this thing that has happened, which the Lord has told us about." So they hurried off and found Mary and Joseph, and the baby, who was lying in the manger. When they had seen him, they spread the word concerning what had been told them about this child, and all who heard it were amazed at what the shepherds said to them. (Luke 2:8–18)

While Samuel was an early example of God revealing his will and his truth to the religious and political establishment through a child, Jesus was the ultimate example of that method of revelation. At the time of his dedication at the temple in Jerusalem, it was prophesied by Simeon concerning him: "This child is destined to cause the falling and rising of many in Israel, and to be a sign that will be spoken against, so that the thoughts of many hearts will be revealed" (Luke 2:33–35).

And although the majority of the scribes and Pharisees ultimately rejected Jesus' testimony, they had a chance to hear and heed him early on when as a twelve-year-old—again, a child in the midst—he sat, according to Luke 2:46–47, "among the teachers, listening to them and asking them questions. Everyone who heard him was amazed at his understanding and his answers."

There is much to learn, therefore, about the management and redirection of ambition from the child in the midst. But what about the application of such teaching to contemporary situations where ambition is a dominant factor, particularly in the area of politics and governance?

The Call to Change and Become Different

Jesus introduced the child in the midst in situations where his disciples were engaged in heated arguments among themselves. And one of its understandable effects was to, at least temporarily, bring the disputation to an end, since it would be unseemly for grown men to continue to carry on in that fashion in the presence of a child, especially one introduced and honored by their Master.

Flash forward to today and contemporary situations—in the board room, the academy, or the political arena—where heated arguments and disputation have arisen. And consider what the effect might be if someone were to simply ask the question, "Would we be carrying on this way if our children were present?"

For example, imagine the House of Commons during the daily Question Period—a cauldron of mistrust, ambition, and self-aggrandizement if there ever was one. The MPs, egged on by the desire for maximum media attention, are hurling loaded questions, clever retorts, and assorted insults across the floor as usual. But imagine if the space between the government and opposition benches were to be occupied, not by the mace and the tables of the house officers, but by scores of young children representing more truly than any Member of Parliament the future hopes of our country. Would we politicians be able to act as we so often do, in the face of the child in the midst? Would it be the presence and actions of the children that would be incongruous and out of place in the Commons, or would it be the harsh words and ambitious actions of the Members that would now appear inappropriate and misdirected?

Jesus used the presence and example of the child in the midst as a call to power-seeking and quarrelsome adults to "change" and to become humble and service-oriented in their ambitions and conduct. Might not a fresh apprehension of the children in our midst have a similar beneficial effect on the power-seeking and quarrelsome adults who so heavily populate our political, economic, and academic institutions?

The Call to Value Character and Purity of Heart

Samuel occupied the unique position in ancient Israel of presiding over two major political and religious transitions—tumultuous times, when the ambition to preserve the old and the ambitions of those who would replace it were both in full bloom. Samuel was the last of the judges at a time when the people were looking for a warrior king to be their head of state, and he also presided over the tumultuous transition from Israel's first king, Saul, to its second king, David.

With respect to the first transition, Samuel was personally opposed to the people's demand for a king but reluctantly acquiesced to it when the Lord said to him, "Listen to all that the people are saying to you; it is not you they have rejected, but they have rejected me as their king . . . Now listen to them; but warn them solemnly and let them know what the king who will reign over them will claim as his rights" (1 Sam 8:6–9).

Samuel is then brought into contact with Saul, the son of Kish, of the tribe of Benjamin. The Lord tells him this is the one to be anointed as Israel's first king, and what is it that most impresses Samuel and the people about Saul? "He was as handsome a young man as could be found anywhere in Israel, and he was a head taller than anyone else" (1 Sam 9:2).

In due time, however, it becomes apparent that while Saul was impressive on the outside he was deficient in character—lacking a faithful heart obedient to God's instructions and becoming increasingly arrogant with the passage of time. Thus the Lord rejects him as king[1] and sends Samuel to look for a successor—leading to another period of unrest and turmoil as Saul's ambition to remain king knows no bounds.

---

1. See 1 Samuel 15:21–23. Samuel to Saul: "Does the Lord delight in burnt offerings and sacrifices as much as in obeying the Lord? To obey is better than sacrifice, and to heed is better than the fat of rams. For rebellion is like the sin of divination, and arrogance like the evil of idolatry. Because you have rejected the word of the Lord, he has rejected you as king."

This time Samuel is led to the household of Jesse, in Bethlehem of Judea. And despite his previous experience with Saul—that outward appearances are not the principal qualification for political or spiritual leadership—Samuel is nevertheless impressed by the appearance of Eliab, Jesse's oldest son. "When Samuel saw Eliab, he thought, 'Surely the Lord's anointed stands here ... But the Lord said to Samuel, 'Do not consider his appearance or his height, for I have rejected him. The Lord does not look at the things people look at. People look at the outward appearance, but the Lord looks at the heart" (1 Sam 16:1–7).

Flash forward to today and contemporary searches for leaders—in business, in the academy, and particularly in politics and government. Are we not still very much swayed by outward appearances, even when we know that modern technologies enable those expert in their use to manufacture and communicate whatever leadership image will be most persuasive with the marketplace or the electorate? Can we not learn—will we not learn— to look for and value character and purity of heart as the most essential prerequisites for leadership in our time?

The Call to Value and Identify with the Humble and Lowly

Jesus used the child in the midst to call his followers to value and serve the humble and the lowly. He not only advocated this course of action, he practiced and demonstrated it. From the very outset of his earthly journey he was immersed among the common people—from his humble birth in a stable, to his apprenticeship in a carpenter's shop, to his declaration to the common people that he was *among* them, not above them, for the purpose of serving not ruling them.

His earliest followers were recruited not from among the elites of Jewish or Roman society, but largely from among lowly fishermen and other Galilean provincials. He was willing to teach any and all who would hear him, including the religious and political leaders of his day. But as the Gospel writer Mark records, it was "the common people", not the members of the religious and political establishment, who "heard him gladly" (Mark 2:36–38, KJV).

Not only did he immerse himself among the common people, he loved them. Matthew tells us that Jesus went through all their towns and villages teaching, proclaiming the good news, and healing (9:35–36). And when he saw the crowds he had compassion on them because they were harassed and helpless, like sheep without a shepherd.

Jesus' relationship to the rank and file of his day is in sharp contrast to the relationship of the religious and political elites of that day to such people. Jesus touches the lepers and even converses with prostitutes and alleged adulteresses. The scribes and Pharisees go home and wash their hands if they have had even the slightest physical contact with any of the great unwashed. Jesus eats with publicans and sinners while the scribes and Pharisees do not and condemn him for doing so. Jesus views the crowd with compassion, as sheep without a shepherd, but the religious elites declare them to be accursed. When even the temple guards are impressed by Jesus' teachings, their masters snarl: "You mean he has deceived you also? . . . Have any of the rulers or of the Pharisees believed in him? No! But this mob that knows nothing of the law—there is a curse on them" (John 7:47–49).

At the same time, while Jesus identifies and sympathizes with the concerns and desires of the common people, he also understands—and this is a very important understanding for us—that "we, the people" have a dark side with which he cannot and will not associate. "Now while he was in Jerusalem at the Passover Festival, many people saw the signs he was performing and believed in his name. But Jesus *would not entrust himself to them*, for he knew all people. He did not need any testimony about mankind, for he knew what was in each person" (John 2:23–25).

When, after one of his miracles (the feeding of the five thousand) he perceives that the people are coming after him for the wrong reasons—to make him their political leader to satisfy their most immediate and obvious desires—what does he do? *He refuses to surrender himself to their political will* and withdraws from their company (John 6:15). Then when he is reunited with them again, he delivers his address on the difference between the earthly bread they seek and the "heavenly bread" he has come to offer. In effect he offers them, not what they want, but what, in his judgment, they need. He tells them not what they want to hear, but what, in his judgment, they need to hear. And he does so in language so clear but unacceptable to them that many say: "This is a hard teaching. Who can accept it?" And, according to the disciple John who witnessed and recorded all this, "From this time on many of his disciples turned back and no longer followed him" (John 6:60, 66).

Are there not lessons in this for our day and generation when the forces of populism are making themselves felt in various way—for example, via the Brexit vote in Great Britain and the election of populist leaders like Donald Trump in the United States, Doug Ford in Ontario, or Jair Bolsonaro in Brazil?

Populism, for better or worse, has its roots among the common people—the humble and lowly—who become estranged from the economic, political, and academic elites of society and reject their leadership. The elites can then react in one of two ways:

1. They can utterly and contemptuously reject these bottom-up expressions of political discontents coming from the lowly and humble—"These ignorant people know not what we know and are therefore to be disregarded"—and even further distance themselves from the populace, or,

2. They can identify and associate with the lowly and humble, walk among them with compassion not contempt, and resolve to understand and respond to their fears and concerns—without deifying them, and offering prescriptions for their ills, different from what the populace favors, but without denying the reality of those ills.

Those who pursue course (1) are tending to follow the path chosen by the scribes and Pharisees; those who pursue course (2) are tending to follow the Jesus way.

What was that way again, translated into a course of action for dealing with populism in our time?

1. Immerse yourself among the common people, establishing a relationship with them that enables you to fully appreciate the roots of their situation and discontents and which enables them to identify with you.

2. Identify and sympathize with those of their concerns and challenges that legitimately cry out for redress, without necessarily embracing the solutions they may immediately propose or favor.

3. Don't destroy any prospect of addressing their concerns and discontents by ignoring them or dismissing the common people as incapable of understanding their own interests and unworthy of your respect.

4. Do not entrust yourself or surrender yourself to their political will, but endeavor to use the rapport and influence that you have previously established to offer them a better path.

5. In proposing that better path, inform their discretion,[2] telling them what they need to hear in order to make a wise decision, as distinct from what they may want to hear.

6. Don't be surprised if they respond by saying, "This is hard advice. Who can accept it?" And no longer want your advice or your leadership. Better, however, that they reject you, than that you reject them.

The Call to Service

One of the most effective ways of showing that you value and care for ordinary people is by serving them, not lecturing them. It is also in serving them—as Jesus demonstrated—that you will gain a moral authority that cannot be obtained in any other way. Thus Jesus not only used the child in the midst as a demonstration to call his followers to change, to be humble, and to identify with the lowly and oppressed, but he also used the occasion to call them to self-sacrificial service.

"I am among you as one who serves," (Luke 22:7) he told them. When the mother of James and John came to him requesting that her sons be given cabinet posts in the government of the coming kingdom, he contrasted the meaning of lordship (rulership) in the political world of his day with its meaning in his kingdom. "The rulers of the Gentiles lord it over them (their people), and their high officials exercise authority over them. But it shall not be so among you: but whosoever will be great among you, let him be your minister; And whosoever will be chief among you, let him be your servant: Even as the Son of man came not to be ministered unto, but to minister, and to give his life a ransom for many" (Matt 20:25-28).

Do faith-oriented participants in the political processes and economy of today, especially those with a Judeo-Christian grounding, have anything unique to contribute when it comes to a service commitment and the outworking of that commitment in practice? Again, we ought to, since service

---

2. "I know of no safe depository of the ultimate powers of society but the people themselves, and if we think them not enlightened enough to exercise control with a wholesome discretion, the remedy is not to take it from them, but to inform their discretion." (Thomas Jefferson, 1820.)

to others, motivated by self-sacrificial love, is again a central theme of the life and teachings of Jesus of Nazareth, the founder of our faith.

One of Jesus' most famous stories was that of the Good Samaritan, the story of an injured man lying helpless by the side of the road (Luke 10:25–37). Several passersby who should have been moved to help him out of their religious convictions ignore him and go by on the other side. Instead it was a Samaritan (a man of a different race and religion that the Jews particularly hated) who stopped and rendered service. Jesus' instruction to his followers, including his followers today? "Go and do thou likewise!" (Luke 10:37). Serve! Especially those in need.

Limitations on time and space do not here permit a full discussion[3] of the role that "service to others" rooted in the Christian concept of self-sacrificial love has already played in Canada in meeting the needs of the injured by the side of the road. But in our day, when the numbers of injured by the side of the road are increasing day by day and when the overwhelmed institutions of the welfare state are passing the point of diminishing social returns, is there not a need for a fresh infusion of and commitment to the "service of others" among our political class, the civil service, and the population at large? And is there not a particular role in the public square for restoring and revitalizing that commitment to "the service of others motivated by love" for people who profess to take seriously Jesus' unequivocal instruction to do something—not leave it to the state or to others—for the injured by the side of the road?

On an even broader scale, the "service sector" of the Canadian economy has become its largest sector—larger in terms of employment and contributions to the gross domestic product (GDP) than the manufacturing and resource sectors combined—employing over 75 percent of Canadians and accounting for 70 percent of the GDP. Talk to employers in that sector and they will often share with you the difficulties they are experiencing in finding employees and managers with a genuine "service ethic." It is the preoccupation with "self" and self-interest—facilitated by so much of the focus of social media—that mitigates against genuine and sincere "service to others."

---

3. Such a discussion would cover the role of Brother Andre in serving the poor in Old Quebec, the role of Edgerton Ryerson in establishing the school system of Ontario, the role of J. S. Woodsworth and Tommy Douglas (both Christian ministers) in laying the foundations of the modern welfare state, and the numerous international service agencies based in Canada and rooted in Christian commitments.

Is this not a gap that the followers of Jesus can and should fill? What if members of the Christian community were known, first and foremost, in the secular world—not for our positions on moral and ethical issues, important as those positions are—but for our capacity to provide genuine, character-rooted, spiritually motivated, effective service to others where such service is required? Would that not be a most effective testimony to the one who said: "I am among you as one who serves" and demonstrated it every day of his sojourn among us?

Was this not what the Apostle Peter—a man not initially suited temperamentally to the service of others—meant when he wrote to the early believers: "If anyone serves, they should do so in the strength that God provides, so that in all things God may be praised through Jesus Christ" (1 Pet 4:11)?

Looking to the Future

Jesus said: "Suffer little children, and forbid them not, to come unto me: for of such is the kingdom of heaven" (Matt 19:14). Not only that, but from such will come the next generation of leaders. Is it not significant that a child (Samuel) was used to signify that the leadership torch in ancient Israel was to be passed on from Eli the priest to the next generation; that a teenager (David) was used to signify that the leadership torch was to be passed on from Israel's first king to the second; and that a twelve-year-old (Jesus in the temple) was used to signify that the old religious order of the Law was to be passed on to the new order of Grace?

The story and the lessons of "the child in the midst" were used by Jesus to teach the necessity of change, humility, and service on the part of his followers and their would-be leaders. They are also linked elsewhere in the Scriptures to related themes such as the importance of character to servant leadership, the right relationship of the leader to those he or she would lead, and the passage of the leadership torch to the next generation.

Looking to the future, it was the prophet Isaiah who sought to describe the peace and tranquility of that future time when all conflicts will cease— those between human beings and God, among human beings themselves, and between human beings and God's creation. He too made reference to the child in the midst, saying that in that day "they will neither harm nor destroy on all my holy mountain, for the earth will be filled with the knowledge of the Lord as the waters cover the sea . . . The wolf will lie down with the lamb, the leopard will lie down with the goat, the calf and the lion and the yearling together, *and a little child will lead them"* (Isa 11:9, 6).

BIBLIOGRAPHY

Abul Abdulcadir, Jasmine, et al. "Care of women with female genital mutilation/cutting." *Swiss Medical Weekly* 140 (January 6, 2011) 131–37.
Aitken, K. T. *Proverbs*. Philadelphia: Westminster John Knox, 1986.
Alexandre-Bidon, Daniele. *Children in the Middle Ages: Fifth to Fifteenth Centuries*. Notre Dame, IN: University of Notre Dame Press, 1997.
Alter, Robert. *The Book of Psalms*. New York: W. W. Norton, 2007.
Anderson, Mark Robert. *The Qur'an in Context: A Christian Exploration*. Downers Grove, IL: IVP Academic, 2016.
———. "What Does the Qur'an Teach About Heaven?" https://understandingislam.today/what-does-the-quran-teach-about-heaven/.
Anderson, Robert D. *Education and Opportunity in Victorian Scotland: Schools and Universities*. Oxford: Clarendon, 1983.
Aries, Philippe. *Centuries of Childhood*. Translated by Robert Baldick. London: Pimlico, 1996.
Aristotle. *Art of Rhetoric*. Translated by J. H. Freese. Loeb Classical Library 193. Cambridge, MA: Harvard University Press, 1926.
———. "On Memory and Recollection." In *On the Soul; Parva Naturalia; On Breath*, translated by W. S. Hett, 285–314. Loeb Classical Library 288. Cambridge, MA: Harvard University Press, 1957.
Arvay, Susan M. "Private Passions: The Contemplation of Suffering in Medieval Affective Devotions." PhD diss., Graduate School—New Brunswick, Rutgers University, 2008.
Athanasius. *On the Incarnation*. Popular Patristics Series. Crestwood, NY: St. Vladimir's Seminary Press, 2011.
Augustine. *Answer to the Pelagians*. New York: New City, 2007.
———. *Confessions*. Translated by Henry Chadwick. Oxford: Oxford University Press, 1991.
———. *The Trinity*. Translated and edited by Edmund Hill. *The Works of Saint Augustine: A Translation for the 21st Century* I/5. 2d ed. Hyde Park, NY: New City, 1991.
Backhouse, Stephen. *Kierkegaard: A Single Life*. Grand Rapids: Zondervan, 2005.
Balthasar, Hans Urs von. "On the Concept of Person." *Communio: International Catholic Review* 13 (1986) 18–26.
———. *Unless You Become Like This Child*. San Francisco: Ignatius, 1991.
Barnett, Christopher B. "Hans Adolph Brorson: Danish Pietism's Greatest Hymn Writer and His Relation to Kierkegaard." In *Kierkegaard and the Renaissance and Early*

Bibliography

Modern Traditions: Tome II: Theology, edited by Jon Stewart, 63–80. Kierkegaard Research: Sources, Reception and Resources, vol. 5. Farnham: Ashgate, 2009.

Barrett, J. E. "Can Scholars Take the Virgin Birth Seriously?" *Bible Review* 4 (October, 1988) 10–15, 29.

Barton, James, and John Muddiman, eds. *Oxford Bible Commentary*. Oxford: Oxford University Press, 2001.

Bauckham, Richard. "Luke's Infancy Narrative as Oral History in Scriptural Form." In *The Christian World Around the New Testament: Collected Essays II*, 131–42. Wissenschaftliche Untersuchungen zum Neuen Testament 386. Tübingen: Mohr Siebeck, 2017.

———. "Markan Christology according to Richard Hays: Some Addenda." *Journal of Theological Interpretation* 11 (2017) 21–36.

Beah, Ishmael. *A Long Way Gone: Memoirs of a Boy Soldier*. New York: Sarah Crichton, 2007.

Beaumont, L. A. *Childhood in Classical Athens: Iconography and Social History*. London: Abingdon, 2012.

Benedict XVI, Pope. *Jesus of Nazareth: The Infancy Narratives*. London: Bloomsbury, 2012.

Berger, Peter. *The Sacred Canopy: Elements of a Social Construction of Religion*. New York: Anchor, 1990.

Bernanos, George. *The Heroic Face of Innocence: Three Stories by George Bernanos*. Grand Rapids: Eerdmans, 2008.

Berryman, Jerome. *Children and the Theologians*. New York: Morehouse, 2009.

Birgitta of Sweden. *Birgitta of Sweden: Life and Revelations*. Classics of Western Spirituality. Edited by Marguerite T. Harris, Albert Tyle Kezel, and Tore Nyberg. Mahwah, NJ: Paulist, 1989.

Blake, William. "Auguries of Innocence." In *William Blake: Selected Poems*, 77–80. Oxford: Oxford University Press, 2019.

Bockmuehl, Markus. *Ancient Apocryphal Gospels*. Interpretation: Resources for the Use of Scripture in the Church. Louisville: Westminster John Knox, 2017.

———. "Scriptural Completion in the Infancy Gospel of James." *Pro Ecclesia* 27 (2018) 180–202.

———. "The Son of David and His Mother." *Journal of Theological Studies* 62 (2011) 476–93.

Bockmuehl, Markus, and Evangeline Kozitza. "The New Testament." In *The Oxford Handbook of Christmas*, edited by T. Larsen, 77–89. Oxford: Oxford University Press, 2020.

Bonhoeffer, Dietrich. *Ethics*. Minneapolis: Fortress, 2015.

———. *Letters and Papers from Prison*. Minneapolis: Fortress, 2010.

Bonner, Stanley F. *Education in Ancient Rome*. London: Methuen, 1977.

Boss, Pauline, *Ambiguous Loss: Learning to Live with Unresolved Grief*. Cambridge, MA: Harvard University Press, 1999.

Bottingheimer, Ruth B. "The Bible for Children: The Emergence and Development of the Genre, 1550–1990." In *The Church and Childhood*, edited by Diana Wood, 347–62. Oxford: Blackwell, 1994.

Brennan, Tad. *The Stoic Life: Emotions, Duties, and Fate*. Oxford: Clarendon, 2005.

Bridges, Charles. *An Exposition of Proverbs*. Evansville, IN: Sovereign Grace Book Club, 1959.

Bibliography

Brooke, George J. *The Dead Sea Scrolls and the New Testament.* Minneapolis: Fortress, 2005.

Brown, Francis, S. R. Driver, and Charles A Briggs. *The Brown, Driver, Briggs Hebrew and English Lexicon.* Peabody, MA: Hendrickson, 1906.

Brown, Raymond E. *The Birth of the Messiah: A Commentary on the Infancy Narratives in the Gospels of Matthew and Luke.* 2d ed. New York: Doubleday, 1993.

Brown, William P. *The Oxford Handbook on the Psalms.* Oxford: Oxford University Press, 2014.

———. "Psalm 139: The Pathos of Praise." *Interpretation* 50 (1996) 280–84.

Brueggemann, Walter. "Bounded by Obedience and Praise: The Psalms as Canon." *Journal for the Study of the Old Testament* 16 (1991) 63–92.

———. *Theology of the Old Testament: Testimony, Dispute, Advocacy.* Minneapolis: Fortress, 2005.

Brueggemann, Walter, and Patrick D. Miller. "Psalm 73 as a Canonical Marker." *Journal for the Study of the Old Testament* 72 (1996) 45–56.

Brunner, Emil. *Christianity and Civilisation.* New York: C. Scribner & Sons, 1949.

Bulfinch, Thomas. *Bulfinch's Mythology.* New York: Jeremy P. Tarcher/Penguin, 2014.

Bunge, Marcia, ed. *The Child in Christian Thought.* Grand Rapids: Eerdmans, 2001.

Bunge, Marcia J., Terence E. Fretheim, and Beverly Roberts Gaventa, eds. *The Child in the Bible.* Grand Rapids: Eerdmans, 2008.

Cainkar, Louise. "Immigrant Palestinian Women Evaluate Their Lives." In *Family and Gender Among American Muslims: Issues Facing Middle Eastern Immigrants and Their Descendants*, edited by Barbara C. Aswad and Barbara Bilgé, 41–58. Philadelphia: Temple University Press, 1996.

Calvo, Patrick A. "Naivety/Nativity." *Crux Journal* 48, no. 4 (Winter 2012) 32.

Cappa, Claudia, et al. *Female Genital Mutilation/Cutting: A Statistical Overview and Exploration of the Dynamics of Change.* New York: United Nations Children's Fund, July 2013.

Carroll, Robert P. *From Chaos to Covenant: Uses of Prophecy in the Book of Jeremiah.* London: SCM, 1981.

———. *Jeremiah: A Commentary.* Philadelphia: Westminster, 1986.

Carruthers, Mary. *The Book of Memory: A Study of Memory in Medieval Culture*, 2d ed. Cambridge: Cambridge University Press, 2008.

———. *The Craft of Thought: Meditation, Rhetoric, and the Making of Images, 400–1200.* Cambridge: Cambridge University Press, 1998.

———. "Hugh of St. Victor: 'The Three Best Memory-Aids for Learning History.'" Appendix A in *The Book of Memory: A Study of Memory in Medieval Culture*, 2d ed., 339–44. Cambridge: Cambridge University Press, 2008.

Carruthers, Mary, and Jan M. Ziolkowski, eds. *The Medieval Craft of Memory: An Anthology of Texts and Pictures.* Philadelphia: University of Pennsylvania Press, 2002.

Cartledge, Paul. *The Cambridge Illustrated History of Ancient Greece.* Cambridge: Cambridge University Press, 1998.

Catholic Education. https://www.catholiceducation.org/en/marriage-and-family/parenting/how-to-ruin-your-children.

Chenu, M.-D. *Nature, Man, and Society.* Translated by Jerome Taylor and Lester K. Little. Toronto: University of Toronto Press, 1997.

BIBLIOGRAPHY

Chesterton, Gilbert K. "Introduction." In *George MacDonald and his Wife*, by Greville MacDonald, 9–15. London: George Allen & Unwin, 1924.
Cicero. *On Invention*. Translated and edited by H. M. Hubbell. Loeb Classical Library 386. Cambridge, MA: Harvard University Press, 1949.
——. *On the Orator: Books I–II*. Translated by E. W. Sutton and H. Rackham. Loeb Classical Library 348. Cambridge, MA: Harvard University Press, 1942.
Clifford, Richard J. *Psalms 73–150*. Nashville: Abingdon, 2003.
Cole, Robert. "An Integrated Reading of Psalms 1 and 2." *Journal for the Study of the Old Testament* 98 (2002) 75–88.
Collins, Adela Yarbro. *Mark: A Commentary*. Hermeneia. Minneapolis: Fortress, 2007.
The Compact Edition of the Oxford English Dictionary. 2 vols. Oxford: Oxford University Press, 1971.
Coolman, Boyd Taylor. *The Theology of Hugh of St. Victor: An Interpretation*. Cambridge: Cambridge University Press, 2010.
Cornhill. "The Scottish Farm Labourer." Vol. X, July–December (1864) 613–16.
Costello, John. *John Macmurray: A Biography*. Edinburgh: Floris, 2002.
Crenshaw, James L. *A Whirlpool of Torment: Israelite Traditions of God as an Oppressive Presence*. Philadelphia: Fortress, 1984.
Culp, Kristine A. *Vulnerability and Glory: A Theological Account*. Louisville: Westminster John Knox, 2010.
Darling-Hammond, Linda. *The Right to Learn: A Blueprint for Creating Schools That Work*. San Francisco: Jossey-Bass, 1997.
Davies, W. D., and Dale C. Allison. *A Critical and Exegetical Commentary on the Gospel According to Saint Matthew*. 3 vols. International Critical Commentary. Edinburgh: T. & T. Clark, 1988–1997.
Davis, Ellen F. *Biblical Prophecy: Perspectives for Christian Theology, Discipleship, and Ministry*. Interpretation. Louisville: Westminster John Knox, 2014.
De La Mare, Walter. *Self to Self*. London: Faber & Gwyer, 1928.
De Mause, Lloyd. *History of Childhood*. New York: Harper and Row, 1974.
Denham, Sir John, et al. *The Psalms in English*, edited by Donald Davie. New York: Penguin, 1996.
De Nogent, Guibert. *Monodies and On the Relics*. Edited by Jay Rubinstein. London: Penguin Classics, 2011.
Dearborn, Kerry. *Baptized Imagination*. Aldershot: Ashgate, 2006.
DeClaissé-Walford, Nancy L. "The Meta-Narrative of the Psalter." In *The Oxford Handbook of The Psalms*, edited by William P. Brown, 363–76. New York: Oxford University Press, 2014.
Diels, H. *Die Fragmente der Vorsokratiker*. 10th ed. Edited by W. Kranz. Berlin: Weidmannsche, 1960.
Eliade, Mircea. *The Myth of the Eternal Return: Or, Cosmos and History*. Princeton, NJ: Princeton University Press, 1974.
El-Islam, M. F. "Cultural aspects of morbid fears in Qatari women." *Social Psychology and Psychiatric Epidemiology* 1994 (29) 671–82.
Elliston, Clark J. *Dietrich Bonhoeffer and the Ethical Self: Christology, Ethics, and Formation*. Minneapolis: Augsburg Fortress, 2016.
Farnsworth, Ward. *The Practicing Stoic*. Jaffrey, NH: David R. Godine, 2018.
Farrell, Kirby. *Post-traumatic Culture: Injury and Interpretation in the Nineties*. Baltimore: Johns Hopkins University Press, 1998.

Bibliography

Farris, Stephen. *The Hymns of Luke's Infancy Narratives: Their Origin, Meaning and Significance*. JSNTSup 9. Sheffield: JSOT, 1985.
Fass, Paula S., ed. *The Routledge History of Childhood in the Western World*. New York: Routledge, 2012.
Fatula, Mary Ann, OP. *Catherine of Siena's Way*. Wilmington, DE: Michael Glazier, 1987.
Fein, Susanna Greer. "Maternity in Aelred of Rievalulx's Letter to His Sister." In *Medieval Mothering*, edited by John Carmi Parsons and Bonnie Wheeler, 139–56. New York: Routledge, 1996.
Fentress-Williams, Judy. *Ruth*. Nashville, TN: Abingdon, 2012.
Firth, David G., and Philip S. Johnstone. *Interpreting the Psalms: Issues and Approaches*. Downers Grove, IL: InterVarsity, 2013.
Fish, Jeffrey, and Kirk R. Sanders. *Epicurus and the Epicurean Tradition*. Cambridge: Cambridge University Press, 2011.
Fitzmyer, Joseph A. *The Acts of the Apostles: A New Translation with Introduction and Commentary*. Anchor Yale Bible 31. New Haven, CT: Yale University Press, 2008.
Folsom, Marty. *Face to Face, Volume 2: Discovering Relational*. Eugene, OR: Wipf and Stock, 2014.
———. *Face to Face, Volume 3: Sharing God's Life*. Eugene, OR: Wipf & Stock, 2014.
Fox, M. V. "The Social Location of the Book of Proverbs." In *Texts, Temples, and Traditions: A Tribute to Menahem Haran*, edited by Michael V. Fox et al., 227–39. Winona Lake, IN: Eisenbrauns, 1996.
Fränkel, Hermann. *Early Greek Poetry and Philosophy: A History of Greek Epic, Lyric, and Prose to the Middle of the Fifth Century*. Translated by Moses Hadas and James Willis. New York: Harcourt, 1975.
Freeland, Jane Patricia, and Agnes Josephine Conway, eds. *St. Leo the Great: Sermons*. The Fathers of the Church 93. Washington, DC: The Catholic University of America Press, 1996.
Frey, Jörg. "How Could Mark and John Do Without Infancy Stories? Jesus' Humanity and his Divine Origins in Mark and John." In *Infancy Gospels: Stories and Identities*, edited by C. Clivaz et al., 189–215. Wissenschaftliche Untersuchungen zum Neuen Testament 281. Tübingen: Mohr Siebeck, 2011.
Gabelman, Daniel. "Organised Innocence: MacDonald, Lewis, and Literature 'For the Childlike.'" In *Informing the Inklings: George MacDonald and the Victorian Roots of Modern Fantasy*, edited by Michael Partridge and Kirstin Jeffrey Johnson, 69–94. Hamden, CT: Winged Lion, 2018.
Garff, Joakim. *Søren Kierkegaard: A Biography*. Princeton, NJ: Princeton University Press, 1996.
Garland, Robert. *The Greek Way of Life: From the Conception to Old Age*. Ithaca, NY: Cornell University Press, 1990.
Garroway, Kristine Henriksen. *Children in the Ancient Near Eastern Households*. Leyden: Eisenbrauns, 2014.
———. *Growing up in Ancient Israel: Children in Material Culture and Biblical Texts*. Archaeology and Biblical Studies 23. Atlanta: SBL, 2018.
Geddert, Timothy J. "The implied YHWH christology of Mark's Gospel: Mark's challenge to the reader to 'connect the dots.'" *Bulletin for Biblical Research* 25 (2015) 325–40.
Georges, Jason, and Mark Baker. *Ministering in Honor-Shame Cultures*. Downers Grove, IL: IVP Academic, 2016.

BIBLIOGRAPHY

Gerstenberger, Erhard S. *Psalms, Part 2, and Lamentations.* Grand Rapids: Eerdmans, 2001.
Globalshopcliq. https://www.globalshopcliq.com/news/advise-on-parenting.
Golden, Mark. *Childhood and Children in Classical Athens.* 2d ed. Baltimore: Johns Hopkins University Press, 2015.
Goldingay, John. *Psalms.* Vol. 3. Grand Rapids: Baker Academic, 1980.
Gould, Graham. "Childhood in Eastern Patristic Thought." In *The Church and Childhood,* edited by Diana Wood, 39–52. Oxford: Blackwell, 1994.
Goulder, Michael D. *The Psalms of the Return (Book V, Psalms 107–150): Studies in the Psalter, IV.* Sheffield; Sheffield Academic, 1998.
Graves, Michael. *Jerome, Commentary on Jeremiah.* Ancient Christian Commentary on Scripture. Edited by Christopher A. Hall, Thomas C. Oden, and Gerald L. Bray. Downers Grove, IL: IVP Academic.
———. *Jerome's Hebrew Philology.* Leiden: Brill, 2007.
Green, William M. "Hugo of St Victor: *De tribus maximis circumstantiis gestorum.*" *Speculum* 18 (1943) 484–93.
Grubbs, Judith Evans, and Tim. G. Parker. *The Oxford Handbook of Childhood and Education in the Classical World.* New York: Oxford University Press, 2013.
Gunton, Colin. *The Promise of Trinitarian Theology.* London: T. & T. Clark, 2003.
Guthrie, George. "Hebrews." In *Commentary on the New Testament Use of the Old Testament,* edited by G. K. Beale and D. A. Carson, 919–96. Grand Rapids: Baker Academic, 2007.
Haddad, Yvonne Y., and Jane I. Smith. "Islamic Values Among American Muslims." In *Family and Gender Among American Muslims: Issues Facing Middle Eastern Immigrants and Their Descendants,* edited by Barbara C. Aswad and Barbara Bilgé, 19–40. Philadelphia: Temple University Press, 1996.
Hale, Rosemary Drage. "Joseph as Mother: Adaptation and Appropriation in the Construction of Male Virtue." In *Medieval Mothering,* edited by John Carmi Parsons and Bonnie Wheeler, 101–16. New York: Routledge, 1996.
Hamlin, John. *Surely There Is a Future: A Commentary in the Book of Ruth.* Grand Rapids: Eerdmans, 1996.
Hanif, L. M. *Sahîh Muslim bisharh al-Nawawî.* Book of Qadr, vol. 16. Al-Matbacat al-Misriyyah bi al-Azhari, 1930.
Harmless Online. http://blog.harmlessonline.net/2003/11/minnesota-crime-commission-wrote.htmld.
Höffe, Otfried. *Aristotle.* Albany, NY: State University of New York Press, 2003.
Hooper, Walter, ed. *They Stand Together: The Letters of C. S. Lewis to Arthur Greeves (1914–1963).* London: Collins and Co., 1979.
Horn, Cornelia, and John H. Martens. *"Let the Little Children Come to Me": Childhood in Early Christianity.* Washington, DC: Catholic University of America Press, 2009.
Houston, James M. "Bernard of Clairvaux: Lover of God as the Lover of Jesus." In *Sources of the Christian Self,* edited by James M. Houston and Jens Zimmerman, 294–311. Grand Rapids: Eerdmans, 2018.
———. *Joyful Exiles: Life in Christ on the Dangerous Edge of Things.* Downers Grove, IL: InterVarsity, 2006.
Hugh of St. Victor. *The Didascalicon of Hugh of Saint Victor: A Medieval Guide to the Arts.* Translated and edited by Jerome Taylor. New York: Columbia University Press, 1991.

Bibliography

———. *A Little Book About Constructing Noah's Ark.* In *The Medieval Craft of Memory: An Anthology of Texts and Pictures,* edited by Mary Carruthers and Jan M. Ziolkowski, translated by Jessica Weiss, 41–70. Philadelphia: University of Pennsylvania Press, 2002.

———. "Noah's Ark: I—*De Arca Noe Morali.*" In *Selected Spiritual Writings,* translated by a Religious of CSMV, introduced by Aelred Squire, 43–153. Eugene, OR: Wipf and Stock, 2009.

———. "The Soul's Three Ways of Seeing." In *Selected Spiritual Writings,* translated by a Religious of CSMV, introduced by Aelred Squire, 183–86. Eugene, OR: Wipf and Stock, 2009.

Illich, Ivan. *In the Vineyard of the Text: A Commentary to Hugh's Didascalicon.* Chicago: University of Chicago Press, 1993.

———. *The Rivers North of the Future: The Testament of Ivan Illich as Told to David Cayley.* Toronto: House of Anansi, 2005.

International Labour Organization. 2012. "Global estimate of forced labour: Executive summary." http:www.ilo.org/wcms_groups/public/---ed_norm/---declaration/documents/publication/wcms_181953.pdf.

Irenaeus. *Against Heresies.* San Francisco: Aetna, 2012.

———. *St Irenaeus of Lyons: Against the Heresies.* Vol. 2. Edited by Dominic J. Unger and John J. Dillon. Ancient Christian Writers 65. Mahwah, NJ: Newman/Paulist, 2012.

El-Islam, M. F. "Cultural aspects of morbid fears in Qatari women." *Social Psychology and Psychiatric Epidemiology* (1994) 671–82.

Jacob, Alan. *Original Sin and Cultural History.* San Francisco: HarperOne, 2009.

Jackson, Peter, dir. *The Lord of the Rings: The Fellowship of the Ring.* 2001; Burbank, CA: New Line Cinema, 2012, DVD.

Jaeger, Werner. *Paideia: The Ideals of Greek Culture.* New York: Oxford University Press, 1945.

James, Carolyn Custin. *The Gospel of Ruth: Loving God Enough to Break the Rules.* Grand Rapids: Eerdmans, 2008.

Jami al-Tirmidhi. Compiled by Abu Isa Muhammad al-Tirmidhi. Sunnah. https://sunnah.com/tirmidhi:2138.

Jarratt, Susan Funderburgh. *Rereading the Sophists: Classical Rhetoric Refigured.* Carbondale, IL: Southern Illinois University Press, 1991.

Jeffrey Johnson, Kirstin. "Rooted in All Its Story, More Is Meant than Meets the Ear: A Study of the Relational and Revelational Nature of George MacDonald's Mythopoeic Art." PhD diss., University of St Andrews, 2010.

Jensen, Robin. "Witnessing the Divine: The Magi in Art and Literature." *Bible Review* 17, no. 6 (2001) 24–32, 59.

John of the Cross. *The Ascent of Mount Carmel.* Translated by David Lewis, with Corrections and a Prefatory Essay on the Development of Mysticism in the Carmelite Order by Benedict Zimmermann. London: Thomas Baker, 1906.

Joyal, Mark, Iain McDougall, and John Yardley. *Greek and Roman Education: A Sourcebook.* New York: Routledge, 2009.

Kass, Leon R. "Educating Father Abraham: The Meaning of Fatherhood." *First Things* 48 (December 1994) 32–43.

Keener, Craig S. *Acts: An Exegetical Commentary: 15:1–23:35.* Vol. 3. Grand Rapids: Baker Academic, 2014.

Bibliography

Kepler, Thomas S., ed. *The Fellowship of the Saints: An Anthology of Christian Devotional Literature.* Nashville: Abingdon, 1948.

Khan, Deeyah. "What We Don't Know About Europe's Muslim Kids." TED video. https://www.ted.com/talks/deeyah_khan_what_we_don_t_know_about_europe_s_muslim_kids/transcript?language=en.

Kidner, Derek. *The Proverbs: An Introduction and Commentary.* Downers Grove, IL: InterVarsity, 1975.

Kierkegaard, Søren. *Johannes Climacus.* Edited by Jane Chamberlain, translated by T. H. Croxall. London: Serpent's Tail, 2001.

———. *Journals and Papers of Soren Kierkegaard.* 6 vols. Edited and translated by Howard V. Hong and Edna H. Hong. Princeton, NJ: Princeton University Press, 1967.

———. *The Sickness unto Death: A Christian Psychological Exposition for Upbuilding and Awakening.* Translated by Howard V. Hong and Edna H. Hong. Princeton, NJ: Princeton University Press, 1983.

Kimball, Katherine McLennan. "Cultivating Christlikeness in and through Suffering: St. Bonaventure's *The Tree of Life* and *The Mystical Vine.*" MA thesis, Regent College, 2018.

Kirmmse, Bruce H., ed. *Encounters with Kierkegaard: A Life as Seen by His Contemporaries* Princeton, NJ: Princeton University Press, 1996.

Koehler, Ludwig, Walter Baumgartner, et al. *The Hebrew and Aramaic Lexicon of the Old Testament.* Leiden: Brill, 2002.

Kozitza, Evangeline. "Legal Exegesis and Historical Narrative in Luke 2:22–24." *Journal of Theological Studies* 71 (2020) 542–80.

Lampard, John S. *Go Forth, Christian Soul: The Biography of a Prayer.* London: Epworth, 2005.

Lazareva, Inna. "Revealed: 'dozens' of girls subjected to breast-ironing in UK." *The Guardian*, January 26, 2019. https://www.theguardian.com/global-development/2019/jan/26/revealed-dozens-of-girls-subjected-to-breast-ironing-in-uk.

Leclercq, Jean. *The Love of Learning and the Desire for God: A Study of Monastic Culture.* 3rd ed. Translated by Catharine Misrahi. New York: Fordham University Press, 1982.

Lee, Laura May. "Youths navigating social networks and social support in settings of chronic crisis: the case of youth-headed households in Rawanda." *African Journal of AIDS Research* 11, no. 3 (2012) 165–75.

Levenson, Jon D. *The Death and Resurrection of the Beloved Son: The Transformation of Child Sacrifice in Judaism and Christianity.* New Haven, CT: Yale University Press, 1993.

Levy, Reuben. *The Social Structure of Islam.* Cambridge: Cambridge University Press, 1969.

Lewis, C. S. *The Weight of Glory and Other Addresses.* New York: HarperOne, 2000.

Lewis, C. S., ed. *George MacDonald: An Anthology.* London: Geoffrey Bles, 1946.

Lichtheim, M. *Ancient Egyptian Literature: A Book of Readings.* Vol. 3. Berkeley, CA: University of California Press, 1980.

Lillegard, Norman. *On Epicurus.* Belmont, CA: Wadsworth/Thompson Learning, 2003.

Lipka, Michael, and Conrad Hackett. "Why Muslims are the world's fastest growing religious group." Pew Research Center, April 6, 2017. https://www.pewresearch.org/fact-tank/2017/04/06/why-muslims-are-the-worlds-fastest-growing-religious-group/.

Bibliography

Lodge, Rupert. *The Philosophy of Plato*. New York: Routledge, 2000.
Long, Seth. "Excavating the Memory Palace: An Account of the Disappearance of Mnemonic Imagery from English Rhetoric, 1550–1650." *Rhetoric Review* 36 (2017) 122–38.
Lucas, E. *Exploring the Old Testament: A Guide to the Psalms and Wisdom Literature*. Downers Grove, IL: InterVarsity, 2003.
MacDonald, George. *Adela Cathcart*. London: Sampson Low, Martston, Searle, and Rivington, 1890.
———. *Alec Forbes*. London: Hurst and Blackett, 1865.
———. *At the Back of the North Wind*. Kila, MT: Kessinger, 2004.
———. *A Book of Strife in the Form of the Diary of an Old Soul*. London: Longmans, Green and Co., 1885.
———. "Browning's Christmas Eve." In *A Dish of Orts*, 195–217. London: Samson Low, 1893.
———. *David Elginbrod*. London: Hurst and Blackett, 1863.
———. *Donal Grant*. London: K. Paul, Trench and Co., 1883.
———. "The Fantastic Imagination. In *A Dish of Orts*, 313–22. London: Samson Low, 1893.
———. *Far Above Rubies*. Whitehorn, CA: Johannesen, 1995.
———. *Heather and Snow*. Whitefish, MT: Kessinger, 2004.
———. *The Hope of the Gospel*. London: Ward, Lock & Co., 1892.
———. "The Imagination: Its Functions and Its Culture." In *A Dish of Orts*, 1–42. London: Samson Low, 1893.
———. *Lilith*. Whitehorn, CA: Johannesen, 1995.
———. *The Princess and Curdie*. Middlesex: Puffin, 1979.
———. *The Princess and the Goblin*. London: Blackie and Son, n.d.
———. *Robert Falconer*. Charleston: Bibliobazaar, 2007.
———. *Sir Gibbie*. Eureka, CA: Sunrise, 1988.
———. "A Sketch of Individual Development." In *A Dish of Orts*, 43–76. London: Samson Low, 1893.
———. *There and Back*. Whitehorn, CA: Johannesen, 1998.
———. *Unspoken Sermons (Series One)*. Eureka, CA: Joseph Flynn Rare Book Publishers, 1989.
———. *Unspoken Sermons (Series Three)*. Eureka, CA: Joseph Flynn Rare Book Publishers, 1989.
"The MacDonalds of the Farm." *Wingfold* 23 (Summer 1998) 41–42.
MacMurray, John. *The Clue to History*. London: SCM, 1938.
———. *Freedom in the Modern World*. London: Faber and Faber, 1932.
———. *Persons in Relation*. London: Faber and Faber, 1961.
———. *Reason and Emotion*. London: Faberand Faber, 1935.
———. *Religion, Art and Science: A Study of the Reflective Activities in Man*. Liverpool: Liverpool University Press, 1961.
———. *To Save From Fear*. Quaker Home Service, 1964.
———. *The Self as Agent*. London: Faber and Faber, 1957.
Malantschuk, Gregor. "Anthropological Contemplation." In *Kierkegaard's Thought*, translated by Howard V. Hong and Edna H. Hong, 2d ed., 11–101. Princeton, NJ: Princeton University Press, 1971.

Bibliography

Marcus, Joel. *Mark: A New Translation with Introduction and Commentary.* 2 vols. The Anchor Yale Bible 27–27A. New Haven, CT: Yale University Press, 2000–2009.

Marrou, Henri Irenee. *A History of Education in Antiquity.* Translated by G. Lamb. New York: Sheed & Ward, 1956.

McCullough, Eleanor. *Julian of Norwich: The Inclusive Christian.* In *Sources of the Christian Self,* edited by James M. Houston and Jens Zimmerman, 341–52. Grand Rapids: Eerdmans, 2018.

McGinn, Bernard, and Patricia Ferris McGinn. *Early Christian Mystics: The Divine Vision of the Spiritual Masters.* New York: Crossroad, 2003.

McInerary, Maud Burnett. "In the Meydens Womb: Julian of Norwich and the Poetics of Enclosure." In *Medieval Mothering,* edited by John Carmi Parsons and Bonnie Wheeler, 157–80. New York: Routledge, 1996.

McIntosh, Esther. *John Macmurray's Religious Philosophy: What It Means to Be a Person.* Ashgate: Farnham and Burlington, 2011.

———. "Science and Objectivity." In *The Personal Universe: Essays in Honor of John Macmurray,* edited by T. E. Wren, 7–23. Atlantic Highlands, NJ: Humanities, 1975.

Melrose, A. R., ed. *Beyond the World of Pooh: Selections from the Memoirs of Christopher Milne.* New York: Dutton, 1968.

Miller, Patrick D. *They Cried to the Lord: The Form and Theology of Biblical Prayer.* Minneapolis: Fortress, 1994.

Miller-McLemore, Bonnie J. *Let the Children Come: Reimagining Childhood from a Christian Perspective.* San Francisco: Jossey-Bass, 2003.

al-Misri, Ahmad ibn an-Naqib. *Reliance of the Traveler.* Rev. ed. Translated by Nun Ha Mim Keller. Beltsville, MD: Amana, 1997.

Missions Fest Vancouver. "Seminar on Women in Islam." January 27, 2018. Vancouver, BC, Canada.

Moberly, R. W. L. *Prophecy and Discernment.* Cambridge: Cambridge University Press, 2006.

Müller, Jörn. "Memory in Medieval Philosophy." In *Memory: A History,* edited by Dmitri Nikulin, 92–124. Oxford: Oxford University Press, 2015.

Noffke, Suzanne. *Catherine of Siena: Vision through a Distinct Eye.* St. Paul, MN: Liturgical, 1996.

Noffke, Suzanne, ed. *Catherine of Siena: The Dialogue.* Mahwah, NJ: Paulist, 1980.

Ogawa, Keiji. *Kierkegaard.* Man's Intellectual Heritage. Tokyo: Kodansha, 1979.

O'Keefe, Tim. *Epicurus.* Oxford: Oxford University Press, 2015.

Palmer, Parker. *To Know as We Are Known.* San Francisco: HarperCollins, 1993.

Pardes, Ilana. "Modern Literature." In *Reading Genesis: Ten Methods,* edited by Ronald S. Hendel, 178–95. Cambridge: Cambridge University Press, 2010.

Parker, Charles. *Expository Thoughts on Ruth.* New York: Tate, 2011.

Parrish, V. Steven. *A Story of the Psalms: Conversation, Canon, Congregation.* Collegeville, MN: Liturgical, 2003.

Pascal, Blaise. *Pensees.* New York: Dover, 2003.

Patmore, Coventry. "A Retrospect." In *Poems,* 439. London: E. Moxon, 1844.

Peguy, Charles. *God Speaks: Religious Poetry.* New York: Pantheon, 1950.

———. *The Portal of the Mystery of Hope.* Translated by David Lovis. Paris: Schlinder, Gallimard, 1926.

Perry, Bruce, and Maia Szalavitz. *The Boy Who Was Raised as a Dog.* New York: Basic, 2017.

Bibliography

Peterson, Jordan B. *12 Rules for Life: An Antidote to Chaos.* Toronto: Penguin Random House Canada, 2018.
Pew Forum. "The World's Muslims: Religion, Politics and Society." https://www.pewforum.org/2013/04/30/the-worlds-muslims-religion-politics-society-beliefs-about-sharia/.
Pew Research. "Many Countries Allow Child Marriage." https://www.pewresearch.org/fact-tank/2016/09/12/many-countries-allow-child-marriage/.
Pieper, Josef. *Leisure: The Basis of Culture.* San Francisco: Ignatius, 2009.
Poulakos, John. *Sophistical Rhetoric in Classical Greece.* Columbia, SC: University of South Carolina Press, 2008.
Prose, Francine. *The Lives of the Muses: Nine Women and the Artists They Inspired.* New York: Harper Perennial, 2003.
Provan, Iain. *Seriously Dangerous Religion.* Waco, TX: Baylor University Press, 2014.
Quintilian. *The Orator's Education: Books 11–12.* Translated and edited by Donald A. Russell. Loeb Classical Library 494. Cambridge, MA: Harvard University Press, 2001.
The Qur'an: A New Annotated Translation. Translated by A. J. Droge. Sheffield, UK: Equinox, 2013.
Rashi. *Rashi's Commentary of the Book of Proverbs.* In *Rashi's Commentary of the Book of Proverbs,* rabbinate thesis by Maurice Lyons, 1936.
Ratanak International. www.ratanak.org.
Reydams-Schils, Gretchen. *The Roman Stoics: Self, Responsibility, and Affection.* Chicago: University of Chicago Press, 2005.
Rhetorica ad Herennium. Translated by Harry Caplan. Loeb Classical Library 403. Cambridge, MA: Harvard University Press, 1954.
Ritter, Constantin, and Adam Alles. *The Essence of Plato's Philosophy.* London: Routledge, 2015.
Robb, Kevin. *Literacy and Paedeia in Ancient Greece.* New York: Oxford University Press, 1994.
Rodd, C. S. "Psalms." In *The Oxford Bible Commentary,* edited by John Barton and John Muddiman, 355–405. Oxford: Oxford University Press 2001.
Rudolph, Conrad. *The Mystic Ark: Hugh of Saint Victor, Art, and Thought in the Twelfth Century.* Cambridge: Cambridge University Press, 2014.
Saanei, Yusuf. "Insemination, Abortion, and Sex Change." Office of Aytullah Sannei. https://saanei.org/index.php?view=02,02,09,248,0.
Sadler, Glenn Edward, ed. *An Expression of Character: The Letters of George MacDonald.* Grand Rapids: Eerdmans, 1994.
Sahih al-Bukhari. Compiled by Muhammad Ibn Isma'il al-Bukhari. Translated by M. Muhsin Khan. Sunnah. https://sunnah.com/ibmajah:76.
Sahih Muslim. Compiled by Muslim ibn al-Naysaburi. Translated by Abdul Hamid Siddiqui. Sunnah. https://sunnah.com/muslim:1403a.
Sallust. *The War with Catiline. The War with Jugurtha.* Edited by John T. Ramsey. Loeb Classical Library 116. Cambridge, MA: Harvard University Press, 1913.
Sandstrom, Aleksandra, and Angelina E. Theodorou. "Many Countries Allow Child Marriage." Pew Research, September 12, 2016. https://www.pewresearch.org/fact-tank/2016/09/12/many-countries-allow-child-marriage.
Schroeder, Joy A., ed. *The Bible in Medieval Tradition: The Book of Jeremiah.* Grand Rapids: Eerdmans, 2017.

Bibliography

Schore, Alan N. "Early Shame Experiences and Infant Brain Development." In *Shame Interpersonal Behavior, Psychopathology, and Culture*, edited by Bernice Andrews and Paul Gilbert, 57–77. New York: Oxford University Press, 1998.

Schwartz, Joshua. "Ishmael at Play: On Exegesis and Jewish Society." *Hebrew Union College Annual* 66 (1995) 203–21.

Scott, A. J. *Notes of Four Lectures on the Literature and Philosophy of the Middle Ages.* Edinburgh: T. Constable, 1857.

———. "On University Education." Introductory Lectures on the Opening of Owens College, Manchester, 1–26. London: T. Sowler, 1852.

Shelton, Jo-Ann. *As the Romans Did: A Source Book in Roman Social History.* New York: Oxford University Press, 1998.

Shields, Christopher J. *Aristotle.* New York: Routledge, 2007.

Snyder, Lisa Gueldenzoph, and Mark J. Snyder. "Teaching Critical Thinking and Problem Solving Skills." *Delta Pi Epsilon Journal* 50 (2008) 90–99.

Soares Prabhu, George M. *The formula quotations in the infancy narrative of Matthew: an enquiry into the tradition history of Mt 1–2.* Analecta biblica 63. Rome: Biblical Institute, 1976.

Soelle, Dorothee. "The Onward Journey Concerning the Problem of Identity: Psalm 139." *European Judaism* 11 (1977) 21–23.

Solomon, Andrew. "Depression: The Secret We Share." TED video. https://www.youtube.com/watch?v=-eBUcBfkVCo.

Southern, R. W. *Saint Anselm: A Portrait in a Landscape.* Oxford: Oxford University Press, 1995.

Speaight, Robert. *George Bernanos: A Study of the Man and the Writer.* New York: Liveright, 1974.

Steinberg, Esther. *The Balance Within: The Science of Connecting Health and the Emotions.* New York: W. H. Freeman & Co., 1970.

Stern, Julian. "John Macmurray, Spirituality, Community and Real Schools." *International Journal of Children's Spirituality* 6, no. 1 (2001) 25–39.

Steward, Jon, ed. *Kierkegaard and the Renaissance & Early Modern Traditions.* Vol.2. Farnham: Ashgate, 2009.

Strawn, Brent A. "Jeremiah's In/Effective Plea: Another Look at רעֻ in Jeremiah 1:6." *Vetus Testamentum* 55, no. 3 (2005) 366–77.

Sugarman, Jeff. "John Macmurray's Philosophy of the Personal and the Irreducibility of Psychological Persons." *Journal of Theoretical and Philosophical Psychology* (January 2006) 172–88.

Sullivan, Shirley. *Aeschylus' Use of Psychological Terminology: Traditional and New.* Montreal: McGill-Queens University Press, 1997.

———. *The Divine Call of Mary: Scriptural Perspectives.* New York: St. Paul's, 2015.

———. *Euripides' Use of Psychological Terminology.* Montreal: McGill-Queens University Press, 2000.

———. *Psychological and Ethical Ideas: What Early Greeks Say.* Leiden: Brill, 1995.

———. *Sophocles' Use of Psychological Terminology: Old and New.* Ottawa: Carleton University Press, 1999.

Sunan Abi Dawud. Complied by Abu Dawud Sulayman al-Sijistani. Sunnah. https://sunnah.com/abudawud:2928.

Sunan al-Nasa'i. Compiled by Ahmad al-Nasa'i. Sunnah. https://sunnah.com/nasai:3104.

Bibliography

Thomas, Matthew J. "Origen on Paul's Authorship of Hebrews." *New Testament Studies* 65 (2019) 598–609.
Thompson, Francis. "The Hound of Heaven." In *The Works of Francis Thompson*, vol. 1, 107. New York: Charles Scribner's Sons, 1908.
Thompson, J. A. *The Book of Jeremiah*. New International Commentary on the Old Testament. Grand Rapids: Eerdmans, 1980.
Tolkien, J. R. R. *The Fellowship of the Ring*. London: HarperCollins, 2011.
———. *The Return of the King*. London: HarperCollins, 2010.
———. *The Tolkien Reader*. New York: Ballantine, 1966.
Torrance, Thomas F. *Divine and Contingent Order*. Edinburgh: T. & T. Clark, 1981.
———. *Theological Science*. Oxford: Oxford University Press, 1969.
Trevarthen, Colwyn "Proof of Sympathy: Scientific Evidence on the Personality of the Infant and Macmurray's 'Mother and Child.'" In *John Macmurray: Critical Perspectives*, edited by David Fergusson and Nigel Dower, 77–118. New York: Peter Lang, 2002.
Tuchman, Barbara W. *A Distant Mirror: The Calamitous 14th Century*. New York: Knopf, 1978.
Tucker, W. Dennis, Jr. *Constructing and Deconstructing Power in Psalms 107–150*. Atlanta: Society of Biblical Literature, 2014.
Tugwell, Simon, OP. *Ways of Imperfection: an Exploration of Christian Spirituality*. Springfield, IL: Templegate, 1985.
UNICEF. "Children make almost one-third of all human trafficking victims worldwide." 2018. https://www.unicef.org/stories/children-make-almost-one-third-all-human-trafficking-victims-worldwide.
———. "Fresh progress toward the elimination of female genital mutilation and cutting in Egypt." Press release, July 2, 2007.
Von Rad, Gerhard. *Genesis: A Commentary*. Philadelphia: Westminster, 1972.
Wainwright, Rufus. "The Tower of Learning." Track 6 on *Poses*. DreamWorks Records, 2001.
Wakefield, Gordon S., ed. *The Westminster Dictionary of Christian Spirituality*. Philadelphia: The Westminster, 1983.
Walker, Jeffrey. *Rhetoric and Poetics in Antiquity*. Oxford: Oxford University Press, 2000.
Waltke, Bruce K. "The Fear of the Lord." In *Alive to God: Studies in Spirituality Presented to James M. Houston*, edited by J. I. Packer and Loren Wilkinson, 17–33. Downers Grove, IL: InterVarsity, 1992.
———. *Proverbs 1–15: A Commentary*. Grand Rapids: Eerdmans, 2005.
———. *Proverbs 15–31: A Commentary*. Grand Rapids: Eerdmans, 2005.
Waltke, Bruce K., and James M. Houston: *The Psalms as Christian Worship: A Historical Commentary*. Grand Rapids: Eerdmans, 2010.
Waltke, Bruce K., and Ivan de Silva. *Proverbs: A Shorter Commentary*. Grand Rapids: Eerdmans, 2021.
Waltke, Bruce K., and Michael Patrick O'Connor. *An Introduction to Biblical Hebrew Syntax*. Winona Lake, IN: Eisenbrauns, 1990.
Walton, John. *The Lost World of Adam and Eve: Genesis 2–3 and the Human Origins Debate*. Downers Grove, IL: IVP Academic, 2015.
Waterfield, Robin. *Creators, Conquerors, and Citizens: A History of Ancient Greece*. New York: Oxford University Press, 2018.

Bibliography

Watson, Nicholas, and Jacqueline Jenkins, eds. *The Writings of Julian of Norwich: A Vision Showed to a Devout Woman and a Revelation of Love*. Brepols Medieval Women Series. College Station, PA: Penn State University Press, 2007.

Wenger, Paul D. "Discipline in the Book of Proverbs: To Spank or Not to Spank?" *Journal of the Evangelical Theological Society* 48, no. 4 (December 2005) 415–32.

Wenham, Gordon J. *Genesis 16–50*. Word Biblical Commentary. Dallas: Word, 1994.

West, M. L., ed. *Iambi et Elegi Graeci*. Vol. 1, 2d ed. Vol. 2. Oxford: Oxford University Press, 1989 and 1971.

Westermann, Claus. *Genesis 12–36: A Commentary*. Translated by John J. Scullion. Minneapolis: Augsburg, 1985.

White, Keith J. "Child Theology as Theology." *ANVIL: Journal of Theology and Mission* 35, no. 1 (2019) 13–20.

Wians, William R., and Ronald M. Polansky. *Reading Aristotle: Argument and Exposition*. Leiden: Brill, 2017.

William of St. Thierry. *Meditations*. In *On Contemplating God; Prayer; Meditations*, 75–86. Translated by Penelope Lawson. Kalamazoo, MI: Cistercian, 1970.

Williams, Rowan. *Being Human: Bodies, Minds, Persons*. Grand Rapids: Eerdmans, 2018.

———. *The Wound of Knowledge: Christian Spirituality from the New Testament to Saint John of the Cross*. 2d ed. London: Darton, Longman and Todd, 1990.

Wilson, Gerald H. "The Shape of the Book of Psalms." *Interpretation* 46 (1992) 129–42.

———. "The Structure of the Psalter." In *Interpreting the Psalms: Issues and Approaches*, edited by David G. Firth and Philip S. Johnston, 229–46. Downers Grove, IL: InterVarsity, 2013.

Wilson, N. G. *Encyclopedia of Ancient Greece*. New York: Routledge, 2006.

World Economic Forum. "Global Gender Gap Report." http://reports.weforum.org/global-gender-gap-report-2016/rankings/.

Wright, Robin. "Iran Now a Hotbed of Islamic Reforms." *Los Angeles Times*, December 29, 2000. https://www.latimes.com/archives/la-xpm-2000-dec-29-mn-5913-story.html.

Yates, Frances A. *The Art of Memory*. London: Pimlico, 1992.

Zenger, Erich, and Frank-Lothar Hossfeld. *Psalms 3: A Commentary on Psalms 101–150*. Hermeneia. Minneapolis: Fortress, 2011.

Zinn, Grover A. "Hugh of Saint Victor and the Art of Memory." *Viator* 5 (1974) 211–34.

Zizioulas, John D. *Being as Communion*. Crestwood, NY: St. Vladimir's Seminary Press, 1985.

———. *Communion and Otherness: Further Studies in Personhood and the Church*. Edited by Paul McPartlan. New York: T. & T. Clark, 2006.

www.ingramcontent.com/pod-product-compliance
Lightning Source LLC
Chambersburg PA
CBHW021649230426
43668CB00008B/561